Transatlantic Rhetoric

Speeches from the American Revolution to the Suffragettes

Edited by Tom F. Wright

EDINBURGH
University Press

Edinburgh University Press is one of the leading university presses in the UK. We publish academic books and journals in our selected subject areas across the humanities and social sciences, combining cutting-edge scholarship with high editorial and production values to produce academic works of lasting importance. For more information visit our website: edinburghuniversitypress.com

Edinburgh University Press Ltd
The Tun – Holyrood Road, 12(2f) Jackson's Entry, Edinburgh EH8 8PJ

Typeset in 10.5/13 Sabon and Gill Sans Nova
by IDSUK (DataConnection) Ltd, and
printed and bound in Great Britain.

A CIP record for this book is available from the British Library

ISBN 978 1 4744 2625 1 (hardback)
ISBN 978 1 4744 2627 5 (webready PDF)
ISBN 978 1 4744 2626 8 (paperback)
ISBN 978 1 4744 2628 2 (epub)

Contents

3 **Slavery and Race**

Acknowledgements

This book is the result of over a decade of reading, teaching and thinking about the spoken words of the past.

It is inspired by my students at the University Sussex with whom I have road-tested the material that follows. Their spirited debates, engaged perspectives and intellectual creativity helped me shape the vast archive of historical speeches into the form you now hold in your hands. Their enthusiasm convinced me that other groups of readers might gain almost as much from this material as we did in our lively classes.

The selection of texts and grasp of the role of oratory in history has been influenced and immeasurably improved by years of fascinating conversations with, among others, Bridget Bennett, Michael J. Collins, Robert Cook, Hillary Emmett, Carolyn Eastman, Fiona Fitzpatrick, Huston Gilmore, Michael Jonik, Thomas C. Jones, Katie McGettigan, Alix Mortimer, Matthew Pethers, Angela Ray, Paul Stob, and Mary and Ronald Zboray.

Finally, thanks also to Michelle Houston at Edinburgh University Press for taking a chance on this project, to the editorial and production team, and to the anonymous reviewers, for their expert guidance in bringing the project to completion.

The book is dedicated to Elf and Lottie, who always see through my rhetoric no matter how finely-wrought I think it is.

Introduction

Between American Independence and World War One, historical turning points on both sides of the Atlantic repeatedly revolved around moments of public speech:

In 1804, in Saint-Domingue, the world's first black republic was born when Louis Boisrond-Tonnerre read aloud the Haitian independence proclamation. In 1819, in Manchester, Britain's journey towards mass democracy was catalysed when Henry 'Orator' Hunt's speech to a sea of workers in St Peter's Field was cut short by the 'Peterloo' cavalry charge. In the 1840s, in meeting rooms from Scotland to Cincinnati, the first global human rights movement was forged through the testimony of fugitive slaves from the American South. In an 1842 Manhattan lecture hall, modern poetry was born when Ralph Waldo Emerson's eloquence inspired the career of a young Walt Whitman. In 1845, in rural Irish fields, the movement for national liberation came alive through the 'monster meetings' of Daniel O'Connell. In 1865, as Abraham Lincoln proclaimed Union victory from the White House balcony, his future assassin John Wilkes Booth vowed from the crowd that it would be 'the last speech he will ever make'.[1] In 1874, in Lancashire, the culminating phase of the women's votes struggle began when the teenage Emmeline Pankhurst left a feminist talk a newly 'conscious and confirmed suffragist'.[2] In the election of 1900, the barnstorming imperialism of Theodore Roosevelt's campaign speeches revolutionised political culture and set the stage for the American Century.

Oratory was central to political and cultural life to an extent not seen before or since. Thanks to the rise of mass democracy, growth in print media, shifts in religious practice and the emergence of a modern culture industry, the antique spoken medium became a cutting-edge centrepiece of the transatlantic public sphere. Uttered in countless settings and disseminated through copious newspaper transcription, public speech was a chief form of nineteenth-century transatlantic modernity, a dynamic medium for communication, and a prominent vehicle for the exchange of ideas.

Too often, however, this body of speech remains silent to us. Because published texts dominate our view of the past, we tend to forget the vigorous vocal worlds that surrounded their creation and reception. Because we

---

1. Louis P. Masur, *Lincoln's Last Speech: Wartime Reconstruction and the Crisis of Reunion* (Oxford: Oxford University Press, 2015), p. xiv.
2. Emmeline Pankhurst, *My Own Story* (New York: Heart, 1914), p. 9.

most often encounter only the historical voices of the powerful, we tend to assume that speeches from marginal perspectives have been forever lost. Since oratory is a medium both functional and expressive – a literary form, and a form of power – it sits uneasily at the crossroads of modern academic disciplines.

This book aims to rectify this neglect. *Transatlantic Rhetoric* brings together seventy-three speeches, mostly but not all delivered in English, to offer a new introduction to nineteenth-century oratory and bring an underexplored body of writing to new readerships. Rather than adding to the tradition of celebratory anthologies of 'great speeches', it builds upon the most up-to-date research to present an unprecedentedly varied range of texts, people, settings and ideas. It is organised around what American and British observers would have called the great 'questions' of the age, including arguments voiced on competing sides of seminal discussions about gender, slavery, empire and war. As befits debates that were under-stood and conducted on transatlantic terms, this book's reach embraces texts from North America, the Caribbean and Mexico, as well as from Scotland, Ireland and England. Famous politicians, celebrity authors and reformers are all to be found, but their voices are placed in dialogue with less familiar perspectives: indigenous women, slave traders, atheists, black female preachers, white supremacists, anarchists and 'race theorists'. The language of high politics is prominent, but so are sermons, treaty negotiations, legal dialogues and what we might now call stand-up comedy. The Senate floor and House of Commons are represented, but this collection also takes readers from the Cherokee tribal lands of rural Georgia to the courtrooms of Dublin, and from the churches of Yorkshire to the street-corner labour rallies of Chicago.

This Introduction provides some essential context for the remarkable prominence of oratory in the long nineteenth century and suggests a number of ways in which this book might be used. Each chapter that follows offers a critical introduction, contextual commentaries on each text, and further reading suggestions. The aim is to provide a unique route into the history of social movements, a guide to political controversies, and an introduction to a host of lesser-known historical figures. The book's juxtapositions offer a way of tracing the evolution of public language, expressive vocabularies, and the ways in which literary, sacred, political, progressive and conservative styles of thought have interacted. Readers can reconnect with the oral origins of some of the most enduring slogans of the era and can trace how metaphors and tropes acted as viral memes, re-echoing from mouth to mouth and cause to cause. Moreover, in an era in which a culture of digital video sharing has brought extended oral communication back to the fore, the public language preserved offers more than just resources for college or classroom but a way of under-standing the enduring currency of spoken ideas.

A Golden Age of Oratory

Publics on both sides of the Atlantic in the period were acutely aware of the ever-increasing prominence for public speech.[3] 'This century', proclaimed one popular Boston anthology of speeches in 1857, 'may be called, with strict propriety, the Golden Age of American Oratory.'[4] Two decades later, the London *Times* observed that, 'in the course of these fifty years we have become a nation of speech-makers. Everyone speaks now.'[5] For some, this new focus on individual voice was a source of cultural pride, with one American magazine reflecting in 1810 that 'greater effects may be produced by it among us than in any nation since the days of antiquity'.[6] To others, this ascendancy of the role of the public speaker was a source of anxiety. Writing in 1869, Charles Dickens thought there was 'everywhere a vast amount too much' speechification, whilst the Scottish historian Carlyle dismissed his age as an 'epoch . . . of babblement'.[7] But what factors explain this resurgence of oratory? The answer lies in a confluence of political, cultural and technological trends.

The most obvious cause was the expansion of mass democracy. In the American republic, and far more gradually in Britain, the growth of a voting public created an ever-increasing role for deliberation, representation and advocacy. As the political nation and civil society grew, the need for consent of the governed made persuasive speech ever more central to the transaction of public life. Oratorical talent went from niche activity to prominent accomplishment and moved, as Sandra Gustafson has put it, 'from the cultural margins (albeit margins where power resided) to a central place in the new order'.[8] It was an order in which the stump, dispatch

---

3. For general treatments of nineteenth-century oratory, see Carolyn Eastman, *A Nation of Speechifiers: Making an American Public After the Revolution* (Chicago: University of Chicago Press, 2009), pp. 12–25; Robert T. Oliver, *Public Speaking in the Reshaping of Great Britain* (Newark: University of Delaware Press, 1987); Joseph S. Meisel, *Public Speech and the Culture of Public Life in the Age of Gladstone* (New York: Columbia University Press, 2002).

4. Edward G. Parker, *The Golden Age of American Oratory* (Boston: Whittemore, Niles and Hall, 1857), p. 1.

5. *The Times* (1873), quoted in Mathew Bevis, *The Art of Eloquence: Byron, Dickens, Tennyson, Joyce* (Oxford: Oxford University Press, 2007), p. 3.

6. 'Adams's Lectures', *Monthly Anthology and Boston Review* (1810), vol. 8, p. 250.

7. Charles Dickens to Mr Ryland, 13 August 1869, quoted in *The Letters of Charles Dickens* (Oxford: Oxford University Press, 2002), p. 394; Thomas Carlyle, 'The Stump-Orator', in *Latter-day Pamphlets*, ed. H. D. Traill (New York: C. Scribner's Sons, 1901), p. 175.

8. Sandra Gustafson, 'Oral Genres and Print', in Mary Saracino Zboray and Ronald J. Zboray, *Oxford History of Popular Print Culture: Volume Five* (Oxford: Oxford University Press, 2019).

boxes and the floors of city and state legislatures were soon iconic spaces (Figures 1, 3, 6). And by the closing decades of the century, the extra-Parliamentary campaigning methods of pioneers such William Gladstone across Britain or William Jennings Bryan across the United States created a new era of outdoor mass persuasion[9] (Figures 12, 14 and 15).

Politicians were not the only orators to turn to this mass 'platform'. A consequence of the increased accountability of leaders was a new focus on social reform. Speaking before large rallies and exploiting the political theatre of mass meetings became one of the most effective means of communicating messages of change to the widest possible audience, and of exerting the influence on rulers known during the era as 'pressure from without'.[10] The great causes of this book, from abolition and women's rights to the labour and peace movements, had lectures, rallies and speeches at the heart of their campaigns.

Broader trends in religious and educational culture also helped encourage this prominence. Transatlantic religious revivals helped make sermons and open-air preaching into something approaching a unifying cultural experience for large groups across denominations. New mass religious practices turned charismatic preachers into celebrities, and offered up emotive performance registers that would in turn influence the styles of reformers and politicians.[11] Though formal oratorical education, and the innate sense of authority required to deliver public speeches, were still the preserve of elite schooling, elocution also became central to the new age of state schools from the mid-century onwards, so that learning became synonymous with presenting a fluent speaking self.[12] All of these developments helped to enlarge what communications theorist Lloyd Bitzer has called 'the rhetorical situation'.[13] New scenes of speech, such as public lectures, after-dinner addresses, political fundraisers, debates and courtroom dialogues meant that oratory was no longer limited to places of worship

----

9. For more on the growth of extra-Parliamentary campaigning see Meisel, *Public Speech and the Culture of Public Life in the Age of Gladstone*.

10. See P. Hollis (ed.), *Pressure from Without in Early Victorian England* (London: Edward Arnold, 1974).

11. See Robert H. Ellison, *The Victorian Pulpit* (Selinsgrove: Susquehanna University Press, 1998).

12. For an account of the elocutionary movement and its legacy see Jay Fliegelman, *Declaring Independence: Jefferson, Natural Language & the Culture of Performance* (Stanford: Stanford University Press, 1993), pp. 28–34; Hugh Blair, *Heads of the Lectures on Rhetorick, and Belles Lettres, in the University of Edinburgh* (Edinburgh: Kincaid, Bell, 1767).

13. Lloyd Bitzer, 'The Rhetorical Situation', *Philosophy & Rhetoric*, 1:1 (January 1968), 3.

or governing, but part of the fabric of public life[14] (Figures 6, 7 and 13). The range of speakers had also changed. Though electoral politics, particularly in Britain, was elite-led, mass reform and religious movements opened up an unprecedented space for female, minority and non-elite speakers (Figures 4 and 10).

Underpinning all of these shifts was a revolution in the print media. The development of new steam-powered printing methods in the 1820s and 1830s lowered costs enormously, transforming the production and availability of newspapers, and by doing so, greatly amplifying the prominence of oratory in their pages[15] (Figure 8). This idea might seem counterintuitive. It seems logical to argue that the early nineteenth-century onset of mass print media marked a transition from 'orality' to literacy. The communication theorist Walter Ong, for example, claims that the era marked a 'new state of consciousness associated with definite interiorisation of print and atrophy of ancient rhetorical traditions'.[16] This notion of a watershed moment has become central to influential understandings of nationalism and literary traditions in British and American contexts.[17] Yet the creation, circulation and endurance of the texts contained in this book are testimony to a moment in which print and speech catalysed each other in profound ways.

Speeches had long been popular material for pamphlets but newspapers now also became vitally important means of broadcasting oratory. Words spoken by notable figures represented ideal content for the hundreds of column inches that needed to be filled in newly affordable newspapers.

---

14. For discussions of these contexts see Martin Hewitt, 'Aspects of Platform Culture in Nineteenth-Century Britain', *Nineteenth-Century Prose*, 29:1 (Spring 2002), 1–32; Angela Ray, *The Lyceum and Public Culture in the Nineteenth-Century United States* (East Lansing: Michigan State University Press, 2005); Donald Scott, 'The Popular Lecture and the Creation of a Public in Mid-Nineteenth-Century America', *Journal of American History*, 66:4 (1980), 791–5; Tom F. Wright (ed.), *The Cosmopolitan Lyceum: Lecture Culture and the Globe* (Amherst: University of Massachusetts Press, 2013); and Tom F. Wright, *Lecturing the Atlantic: Speech, Print and an Anglo-American Commons 1830–1870* (Oxford: Oxford University Press, 2017).

15. Joanne Shattock (ed.), *Journalism and the Periodical Press in Nineteenth-Century Britain* (Cambridge: Cambridge University Press, 2017); Aled Jones, *Powers of the Press: Newspapers, Power and the Public in Nineteenth-Century England* (London: Routledge, 2016).

16. Walter J. Ong, with additional chapters by John Hartley, *Orality and Literacy: The Technologizing of the Word: 30th Anniversary Edition* (London: Routledge, 2012), p. 162.

17. Larzer Ziff, *Writing in the New Nation: Prose, Print, and Politics in the Early United States* (New Haven, CT: Yale University Press, 1991); Michael Warner, *The Letters of the Republic: Publication and the Public Sphere in Eighteenth-Century America* (Cambridge, MA: Harvard University Press, 1990).

The legitimacy of such printing was often controversial. As recently as the 1770s, British reporters transcribing the words of statesmen would have been jailed for breaching Parliamentary privilege, and a hundred years later, speakers routinely complained about the intellectual theft of their words.[18] Yet there was a gradual move towards recognising public utterances as common property. By mid-century, almost all newspapers, from national and regional titles to the very smallest outlets, had routinised the printing of speeches, sometimes by requesting the speaker's own script but far more often through increasingly sophisticated shorthand and stenography methods (Figures 3 and 12).

Printed versions of speeches reached audiences far greater than ever heard them spoken. As one historian recalls, 'a speech delivered in the House of Commons in the evening was read next morning at a million breakfast tables, and discussed in the afternoon in thousands of workshops and mills'.[19] Such oratory became an absorbing spectacle of the page through accounts that typically captured not only speaker but audience response, including laugher, applause, murmurs and heckles. If newspaper consumption, in Benedict Anderson's classic account of nationalism, allowed the republic to conceive of itself as 'a deep, horizontal comradeship', then reporting of oratorical events allowed citizens to become part of an abstract community of listeners.[20] The speakers contained in this book therefore composed and delivered their words conscious of the dynamics of this new mediascape of capture and dissemination. Such coverage was, after all, one of the reasons that speechmaking came to occupy such a crucial cultural role, one in which, as the lecturer–celebrity Emerson put it, 'the highest bribes of society are all at the feet of the successful orator'.[21]

Why Study Oratory?

Given this former prominence, the marginal place that the study of oratory now occupies might seem surprising. There are various traditions underpinning this. The oldest is the dismissal of rhetoric as merely instrumental

---

18. Christopher Reid, 'Whose Parliament? Political Oratory and Print Culture in the Later Eighteenth Century', *Language and Literature*, 9 (May 2000), 122–34; John Vice and Stephen Farrell, *The History of Hansard* (London: Hansard, 2017).

19. William S. Murphy, *The Genesis of British War Poetry* (London: Simpkin, Marshall, 1918), p. 11. For cultures of revocalisation see Philip Collins, *Reading Aloud: A Victorian Metier* (Lincoln: Tennyson Research, 1972).

20. Benedict Anderson, *Imagined Communities: Reflections on the Origin and Spread of Nationalism* (London: Verso, 1991), p. 7.

21. Ralph Waldo Emerson, 'Eloquence', in *The Collected Works of Ralph Waldo Emerson*, ed. Robert E. Spiller, Alfred R. Ferguson, Joseph Slater and Jean F. Carr (Cambridge, MA: Belknap Press, 1971), p. 31.

and innately suspect, a note sounded as early as Plato. It was re-echoed at the beginning of our period by Immanuel Kant, who made the influential distinction that, whereas 'poetry expands the mind by setting the imagination free; rhetoric borrows from the art of poetry to win minds [and] to rob them of their freedom'.[22] Future US President and Harvard Professor of Rhetoric John Quincy Adams acknowledged in 1810 the prevailing view that it was

> a frivolous science, substituting childish declamation instead of manly sense, and adapted rather to the pageantry of a public festival than to the sober concerns of real life . . . and it is a pernicious science; the purpose of which is to mislead the judgement by fascinating the imagination.[23]

Especially in North America, oratory was still often discussed and published as part of literary tradition. But by the late nineteenth century, oral language had become associated primarily with agitation and statecraft, more a matter of ideology and persuasion than intrinsic aesthetic or cultural value. The professionalisation of higher education helped further this separation. During the foundational canon-forming moments of British and American literary studies, evanescent ephemeral forms, such as speeches, sermons and lectures, were seen as detached from the permanence and gravity of novels, drama, poetry and the essay. Though spoken eloquence had been central to humanistic education and artistic endeavour for centuries, gradually the two subjects of 'Rhetoric and Communication' and 'English' developed quite distinct institutional identities, with the former disappearing entirely from British university life.

A series of twentieth-century intellectual trends helped perpetuate this neglect. The New Criticism distrusted the ephemeral, contextual nature of the spoken word and the kind of questions that emerge from rhetorical situations.[24] Social historians have tended to dismiss attention to oratory that has survived the processes of erasure as primarily the connoisseurship of elite male discourse. History of the book scholarship, with its emphasis on the materiality of texts, also tended to marginalise the spoken word.[25]

---

22. Immanuel Kant, *Critique of the Power of Judgment*, trans. Paul Guyer (Cambridge: Cambridge University Press, 2007), p. 203.

23. John Quincy Adams, *Lectures on Rhetoric and Oratory: Delivered to the Classes of Senior and Junior Sophisters in Harvard University* (Cambridge: Hilliard and Metcalf, 1810), p. 54.

24. Walter Ong rightly considers the New Critical stance 'a prime example of text-bound thinking . . . [which] assimilated the verbal artwork to the visual object-world of texts rather than to the oral–aural event-world' (Ong, with Hartley, *Orality and Literacy*).

25. See Paul Erickson, 'Help or Hindrance? The History of the Book and Electronic Media', in Henry Jenkins and David Thorburn (eds), *Rethinking Media Change: The Aesthetics of Transition* (Cambridge, MA: MIT Press, 2003).

Meanwhile, Jacques Derrida's influential poststructuralist critique of Western overemphasis of the 'presence' of speech raised the ideological stakes involved in the very act of contemplating spoken texts.[26] These tendencies enabled a generation of scholars to view oratorical expression with suspicion. During recent decades, however, there has been a return to the world of speech. The New Historicism advocated a less sharp divide between 'literary' and 'rhetorical', and made possible the study of a wider range of texts, while postcolonial history and multicultural literary studies have both encouraged scholars to revisit the archives of non-literate peoples.[27] Contemporary media studies has reclaimed voice and performance as best understood as part of the 'emerging media' of industrial modernity.[28]

Reintegrating oratory back into transatlantic cultural, literary and political history enables a number of vital new perspectives. It reconnects us to the ways in which large groups of people encountered and employed language and helps us access the imaginative horizons of a more orally orientated. Since, as the British essayist and Parliamentary observer William Hazlitt noted in 1804, 'the business of the orator' was to match 'action to feeling', the act of tracing this process in action yields fascinating insights into the history of emotions.[29] Finally, an understanding of oratorical history can enrich the appreciation of the period's literature. Cultures of speechmaking marked the great writing of the age in multiple stylistic and intellectual ways. Thomas Paine's pamphleteering makes more sense when considered as transcribed stump preaching; Whitman's *Leaves of Grass* acquires new layers by seeing it as the product of a speech-fevered New York. As Matthew Bevis has shown, grasping the importance of oratory to the Victorian public sphere can also enrich readings of Lord Byron, Charles Dickens and the stream-of-consciousness rhythms of James Joyce.[30]

---

26. For a useful summary of Derridean attitudes to orality see Christopher Norris, 'Derrida and Oralcy: Grammatology Revisited'. Available at: <http://www2.lingue.unibo.it/acume/acumedvd/Essays%20ACUME/Norris.pdf> (last accessed 23 July 2013).

27. See especially Lora Romero, 'Vanishing Americans: Gender, Empire and New Historicism', in Michael A. Elliott and Claudia Stokes (eds), *American Literary Studies: A Methodological Reader* (New York: New York University Press, 2003).

28. For a survey of this work see Sandra Gustafson, 'American Literature and the Public Sphere', *American Literary History*, 20:3 (2008), 465–78.

29. William Hazlitt, *The Eloquence of the British Senate: Being a Selection of the Best Speeches of the Most Distinguished Parliamentary Speakers, from the Beginning of the Reign of Charles I. to the Present Time: With Notes, Biographical, Critical, and Explanatory* (London: J. Murray, 1808), p. 4.

30. Bevis, *The Art of Eloquence.*

How to Use This Book

Books such as *Transatlantic Rhetoric* are the latest in a long and varied line of speech anthologies, a tradition that has been imagined in multiple ways. During the nineteenth century, many were published as elocutionary manuals, to train young readers for democratic participation. The most famous was Caleb Bingham's *The Columbian Orator*, a collection first published in 1797 that became a touchstone for generations of American autodidacts, most notably the young Frederick Douglass, who claimed its contents helped 'give tongue' to his own radical thoughts.[31] Countless other volumes appeared during the century, conceived variously as inspirational patriotic documents reconnecting readers to 'the history and original spirit of our government', or in other cases as a 'fund of philosophy' and 'well of wisdom' to uplift the casual reader.[32] The compilers of such books were typically content with a radically limited sense of notable speakers and topics, something that often continues into today's popular speech anthologies.[33] A number of contemporary collections, however, have explicitly sought to redress these archival imbalances. *Lift Every Voice* (1998), a pioneering collection of early African American oratory, is presented in terms of its 'indispensable access to the actual voices of historical actors . . . denied the critical attention they deserve'.[34] Similarly, *Women at the Podium* (2000) is framed as 'a stirring tribute to the many women who fought so hard to be heard'.[35] These ambitions of multicultural recovery have become the norm

---

31. Quoted in David Blight, *Frederick Douglass: Prophet of Freedom* (New York: Simon and Schuster, 2018), p. 45.

32. G. M. Whitman, *American Orators and Oratory* (New York: Occidental, 1884), p. 4; Godfrey Locker-Lampson, *Oratory, British and Irish: The Great Age* (London: Arthur Humphries, 1918), p. 6.

33. Recent examples of this genre include Lewis Copeland, Lawrence W. Lamm and Stephen J. McKenna (eds), *The World's Great Speeches: Fourth Enlarged Edition* (Newburyport, MA: Dover, 2012); William Safire, *Lend Me Your Ears: Great Speeches in History* (Newburyport, MA: Rosetta, 2014); Brian MacArthur, *The Penguin Book of Historic Speeches* (London: Penguin, 1995); Brian MacArthur, *The Penguin Book of Modern Speeches* (London: Penguin, 2017). Recent, more critical, collections include Andrew Burnett, Nancy Bailey, Alan Burnett, Andrew Campbell, Steve Cramer and Catherine Gaunt (eds), *50 Speeches that Made the Modern World* (2016); and Shaun Usher, *Speeches of Note: A Celebration of the Old, New and Unspoken* (London: Hutchison, 2018).

34. Philip S. Foner and Robert J. Branham, *Lift Every Voice: African American Oratory, 1787–1900* (Tuscaloosa: University of Alabama Press, 1998).

35. S. M. Nix, *Women at the Podium: Memorable Speeches in History* (New York: Harper, 2000).

in the most prominent inheritors of the speech anthology tradition that is now a hybrid genre of uplift, inclusion and historical curiosity.

This book adopts a more focused format in order to allow for a number of historical and conceptual approaches. Rather than being chronological, the book is structured thematically around the major debates of the era. As Holly Case has argued, 'the nineteenth century drive to *settle* or *solve* questions' was one of the defining features of how intellectual progress was imagined: 'the question had become an instrument of thought with special potency, structuring ideas about society, politics and states'.[36] In keeping with this, the chapters that follow organise speeches into six chapters, loosely arranged around the great 'questions' of the century: Nationalisms and Independence; Gender, Suffrage and Sexuality; Slavery and Race; Faith, Culture and Society; Empire and Manifest Destiny; and War and Peace. Within these chapters, smaller sections treat issues such as the Irish Question, the suffrage debate and the American sectional crisis. These chapters allow readers to navigate key controversies and form a sense of the content and style of arguments mounted on either sides, and provides a point of entry into key figures, movements and contexts.

Structuring these texts in terms of 'questions' foregrounds an agonistic model of political action, with rhetoric as a flawed means of solving social problems. It also reveals illuminating points of connection and dissonance in how different rhetorical traditions have sought to do this: the varying tone of Irish, Haitian and American nationalisms; the shared metaphors of abolition and the women's movement; the differences between Seneca, Cherokee and Delaware oral styles. Chief among these is the broad comparison between British and American speechmaking, whose supposed distinctions understandably fascinated contemporaries.[37] As the selections and introductions make clear, the key intellectual discourses of the period, from abolition and women's suffrage to science and spiritualism, were explicitly transatlantic affairs, reliant upon a shared network of settings, speakers, goals, tropes and discourses. However, readers can see how certain fascinating distinctions none the less emerge. For example, as Stephen Fender has argued, whereas American rhetoric of the period characteristically turns on broad points of principle, 'speeches work differently in British culture' and tend towards less abstract problems and solutions.[38]

---

36. Holly Case, *The Age of Questions: Or, a First Attempt at an Aggregate History of the Eastern, Social, Woman, American, Jewish, Polish, Bullion, Tuberculosis, and Many Other Questions Over the Nineteenth Century, and Beyond* (Princeton: Princeton University Press, 2018).

37. For a good example of comparative assessments of oratorical traditions see Edward Everett, 'Speeches of Henry Clay', *North American Review*, 25 (October 1827): 425–51. Also see the commentary in Adams, *Lectures on Rhetoric and Oratory*, and Charles Dickens, *American Notes* (London: Chapman and Hall), pp. 141–5.

38. Stephen Fender, *The Great American Speech: Words and Monuments* (London: Reaktion, 2015).

However, an equally productive means of using this book is by working backwards from the extensive index. Entries for movements, figures, ideas and contexts will allow readers to range freely through the texts and to appreciate this body of work as a story of interlinking ideas that mutate, reappear and take on new resonances. Take, for example, the fundamental keyword of *liberty*. The book's first chapter includes Edmund Burke's discussion of the 'fierce spirit of liberty' (p. 35) of the American colonists; the 'spectre of liberty' (p. 50) of the Haitian uprising; and the famous antithesis of Patrick Henry's speech urging war with Britain: 'give me liberty or give me death!' (p. 40). The word flows through the book, often ironically, as when Douglass in the 1850s dismisses the 'shoots of liberty and equality' as 'hollow mockery' (p. 131). Elsewhere, it is used despairingly to describe what is being lost, as when Lewis C. Levin's claims that Irish immigrants of the 1840s have made his 'fair land of liberty . . . a battle ground of tyrants' (p. 223), or when Robert Ingersoll tells his 1870s audience that 'there can be little liberty on earth while men worship a tyrant in heaven' (p. 161). By the end of the period covered by the book, we have come full circle, with Emmeline Pankhurst's 1913 address in Connecticut explicitly reviving Henry's 'liberty or death' antithesis for a new struggle and a new century.

Diving even deeper, readers might adopt a literary focus on tropes and phrases as subtle bearers of meaning. A fascinating example might be the multiple roles played by the word *voice*. Using the index, we can see how often speakers invoke imagined *voices* as participants triangulating between audience and speaker: for example, when Tecumseh urges his fellow Native Americans to 'listen to the voice . . . of your endangered country' (p. 56), when Gladstone reminds Parliament that 'we have given Ireland a voice, we must all listen for a moment to what she says' (p. 228), when Elizabeth Cady Stanton claims that 'the voice of woman has been silenced' or when Thomas Jefferson claims that the British have been 'deaf to the voice of justice' (p. 46). Others use it to frame their own power, as when Angelina Grimké aims to 'lift up my voice like a trumpet' (p. 123) or when Henry David Thoreau proclaims that 'voices in prison can still afflict the ear of the state' (p. 277). A similar dynamic is at work in the ubiquitous tropes centred on ideas of *awakening* and *rousing*: John Calhoun calls upon 'the power of mortal voice to awaken' (p. 119) the South; Emerson urges the 'voice of the mind' (p. 166) to bring us to consciousness; Stanton aims to 'rouse a nation to a sense of its sins' (p. 67); and Ida Wells longs for a voice that will 'rouse this nation', just as Douglass claims that 'the conscience of the nation must be roused' (p. 130). In each case, uses of *voice* or *rousing* become revealing meta-rhetorical commentaries on the relationship of individual agency to collective will.

Even more abstractly, readers can trace the subtleties involved in the fascinating use of natural imagery. Flows of water reappear in multiple speeches as telling metaphors for complex historical processes: they indicate inevitability when Douglass talks of the 'great streams' and 'angry waves' of justice (p. 127) and Gladstone warns the opponents of Irish Home Rule that the 'ebbing tide is with you, and the flowing tide is with us' (p. 228); or are suggestive of harmony when Swami Vivekananda describes racial mixing in terms of the 'different streams' that 'mingle their waters in the sea' (p. 163). A final example might the metaphor of the *storm*. Some speakers figure gales and squalls entirely negatively: Henry claims to have 'done everything that could be done to avert the storm which is now coming on' (p. 39); Tecumseh laments how tribes are 'driven before the wintry storms' (p. 55), as does Henry Ward Beecher when he speaks of how Civil War America is 'rolling, helplessly in a great tempest' (p. 132). Yet the rhetoric of others embraces the very condition of the storm. Douglass defiantly states that the cause of abolition needs 'the storm, the whirlwind, and the earthquake' (p. 131); Pankhurst draws power from her proud place 'in the storm centre of the suffragette movement' (p. 86). The entries in the index present many other examples of tropes, metaphors and phrases through which the book might be read.

Finally, the paramount task is to remember to read these words as both *speeches* and *texts*. The former requires an imaginative leap, re-entering the rhetorical situation in all its vivid performative dimensions, conjuring up rooms, faces, stages, settings, faces, reactions, gestures, bodies, responses and noises. It also requires an auditory leap, compelling us to hear the sounds, rhythms and flow of sentences, vowels and syllables. As the editorial note that follows this Introduction reminds us, most of the texts are excerpted for concision from longer pieces, and readers would do well to imagine the place of the selection within the broader dramatic structure of the performance. Reconstructing atmosphere is often helped along by transcriptions that include references to audience reaction: from 'applause', 'cheers' and 'laughter' to 'disapprobation' and heckles. However, such additions should also remind us of the compromised nature of all transcribed oratory. In the contextual headnotes to each speech, readers are encouraged to think of the very act of reading oratory as problematic. Transcripts are partial reconstructions of ephemeral moments of performance at best, and mere wilful misrepresentations at worst. Each new publication wrests control of message and meaning, a process continued, of course, by the book you hold in your hands. Readers should be sure to recall how important the journey of publication, recirculation and juxtaposition was to a text's ultimate meaning and reception in ways that were largely out of the speakers' control.

These approaches can bring the richness of public language alive and illuminate both the role speech has played historically and the role it continues to play in culture and society. By making Anglo-American oratory resonate, we reconnect to the fascination and potential of a timeless human activity. After all, this is a body of work with myriad lessons for contemporary political debates: from controversies over immigration, human rights, the role of race in American society or the enduring constitutional issues of the British Isles. Reflecting upon the power of voice is therefore by no means merely a nostalgic task. Rhetoric is open-source software that might just provide a manual for future political action.

Note on Texts and Editorial Policy

The book collects seventy-three speeches delivered between 1774 and 1913, in six chapters structured around what those in the period would have called great 'questions' of the day. The focus is on the English-speaking North Atlantic, but also embraces a handful of speeches translated from indigenous languages, and texts from Mexico, the Caribbean and Germany. Each chapter begins with a brief introduction, and each speech is presented with a contextual headnote, explanatory footnotes, and details of where to find the full original source.

The aim has been to broaden an understanding of nineteenth-century speechmaking through a newly diverse canon. By drawing on the most up-to-date research, the book offers an unprecedently rounded view of the most consequential spoken words of the era. This is, in part, a matter of the balance between well-known and more unexpected orators. Some selections present texts by famous orators, other by fascinating neglected figures; there are some by those famous for their eloquence, others renowned for different things but whose spoken words had significance. Some selections have been published before many times; others present previously unpublished or hard-to-find texts. For the most canonical speakers I have tried to include lesser-known pieces: not just Sojourner Truth's celebrated 1851 Ohio address but her wider reform speeches; not just Gladstone's Parliamentary oratory but his more controversial campaign-trail interventions in the American Civil War. Just as important was a consideration of diverse arguments. Care has been given to present spoken arguments both for and against some of the key issues of the day, including voices against female suffrage or racial equality, and argument in favour of the slave trade, imperial expansion and the cause of the Confederacy.

Nineteenth-century audiences were famously tolerant of length, and appreciative of speeches of over two hours in duration. Inevitably, therefore, the texts that follow are, for the most part, heavily excerpted. The guiding principle has been to present the most resonant or powerful passages, to allow readers to grasp the argument, tone and emotional pitch of each given speech. However, readers aiming to place these moments back into their original structures or gain a fuller sense of the whole can use the citation provided to go back to the full source text.

Throughout, readers are encouraged to think of reading oratory as inherently problematic. No matter how seemingly polished, these are only ever imperfect reconstructions of ephemeral moments. Since many of these texts were not originally intended for publication, decisions had to be made by their first publishers and editors to render them comprehensible as printed artefacts. Some texts were scripts prepared by their speakers, others verbatim transcriptions by audience members, and yet others reconstructed in more impressionistic fashion by listeners. Some capture prepared words uttered in grand formal venues, others the improvised interventions, riffs of street corners, muddy fields and courtrooms. No selection can do justice to a diffuse historical record over a century long. Instead, this book is a resource that will allow scholars and general readers to begin a rewarding and unexpected journey through a world of speech.

Figure 1 'Edmund Burke, the Great Orator', from Coleman E. Bishop, *Pictures of English History*, 1850.

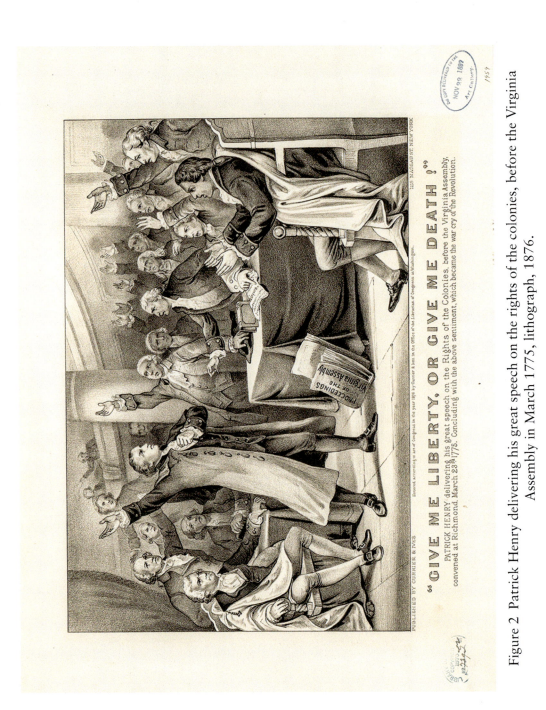

Figure 2 Patrick Henry delivering his great speech on the rights of the colonies, before the Virginia Assembly in March 1775, lithograph, 1876.

Figure 3 George Caleb Bingham, *Stump Speaking*, 1854.

Figure 4 John Mix Stanley, *The Trial of Red Jacket*, 1869.

Destruction by Fire of Pennsylvania Hall,

On the night of the 17th May, **1838**

Figure 5 The hall was burned to the ground by an anti-abolitionist crowd two days after a speech against slavery by Angelina Grimke.

Figure 6 'Exeter Hall, the great anti-slavery meeting', engraving, Henry Melville, 1841.

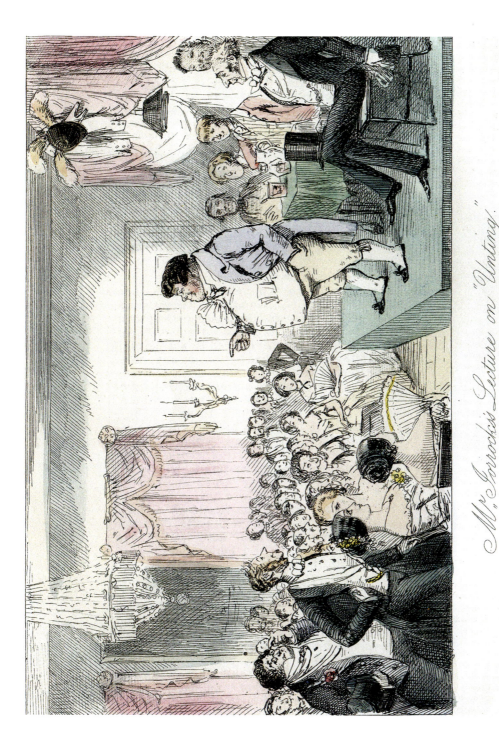

Mr Jorrocks' Lecture on "Unting".

Figure 7 'Victorian Man Giving a Lecture', illustration, John Leech, 1854.

THE ORATION.

We regret that our limited space will not permit us to lay before our readers this splendid effort of Mr. Everett. In it he gives a graphic and eloquent description of the battle of Gettysburg and an admirable dissertation upon the wicked rebellion of which it was one of the bloody fruits. The oration will be read with interest by every loyal man and woman in the land.

When Mr. Everett had concluded, a hymn composed by Hon. B. B. French, was sung with excellent effect by the Baltimore Glee Club, after which, Marshal Lamon introduced to the assemblage, the President of the United States, who delivered the following dedicatory remarks:

SPEECH OF THE PRESIDENT.

Four score and seven years ago our fathers brought forth upon this continent a new nation, conceived in liberty and dedicated to the proposition that all men are created equal. [Applause.] Now, we are engaged in a great civil war, testing whether that nation, or any other nation so conceived and so dedicated, can long endure. We are met on a great battle-field of that war; we are met to dedicate a portion of it as the final resting-place of those who here gave their lives that that nation might live. It is altogether fitting and proper that we should do this. But, in a larger sense, we cannot dedicate, we cannot consecrate, we cannot hallow this ground. The brave men, living and dead, who struggled here have consecrated it far above our poor power to add or detract. [Applause.] The world will little note nor long remember what we say here; but it can never forget what they did here. [Applause.]

It is for us, the living, rather to be dedicated here to the unfinished work that they have thus far so nobly carried on. [Applause.] It is rather for us here to be dedicated to the great task remaining before us; that from these honored dead we take increased devotion to that cause for which they here gave the last full measure of devotion; that we here highly resolve that those dead shall not have died in vain. [Applause.] That the nation shall, under God, have a new birth of freedom; and that Governments of the people, by the people and for the people, shall not perish from the earth. [Long continued applause.]

Figure 8 Lincoln's 'Gettysburg Address' in the Washington, DC, *National Republican*, 19 November 1863.

I Sell the Shadow to Support the Substance.

SOJOURNER TRUTH.

Figure 9 Sojourner Truth *carte de visite* c.1864.

THE NATIONAL COLORED CONVENTION IN SESSION AT WASHINGTON, D. C.—SKETCHED BY THEO. R. DAVIS.—[SEE FIRST PAGE.]

Figure 10 National Convention of the Colored Men of America in session at Washington, DC, January 1869. Among the speakers was Frederick Douglass.

Figure 11 Charles Spurgeon preaching at the South London Tabernacle, 1876.

Figure 12 William Gladstone at Blackheath, *Illustrated London News*, 7 February 1874.

PREHISTORIC PEEPS.

A NIGHT LECTURE ON EVOLUTION.

Figure 13 'Prehistoric Peeps: A Night Lecture on Evolution', satirical engraving, 1894.

Figure 14 Emmeline Pankhurst addressing a crowd in Trafalgar Square, London, October 1908.

Figure 15 Emma Goldman addressing garment workers in Union Square, New York, 1916.

1 Nationalisms and Independence

Introduction

The great age of nationalism ushered in potent new ways of describing social bonds. The three great Atlantic revolutions with which this book's period begins – the American (1775–83), French (1789–99) and Haitian (1791–1804) – turned on the novel proposition that scattered peoples could be united through emotional allegiance to the idea of a sovereign state. This coming together of these peoples into new 'nations' was driven by economic development, encouraged by religious revivals and sharpened by oppression and political grievance. But first these new connections had to be imagined and described. A new language had to be forged for what Edmund Burke, in his speech below, calls 'the things that hold together the great contexture of the mysterious whole' (p. 36). Replacing older local traditions and ideals of dynastic stability, national movements achieved emotional legitimacy in part thanks to the quasi-religious symbolic language rich in metaphor and mystification, centred on land, blood, honour and liberty.

Orators played a symbolic role in this process. The development of print capitalism allowed pamphleteers to help the infectious language of nationhood take root, but it was nationalist oratory that offered the purest means by which live crowds and secondary readerships could imagine the spirit of the *Volk* condensed into a single voice. In the 1750s, the Scottish philosopher David Hume predicted that the revival of interest in speechmaking might serve to 'rouse the genius of the nation'.[1] And, as historian Daniel Boorstin has written of the period, at the moment that nations 'struggled into self-consciousness, the orator – the man standing to or for or with his community – acquired a mythic role'.[2] This was not least because the antique symbolism of oratory matched the pretentions to antiquity that obscured the artifice involved in inventing national traditions. When transcribed, the speeches given by leaders of revolutionary America, Haiti and Mexico, and

---

1. David Hume, 'Of Eloquence' (1742), in *Essays and Treatises on Several Subjects: In Two Volumes* (London: Printed for T. Cadell, 1788), p. 91.
2. Daniel Boorstin, *The Americans: The National Experience* (New York: Random House, 1965), p. 276.

those of would-be liberators of Ireland, were available for viral repetition as part of a sacred canon that schoolchildren from Virginia to Dublin would be encouraged to recite and preserve for much of the next century.[3]

The selections below gather a range of the most important or indicative speeches of those seeking to direct the passions loosed by nationalism. The first part ('Debating American Freedom') voices four different positions over the fate of the British colonies. The first two urge compromise. Pennsylvania loyalist Joseph Galloway's speech (1774) vainly attempted to dissuade his fellow delegates in the first Continental Congress from severing bonds with the mother country, whilst Edmund Burke's words in Parliament (1775) capture the doomed attempt of sympathetic British observers to prevent escalation. By contrast, in the next selection, Patrick Henry's 'Give Me Liberty' speech (1775) adapted the language of religious revivalism to stir his fellow Virginians to resist the British, in what would become the era's most famous example of nationalist oratory. The conflict on the ground between loyalists and revolutionaries did not, of course, take place in a vacuum. The section ends with a speech from Delaware Chief Buckongahelas, from one of many groups caught in the 'family quarrel' (p. 41) between settlers and their former masters, offering his people a vision of how to adapt to new realities.

The next part ('Declaring Independence') brings together proclamations intended for oral transmission that, in various ways, announced the arrival of self-determination. Two of these – Thomas Jefferson's 'Declaration of Independence' (1776) and Jean-Jacques Dessalines's 'Haitian Declaration of Independence' (1804) were performative utterances with ultimate legal force. The very brief 'Cry of Dolores' ('El Grito de Dolores') (1810) of Miguel Hidalgo y Costilla has a more symbolic status as the opening rhetorical shot of the Mexican War of Independence. Robert Emmet's 'Speech from the Dock' (1803) marks not a successful anti-colonial rebellion but the words of a leader about to give his life for an unrealised Irish freedom, carefully fashioning his posthumous martyrdom.

The final part ('Pan- and Transnationalisms') ends with examples of speeches that called for forms of belonging that transcended the literal nation. Given the racial underpinnings of ideologies of nationhood, it is no surprise that the selections here all come from non-white groups eager to imagine alternative universalist communities based on cosmopolitan diasporas. In what follows, the Shawnee warrior Tecumseh calls (1811) for a Native American tribal confederacy to resist Euro-American encroachment. The Cuban patriot–poet José Martí argues (1889) for a coming together of the peoples of Caribbean and Latin America, just as the African American

---

3. See Carolyn Eastman, *A Nation of Speechifiers: Making an American Public After the Revolution* (Chicago: University of Chicago Press, 2009), pp. 20–5; and James Perrin Warren, *Culture of Eloquence: Oratory and Reform in Antebellum America* (University Park: Penn State University Press, 1999).

intellectual W. E. B. Du Bois urges (1900) a London audience of fellow black statesmen to unify a global diaspora against what he momentously terms 'the color line' (p. 59). Ranging from one end of the nineteenth century to the other, these addresses all repurpose nationalism's own rhetoric to persuade peoples 'scattered as autumn leaves' (p. 55) to use racial solidarity as a counterweight to overbearing Euro-nationalism.

Beginning this book with these speeches allows us to see how, as Benedict Anderson has shown, tropes of nationalism were 'modular' and capable of radical reproducibility.[4] The words that follow provided a repertoire of gestures that were transferrable, not just for other movements for national liberation, such as those throughout the Americas in the early nineteenth century or Africa into the twentieth, but also for broader emancipatory movements such as that for gender equality.[5] In successive chapters, the distinctively masculinist tropes and emotional register of nationalism will be constantly repurposed, sometimes sincerely sometimes with pointed irony, for new and unexpected ends.

---

4. Benedict Anderson, *Imagined Communities* (London: Verso, 1982), p. 4.
5. See David Armitage, *The Declaration of Independence: A Global History* (Cambridge, MA: Harvard University Press, 2008).

Part A: Debating American Freedom

1. Joseph Galloway, 'A Plan to Avoid War' (Philadelphia, 1774)

In September 1774, prominent Pennsylvania loyalist Joseph Galloway (1731–1803) made an impassioned plea to fellow members of the Continental Congress in Philadelphia, urging them to support compromise with the British crown.

Galloway served as speaker of the colonial assembly from 1766 to 1775, and as discussions in that body moved towards political separation, his became a notable moderate voice against formal independence. The speech below, with its familial language of virtue and duty, expressed an exasperated loyalist's proposal for reconciliation. Yet sentiment in the assembly had already shifted too far along the road to separation for his pleas to have an effect, and his plan was defeated by one vote. Galloway left Philadelphia to join the British army before fleeing the colonies for England in 1778.

Source

'Galloway's Plan', in 'Journals of the Continental Congress', September 1774, at *A Century of Lawmaking for the New Nation*, Library of Congress. Available at: <http://memory.loc.gov/ammem/amlaw/lawhome.html> (last accessed 11 July 2019).

These advocates also assert, what we cannot deny – That the discovery of the Colonies was made under a commission[6] granted by the supreme authority of the British State, that they have been settled under that authority, and therefore are truly the property of that State. Parliamentary jurisdiction has been constantly exercised over them from their first settlement; its executive authority has ever run through all their inferior political systems: the Colonists have ever sworn allegiance to the British State, and have been considered, both by the State and by themselves, as subjects of the British Government. Protection and allegiance are reciprocal duties; the one cannot exist without the other. The Colonies cannot claim the protection of Britain upon any principle of reason or law, while they deny its supreme authority. Upon this ground the authority of Parliament stands too firm to be shaken by any arguments whatever; and therefore to deny that authority, and at the same time to declare their incapacity to be represented, amounts to a full and explicit declaration of independence ...

---

6. British colonies in North America were established through the granting of commercial charters by successive administrations from King James I to Charles II.

In regard to the political state of the Colonies, you must know that they are so many inferior societies, disunited and unconnected in polity. That while they deny the authority of Parliament, they are, in respect to each other, in a perfect state of nature, destitute of any supreme direction or decision whatever, and incompetent to the grant of national aids, or any other general measure whatever, even to the settlement of differences among themselves ...

You also knew that the seeds of discord are plentifully sowed in the constitution of the Colonies; that they are already grown to maturity, and have more than once broke out into open hostilities. They are at this moment only suppressed by the authority of the Parent State; and should that authority be weakened or annulled, many subjects of unsettled disputes, and which in that case, can only be settled by an appeal to the sword, must involve us in all the horrors of civil war ...

Desirous as I am to promote the freedom of the Colonies, and to prevent the mischiefs which will attend a military contest with Great-Britain, I must intreat you to desert the measures which have been so injudiciously and ineffectually pursued by antecedent Assemblies. Let us thoroughly investigate the subject matter in dispute, and endeavour to find from that investigation the means of perfect and permanent redress ... I would therefore acknowledge the necessity of the supreme authority of Parliament over the Colonies, because it is a proposition which we cannot deny without manifest contradiction, while we confess that we are subjects of the British Government; and if we do not approve of a representation in Parliament, let us ask for a participation in the freedom and power of the English constitution in some other mode of incorporation: for I am convinced, by long attention to the subject, that let us deliberate, and try what other expedients we may, we shall find none that can give to the Colonies substantial freedom, but some such incorporation.

I therefore beseech you, by the respect you are bound to pay to the instructions of your constituents, by the regard you have for the honour and safety of your country, and as you wish to avoid a war with Great-Britain, which must terminate, at all events in the ruin of America, not to rely on a denial of the authority of Parliament, a refusal to be represented, and on a non-importation agreement; because whatever protestations, in that case, may be made to the contrary, it will prove to the world that we intend to throw off our allegiance to the State, and to involve the two countries in all the horrors of a civil war.

2. Edmund Burke, 'On Conciliation with the Colonies' (London, 1775)

On the other side of the Atlantic the following Spring, legislators would hear a far more famous argument in favour of moderation. As hostilities moved toward war, in March 1775, Anglo-Irish statesman Edmund Burke (1729–97) delivered a dramatic speech to the House of Commons, presenting a plan to 'conciliate and concede' to America without the appearance of Britain having been defeated.

Burke was not just a respected philosopher and theorist but one of the outstanding orators of his day. A leading speaker in Parliament for over thirty years, his impassioned speeches helped shape English public life in the second half of the eighteenth century. His epic orations found a second audience as printed documents, and through the century following his death in 1797 were often studied and recited in schools and colleges in both Europe and the United States (Figure 1).

In this, perhaps his most famous, Parliamentary speech, he attempted to persuade the Commons of the validity of the grievances expressed by the colonists. It was based on the optimistic assumption that the American colonists were interested in reforming and renewing the imperial relationship. Yet only one month after Burke delivered the speech, the Battles of Lexington and Concord of 19 April 1775 meant that little prospect of reconciliation survived. In the extract below we pick up mid-point in the lengthy, ornate address, as Burke concludes his prefatory arguments and proceeds to the plan, a scheme that was heavily defeated when the vote was taken in the House of Commons.

Source

Edmund Burke, *The Works of the Right Honourable Edmund Burke*, 6 vols (London: Henry G. Bohn, 1854), vol. 1, pp. 17–93.

A fierce spirit of liberty has grown up [in America]. It has grown with the growth of the people in your colonies, and increased with the increase of their wealth; a spirit, that unhappily meeting with an exercise of power in England, which, however lawful, is not reconcilable to any ideas of liberty, much less with theirs, has kindled this flame that is ready to consume us.

I do not mean to commend either the spirit in this excess, or the moral causes which produce it. Perhaps a more smooth and accommodating spirit of freedom in them would be more acceptable to us. Perhaps ideas of liberty might be desired, more reconcilable with an arbitrary and boundless authority. Perhaps we might wish the colonists to be persuaded, that their liberty is more secure when held in trust for them by us (as their guardians during a perpetual minority) than with any part of it in their own hands. The question is, not whether their spirit deserves praise or blame, but – what, in the name of God, shall we do with it? . . .

Do not entertain so weak an imagination, as that your registers and your bonds, your affidavits and your sufferances, your cockets and your clearances, are what form the great securities of your commerce. Do not dream that your letters of office, and your instructions, and your suspending clauses, are the things that hold together the great contexture of the mysterious whole. These things do not make your government. Dead instruments, passive tools as they are, it is the spirit of the English communion that gives all their life and efficacy to them. It is the spirit of the English Constitution,[7] which, infused through the mighty mass, pervades, feeds, unites, invigorates, vivifies every part of the empire, even down to the minutest member.

Is it not the same virtue which does everything for us here in England? Do you imagine then, that it is the Land Tax Act[8] which raises your revenue? that it is the annual vote in the Committee of Supply which gives you your army? or that it is the Mutiny Bill[9] which inspires it with bravery and discipline? No! surely no! It is the love of the people; it is their attachment to their government, from the sense of the deep stake they have in such a glorious institution – which gives you your army and your navy, and infuses into both that liberal obedience, without which your army would be a base rabble, and your navy nothing but rotten timber.

All this, I know well enough, will sound wild and chimerical to the profane herd of those vulgar and mechanical politicians, who have no place among us; a sort of people who think that nothing exists but what is gross and material; and who therefore, far from being qualified to be directors of the great movement of empire, are not fit to turn a wheel in the machine. But to men truly initiated and rightly taught, these ruling and master principles, which, in the opinion of such men as I have mentioned, have no substantial existence, are in truth every thing, and all in all. Magnanimity in politicks is not seldom the truest wisdom; and a great empire and little minds go ill together. If we are conscious of our station, and glow with zeal to fill our places as becomes our situation and ourselves, we ought to auspicate all our public proceedings on America with the old warning of the church, *Sursum corda!*[10]

We ought to elevate our minds to the greatness of that trust to which the order of Providence has called us. By adverting to the dignity of this high calling, our ancestors have turned a savage wilderness into a glorious empire; and have made the most extensive, and the only honourable conquests, not by destroying, but by promoting the wealth, the number, the happiness, of the human race. Let us get an American revenue as we have got an American empire. English privileges have made it all that it is; English privileges alone will make it all it can be.

---

7. Rather than a written constitution, the body politic of Great Britain consisted of statue law, common law and acts of Parliament.
8. A national property tax introduced by Parliament in 1692.
9. The 1774 Quartering Act required local governments in the American colonies to provide the British soldiers with housing and food.
10. 'Lift up your hearts'.

3. Patrick Henry, 'Give Me Liberty or Give Me Death' (Richmond, Virginia, 1775)

Voices of moderation such as those of Galloway and Burke were set against the contagious passion of those who urged audiences towards conflict. The most famous speech of all took place in a small hilltop parish church in St John, Richmond, Virginia. Before an audience of 122 delegates of the Second Virginia Convention, a grouping that included future Presidents George Washington and Thomas Jefferson, local attorney Patrick Henry (1736–99) delivered what was eventually to become the most quoted speech of the era (Figure 2).

The delegates for the Commonwealth of Virginia had met to debate whether to mobilise the state's troops against the British. On the fourth day of the conference, a number of speakers had urged caution, but Henry's speech in favour of raising a militia was credited with swinging the balance in convincing the Convention. As he had done in that assembly for over a decade, Henry spoke powerfully against pacifying the British. Connecting passionate adherence to ideals of liberty and natural rights to a rhetoric of martyrdom, Henry goaded his audience into martial readiness.

Henry is now remembered as the quintessential public speaker of the Revolution, recalled by Jefferson as 'the man who gave the first impulse to the ball of revolution, and the greatest orator that ever lived'.[11] Yet this posthumous fame was slow to develop and his actual words built on uncertain foundations. It was not until a generation after his death, when a biographer interviewed those present in 1775 and reconstructed the supposed words for a wider audience, that the speech took on an afterlife of its own.[12] The abiding resonance of the phrase for which the speech is cherished – 'Give me Liberty or Give me Death! – weave their way through this anthology, ending up in the rhetoric of British suffragette Emmeline Pankhurst, who found Henry's uncompromising antithesis useful in her own struggle for gender equality.

Source

William Wirt, *Sketches of the Life and Character of Patrick Henry* (Philadelphia: Webster, 1817), pp. 119–23.

---

11. Thomas Jefferson to William Wirt, 4 August 1805, quoted in Sandra M. Gustafson, *Eloquence is Power: Oratory and Performance in Early America* (Chapel Hill: University of North Carolina Press, 2001), p. 160.
12. William Wirt, *Sketches of the Life and Character of Patrick Henry* (Philadelphia: Webster, 1817), pp. 119–23.

No man thinks more highly than I do of the patriotism, as well as abilities, of the very worthy gentlemen[13] who have just addressed the House. But different men often see the same subject in different lights; and, therefore, I hope it will not be thought disrespectful to those gentlemen if, entertaining as I do opinions of a character very opposite to theirs, I shall speak forth my sentiments freely and without reserve. This is no time for ceremony. The question before the House is one of awful moment to this country. For my own part, I consider it as nothing less than a question of freedom or slavery; and in proportion to the magnitude of the subject ought to be the freedom of the debate. It is only in this way that we can hope to arrive at truth, and fulfill the great responsibility which we hold to God and our country. Should I keep back my opinions at such a time, through fear of giving offense, I should consider myself as guilty of treason towards my country, and of an act of disloyalty toward the Majesty of Heaven, which I revere above all earthly kings.

Mr. President,[14] it is natural to man to indulge in the illusions of hope. We are apt to shut our eyes against a painful truth, and listen to the song of that siren till she transforms us into beasts. Is this the part of wise men, engaged in a great and arduous struggle for liberty? Are we disposed to be of the number of those who, having eyes, see not, and, having ears, hear not, the things which so nearly concern their temporal salvation? For my part, whatever anguish of spirit it may cost, I am willing to know the whole truth; to know the worst, and to provide for it.

I have but one lamp by which my feet are guided, and that is the lamp of experience. I know of no way of judging of the future but by the past. And judging by the past, I wish to know what there has been in the conduct of the British ministry for the last ten years to justify those hopes with which gentlemen have been pleased to solace themselves and the House. Is it that insidious smile with which our petition has been lately received? Trust it not, sir; it will prove a snare to your feet. Suffer not yourselves to be betrayed with a kiss. Ask yourselves how this gracious reception of our petition comports with those warlike preparations which cover our waters and darken our land. Are fleets and armies necessary to a work of love and reconciliation? Have we shown ourselves so unwilling to be reconciled that force must be called in to win back our love? Let us not deceive ourselves, sir. These are the implements of war and subjugation; the last arguments to which kings resort. I ask gentlemen, sir, what means this martial array, if its purpose be not to force us to submission? Can gentlemen assign any other possible motive for it? Has Great Britain any enemy, in this quarter of the world, to call for all this accumulation of navies and armies?

No, sir, she has none. They are meant for us: they can be meant for no other. They are sent over to bind and rivet upon us those chains which the British

---

13. Other members of the Virginia House of Burgesses.
14. Peyton Randolph (1722–55), Speaker of the House of Burgesses and Virginia Convention.

ministry have been so long forging. And what have we to oppose to them? Shall we try argument? Sir, we have been trying that for the last ten years. Have we anything new to offer upon the subject? Nothing. We have held the subject up in every light of which it is capable; but it has been all in vain. Shall we resort to entreaty and humble supplication? What terms shall we find which have not been already exhausted? Let us not, I beseech you, sir, deceive ourselves. Sir, we have done everything that could be done to avert the storm which is now coming on. We have petitioned; we have remonstrated; we have supplicated; we have prostrated ourselves before the throne, and have implored its interposition to arrest the tyrannical hands of the ministry and Parliament. Our petitions have been slighted; our remonstrances have produced additional violence and insult; our supplications have been disregarded; and we have been spurned, with contempt, from the foot of the throne! In vain, after these things, may we indulge the fond hope of peace and reconciliation. There is no longer any room for hope. If we wish to be free – if we mean to preserve inviolate those inestimable privileges for which we have been so long contending – if we mean not basely to abandon the noble struggle in which we have been so long engaged, and which we have pledged ourselves never to abandon until the glorious object of our contest shall be obtained – we must fight! I repeat it, sir, we must fight! An appeal to arms and to the God of hosts is all that is left us!

They tell us, sir, that we are weak; unable to cope with so formidable an adversary. But when shall we be stronger? Will it be the next week, or the next year? Will it be when we are totally disarmed, and when a British guard shall be stationed in every house? Shall we gather strength by irresolution and inaction? Shall we acquire the means of effectual resistance by lying supinely on our backs and hugging the delusive phantom of hope, until our enemies shall have bound us hand and foot? Sir, we are not weak if we make a proper use of those means which the God of nature hath placed in our power. The millions of people,[15] armed in the holy cause of liberty, and in such a country as that which we possess, are invincible by any force which our enemy can send against us. Besides, sir, we shall not fight our battles alone. There is a just God who presides over the destinies of nations, and who will raise up friends to fight our battles for us. The battle, sir, is not to the strong alone; it is to the vigilant, the active, the brave. Besides, sir, we have no election. If we were base enough to desire it, it is now too late to retire from the contest. There is no retreat but in submission and slavery![16] Our chains are forged! Their clanking

---

15. The population of the thirteen British colonies is estimated to have been 2.4 million.
16. Henry was a slave-owner, whose deep ambivalence did not lead him to renounce the peculiar institution. 'I am the master of slaves of my own purchase,' he wrote in 1773. 'I am drawn along by the general inconvenience of living here without them. I will not, I cannot justify it' (quoted in Jon Kukla, *Patrick Henry: Champion of Liberty* (New York: Simon & Schuster), p. 124).

may be heard on the plains of Boston![17] The war is inevitable – and let it come!
I repeat it, sir, let it come.

It is in vain, sir, to extenuate the matter. Gentlemen may cry, Peace, Peace –
but there is no peace. The war is actually begun! The next gale that sweeps
from the north will bring to our ears the clash of resounding arms! Our
brethren are already in the field! Why stand we here idle? What is it that
gentlemen wish? What would they have? Is life so dear, or peace so sweet, as
to be purchased at the price of chains and slavery? Forbid it, Almighty God!
I know not what course others may take; but as for me, give me liberty or
give me death!

4. Buckongahelas, 'You See a Great and Powerful Nation Divided!' (Delaware, 1781)

The final speech of this part allows us to hear the rarely heard voice
of the many groups caught amidst the currents of the Anglo-American
crisis. Buckongahelas (1750s–1804), also known as 'Pachgantschihilas'
('fulfiller') and 'Petchnanalas' ('one who succeeds in all he undertakes')
was a representative of the Algonquin-speaking Lenape tribe native to
the Delaware river region. Constantly pushed west from his ancestral
Delaware, his people joined a Shawnee-led confederacy against American settlements in the Ohio river, and after the Revolution took part in
many anti-settler wars in the Old Northwest.

In the speech below from 1781, delivered several years into the
War of Independence, he reluctantly undertook to persuade those
under his control to abandon the neutrality of Lenape leader White
Eyes and lend qualified support to the British. Like Galloway, he
framed the debate as domestic and familial, and this short extract
captures the fraught emotional stakes faced by those forced to
navigate the perilous and violent birth of the American republic.
Following American independence, Buckongahelas continued to fight
against the encroachment of the republic's forces in many wars in the
Old Northwest territories.

Source

Bob Blaisdell (ed.), *Great Speeches by Native Americans* (New York:
Dover, 2000).

17. Following the public sabotage of British property at the Boston Tea Party of
December 1773, the British ended self-government and imposed a series of punitive
restrictions.

Friends! Listen to what I say to you! You see a great and powerful nation divided! You see the father fighting against the son, and the son against the father! The father has called on his Indian children, to assist him in punishing his children, the Americans, who have become refractory. I took time to consider what I should do; whether or not I should receive the hatchet of my father to assist him. At first I looked upon it as a family quarrel, in which I was not interested.

However, at length, it appeared to me that the father was in the right; and his children deserved to be punished a little. That this must be the case, I concluded from the many cruel acts his offspring had committed from time to time on his Indian children, in encroaching on their land, stealing their property, shooting at, and murdering, without cause, men, women, and children.

Yes! even murdering those, who at all times, had been friendly to them, and were placed for protection under the roof of their father's house – the father himself standing sentry at the door at the time. Friends! often has the father been obliged to settle, and make amends for the wrongs and mischiefs done to us by his refractory children; yet these do not grow better. No; they remain the same; and will continue to be so, as long as we have any land left us. Look back at the murders committed by the Long-knives [English colonists] on many of our relations, who lived peaceable neighbors to them on the Ohio. Did they not kill them without the least provocation? Are they, do you think, better now than they were then?

Part B: Declaring Independence

5. Thomas Jefferson et al., 'The Unanimous Declaration of the United States of America' (Philadelphia, 1776)

Formal separation of the American colonies was enacted through a choreographed moment of speech. On Thursday, 4 July 1776, copies of a text announcing American independence were printed in Philadelphia and the Continental Congress ordered that they be rushed by horseback to be 'proclaimed in each of the United States, and at the head of the Army'.[18] On Monday, 8 July, the 'Unanimous Declaration of the Thirteen United States of America' was read aloud for the first time by Colonel John Nixon of the Committee of Safety at the State House in Philadelphia. In towns and cities across the nation, similar readings marked the first Independence Day celebrations, often accompanied by revelry and the tearing down of British emblems.

Audiences listening to this momentous proclamation heard that the thirteen American colonies, then at war with Great Britain, regarded themselves as independent states and no longer a part of the British Empire. Instead, they had formed a union that would become a new nation – the United States of America.

The text had been commissioned by John Adams, the representative from Massachusetts, and was essentially composed by the Virginian Thomas Jefferson, modified only slightly by the Congress. His text is customarily seen as possessing at least three parts. The first twenty-nine lines constitute a preamble, offering justification for the separation through deductive reasoning grounded in natural rights theory. The lengthy central section consists of a list of grievances, before the third and final section moves towards the ultimate declaration. The opening and closing sections were deliberately composed in a manner characteristic of what eighteenth-century rhetoricians called style périodique, with expansive, oratorical sentences whose sense is often grammatically deferred until their close, and were thus ideally suited to being read aloud.[19]

The importance of its framing of ideas, however, was to prove far more versatile and global. David Armitage has written of how the Declaration,

---

18. Pauline Maier, *American Scripture: Making the Declaration of Independence* (New York: Vintage/Knopf, 1998), p. 159.

19. Stephen E. Lucas, 'The Stylistic Artistry of the Declaration of Independence', *Prologue*, 22:1 (1990).

explicitly addressed as it was over the heads of the British to 'the candid world' at large, was variously 'an event, a document, and the beginning of a genre', whose ripples circled the globe'.[20] Its language and ideas became what Jefferson came to call 'an instrument', readily applicable not just to other self-determination movements throughout world history since, including the dawning of independence across Latin America and the Caribbean, in Vietnam, Liberia and New Zealand, but also to the struggle for gender equality and global civil rights.

Source

'The Unanimous Declaration of the Thirteen United States of America', *Primary Documents in American History*, Library of Congress. Available at: <https://www.loc.gov/rr/program/bib/ourdocs/DeclarInd.html> (11 July 2019).

When, in the course of human events, it becomes necessary for one people to dissolve the political bonds which have connected them with another, and to assume among the powers of the earth, the separate and equal station to which the laws of nature and of nature's God entitle them, a decent respect to the opinions of mankind requires that they should declare the causes which impel them to the separation.[21]

We hold these truths to be self-evident, that all men are created equal, that they are endowed by their Creator with certain unalienable rights, that among these are life, liberty and the pursuit of happiness.[22] That to secure these rights, governments are instituted among men, deriving their just powers from the consent of the governed. That whenever any form of government becomes destructive to these ends, it is the right of the people to alter or to abolish it, and to institute new government, laying its foundation on such principles and organizing its powers in such form, as to them shall seem most likely to effect their safety and happiness. Prudence, indeed, will dictate that governments long established should not be changed for light and transient causes; and accordingly

---

20. David Armitage, *The Declaration of Independence: A Global History* (Cambridge, MA: Harvard University Press, 2007).

21. This paragraph is a famous example of a periodic sentence, in which the main idea is postponed until the very end of a sentence. The main verb ('declare') comes sixty-three words into the construction, forcing a radical suspension of listeners' comprehension when spoken.

22. This most famous of sentences is usually seen as a reworking of John Locke's 'life, the liberty, health, limb, or goods of another' (John Locke, *Two Treatises of Government* (London: Awnsham Churchill, 1690)).

all experience hath shown that mankind are more disposed to suffer, while evils are sufferable, than to right themselves by abolishing the forms to which they are accustomed. But when a long train of abuses and usurpations, pursuing invariably the same object evinces a design to reduce them under absolute despotism, it is their right, it is their duty, to throw off such government, and to provide new guards for their future security. – Such has been the patient sufferance of these colonies; and such is now the necessity which constrains them to alter their former systems of government. The history of the present King of Great Britain is a history of repeated injuries and usurpations, all having in direct object the establishment of an absolute tyranny over these states. To prove this, let facts be submitted to a candid world.[23]

He has refused his assent to laws, the most wholesome and necessary for the public good.

He has forbidden his governors to pass laws of immediate and pressing importance, unless suspended in their operation till his assent should be obtained; and when so suspended, he has utterly neglected to attend to them.

He has refused to pass other laws for the accommodation of large districts of people, unless those people would relinquish the right of representation in the legislature, a right inestimable to them and formidable to tyrants only.

He has called together legislative bodies at places unusual, uncomfortable, and distant from the depository of their public records, for the sole purpose of fatiguing them into compliance with his measures.

He has dissolved representative houses repeatedly, for opposing with manly firmness his invasions on the rights of the people.

He has refused for a long time, after such dissolutions, to cause others to be elected; whereby the legislative powers, incapable of annihilation, have returned to the people at large for their exercise; the state remaining in the meantime exposed to all the dangers of invasion from without, and convulsions within.

He has endeavored to prevent the population of these states; for that purpose obstructing the laws for naturalization of foreigners; refusing to pass others to encourage their migration hither, and raising the conditions of new appropriations of lands.

He has obstructed the administration of justice, by refusing his assent to laws for establishing judiciary powers.

He has made judges dependent on his will alone, for the tenure of their offices, and the amount and payment of their salaries.

He has erected a multitude of new offices, and sent hither swarms of officers to harass our people, and eat out their substance.

He has kept among us, in times of peace, standing armies without the consent of our legislature.

---

23. A pointed phrase, which might include those subscribing to Enlightened principles, encompassing the Dutch Republic and the Kingdom of France.

He has affected to render the military independent of and superior to civil power.

He has combined with others to subject us to a jurisdiction foreign to our constitution, and unacknowledged by our laws; giving his assent to their acts of pretended legislation:

For quartering large bodies of armed troops among us:

For protecting them, by mock trial, from punishment for any murders which they should commit on the inhabitants of these states:

For cutting off our trade with all parts of the world:

For imposing taxes on us without our consent:

For depriving us in many cases, of the benefits of trial by jury:

For transporting us beyond seas to be tried for pretended offenses:

For abolishing the free system of English laws in a neighboring province, establishing therein an arbitrary government, and enlarging its boundaries so as to render it at once an example and fit instrument for introducing the same absolute rule in these colonies:

For taking away our charters, abolishing our most valuable laws, and altering fundamentally the forms of our governments:

For suspending our own legislatures, and declaring themselves invested with power to legislate for us in all cases whatsoever.

He has abdicated government here, by declaring us out of his protection and waging war against us.

He has plundered our seas, ravaged our coasts, burned our towns, and destroyed the lives of our people.

He is at this time transporting large armies of foreign mercenaries[24] to complete the works of death, desolation and tyranny, already begun with circumstances of cruelty and perfidy scarcely paralleled in the most barbarous ages, and totally unworthy the head of a civilized nation.

He has constrained our fellow citizens taken captive on the high seas to bear arms against their country, to become the executioners of their friends and brethren, or to fall themselves by their hands.

He has excited domestic insurrections amongst us, and has endeavored to bring on the inhabitants of our frontiers, the merciless Indian savages, whose known rule of warfare, is undistinguished destruction of all ages, sexes and conditions.

In every stage of these oppressions we have petitioned for redress in the most humble terms: our repeated petitions have been answered only by repeated injury. A prince, whose character is thus marked by every act which may define a tyrant, is unfit to be the ruler of a free people.

------

24. The British army relied during the 1770s upon the service of Hessian mercenaries, a mostly German pool of auxiliary soldiers, ultimately forming a quarter of all forces mobilised against the rebel colonists.

Nor have we been wanting in attention to our British brethren. We have warned them from time to time of attempts by their legislature to extend an unwarrantable jurisdiction over us. We have reminded them of the circumstances of our emigration and settlement here. We have appealed to their native justice and magnanimity, and we have conjured them by the ties of our common kindred to disavow these usurpations, which, would inevitably interrupt our connections and correspondence. They too have been deaf to the voice of justice and of consanguinity. We must, therefore, acquiesce in the necessity, which denounces our separation, and hold them, as we hold the rest of mankind, enemies in war, in peace friends.

We, therefore, the representatives of the United States of America,[25] in General Congress, assembled, appealing to the Supreme Judge of the world for the rectitude of our intentions, do, in the name, and by the authority of the good people of these colonies, solemnly publish and declare, that these united colonies are, and of right ought to be free and independent states; that they are absolved from all allegiance to the British Crown, and that all political connection between them and the state of Great Britain, is and ought to be totally dissolved; and that as free and independent states, they have full power to levy war, conclude peace, contract alliances, establish commerce, and to do all other acts and things which independent states may of right do. And for the support of this declaration, with a firm reliance on the protection of Divine Providence, we mutually pledge to each other our lives, our fortunes and our sacred honor.

6. Robert Emmet, 'Speech from the Dock' (Dublin, 1803)[26]

On 19 September 1803, the young Irish nationalist Robert Emmet (1778–1803) was sentenced to death for treason for his part in an uprising in Dublin, and delivered a speech from the dock that was to become an iconic text in the long Irish independence struggle that would follow.

Emmet was a Republican rebel leader from a wealthy Protestant family who had sympathised with the American colonists, and who viewed redress of Irish Catholics' lack of Parliamentary representation as part of the same struggle. During the unsuccessful 1803 uprising, the rebels had issued a 'Proclamation' of independence, outlining their aims, but it was to be the words apparently spoken by Emmet in the dock that would have the more lasting significance.

The extract below conveys the sense of the version of Emmet's words that was mostly commonly reprinted in the decades to follow. With its

---

25. That is, the fifty-six signatories to the Second Continental Congress.
26. Josef L. Altholz, *Selected Documents in Irish History* (Armonk, NY: M. E. Sharpe, 2000).

resonant call to place Ireland's 'independence beyond the reach of any power' and for it to take its place 'among the nations of the earth', it can be read as an independence declaration in the form of prophecy. And as such it was treated by later Irish patriots, who reprinted, amplified and edited the condemned man's speech in editions on both sides of the Atlantic, building upon the glamour of Emmet's words to sustain a movement for an independent Irish future.[27]

Source

Speeches from the Dock, or Protests of Irish Patriotism (Dublin: Gill, 1878).

I acted as an Irishman, determined on delivering my country from the yoke of a foreign and unrelenting tyranny,[28] and from the more galling yoke of a domestic faction,[29] its joint partner and perpetrator in the patricide, whose reward is the ignominy of existing with an exterior of splendour and a consciousness of depravity. It was the wish of my heart to extricate my country from this doubly-riveted despotism – I wish to place her independence beyond the reach of any power on earth. I wish to exalt her to that proud station in the world which Providence had destined her to fill. Connection with France was, indeed, intended, but only so far as mutual interest would sanction or require.

Were the French to assume any authority inconsistent with the purest independence, it would be the signal for their destruction. We sought their aid – and we sought it as we had assurances we should obtain it – as auxiliaries in war, and allies in peace. Were the French to come as invaders or enemies, uninvited by the wishes of the people, I should oppose them to the utmost of my strength.

Yes! My countrymen, I should advise you to meet them on the beach with a sword in one hand and a torch in the other. I would meet them with all the destructive fury of war, and I would animate my countrymen to immolate them in their boats before they had contaminated the soil of my country. If they succeeded in landing, and if forced to retire before superior discipline, I would

27. The speech was also frequently included in popular elocutionary anthologies of speeches intended for general American audiences, such as Abraham Small (ed.), *The American Speaker: A Selection of Popular, Parliamentary and Forensic Eloquence* (Philadelphia: Abraham Small, 1816) or James Kay (ed.), *The American Orator's Own Book: A Manual of Extemporaneous Eloquence* (Philadelphia: Kay & Troutman, 1846).

28. In Irish nationalist rhetoric, the English 'yoke' is typically traced back to the Norman invasion of 1169.

29. The Protestant Ascendancy, or the minority of landowners and professions loyal to the Church of Ireland and England, who had dominated Irish society during the eighteenth century.

dispute every inch of ground, raze every house, burn every blade of grass; the last spot on which the hope of freedom should desert me, there would I hold, and the last of liberty should be my grave.

. . .

Let no man dare, when I am dead, to charge me with dishonour; let no man attaint my memory by believing that I could have engaged in any cause but that of my country's liberty and independence; or that I could have become the pliant minion of power in the oppression and misery of my countrymen. The proclamation of the Provisional Government[30] speaks for my views; no inference can be tortured from it to countenance barbarity or debasement at home, or subjection, humiliation, or treachery from abroad.

I would not have submitted to a foreign oppressor, for the same reason that I would resist the domestic tyrant. In the dignity of freedom, I would have fought upon the threshold of my country, and its enemy should only enter by passing over my lifeless corpse. And am I, who lived but for my country, who have subjected myself to the dangers of the jealous and watchful oppressor, and now to the bondage of the grave, only to give my countrymen their rights, and my country her independence – am I to be loaded with calumny and not suffered to resent it? No, God forbid!

Here Lord Norbury told Emmet that his sentiments and language disgraced his family and his education, but more particularly his father, Dr Emmet, who was a man, if alive, that would not countenance such opinions. To which Emmet replied: –

If the spirits of the illustrious dead participate in the concerns and cares of those who were dear to them in this transitory life, O! ever dear and venerated shade of my departed father, look down with scrutiny upon the conduct of your suffering son, and see if I have, even for a moment, deviated from those principles of morality and patriotism which it was your care to instil into my youthful mind, and for which I am now about to offer up my life. My lords, you seem impatient for the sacrifice. The blood for which you thirst is not congealed by the artificial terrors which surround your victim

[the soldiery filled and surrounded the Sessions House]

– it circulates warmly and unruffled through the channels which God created for noble purposes, but which you are now bent to destroy, for purposes so grievous that they cry to heaven.

Be yet patient! I have but a few words more to say. I am going to my cold and silent grave; my lamp of life is nearly extinguished; my race is run; the grave opens to receive me, and I sink into its bosom. I have but one request to ask at my departure from this world; it is – THE CHARITY OF ITS SILENCE. Let no man write my epitaph; for as no man who knows my motives dare now vindicate them, let not prejudice or ignorance asperse them. Let them and me

---

30. A proclamation issued in Dublin by Emmet in the name of the 'Provisional Government of Ireland' in July 1803.

rest in obscurity and peace, and my name remain uninscribed, until other times and other men can do justice to my character. When my country takes her place among the nations of the earth, then, and not till then, let my epitaph be written. I have done.

7. Jean-Jacques Dessalines, 'The Haitian Declaration of Independence' (Gonaïves, Saint-Domingue, 1804)

On 1 January 1804, a group of military generals led by former slave Jean-Jacques Dessalines (1758–1806) gathered in the city of Gonaïves in the west of the island of Saint-Dominique. As they listened to a public reading by the official secretary, Louis Boisrond-Tonnerre, of a declaration ending French rule, the state soon to be known as Haiti began its modern existence as only the second independent state in the Western hemisphere. As the third in the trio of Atlantic revolutions, the Haitian Revolution was, in the words of Michel-Rolph Trouillot, an 'unthinkable' event, in ways that even its American and French counterparts were not'.[31] The world's only successful slave revolution had defied all precedent, and created a new leadership class of what C. L. R. James called 'Black Jacobins'.[32] Though the most famous of these was the charismatic leader Toussaint L'Ouverture, the revolution's most momentous words were those authored by Dessalines.

French control of the island, the most profitable possession of its empire, had come to an end with the rebel victory at the Battle of Vertières in November the previous year. Yet the reading of the Declaration below was a climactic act of a bitter war against Napoleonic forces. Unlike in the rights-based republican framing of its American equivalent, separation here was articulated in terms of a vision of racial equality. Rather than marking the beginning of an aspirational revolt, it presented itself as cementing the end of a process. However, despite warning against 'vengeance', the speech marked the onset not of peace but of a period of continued struggle that would involve Dessalines's assassination in 1806.

Source

Laurent Dubois and John D. Garrigus, *Slave Revolution in the Caribbean, 1789–1804: A Brief History with Documents* (Boston: Bedford/St Martin's, 2006).

---

31. Michel-Rolph Trouillot, 'An Unthinkable History: The Haitian Revolution as a Non-Event', in *Silencing the Past: Power and the Production of History* (Boston: Beacon Press, 1995), pp. 70–107.
32. C. L. R. James, *Black Jacobins: Toussaint L'Ouverture and the San Domingo Revolution* (London: Sacker and Warburg, 1938).

The Commander in Chief to the People of Haiti
Citizens:

It is not enough to have expelled the barbarians who have bloodied our land for two centuries;[33] it is not enough to have restrained those ever-evolving factions that one after another mocked the specter of liberty that France dangled before you. We must, with one last act of national authority, forever assure the empire of liberty in the country of our birth; we must take any hope of re-enslaving us away from the inhuman government that for so long kept us in the most humiliating torpor. In the end we must live independent or die.

Independence or death ... let these sacred words unite us and be the signal of battle and of our reunion.

Citizens, my countrymen, on this solemn day I have brought together those courageous soldiers who, as liberty lay dying, spilled their blood to save it; these generals who have guided your efforts against tyranny have not yet done enough for your happiness; the French name still haunts our land.

Everything revives the memories of the cruelties of this barbarous people: our laws, our habits, our towns, everything still carries the stamp of the French. Indeed! There are still French in our island, and you believe yourself free and independent of that Republic which, it is true, has fought all the nations, but which has never defeated those who wanted to be free.

What! Victims of our [own] credulity and indulgence for 14 years; defeated not by French armies, but by the pathetic eloquence of their agents' proclamations; when will we tire of breathing the air that they breathe? What do we have in common with this nation of executioners? The difference between its cruelty and our patient moderation, its color and ours the great seas that separate us, our avenging climate, all tell us plainly that they are not our brothers, that they never will be, and that if they find refuge among us, they will plot again to trouble and divide us.

Native citizens, men, women, girls, and children, let your gaze extend on all parts of this island: look there for your spouses, your husbands, your brothers, your sisters. Indeed! Look there for your children, your suckling infants, what have they become? ... I shudder to say it ... the prey of these vultures.

Instead of these dear victims, your alarmed gaze will see only their assassins, these tigers still dripping with their blood, whose terrible presence indicts your lack of feeling and your guilty slowness in avenging them. What are you waiting for before appeasing their spirits? Remember that you had wanted your remains to rest next to those of your fathers, after you defeated tyranny; will you descend into their tombs without having avenged them? No! Their bones would reject yours.

---

33. European control of the island the Taíno and Arawak people had called 'Ayiti' began in 1492, when Christopher Columbus landed, renaming the island *La Isla Española*. By 1660, the French controlled the territory, renamed it Saint-Domingue and began the importation of slaves in the same period.

And you, precious men, intrepid generals, who, without concern for your own pain, have revived liberty by shedding all your blood, know that you have done nothing if you do not give the nations a terrible, but just example of the vengeance that must be wrought by a people proud to have recovered its liberty and jealous to maintain it. Let us frighten all those who would dare try to take it from us again; let us begin with the French. Let them tremble when they approach our coast, if not from the memory of those cruelties they perpetrated here, then from the terrible resolution that we will have made to put to death anyone born French whose profane foot soils the land of liberty.

We have dared to be free, let us be thus by ourselves and for ourselves. Let us imitate the grown child: his own weight breaks the boundary that has become an obstacle to him. What people fought for us? What people wanted to gather the fruits of our labor? And what dishonorable absurdity to conquer in order to be enslaved. Enslaved? ... Let us leave this description for the French; they have conquered but are no longer free.

Let us walk down another path; let us imitate those people who, extending their concern into the future, and dreading to leave an example of cowardice for posterity, preferred to be exterminated rather than lose their place as one of the world's free peoples.

Let us ensure, however, that a missionary spirit does not destroy our work; let us allow our neighbors to breathe in peace; may they live quietly under the laws that they have made for themselves, and let us not, as revolutionary firebrands, declare ourselves the lawgivers of the Caribbean, nor let our glory consist in troubling the peace of the neighboring islands. Unlike that which we inhabit, theirs has not been drenched in the innocent blood of its inhabitants; they have no vengeance to claim from the authority that protects them.

Fortunate to have never known the ideals that have destroyed us, they can only have good wishes for our prosperity.

Peace to our neighbors; but let this be our cry: 'Anathama to the French name! Eternal hatred of France!'

Natives of Haiti! My happy fate was to be one day the sentinel who would watch over the idol to which you sacrifice; I have watched, sometimes fighting alone, and if I have been so fortunate as to return to your hands the sacred trust you confided to me, know that it is now your task to preserve it. In fighting for your liberty, I was working for my own happiness. Before consolidating it with laws that will guarantee your free individuality, your leaders, who I have assembled here, and I, owe you the final proof of our devotion.

Generals and you, leaders, collected here close to me for the good of our land, the day has come, the day which must make our glory, our independence, eternal.

If there could exist among us a lukewarm heart, let him distance himself and tremble to take the oath which must unite us. Let us vow to ourselves, to posterity, to the entire universe, to forever renounce France, and to die rather than live under its domination; to fight until our last breath for the independence of our country.

And you, a people so long without good fortune, witness to the oath we take, remember that I counted on your constancy and courage when I threw myself into the career of liberty to fight the despotism and tyranny you had struggled against for 14 years. Remember that I sacrificed everything to rally to your defense; family, children, fortune, and now I am rich only with your liberty; my name has become a horror to all those who want slavery. Despots and tyrants curse the day that I was born. If ever you refused or grumbled while receiving those laws that the spirit guarding your fate dictates to me for your own good, you would deserve the fate of an ungrateful people. But I reject that awful idea; you will sustain the liberty that you cherish and support the leader who commands you. Therefore vow before me to live free and independent, and to prefer death to anything that will try to place you back in chains. Swear, finally, to pursue forever the traitors and enemies of your independence.

8. Miguel Hidalgo y Costilla, 'The Cry of Dolores' ('El Grito de Dolores') (Dolores, Mexico, 1810)

On 16 September 1810, Miguel Hidalgo y Costilla, parish priest of Dolores in what was then the territory of New Spain, rang the church bells intended to initiate a revolt against Spanish rule. Before a crowd gathered in front of the church, he uttered a short series of passionate republican slogans that would become known as *'The Cry of Dolores'* (*'El Grito de Dolores'*).[34]

During 1810, Hidalgo had been involved in a plot against the Spanish colonial government and had helped to arm a large popular militia. When the plot was betrayed, he decided to act immediately by initiating the uprising. Though his movement was suppressed and Hidalgo captured and executed the following year, his 'Grito' was to become a legendary icon of Mexican independence.

Each year on the night of 15 September – the eve of Mexican Independence Day – the President of the Republic reads a version of 'el Grito' from the balcony of the National Palace in Mexico City. The ceremony is broadcast throughout the country and is repeated on a smaller scale in many towns and villages. The exact text of this most symbolic of Mexican speeches is not known and a wide variety of 'reconstructed' versions have been published. The most widely accepted version is translated below.

Source

Burton Kirkwood, *History of Mexico* (Westport, CT: Greenwood Press, 2000).

---

34. Virginia Guedea, 'Miguel Hidalgo y Costilla', in Michael S. Werner (ed.), *Encyclopedia of Mexico* (Chicago: Fitzroy Dearborn, 1997), p. 640.

My children: a new dispensation comes to us today. Will you receive it? Will you free yourselves? Will you recover the lands stolen three hundred years ago from your forefathers by the hated Spaniards? We must act at once … Will you not defend your religion and your rights as true patriots? Long live our Lady of Guadalupe! Death to bad government! Death to the *gachupines*![35]

---

35. A disparaging term for Spanish settlers in the Americas.

Part C: Pan- and Transnationalisms

9. Tecumseh, 'Sleep No Longer, O Choctaws and Chickasaws' (Mississippi, 1811)

In 1811, the Shawnee chief Tecumseh (1768–1813) travelled south from his native Ohio to meet with other Indian nations to persuade them to embrace their 'one common cause' and join him in a pan-Indian alliance against settler encroachment. In the preceding years, along with his brother Tenskwatawa, Tecumseh had managed to build a confederation of more than two dozen Indian nations in the Old Northwest area. He now aimed for a greater alliance of all remaining native people, from Canada to the Gulf of Mexico, setting aside ancestral rivalries to defend their homelands.

His speech below to a council of Choctaw and Chickasaw, communicated through his interpreters, was ultimately unsuccessful. Instead of heeding his call for union, the tribes instead followed the arguments of Choctaw chief Pushamatah, who contended that the United States was too strong to resist with force. With his grand confederacy unrealised, Tecumseh formed an alliance with the British in the War of 1812 and was killed fighting General William Henry Harrison's US forces in Ontario in October 1813. He was posthumously venerated as 'an Indian Moses' for his military and oratorical prowess, and speeches such as the one below became canonised through later reprintings as a touchstone of Native American eloquence.[36]

Source

H. B. Cushman, *History of the Choctaw, Chickasaw and Natchez Indians* (Greenville, TX: Headlight Printing House, 1899).

In view of questions of vast importance, have we met together in solemn council tonight. Nor should we here debate whether we have been wronged and injured, but by what measures we should avenge ourselves; for our merciless oppressors, having long since planned out their proceedings, are not about to make, but have and are still making attacks upon our race who have as yet come to no resolution. Nor are we ignorant by what steps, and by what gradual advances, the whites break in upon our neighbors. Imagining themselves

---

36. John Sugden, 'Early Pan-Indianism: Tecumseh's Tour of the Indian Country, 1811–1812', *American Indian Quarterly*, 10 (1986), 273. For details of this afterlife see William H. Van Hoose, *Tecumseh, an Indian Moses* (Canton, OH: Daring, 1984).

to be still undiscovered, they show themselves the less audacious because you are insensible. The whites are already nearly a match for us all united, and too strong for any one tribe alone to resist; so that unless we support one another with our collective and united forces; unless every tribe unanimously combines to give check to the ambition and avarice of the whites, they will soon conquer us apart and disunited, and we will be driven away from our native country and scattered as autumnal leaves before the wind.

But have we not courage enough remaining to defend our country and maintain our ancient independence? Will we calmly suffer the white intruders and tyrants to enslave us? Shall it be said of our race that we knew not how to extricate ourselves from the three most dreadful calamities – folly, inactivity and cowardice? But what need is there to speak of the past? It speaks for itself and asks, Where today is the Pequod? Where the Narragansetts, the Mohawks, Pocanokets, and many other once powerful tribes of our race? They have vanished before the avarice and oppression of the white men, as snow before a summer sun. In the vain hope of alone defending their ancient possessions, they have fallen in the wars with the white men. Look abroad over their once beautiful country, and what see you now? Naught but the ravages of the paleface destroyers meet our eyes. So it will be with you Choctaws and Chickasaws![37] Soon your mighty forest trees, under the shade of whose wide spreading branches you have played in infancy, sported in boyhood, and now rest your wearied limbs after the fatigue of the chase, will be cut down to fence in the land which the white intruders dare to call their own. Soon their broad roads will pass over the grave of your fathers, and the place of their rest will be blotted out forever.

The annihilation of our race is at hand unless we unite in one common cause against the common foe. Think not, brave Choctaws and Chickasaws, that you can remain passive and indifferent to the common danger, and thus escape the common fate. Your people, too, will soon be as falling leaves and scattering clouds before their blighting breath. You, too, will be driven away from your native land and ancient domains as leaves are driven before the wintry storms.

Sleep not longer, O Choctaws and Chickasaws, in false security and delusive hopes. Our broad domains are fast escaping from our grasp. Every year our white intruders become more greedy, exacting, oppressive and overbearing. Every year contentions spring up between them and our people and when blood is shed we have to make atonement whether right or wrong, at the cost of the lives of our greatest chiefs, and the yielding up of large tracts of our lands. Before the palefaces came among us, we enjoyed the happiness of unbounded freedom, and were acquainted with neither riches, wants nor oppression. How is it now? Wants and oppression are our lot; for are we not controlled in everything, and dare we move without asking, by your leave? Are we not being

---

37. Two of the 'Five Civilized Tribes' based in the south-eastern United States between Mississippi and Florida.

stripped day by day of the little that remains of our ancient liberty? Do they not even kick and strike us as they do their blackfaces? How long will it be before they will tie us to a post and whip us, and make us work for them in their cornfields as they do them? Shall we wait for that moment or shall we die fighting before submitting to such ignominy?

Have we not for years had before our eyes a sample of their designs, and are they not sufficient harbingers of their future determinations? Will we not soon be driven from our respective countries and the graves of our ancestors? Will not the bones of our dead be plowed up, and their graves be turned into fields? Shall we calmly wait until they become so numerous that we will no longer be able to resist oppression? Will we wait to be destroyed in our turn, without making an effort worthy of our race? Shall we give up our homes, our country, bequeathed to us by the Great Spirit, the graves of our dead, and everything that is dear and sacred to us, without a struggle? I know you will cry with me: Never! Never! Then let us by unity of action destroy them all, which we now can do, or drive them back whence they came. War or extermination is now our only choice. Which do you choose? I know your answer. Therefore, I now call on you, brave Choctaws and Chickasaws, to assist in the just cause of liberating our race from the grasp of our faithless invaders and heartless oppressors. The white usurpation in our common country must be stopped, or we, its rightful owners, be forever destroyed and wiped out as a race of people. I am now at the head of many warriors backed by the strong arm of English soldiers.[38] Choctaws and Chickasaws, you have too long borne with grievous usurpation inflicted by the arrogant Americans. Be no longer their dupes. If there be one here tonight who believes that his rights will not sooner or later be taken from him by the avaricious American pale-faces, his ignorance ought to excite pity, for he knows little of the character of our common foe.

And if there be one among you mad enough to undervalue the growing power of the white race among us, let him tremble in considering the fearful woes he will bring down upon our entire race, if by his criminal indifference he assists the designs of our common enemy against our common country. Then listen to the voice of duty, of honor, of nature and of your endangered country. Let us form one body, one heart, and defend to the last warrior our country, our homes, our liberty, and the graves of our fathers.

Choctaws and Chickasaws, you are among the few of our race who sit indolently at ease. You have indeed enjoyed the reputation of being brave, but will you be indebted for it more from report than fact? Will you let the whites encroach upon your domains even to your very door before you will assert your rights in resistance? Let no one in this council imagine that I speak more from malice against the paleface Americans than just grounds of complaint. Complaint is just toward friends who have failed in their duty; accusation is against enemies

---

38. Tecumseh's forces had been backed by the promise of British military support.

guilty of injustice. And surely, if any people ever had, we have good and just reasons to believe we have ample grounds to accuse the Americans of injustice; especially when such great acts of injustice have been committed by them upon our race, of which they seem to have no manner of regard, or even to reflect. They are a people fond of innovations, quick to contrive and quick to put their schemes into effectual execution no matter how great the wrong and injury to us; while we are content to preserve what we already have. Their designs are to enlarge their possessions by taking yours in turn; and will you, can you longer dally, O Choctaws and Chickasaws?

Do you imagine that that people will not continue longest in the enjoyment of peace who timely prepare to vindicate themselves, and manifest a determined resolution to do themselves right whenever they are wronged? Far otherwise. Then haste to the relief of our common cause, as by consanguinity of blood you are bound; lest the day be not far distant when you will be left single-handed and alone to the cruel mercy of our most inveterate foe.

10. José Martí, 'Our America' (New York City, 1889)

On 19 December 1889, the Cuban activist, poet and political theorist José Martí (1853–95) delivered an address to the Latin American Society of New York, crystallising his ideas about the unity of the Spanish-speaking peoples of the Western Hemisphere.

Active from an early age in radical circles throughout Europe, South America and the United States, Martí gained fame as a passionate advocate for independence from Spanish rule. Martí's gift for expansive, dramatic oratory earned him the nickname 'el Doctor Torrente'.[39] One of his central tenets, expressed in his New York speech below, was that Latin American countries needed to develop a historically conscious pan-national identity as 'los hombres del sur' (men of the South).

Source

José Martí, Our America: Writings on Latin America and the Struggle for Cuban Independence (New York: Monthly Review Press, 1977).

Where is America going, and who will unite her and be her guide? Alone and as one people she is rising. Alone she is fighting. Alone she will win.

And we have transformed his venom into sap! Never was there such a precocious, persevering and generous people born out of so much opposition

---

39. Alfred J. López, José Martí: A Revolutionary Life (Austin: University of Texas Press, 2014), p. 163.

and unhappiness. We were a den of iniquity and are beginning to be a crucible. We built upon hydras. Our railroads have demolished the pikes of Alvarado.[40] In the public squares where they used to burn heretics, we built libraries. We have as many schools now as we had officers of the Inquisition before. What we have not yet done, we have not had time to do, having been busy cleansing our blood of the impurities bequeathed to us by our ancestors. The religious and immoral missions have nothing left but their crumbling walls where an occasional owl shows an eye, and where the lizard goes his melancholy way. The new American has cleared the paths among the dispirited breeds of men, the ruins of convents, and the horses of barbarians, and he is inviting the youth of the world to pitch their tents in his fields.

. . .

We are taking Our America, as host and inspiration, to where there is no forgetting and no death! And neither corruptive interests nor certain new fashions in fanaticism will let us be uprooted from her! We must show our soul as it is to these illustrious messengers who have come here from our nations, so they may see that we consider it faithful and honourable. We must convince these delegates that a just admiration and a sincere study of other nations – a study neither too distant nor myopic – does not weaken the ardent, redemptive and sacred love for what is our own. Let us allow them to see that for our personal good – if there is in any good in the conscience without peace – we will not be traitors to that which Nature and humanity demand of us.

And thus, when each of them, content with our integrity, returns to the shores that we may never see again, he will be able to say to her who is our mistress, hope and guide: 'Mother America, we found brothers there! Mother America, you have sons there!'

11. W. E. B. Du Bois, 'To the Nations of the World' (London, 1900)

When the Pan-African Congress met at Westminster Town Hall, London, in July 1900, among the speakers at the closing session was the American sociologist and historian W. E. B. Du Bois (1868–1963). Du Bois was one of the most important transatlantic intellectuals of his age, the first African American to graduate with a PhD from Harvard and co-founder of the National Association for the Advancement of Colored People (NAACP).

In his London speech, before an audience including the feminist Anna Julia Cooper, former fugitive slave Henry 'Box' Brown, Haitian politician

---

40. Pedro de Alvarado y Contreras (c.1485–1541), Spanish *conquistador* and leader of the conquest of Cuba.

Benito Sylvain and Indian former Liberal Party MP Dadabhai Naoroji[41], Du Bois called upon 'blacks of all nations' to combine as one political movement.[42] Using powerful familial metaphors and consciously invoking the Declaration of Independence, Du Bois's speech promoted the idea that a common history of oppression and discrimination could create a viable common identity. His influential ideas represented what David Lewis has called a 'movement exploding into the twentieth century, like a stick of dynamite', helping to set the tone for generations of black expression and political action.[43]

Source

Philip S. Foner and Robert J. Branham, *Lift Every Voice: African American Oratory, 1787–1900* (Tuscaloosa: University of Alabama Press, 1998).

In the metropolis of the modern world, in this the closing year of the nineteenth century, there has been assembled a congress[44] of men and women of African blood, to deliberate solemnly upon the present situation and outlook of the darker races of mankind. The problem of the twentieth century is the problem of the color line, the question as to how far differences of race – which show themselves chiefly in the color of the skin and the texture of the hair – will hereafter be made the basis of denying to over half the world the right of sharing to utmost ability the opportunities and privileges of modern civilization.

To be sure, the darker races are today the least advanced in culture according to European standards. This has not, however, always been the case in the past. And certainly the world's history, both ancient and modern, has given many instances of no despicable ability and capacity among the blackest races of men. In any case, the modern world must remember that in this age when the ends of the world are being brought so near together the millions of black men in Africa, America and the Islands of the Sea, not to speak of the brown and yellow myriads elsewhere, are bound to have a great influence upon the world in the future, by reason of sheer numbers and physical contact.

----

41. For Naoroji's own oratory of this period, see Chapter 5 (pp. 237–8).
42. Brent H. Edwards, *The Practice of Diaspora: Literature, Translation, and the Rise of Black Internationalism* (Cambridge, MA: Harvard University Press, 2009), pp. 2–3.
43. David Levering Lewis, *WEB Du Bois, 1868–1919: Biography of a Race* (New York: Henry Holt and Company, 1994), pp. 249–50.
44. The convention was organised by Trinidadian barrister and Pan-Africanist Henry Sylvester Williams (1867–1911).

If now the world of culture bends itself towards giving Negroes and other dark men the largest and broadest opportunity for education and self-development, then this contact and influence is bound to have a beneficial effect upon the world and hasten human progress. But if, by reason of carelessness, prejudice, greed and injustice, the black world is to be exploited and ravished and degraded, the results must be deplorable, if not fatal – not simply to them, but to the high ideals of justice, freedom and culture which a thousand years of Christian civilization have held before Europe.

And now, therefore, to these ideals of civilization, to the broader humanity of the followers of the Prince of Peace, we, the men and women of Africa in world congress assembled, do now solemnly appeal: Let the world take no backward step in that slow but sure progress which has successively refused to let the spirit of class, of caste, of privilege, or of birth, debar from life, liberty and the pursuit of happiness a striving human soul. Let no color or race be a feature of distinction between white and black men, regardless of worth or ability.

Let not the natives of Africa be sacrificed to the greed of gold, their liberties taken away, their family life debauched, their just aspirations repressed, and avenues of advancement and culture taken from them. Let not the cloak of Christian missionary enterprise be allowed in the future, as so often in the past, to hide the ruthless economic exploitation and political downfall of less developed nations, whose chief fault has been reliance on the plighted faith of the Christian church.

Let the British nation, the first modern champion of Negro freedom, hasten to crown the work of Wilberforce, and Clarkson, and Buxton, and Sharp, Bishop Colenso, and Livingston,[45] and give as soon as practicable, the rights of responsible government to the black colonies of Africa and the West Indies. Let not the spirit of Garrison, Phillips, and Douglass wholly die out in America; may the conscience of a great nation rise and rebuke all dishonesty and unrighteous oppression toward the American Negro, and grant to him the right of franchise, security of person and property, and generous recognition of the great work he has accomplished in a generation toward raising nine millions of human beings from slavery to manhood.

Let the German Empire, and the French Republic,[46] true to their great past, remember that the true worth of colonies lies in their prosperity and progress, and that justice, impartial alike to black and white, is the first element of prosperity. Let the Congo Free State become a great central Negro state of the

---

45. William Wilberforce (1759–1833) (see pp. 105–9), Thomas Clarkson (1760–1846), Thomas Fowell Buxton (1786–1845) and Granville Sharp (1735–1810) were leading British anti-slavery activists. Bishop John William Colenso (1814–83) was a noted advocate for African causes. David Livingstone (1813–73) was a celebrity missionary and explorer.

46. Both of these empires were part of the 'Scramble for Africa', or the intensification of the colonisation of Africa between the 1880s and World War One.

world, and let its prosperity be counted not simply in cash and commerce, but in the happiness and true advancement to its black people.

Let the nations of the world respect the integrity and independence of the free Negro states of Abyssinia, Liberia, Haiti, and the rest, and let the inhabitants of these states, the independent tribes of Africa, the Negroes of the West Indies and America, and the black subjects of all nations take courage, strive ceaselessly, and fight bravely, that they may prove to the world their incontestable right to be counted among the great brotherhood of mankind. Thus we appeal with boldness and confidence to the Great Powers of the civilized world, trusting in the wide spirit of humanity, and the deep sense of justice and of our age, for a generous recognition of the righteousness of our cause.

2 Gender, Suffrage and Sexuality

Introduction

As the nineteenth century began, women in Britain and the US enjoyed few legal, social, or political rights. In neither nation could a woman retain her earnings, make a contract or will, bring a lawsuit, or fully control personal property or children. For non-elites, notably the enslaved, ethnic minority, indigenous women and sex workers, restrictions were even more acute. Underpinning this legal inequality were broader cultural assumptions that held marriage, motherhood and subservience to men to be the sole route to emotional and spiritual fulfilment. As women gained greater prominence in the workforce and the franchise for men expanded, the contradictions of these injustices became untenable for an increasingly vocal group of individuals, convinced that, as American feminist Margaret Fuller put it in 1844, in this 'new age' woman must 'now take her turn in the full pulsation of life'.[1]

Though feminist arguments had been articulated long before, the mainstream gender equality movement is traditionally seen as bursting into transatlantic prominence with the 1848 Seneca Falls movement in upstate New York. During the years that followed, petition drives, lobbying and resistance both passive and violent helped make the spectre of 'the new woman' one of the era's most contentious political disputes. Some leading figures in this struggle were men, including the Irish reformer William Thompson and English philosopher and MP John Stuart Mill. However, the most important texts of nineteenth-century feminism were authored by women: articles, pamphlets and novels that described oppression, decried conflicting social expectations, and voiced long-silenced aspirations. Most contentious of all were from those women who overcame what Elizabeth Cady Stanton calls in her speech below 'dark storm clouds of opposition' (p. 68), in order to deliver their views in public .

Cultural resistance to women speakers took several forms. Most common was the claim that female forays into the public sphere were simply unnatural;

---

1. Margaret Fuller, *Woman in the Nineteenth Century*, ed. Larry Reynolds (New York: W. W. Norton, 1998), p. 25.

that, in the words of one anti-suffragist below, the very idea of gender equality represented 'vain combat with nature' (p. 82). This was Queen Victoria's view: reading in 1870 of a feminist lecture, she attacked the 'mad, wicked folly of women's rights', fearing that women would '"unsex" themselves' and 'become the most hateful, heathen, and disgusting of beings'.[2] There was also the notion of ethical propriety. As American reformer Hannah Crocker put it in 1815, it was thought 'morally improper, and physically very incorrect, for the female character to . . . ascend the rostrum to gain the loud applause of men, although their powers of mind may be equal to the task'.[3] Finally, there was what US reformer Lucretia Mott called simple 'ridicule, satire and sarcasm', with opponents of women's activism routinely rehearsing Dr Johnson's quip that 'a woman preaching is like a dog walking on its hinder legs. It is not done well; but you are surprised to find it done at all.'[4]

Women's rights oratory therefore had a dual burden: to make a case on its own merits, and to counter prejudices against women as their own messengers. The speeches that follow offer an outline of the ways in which these twin demands were met. The first part ('Gender Equality') begins with Stanton's foundational keynote address at the 1848 Seneca Falls convention. This is followed by two speeches by Sojourner Truth, one of the legendary figures of nineteenth-century American reform: her Ohio Women's Rights Convention address (1851) and her lesser-known 'Address to the Equal Rights Association' (1867), both of which underline the unity of abolition, anti-racist and women's crusades. The final speech (1870), from British reformer Josephine Butler, uses a language of patriotic shame to protest against the mistreatment of women suspected of prostitution.

The following part of the chapter ('Suffrage for Women') collects contributions to what Emmeline Pankhurst calls below 'the hardest of all fights' (p. 87). In the US, despite cherished democratic ideals, the path to universal suffrage was slow and uneven, and with the exception of pioneer states such as Wyoming and Utah, women had to wait until the 1910s for the vote. In Britain, the struggle was even slower, as women were excluded from the electoral expansions of the Great Reform Acts of 1832, 1867 and 1884. However, after John Stuart Mill delivered a suffrage petition to Parliament in 1866, debates began to grow in frequency. One of the selections in this part of the chapter captures the arguments made in one such debate (1871)

---

2. Queen Victoria to Theodore Martin, 29 May 1870, quoted in Martin, *Queen Victoria as I Knew Her* (London: William Blackwood, 1901), p. 122.
3. Hannah M. Crocker and Constance J. Post, *Observations on the Real Rights of Women and Other Writings* (Lincoln: University of Nebraska Press, 2011), p. 84.
4. Lucretia Mott, *Discourse on Woman, Delivered at the Assembly Buildings, December 17, 1849* (Philadelphia: Peterson, 1850), p. 3; James Boswell, *The Life of Samuel Johnson* (London: Penguin, 2008), p. 327.

from two leading anti-suffrage MPs. This is preceded by a speech made by Susan B. Anthony on a lecture tour of upstate New York, following her provocative attempt to vote in the 1872 Presidential election. The section ends with Emmeline Pankhurst's famous 1913 address in Hartford, Connecticut, delivered whilst a fugitive from the British police (Figure 14).

Often underpinning these debates was the supposed relationship of reproduction to gender identity. In debates over women's social role, the case was often made, even by those sympathetic to the women's cause such as English MP and social scientist George Hastings, that 'man is eminently a working animal . . . whereas a married woman is eminently, essentially, and primarily, a child-bearing animal'.[5] This chapter's final part ('Sexuality and Reproduction') brings together a range of speeches that turned on this issue, and by doing so offers a tantalising glimpse of an embryonic modern rhetoric for lesbian, gay, bisexual, transgender and queer (LGBTQ) rights. In the first speech, Frances Ellen Watkins Harper makes a conservative case for 'Enlightened Motherhood' (1892) as a means to restrain male sexuality, whereas Theodore Roosevelt a decade later in 1905 frames the issue of reproductive capacity in patriotic terms, dismissing as anti-American the 'selfish and sordid' life of the wilfully childless.

This part of the chapter's other speeches offer seminal contributions to the mostly invisible debate over same-sex relationships. In an extract from his testimony in his 1895 Indecency Trial, Oscar Wilde affirms affection between men as part of an ancient and beneficial cultural tradition. In her speech to a 1904 Berlin convention, the German activist Anna Rüling extends the claims of the women's movement to the group she calls 'Urnings', or those in same-sex female relationships. Women's rights advocacy frequently invoked rival movements such as abolition, temperance or even nationalism rather instrumentally, as a way to construct arguments based on analogy. However, examining Rüling's speech allows us to see how, just as in the rhetoric of Harper and Truth, there was also a genuine progressive vision of how to weave together overlapping claims, causes and inequalities.

---

5. Quoted in Mary L. Shanley, *Feminism, Marriage, and the Law in Victorian England, 1850–1895* (Princeton: Princeton University Press, 1989), p. 101.

Part A: Gender Equality

1. Elizabeth Cady Stanton, 'Keynote Address at Seneca Falls Convention' (Seneca Falls, New York, 1848)

At eleven in the morning on Wednesday, 19 July 1848, the thirty-three-year-old activist Elizabeth Cady Stanton (1815–1902) rose to the lectern in the Wesleyan Methodist Chapel of Seneca Falls, a small town in upstate New York. She was to deliver the principal remarks before a convention of women's rights reformers, a speech that is often seen as inaugurating the modern American women's movement.

Together with her fellow activist Lucretia Mott, Stanton had convened the event to provide a focal point for reformist energies on the question of gender equality. It was the first time that men and women had ever assembled explicitly to discuss gender injustice, and it attracted some of the era's leading reformers, including male activists such as Frederick Douglass. The intense discussion at the event on how to approach issues such as legal oppression, inequality in education and women's right to vote was to culminate in the Seneca Falls 'Declaration of Sentiments', a document drafted by Stanton that creatively repurposed Jefferson's independence text as a toolkit for female liberation.

Thanks to the prominence of the event in Stanton's *History of Women's Suffrage* (1869), Seneca Falls and the energies it galvanised have become enshrined as a turning point in women's rights rhetoric.[6] As historian Sally McMillen puts it, 'the meeting changed the way American society (and much of the Western world) thought about and treated women . . . unleashing a complicated lengthy struggle that continues to this day'.[7] The text below represents the entirety of Stanton's keynote remarks.

Source

Elizabeth C. Stanton and Susan B. Anthony, *The Elizabeth Cady Stanton–Susan B. Anthony Reader: Correspondence, Writings, Speeches*, ed. Ellen C. Dubois (Boston: Northeastern University Press, 1992), pp. 27–40.

---

6. For more on this myth-making, see Lisa Tetraul, *The Myth of Seneca Falls: Memory and the Women's Suffrage Movement, 1848–1898* (Chapel Hill: University of North Carolina Press, 2014).

7. Sally McMillen, *Seneca Falls and the Origins of the Women's Rights Movement* (Oxford: Oxford University Press, 2009), p. 3.

We have met here today to discuss our rights and wrongs, civil and political, and not, as some have supposed, to go into the detail of social life alone. We do not propose to petition the legislature to make our husbands just, generous, and courteous, to seat every man at the head of a cradle, and to clothe every woman in male attire.

None of these points, however important they may be considered by leading men, will be touched in this convention. As to their costume, the gentlemen need feel no fear of our imitating that, for we think it in violation of every principle of taste, beauty, and dignity; notwithstanding all the contempt cast upon our loose, flowing garments, we still admire the graceful folds, and consider our costume far more artistic than theirs. Many of the nobler sex seem to agree with us in this opinion, for the bishops, priests, judges, barristers, and lord mayors of the first nation on the globe, and the Pope of Rome, with his cardinals, too, all wear the loose flowing robes, thus tacitly acknowledging that the male attire is neither dignified nor imposing.

No, we shall not molest you in your philosophical experiments with stocks, pants, high-heeled boots, and Russian belts. Yours be the glory to discover, by personal experience, how long the kneepan can resist the terrible strapping down which you impose, in how short time the well-developed muscles of the throat can be reduced to mere threads by the constant pressure of the stock, how high the heel of a boot must be to make a short man tall, and how tight the Russian belt may be drawn and yet have wind enough left to sustain life.

But we are assembled to protest against a form of government existing without the consent of the governed – to declare our right to be free as man is free, to be represented in the government which we are taxed to support, to have such disgraceful laws as give man the power to chastise and imprison his wife, to take the wages which she earns, the property which she inherits, and, in case of separation, the children of her love; laws which make her the mere dependent on his bounty. It is to protest against such unjust laws as these that we are assembled today, and to have them, if possible, forever erased from our statute books, deeming them a shame and a disgrace to a Christian republic in the nineteenth century. We have met to uplift woman's fallen divinity upon an even pedestal with man's. And, strange as it may seem to many, we now demand our right to vote according to the declaration of the government under which we live.

This right no one pretends to deny. We need not prove ourselves equal to Daniel Webster[8] to enjoy this privilege, for the ignorant Irishman in the ditch has all the civil rights he has.[9] We need not prove our muscular power equal

---

8. Daniel Webster (1782–1852), the US Senator from Massachusetts representing the Whig Party, celebrated in his time as the archetype of a powerful orator. For his landmark 1830 'Reply to Hayne' speech, see Chapter 6 (pp. 244–7).

9. Casual vilification of the 'ignorant Irish', the 'Chinese heathen' and 'the Hebrew' were frequent rhetorical tropes invoked in the early American women's movement's arguments for equality.

to this same Irishman to enjoy this privilege, for the most tiny, weak, ill-shaped stripling of twenty-one has all the civil rights of the Irishman. We have no objection to discuss the question of equality, for we feel that the weight of argument lies wholly with us, but we wish the question of equality kept distinct from the question of rights, for the proof of the one does not determine the truth of the other. All white men in this country have the same rights, however they may differ in mind, body, or estate.

The right is ours. The question now is: how shall we get possession of what rightfully belongs to us? We should not feel so sorely grieved if no man who had not attained the full stature of a Webster, Clay, Van Buren, or Gerrit Smith could claim the right of the elective franchise.[10] But to have drunkards, idiots, horse-racing, rum-selling rowdies, ignorant foreigners, and silly boys fully recognized, while we ourselves are thrust out from all the rights that belong to citizens, it is too grossly insulting to the dignity of woman to be longer quietly submitted to.

The right is ours. Have it, we must. Use it, we will. The pens, the tongues, the fortunes, the indomitable wills of many women are already pledged to secure this right. The great truth that no just government can be formed without the consent of the governed we shall echo and re-echo in the ears of the unjust judge, until by continual coming we shall weary him.

There seems now to be a kind of moral stagnation in our midst. Philanthropists have done their utmost to rouse the nation to a sense of its sins. War, slavery, drunkenness, licentiousness, gluttony, have been dragged naked before the people, and all their abominations and deformities fully brought to light, yet with idiotic laugh we hug those monsters to our breasts and rush on to destruction. Our churches are multiplying on all sides, our missionary societies, Sunday schools, and prayer meetings and innumerable charitable and reform organizations are all in operation, but still the tide of vice is swelling, and threatens the destruction of everything, and the battlements of righteousness are weak against the raging elements of sin and death.

Verily, the world waits the coming of some new element, some purifying power, some spirit of mercy and love. The voice of woman has been silenced in the state, the church, and the home, but man cannot fulfill his destiny alone, he cannot redeem his race unaided. There are deep and tender chords of sympathy and love in the hearts of the downfallen and oppressed that woman can touch more skillfully than man.

The world has never yet seen a truly great and virtuous nation, because in the degradation of woman the very fountains of life are poisoned at their source. It is vain to look for silver and gold from mines of copper and lead.

---

10. Henry Clay (1777–1852), US Senator from Kentucky and 1844 Whig Presidential candidate; Martin Van Buren (1782–1862), President of the US, 1837–41; Gerrit Smith (1797–1874), New York Congressman and Presidential candidate on the Liberty Party ticket for 1848, the year of the Seneca Falls Convention.

It is the wise mother that has the wise son. So long as your women are slaves you may throw your colleges and churches to the winds. You can't have scholars and saints so long as your mothers are ground to powder between the upper and nether millstone of tyranny and lust. How seldom, now, is a father's pride gratified, his fond hopes realized, in the budding genius of his son!

The wife is degraded, made the mere creature of caprice, and the foolish son is heaviness to his heart. Truly are the sins of the fathers visited upon the children to the third and fourth generation. God, in His wisdom, has so linked the whole human family together that any violence done at one end of the chain is felt throughout its length, and here, too, is the law of restoration, as in woman all have fallen, so in her elevation shall the race be recreated.

'Voices' were the visitors and advisers of Joan of Arc.[11] Do not 'voices' come to us daily from the haunts of poverty, sorrow, degradation, and despair, already too long unheeded? Now is the time for the women of this country, if they would save our free institutions, to defend the right, to buckle on the armor that can best resist the keenest weapons of the enemy – contempt and ridicule. The same religious enthusiasm that nerved Joan of Arc to her work nerves us to ours. In every generation God calls some men and women for the utterance of truth, a heroic action, and our work today is the fulfilling of what has long since been foretold by the Prophet – Joel 2: 28:

> 'And it shall come to pass afterward, that I will pour out my spirit upon all flesh; and your sons and your daughters shall prophesy.'

We do not expect our path will be strewn with the flowers of popular applause, but over the thorns of bigotry and prejudice will be our way, and on our banners will beat the dark storm clouds of opposition from those who have entrenched themselves behind the stormy bulwarks of custom and authority, and who have fortified their position by every means, holy and unholy. But we will steadfastly abide the result. Unmoved we will bear it aloft. Undauntedly we will unfurl it to the gale, for we know that the storm cannot rend from it a shred, that the electric flash will but more clearly show to us the glorious words inscribed upon it, 'Equality of Rights'.

2. Sojourner Truth, 'Speech to the Women's Rights Convention' (Akron, Ohio, 1851)

In the years following the Seneca Falls meeting, many more women's rights conventions took place across the US. Of all the speeches they witnessed, it would be some brief impromptu remarks spoken in

---

11. Joan of Arc (1412–31), the French heroine of the Hundred Years' War, famous for her claims to have experienced the voices of angels and saints.

Akron, Ohio, in 1851 by a former slave calling herself Sojourner Truth (c.1797–1883) that would prove the most enduring.

Born Isabella Van Wagenen into slavery in upstate New York and raised speaking Dutch, she escaped to freedom with her children in the 1820s; upon converting to Methodism, she adopted her new name to mark her fresh calling as a travelling speaker against the evils of slavery (Figure 9).

At Akron she spoke unannounced, making an off-the-cuff speech urging for the broadening of the gender equality movement to include the black experience. Like other black activists, such as Maria W. Stewart (1803–79), who had made a similar rhetorical gesture a decade earlier, Truth inverted the gender of the interrogatory abolitionist motto 'Am I not a man and a brother?'[12] By doing so, her words spoke powerfully to intersectional inequalities of American society, and asserted the complexity of gender, race and class before her mostly white, well-educated crowd.

Yet as powerful as the commonly received version of Truth's speech remains, it is impossible to read as entirely transparent. Even more than with most other texts in this book, the attribution and exact wording remain controversial, due to the speech's publication in two quite distinct versions, both of which are included below. The first, printed in the *Anti-Slavery Bugle* in June 1851, was taken by the convention's recording secretary, and made no mention of the famous rhetorical question. Twelve years later, the second, more famous, version was published by Frances Dana Barker Gage (1808–84), an Ohio reformer with progressive views on racial equality. Her version added an evocative description of the audience response, but also rendered the words of Truth – a northerner who took pride in her graceful spoken English – in a pungent Southern slave vernacular. Though the problematic dialect politics of Gage's rendition has led many to question its documentary value, the combined force of the two versions here reaffirm the seminal place of the speech in the history of American civil rights rhetoric.[13]

---

12. See Valerie Cooper, *Word, Like Fire: Maria Stewart, the Bible, and the Rights of African Americans* (Charlottesville: University of Virginia Press, 2011), p. 16. For a comparison of Stewart and Truth's rhetoric and careers, see Carla L. Peterson, *'Doers of the Word': African American Women Speakers and Writers in the North, 1830–1880* (New Brunswick, NJ: Rutgers University Press, 1998), pp. 57–60.
13. The classic study of the culture of dialect in the period is Gavin Jones, *Strange Talk: The Politics of Dialect Literature in Gilded Age America* (Berkeley: University of California Press, 1999).

Text A: 'Woman's Rights Convention' (*Anti-Slavery Bugle*, Salem, Ohio, 21 June 1851)

One of the most unique and interesting speeches of the convention was made by Sojourner Truth, an emancipated slave. It is impossible to transfer it to paper, or convey any adequate idea of the effect it produced upon the audience. Those only can appreciate it who saw her powerful form, her whole-souled, earnest gesture, and listened to her strong and truthful tones. She came forward to the platform and addressing the President said with great simplicity: 'May I say a few words?' Receiving an affirmative answer, she proceeded.

'May I say a few words? I want to say a few words about this matter.

I am for woman's rights. I have as much muscle as any man, and can do as much work as any man. I have plowed and reaped and husked and chopped and mowed, and can any man do more than that? I have heard much about the sexes being equal; I can carry as much as any man, and can eat as much too, if I can get it. I am as strong as any man that is now. As for intellect, all I can say is, if a woman have a pint and man a quart – why cant she have her little pint full? You need not be afraid to give us our rights for fear we will take too much, – for we cant take more than our pint'll hold. The poor men seem to be all in confusion, and dont know what to do.

Why children, if you have woman's rights give it to her and you will feel better. You will have your own rights, and they wont be so much trouble. I cant read, but I can hear. I have heard the bible and have learned that Eve caused man to sin. Well if woman upset the world, do give her a chance to set it right side up again. The Lady has spoken about Jesus, how he never spurned woman from him, and she was right.

When Lazarus[14] died, Mary and Martha came to him with faith and love and besought him to raise their brother. And Jesus wept – and Lazarus came forth. And how came Jesus into the world? Through God who created him and woman who bore him. Man, where is your part? But the women are coming up blessed by God and a few of the men are coming up with them. But man is in a tight place, the poor slave is on him, woman is coming on him, and he is surely between a hawk and a buzzard.

Text B: 'Sojourner Truth's Speech' [Reminiscence by Francis Gage] (*New York Independent*, 23 April 1863)

The leaders of the movement trembled on seeing a tall, gaunt black woman in a gray dress and white turban, surmounted with an uncouth sunbonnet, march

---

14. The Gospel of John (11: 1–44) recalls how Jesus restored Lazarus of Bethany back to life four days after his burial.

deliberately into the church, walk with the air of a queen up the aisle, and take her seat upon the pulpit steps. A buzz of disapprobation was heard all over the house, and there fell on the listening ear, 'An abolition affair!' 'Woman's rights and niggers!' 'I told you so!' 'Go it, darkey!' ... Again and again, timorous and trembling ones came to me and said, with earnestness, 'Don't let her speak, Mrs. Gage, it will ruin us. Every newspaper in the land will have our cause mixed up with abolition and niggers, and we shall be utterly denounced.' My only answer was, 'We shall see when the time comes.'

The second day the work waxed warm. Methodist, Baptist, Episcopal, Presbyterian, and Universalist minister came in to hear and discuss the resolutions presented. One claimed superior rights and privileges for man, on the ground of 'superior intellect'; another, because of the 'manhood of Christ; if God had desired the equality of woman, He would have given some token of His will through the birth, life, and death of the Saviour.' Another gave us a theological view of the 'sin of our first mother.'

There were very few women in those days who dared to 'speak in meeting'; and the august teachers of the people were seemingly getting the better of us, while the boys in the galleries, and the sneerers among the pews, were hugely enjoying the discomfiture as they supposed, of the 'strong-minded.' Some of the tender-skinned friends were on the point of losing dignity, and the atmosphere betokened a storm. When, slowly from her seat in the corner rose Sojourner Truth, who, till now, had scarcely lifted her head. 'Don't let her speak!' gasped half a dozen in my ear. She moved slowly and solemnly to the front, laid her old bonnet at her feet, and turned her great speaking eyes to me. There was a hissing sound of disapprobation above and below. I rose and announced, 'Sojourner Truth,' and begged the audience to keep silence for a few moments.

The tumult subsided at once, and every eye was fixed on this almost Amazon form, which stood nearly six feet high, head erect, and eyes piercing the upper air like one in a dream. At her first word there was a profound hush. She spoke in deep tones, which, though not loud, reached every ear in the house, and away through the throng at the doors and windows.

'Wall, chilern, whar dar is so much racket dar must be somethin' out o' kilter. I tink dat 'twixt de niggers of de Souf and de womin at de Norf, all talkin' 'bout rights, de white men will be in a fix pretty soon. But what's all dis here talkin' 'bout?'

'Dat man ober dar say dat womin needs to be helped into carriages, and lifted ober ditches, and to hab de best place everywhar. Nobody eber helps me into carriages, or ober mud-puddles, or gibs me any best place!' And raising herself to her full height, and her voice to a pitch like rolling thunder, she asked. 'And ain't I a woman? Look at me! Look at my arm! *(and she bared her right arm to the shoulder, showing her tremendous muscular power).* I have ploughed, and planted, and gathered into barns, and no man could head me! And ain't I a woman? I could work as much and eat as much as a man – when I could get it – and bear de lash as well! And ain't I a woman? I have borne thirteen chilern, and seen 'em mos' all sold off to slavery, and when I cried out with my mother's grief, none but Jesus heard me! And ain't I a woman?'

'Den dey talks 'bout dis ting in de head; what dis dey call it?' (*'Intellect,' whispered someone near.*)

'Dat's it, honey. What's dat got to do wid womin's rights or nigger's rights? If my cup won't hold but a pint, and yourn holds a quart, wouldn't ye be mean not to let me have my little half-measure full?' And she pointed her significant finger, and sent a keen glance at the minister who had made the argument. The cheering was long and loud.

'Den dat little man in back dar, he say women can't have as much rights as men, 'cause Christ wan't a woman! Whar did your Christ come from?' *Rolling thunder couldn't have stilled that crowd, as did those deep, wonderful tones, as she stood there with out-stretched arms and eyes of fire. Raising her voice still louder, she repeated,* 'Whar did your Christ come from? From God and a woman! Man had nothin' to do wid Him.'

Oh, what a rebuke that was to that little man. Turning again to another objector, she took up the defense of Mother Eve. I can not follow her through it all. It was pointed, and witty, and solemn; eliciting at almost every sentence deafening applause; and she ended by asserting:

'If de fust woman God ever made was strong enough to turn de world upside down all alone, dese women togedder (and she glanced her eye over the platform) ought to be able to turn it back, and get it right side up again! And now dey is asking to do it, de men better let 'em.' Long-continued cheering greeted this. ''Bleeged to ye for hearin' on me, and now ole Sojourner han't got nothin' more to say.'

Amid roars of applause, she returned to her corner leaving more than one of us with streaming eyes, and hearts beating with gratitude. She had taken us up in her strong arms and carried us safely over the slough of difficulty turning the whole tide in our favor. I have never in my life seen anything like the magical influence that subdued the mobbish spirit of the day, and turned the sneers and jeers of an excited crowd into notes of respect and admiration. Hundreds rushed up to shake hands with her, and congratulate the glorious old mother, and bid her God-speed on her mission of 'testifyin' agin concerning the wickedness of this 'ere people.'

3. Sojourner Truth, 'Address to the American Equal Rights Association' (New York City, 1867)

Like Frederic Douglass, Truth cautiously welcomed the Civil War as a necessary spiritual purge. But she too feared that defeat of the South would leave much undone. Following the war, she continued her activism into her eighth decade, declaring in the key 1867 speech excerpted below that she remained alive only 'because something remains for me to do'. By the late 1860s, as Margaret Washington has put it, Truth's 'lived experience was already competing with myth.

Yet even this myth-making illuminates the magnitude of Sojourner Truth's place in national history and reveals the extent to which she transcends the era.'[15]

After the war, Truth had joined the American Equal Rights Association, a body formed in 1866 from the National Woman's Rights Convention to ensure that the Civil War led to 'equal Rights to all American citizens, especially the right of suffrage irrespective of race, color, or sex'.[16] The organisation had become split over the relative priorities of women's suffrage versus that of black males. Led largely by white feminists such as Lucretia Mott and Lucy Stone, the body aimed to persuade states to accept the goal of universal suffrage, a position that put them in conflict with key African American reformers such as Charles Remond and George T. Downing.

This second extract gives a sense of her interventions in the organisation's debates. Speaking at its first convention in New York on 9 May 1867, Truth reminded her largely white, middle-class audience of the intersectional pressures on 'colored women'. As Truth realised, the ferment of postwar Reconstruction offered a unique and limited window during which the rights and material conditions of the formerly enslaved could remain visible. Her aim was to 'keep the whole thing stirring, now that the ice is a little cracked', fighting against the incessant invisibility of black women in republican discourse.

Source

Philip S. Foner and Robert J. Branham, *Lift Every Voice: African American Oratory, 1787–1900* (Tuscaloosa: University of Alabama Press, 1998).

[Arising to cheers] My friends, I am rejoiced that you are glad, but I don't know how you will feel when I get through. I come from another field – the country of the slave. They have got their liberty – so much good luck to have slavery partly destroyed; not entirely. I want it root and branch destroyed. Then we will all be free indeed.

I feel that if I have to answer for the deeds done in my body just as much as man, I have a right to have as much as a man. There is a great stir about colored men getting their rights, but not a word about the colored women;

---

15. Margaret Washington, *Sojourner Truth's America* (Urbana: University of Illinois Press, 2009), p. 5.
16. Henry M. Parkhurst, *Proceedings of the First Anniversary of the American Equal Rights Association: Held at the Church of the Puritans, New York, May 9 and 10, 1867* (New York: R. J. Johnston, 1867), p. 3.

and if colored men get their rights, and not colored women theirs, you see the colored men will be masters over the women, and it will be just as bad as it was before.

So I am for keeping the thing going while things are stirring; because if we wait till it is still, it will take a great while to get it going again. White women are a great deal smarter, and know more than colored women, while colored women do not know scarcely anything. They go out washing, which is about as high as a colored woman gets, and their men go about idle, strutting up and down; and when the women come home, they ask for their money and take it all, and then scold you because there is no food.

I want you to consider on that chil'n. I call you chil'n; you are somebody's chil'n, and I am old enough to be mother of all that is here. I want women to have their rights. In the courts women have no right, no voice; nobody speaks for them. I wish woman to have her voice there among the pettifoggers. If it is not a fit place for women, it us unfit for men to be there.

I am above eighty years old; it is about time for me to be going. I have been forty years a slave and forty years free, and would be here forty years more to have equal rights for all. I suppose I am kept here because something remains for me to do; I suppose I am yet to help to break the chain. I have done a great deal of work; as much as a man, but did not get so much pay. I used to work in the field and bind grain, keeping up with the cradler, but men doing no more, got twice as much pay; so with the German women. They work in the field and do as much work but do not get the pay. We do as much, eat as much, we want as much.

I suppose I am about the only colored woman who goes about to speak for the rights of the colored women.[17] I want to keep the thing stirring, now that the ice is cracked. What we want is a little money. You men know that you get as much again as women when you write, or for what you do. When we get our rights we shall not have to come to you for money, for then we shall have money enough in our pockets; and may be you will ask us for money.

But help us now until we get it. It is a good consolation to know that when we have got this battle once fought we shall not be coming to you any more. You have been having our rights so long, that you think, like a slave-holder, that you own us. I know that it is hard for one who has held the reins for so long to give up; it cuts like a knife. It will feel all the better when it closes up again. I have been in Washington about three years, seeing about these colored people.

Now colored men have the right to vote. There ought to be equal rights now more than ever, since colored people have got their freedom. I am going to talk several times while I am here; so now I will do a little singing. I have not heard any singing since I came here.

―――――

17. Sojourner Truth was a pioneer but far from alone in her activities as a black feminist activist. For career biographies of some of her counterparts see Shirley J. Yee, *Black Women Abolitionists: A Study in Activism, 1828–1860* (Knoxville: University of Tennessee Press, 1993).

4. Josephine Butler, 'Speech on Sex Workers' Rights' (Wigan, 1870)

On the other side of the Atlantic, the women's movement began to gather new momentum in the 1870s. One of its key figures was Josephine Butler (1828–1906), a prolific campaigner who framed some of the influential arguments for women's education and legal protection. Born into a wealthy and prominent Northumberland family related to the Whig Prime Minister of the 1830s, Earl Grey, she was brought up in a climate of liberal reform. Marrying an Oxford academic, Butler became a dynamic campaigner against child prostitution, human trafficking and the raising of the age of consent.

When a new Contagious Diseases Act was introduced in 1869 and brought with it the right of police to arrest and search any women suspected of the illness, Butler toured the country denouncing the legislation and the 'steel rape' that such searches represented. In the speech below we see her addressing a crowded meeting hall in Wigan in the North of England at the beginning of what was to be a long and controversial career of agitation. Though facing intense opposition as a woman speaking about sexual matters in public, Butler helped secure successful repeal of the acts in 1883.

Source

'Speech Given by Josephine E. Butler at Wigan', Friday, 20 May 1870, *Shield* (13 June 1870), pp. 124–5.

I had just returned from abroad when I heard that these Acts[18] had been passed, and it was some time before I could believe it. When at least convinced that our country was to be thus degraded and made like most of the Continental countries, it seemed as if a thunderclap had broken on my head.

I was filled with the deepest agony of soul. For nights I could not sleep; my pillow was literally wet with my tears. I thought if this was to be the case God has indeed forsaken our country. The pain which it has given me to stand up and speak, as I am now compelled to do, is nothing to the anguish I endured when I found that vice was acknowledged as a necessity and license to sin had obtained the sanction of the law. I am the mother of a family of sons growing up into life, and, rather than they should live to grow up under the foul influences which such laws engender, I would see them die in their purity and innocence

   . . .

---

18. Contagious Diseases Acts were introduced in 1864 to regulate prostitution and reduce the prevalence of sexually transmitted diseases. A further 1869 Act extended the prison sentence involved to one year.

Such, my friends, is the history and character of the awful slavery of women in modern times. It is a slavery and a slave trade as hideous as that which England so nobly contributed to put an end to in America and Africa, Shall the same country which paid its millions for the abolition of negro Maven[19] now pay its millions for the establishment of white slavery within its own bosom? the country of Wilberforce and Clarkson, and the noble heroes of the anti-slavery cause, now endure to see women degraded as the negro women in the plantations of Carolina?

My friends, it is not England that has done this thing, it is not my country which has established this shameful, impious, and oppressive law in our midst. That it is not England which has done it is proved by the strong, steady, holy, indignation which has burst from the heart of the people, by that distant murmur which we hear or rising wrath coming nearer and louder every day. No, the conscience of England is not dead – her heart is not stone, I thank God still that England is my country, amid the land of the free, not the slave.

The people had no voice in making this law, which has been now established for several years in some of our towns. It was secretly made, and has been secretly administered, by persons who seem to have lost the power to discern good and evil.

---

19. A reference to the 1833 Slavery Abolition Act, which compensated Caribbean and British slave-owners for their loss of property.

Part B: Suffrage for Women

5. Susan B. Anthony, 'Is It a Crime for a US Citizen to Vote?' (Rochester, New York, 1873)

In 1871, the National Women's Suffrage Association began urging American women to attempt to register to vote, using the Fourteenth Amendment as a legal basis for their claim. Many attempts were made across the country during the years that followed. The most consequential occurred when the veteran activist Susan B. Anthony (1820–1906) and a group of fifteen other women presented themselves to vote in the 1872 Presidential election in Rochester, New York. For 'all the women who took part in this action of mass civil disobedience', Elaine Weiss notes in her history of the women's movement, 'the consequences they faced, including heavy fines, public rebuke, and possibly prison, paled in comparison with the thrill of demanding a ballot and taking the law into their own hands'.[20]

Upon being charged with an illegal attempt to vote, Anthony transformed her trial into an opportunity for political theatre. That winter, Anthony took to the stump in every town across the upstate New York County, where the trial was to be held, delivering a speech that posed the question: 'Is it a Crime for a Citizen of the United States to Vote?' Her public relations strategy worked as planned and the case was covered daily in the national press. So concerned was the prosecution about the threat that Anthony's activism posed, the US Attorney fought to have the trial moved, only for Anthony to continue her tour into the new upstate county. When eventually found guilty and fined $100, she declared to the judge. 'I shall never pay a dollar of your unjust penalty,' calling the bluff of the court, who set her free without payment.

Source

Ann D. Gordon (ed.), *The Selected Papers of Elizabeth Cady Stanton and Susan B. Anthony, Volume II: An Aristocracy of Sex, 1866–1873.* Copyright © 2000 by Rutgers, the State University of New Jersey.

Friends and Fellow-citizens: I stand before you to-night, under indictment for the alleged crime of having voted at the last Presidential election,[21] without

---

20. Elaine Weiss, *The Woman's Hour: The Great Fight to Win the Vote* (New York: Hachette, 2019), p. 120.
21. In the 1872 election, incumbent Republican President Ulysses S. Grant (1822–85) won re-election over Liberal Republican candidate Horace Greeley (1811–72). In the election, Victoria Woodhull also ran a half-campaign for President on a National Woman's Suffrage Association ticket.

having a lawful right to vote. It shall be my work this evening to prove to you that in thus voting, I not only committed no crime, but, instead, simply exercised my citizen's right, guaranteed to me and all United States citizens by the National Constitution, beyond the power of any State to deny. . . .

Though the words persons, people, inhabitants, electors, citizens, are used indiscriminately in the national and state constitutions, there was always a conflict of opinion, prior to the war, as to whether they were synonymous terms. As for instance: 'No person shall be a representative who shall not have been seven years a citizen, and who shall not, when elected, be an inhabitant of that state in which he is chosen.' 'No person shall be a senator who shall not have been a citizen of the United States, and an inhabitant of the state of which he is chosen.'

But whatever room there was for a doubt under the old regime, the adoption of the fourteenth amendment settled the question forever in its first sentence. 'All persons born or naturalized in the United States, and subject to the jurisdiction thereof, are citizens of the United States, and of the state wherein they reside.'

And the second settles the equal status of all persons – all citizens. 'No state shall make or enforce any law which shall abridge the privileges or immunities of citizens; nor shall any state deprive any person of life, liberty, or property, without due process of law; nor deny to any person within its jurisdiction the equal protection of the laws.'

The only question left to be settled here is, are women persons? And I hardly believe any of our opponents will have the hardihood to say they are not! Being persons, then women are citizens; and no state has a right to make any new law, or enforce any old law, that shall abridge their privileges or immunities. Hence every discrimination against women in constitutions and laws of the several states is to-day null and void – precisely as is every one against negros.

Is the right to vote one of the privileges and immunities of citizens? I think the disfranchised ex-rebels and ex-state prisoners will all agree with me that it is not only one of them, but the one without which all the others are nothing. Seek first the kingdom of the ballot and all things else shall be given thee, is the political injunction. Webster, Worchester, and Bouvier all define citizen to be a person in the United States entitled to vote and hold office.

Prior to the adoption of the 13th amendment, by which slavery was forever abolished, and black men transformed from property to personality, the judicial decisions of the country were in harmony with these definitions. To be a person was to be a citizen; and to be a citizen was to be a voter.[22]

---

22. The Thirteenth Amendment to the US Constitution, the first of three Reconstruction Amendments, passed the Senate in April 1864 and was ratified by the states in December 1865.

Associate Justice Washington, one of the most distinguished judges of the Supreme Court, in defining the privileges and immunities of the citizen, more than fifty years ago, said: 'they include all such privileges as are fundamental in their nature.' And 'among them is the right to exercise the elective franchise and to hold office, as provided for by the laws of the various states.'

Even the 'Dred Scott' decision, pronounced by abolitionists and republicans infamous, because it virtually declared 'black men had no rights white men were bound to respect,' gave this true and logical conclusion, that to be one of the people was to be a citizen and a voter.[23]

. . .

Is anything further needed to prove woman's 'condition of servitude' sufficiently orthodox to entitle her to the guarantees of the fifteenth amendment ?

Is there a man who will not agree with me, that to talk of 'freedom without the ballot' is mockery, is slavery, to the women of this republic, precisely as New England's orator, Wendell Phillips,[24] at the close of the late war declared it to be to the newly emancipated black men?

Prior to the rebellion, by common consent, the right to enslave as well as to disfranchise both native and foreign born citizens, was conceded to the states. But the one grand principle, settled by the war and the reconstruction legislation, is, the supremacy of national power to protect the citizens of the United States in their right to freedom and the elective franchise, against any and every interference on the part of the several states. And again and again, have the American people asserted the triumph of this principle, by their own overwhelming majorities for Lincoln and Grant.

The one issue of the last two presidential elections was, whether the 14th and 15th amendments should be considered the irrevocable will of the people; and the decision was, they shall be – and that it is not only the right, but the duty of the national government to protect all United States citizens in the full enjoyment and free exercise of all their privileges and immunities against any attempt of any state to deny or abridge.

And in this conclusion, Republicans and Democrats alike agree. Senator Frelinghuysen[25] said, 'The heresy of state rights has been completely buried in these amendments; that as amended the Constitution confers not only national, but state citizenship upon all persons born or naturalized within our limits.' The National Republican Convention Call said, 'Equal suffrage has been engrafted on

---

23. In *Dred Scott* v. *Sandford* (1857), the Supreme Court ruled that negros whose ancestors were slaves could never be American citizens or lay claim to representation in federal court.

24. Wendell Phillips (1811–84), the leading abolition activist and women's rights campaigner from Massachusetts, was also a prominent supporter of women's rights.

25. Frederick Theodore Frelinghuysen (1817–85), US Senator from New Jersey for the Democrat Party.

the national Constitution; the privileges and immunities of American citizenship have become a part of the organic law.' The National Republican Platform said, 'Complete liberty and exact equality in the enjoyment of all civil, political, and public rights, should be established and maintained throughout the Union by efficient and appropriate state and federal legislation.'

If that means anything, it is that Congress should pass a law to require the states to protect women in their equal political rights; and that the states should enact laws making it the duty for the inspectors of elections to receive women's votes, on precisely the same conditions they do those of men.

. . .

We ask the courts to render true and unprejudiced opinions of the law, and wherever there is room for a doubt to give its benefit on the side of liberty and equal rights to all citizens, remembering that the true rule of interpretation under our national constitution, especially since its amendments, is that anything for human rights is constitutional, everything against human rights unconstitutional.

We ask the juries to fail to return a verdict of 'guilty' against honest, law-abiding, tax paying United States citizens for offering their votes, at our elections. Or against intelligent, worthy young men, inspectors of elections, for receiving and counting such citizens' votes. And it is on this line that we propose to fight our battle for the ballot – all peaceably, but nevertheless persistently through to complete triumph, when all United States citizens shall be recognized as equals before the law.

6. Sir Henry James and W. E. Forster, 'The Anti-Suffrage Case' (London, 1879)

While reformers such as Butler were taking the women's rights message to the meeting halls and lecterns of Britain, the debate over female suffrage was also becoming more prominent in Parliament. Beginning in 1866, pro-suffrage members, such as liberal philosopher John Stuart Mill (1806–73), had begun to present multiple bills to Parliament urging that the case for votes for women be reviewed. Yet such reformers found themselves on the losing side of an increasingly heated debate. In the early Parliamentary debates on women's suffrage, its opponents relied on ridicule and sarcasm, and anecdotal evidence that women did not desire the vote.[26]

The extract below, from March 1879, comes from a later stage of the debate, featuring more substantive arguments. It comes midway

---

26. Sophia A. Van Wingerden, *The Women's Suffrage Movement in Britain, 1866–1928* (London: Palgrave Macmillan, 1999), pp. 45–6.

through a Commons debate on the 'Election Disabilities of Women Resolution', whose motion was that it was 'injurious to the best interests of the Country that women . . . should be disabled from voting in Parliamentary elections . . . and that it is expedient that this disability should be forthwith repealed'. Amongst those making the case against the motion were the Quaker industrialist W. E. Forster (1818–86) and fellow Liberal MP, the Solicitor-General Henry James (1828–1911), who was to become the most important Parliamentary anti-suffragist of the period.

Source

'Electoral Disabilities Of Women. – Resolution', HC Deb 07 March 1879, *Hansard*, vol. 244 cc405–507.

Sir Henry James: Sir, it is some years ago that I formed the opinion that very little that was novel could be added to any debate on this subject, and I certainly have come to the conclusion that I cannot say anything that is new. . . .

. . . Perhaps it is better not to speak of one's own experience; but surely the majority of Members in this House will be disposed to think how much better it would have been if they had learnt those mother's lessons more and forgotten them less. Again, of those who enter into the married relations of life, my hon. Friend, in the same speech, said – 'How constantly does it happen that the man's freedom of intellect is a thing kept to himself, that he is incapable of imparting to the woman with whom so much of his life is spent any conception of the range of his thoughts?' Sir, on that subject I can offer no information. I have had no experience on that subject; but if this so constantly occurs, and if the results of a mother's lessons are such as my hon. Friend represents them, and if the wife is of such a nature that the husband is incapable of imparting to her any conception of the range of his thoughts, is it not strange that that mother who teaches wrongly, and that the wife who has such a degraded intellect should be the very persons to whom the hon. Member is now asking us to give the franchise? He has asked us to give the franchise to the mother who teaches wrongly, and to the wife who drags down her husband's intellect.

The hon. Member, in effect, says – 'I would give it to them because they are unfit, and the more unfit they are, the more they want the franchise.' Why – and I appeal especially to hon. Members opposite – if you are to give the franchise to people because they are unfit to exercise it, to whom are you to refuse the franchise? Are you to refuse it to the agricultural labourer? You tell us he is so unfit that he cannot be enfranchised; and to-night we have heard the argument which was substantially used last year – that the more unfit the person is, the more it is your duty to give the franchise, in order to remedy that unfitness. But what is to become of the country if that doctrine is accepted? What is to become of the government whilst this unfitness is being cured? It will not be remedied by the fact of women being registered. Time must roll on; years must pass by; generations must go and come, before the nature of the thoughts and minds of a sex can be changed. What, I ask, is to become of the government of this country in the meantime? Why, the whole country, the entire community, must suffer grievously – I think almost to their destruction – whilst this vain combat with nature is being carried on.

My hon. Friend[27] spoke but lightly of some subjects, which I should have thought would have been more pertinent and relevant to the matter than this attempt to alter a woman's nature and condition. Did it ever occur to him that after women had been enfranchised – and then, of course, by natural conse-quence, they must come to this House – that that unfitness must still continue? It is not only a question of the franchise. It is a question of the habits of life, of knowledge, and of practical study. When men go forth for the work of their daily life, they gain knowledge on practical subjects; in their different callings they gain knowledge, which they bring into this House, and which they use at the polling booths. They form judgments not only from mere study, but from practi-cal knowledge, resulting from their different occupations in life. Well, Sir, can a woman ever learn practical subjects as we have learnt them? What is her profes-sion? I say it with some diffidence, but I fancy that a woman's profession, perhaps her only profession, is marriage. ['Oh!'] Sir, I hear dissent behind me. I knew the danger of making that assertion without having an authority to support it. I can foresee that, in some of these itinerant lectures we hear so much of, I shall be figuratively pulled to pieces for making that statement, and I shall have dissent more loudly expressed than that of the hon. Member for Liskeard. I am anxious, therefore, to support my statement, almost for my safety, as well as for any weight that is to be given to what I say, by what I find in the records of this House.

. . .

Mr. W. E. Forster: I think we must all admit – that the country, that England at present, England in past times, has gained good and had done good by no class more than single women, from Queen Elizabeth to Florence Night-ingale; but what we find women saying and thinking is, not that marriage is specially the vocation of women, but that when there is marriage the husband has one thing to do and the wife has another thing to do. My hon. and learned Friend says what a great advantage it would be to bring women in to the vote, because they would always give a vote in favour of peace. I do not admit it.

Mr. Sullivan: If the right hon. Gentleman would allow me, I am sure they would often deter us from unnecessary wars.

Mr. W. E. Forster: I think just the contrary. I think if the women had to vote, it would be a vote in favour of war rather than peace. I remember when I

_____

27. Leonard Henry Courtney (1832–1918), Liberal MP for Liskeard, who had made the radical argument that the vote itself would confer political education.

was travelling in the Southern States of America, I asked how they were getting over the Civil War, and they told me the men who fought wished to be at peace with the North; they had had quite enough of it; and they had had quite enough of it long before, if it had not been for the women. And why? Because the women did not do the fighting, and the men did. And we must, when we come to the different duties, and the different walks of life – we must consider what it is, what Government depends upon, and what the administration of public affairs depends on. It depends on the force and power of getting the verdict of the Government of the country carried out, and that must be done by men, for my hon. Friend the Member for Liskeard surely does not wish women to be subjected to the conscription. We have no conscription here; but if we had, surely he would not wish them to be subjected to the conscription.

I do not wish to detain the House; but I want simply to say that I believe the enormous majority of women, and the best of women, do not wish to have the vote, on the ground on which I agree with them, and which can be simply expressed in three words – that women are not men, and that the business of public affairs belongs to men rather than women. And, remember, that it is not a question merely of giving them a thing which they do not wish for; but it is a question of forcing on them difficulties and responsibilities and duties which they do not desire, and that the women who do not wish for the vote, if my hon. Friend's Motion was carried out, and they were thus forced to have the vote, would be actually injured by having a vote given them they would rather be without – they would not like the duty imposed upon them, or the difficulties and dangers in connection with it.

I have only one further remark to make. It is not very desirable, for many reasons, for any man to prophesy upon any sort of public question. But I do venture to say this – that I feel certain that, although we shall probably have this Motion year by year, that it never will be carried.

I ask my hon. Friend to look at America. I recollect, many years ago, in England and Wales, almost before many of you were born, that this question was so much talked of that it looked as if it might be passed; but then it suddenly stopped.[28] That happened in America which is happening here, and will happen every where, according to my opinion. People will play with it, men will play with it, they will seldom deal with it seriously; but the moment they find there is any possibility of the question being carried, that will happen that happened in the United States – the large majority of men, backed by a larger majority of women, will say that this hard work of government, this law-making, belongs to men; it is their duty to do it, and we women would rather not have the franchise.

---

28. Three years following the failure of Susan B. Anthony's voting strategy, in *Minor v. Happersett* (1875), the Supreme Court rejected women's suffrage, ruling that the Constitution did not confer suffrage on any citizens. Some contemporaries saw these twin defeats as having drained momentum from the US women's movement.

7. Emmeline Pankhurst, 'Freedom or Death' (Hartford, Connecticut, 1913)

British activist Emmeline Pankhurst (1857–1928) was the most famous figure in the final stage of the British women's suffrage struggle (Figure 14). As a teenager in Manchester, she had been inspired by the lectures of feminist pioneer Lydia Becker to join the cause, founding the Women's Franchise League in 1889 to fight for the vote for married women. Having grown dissatisfied with its slow progress, in 1903 Pankhurst established the more militant Women's Social and Political Union, and the civil disobedience career of the 'suffragettes' began. Its notorious activities over the next decade, including arson, vandalism and hunger strikes, occurred alongside the elaborate rhetorical tactic of disrupting political meetings and heckling speakers at rallies and gatherings until forcibly ejected.

As figurehead for the movement, Pankhurst was repeatedly imprisoned and her own many public speeches to groups of largely working-class women were heavily surveilled and increasingly disrupted. Channelling the frustration of a movement that feared it would never meet its objectives, her rhetoric was often fierce – she famously declared to a Royal Albert Hall crowd, 'I incite this meeting to rebellion!'

Her most famous address was to take place on the other side of the Atlantic, where she had sailed in October 1913 on a fund-raising lecture tour to avoid police attention in London. With news of her radical methods preceding her, she was initially detained and barred from entry at Ellis Island as a wanted fugitive, before President Woodrow Wilson intervened to allow her access. On 13 November, she spoke at Parson's Theatre in Hartford, Connecticut, framing the demands of the movement by reaching back to the iconic rhetoric of Patrick Henry, repurposing his cry of 'freedom or death' as part of a new century's defining struggle.

Source

Verbatim Report of Mrs. Pankhurst's Speech, delivered Nov. 13, 1913 at Parson's Theatre, Hartford, Conn. (Hartford: Connecticut Woman Suffrage Association, 1913).

I am here as a soldier who has temporarily left the field of battle in order to explain – it seems strange it should have to be explained – what civil war is like when civil war is waged by women. I am not only here as a soldier temporarily absent from the field at battle; I am here – and that, I think, is the strangest part of my coming – I am here as a person who, according to the law courts of my country, it has been decided, is of no value to the community at all: and I am adjudged because of my life to be a dangerous person, under sentence of penal servitude in a convict prison. So you see there is some special interest in hearing so unusual a person address you. I dare say, in the minds of many of you – you will perhaps forgive me this personal touch – that I do not look either very like a soldier or very like a convict, and yet I am both.

... Women are very slow to rouse, but once they are aroused, once they are determined, nothing on earth and nothing in heaven will make women give way; it is impossible. And so this 'Cat and Mouse Act'[29] which is being used against women today has failed: and the home secretary has taken advantage of the fact that parliament is not sitting, to revive and use alongside of it the forcible feeding. At the present time there are women lying at death's door, recovering enough strength to undergo operations, who have had both systems applied to them, and have not given in and won't give in, and who will be prepared, as soon as they get up from their sick beds, to go on as before. There are women who are being carried from their sick beds on stretchers into meetings. They are too weak to speak, but they go amongst their fellow workers just to show that their spirits are unquenched, and that their spirit is alive, and they mean to go on as long as life lasts.

Now, I want to say to you who think women cannot succeed, we have brought the government of England to this position, that it has to face this alternative: either women are to be killed or women are to have the vote. I ask American men in this meeting, what would you say if in your state you were faced with that alternative, that you must either kill them or give them their citizenship – women, many of whom you respect, women whom you know have lived useful lives, women whom you know, even if you do not know them personally, are animated with the highest motives, women who are in pursuit of liberty and the power to do useful public service? Well, there is only one answer to that alternative; there is only one way out of it, unless you are prepared to put back civilisation two or three generations: you must give those women the vote. Now that is the outcome of our civil war.

You won your freedom in America when you had the revolution, by bloodshed, by sacrificing human life. You won the civil war by the sacrifice of human life when you decided to emancipate the negro. You have left it to women in your land, the men of all civilised countries have left it to women, to work out their own salvation. That is the way in which we women of England are doing. Human life for us is sacred, but we say if any life is to be sacrificed it shall be ours; we won't do it ourselves, but we will put the enemy in the position where they will have to choose between giving us freedom or giving us death.

---

29. The name given to the police tactic used against the British suffragette activists involving repeat imprisonment, force-feeding and release, in a cycle intended to weaken the will of the movement.

Now whether you approve of us or whether you do not, you must see that we have brought the question of women's suffrage into a position where it is of first rate importance, where it can be ignored no longer. Even the most hardened politician will hesitate to take upon himself directly the responsibility of sacrificing the lives of women of undoubted honour, of undoubted earnestness of purpose. That is the political situation as I lay it before you today.

Now then, let me say something about what has brought it about because you must realise that only the very strongest of motives would lead women to do what we have done. Life is sweet to all of us. Every human being loves life and loves to enjoy the good things and the happiness that life gives: and yet we have a state of things in England that has made not two or three women but thousands of women quite prepared to face these terrible situations that I have been trying without any kind of passion or exaggeration to lay before you.

. . .

There hasn't been a victory that the women of America have won that we have not rejoiced in. I think as we have read month by month of the new States that have been added to the list of fully enfranchised states, perhaps we who know how hard the fight is, have rejoiced even more than American women themselves.

I have heard cheers ring out in a meeting in London when the news of some new state being added to the list was given, cheers louder and more enthusiastic than I have ever heard for any victory in an American meeting. It is very true that those who are fighting a hard battle, those who are sacrificing greatly in order to win a victory, appreciate victories and are more enthusiastic when victories are won. We have rejoiced wholeheartedly in your victories. We feel that those victories have been easier perhaps because of the hard times that we were having, because out of our militant movement in the storm centre of the suffrage movement have gone waves that have helped to rouse women all over the world.

You could only explain the strange phenomena in that way. Ten years ago there was hardly any woman suffrage movement at all. Now even in China and Japan, in India, in Turkey, everywhere women are rising up and asking for these larger opportunities, which modern conditions demand that women should have: and we women think that we have helped. Well, if we have helped at all, if, as has been said from the chair tonight, we have even helped to rouse suffrage enthusiasm in Connecticut, can you blame me very much if I come and tell you of the desperate struggle we are having, of how the government is trying to break us down in every possible way, even by involving us in lawsuits, and trying to frighten our subscribers by threatening to prosecute even people who help us by subscribing money? Can you wonder I come over to America? Have you read about American dollars that have been given the Irish law-breakers?

So here am I. I come in the intervals of prison appearance: I come after having been four times imprisoned under the 'Cat and Mouse Act', probably going back to be rearrested as soon as I set my foot on British soil. I come to ask you to help to win this fight. If we win it, this hardest of all fights, then, to be sure, in the future it is going to be made easier for women all over the world to win their fight when their time comes. So I make no apologies for coming, and I make no apologies, Mrs Hepburn,[30] for asking this audience if any of them feel inclined to help me to take back some money from America and put it with the money that I know our women are raising by desperate personal sacrifice at home, so that when we begin our next year's campaign, facing a general election, as probably we shall face next year, our anxieties on the money side will not be so heavy as they would have been if I had not found strength and health enough to come and carry out this somewhat arduous tour in the United States of America.

---

30. Katharine Houghton Hepburn (1881–1951), President of the Connecticut Woman's Suffrage Association, and mother of the film actress of the same name.

Part C: Sexuality and Reproduction

8. Frances Ellen Watkins Harper, 'Enlightened Motherhood' (Brooklyn, 1892)

The relationship of sexuality to freedom was a prominent yet under-appreciated undercurrent to women's movement rhetoric of the period. Some of the most powerful arguments on this taboo topic were made as part of the civil rights struggle. Francis Ellen Watkins Harper (1825–1911) was one such reformer who made the desire to reform sexual mores and moral standards a key part of black uplift rhetoric. Born free in Maryland, Harper had found fame as a poet and author, before embarking on a half-century-long career as an educator and moral reformer. With one daughter herself, Harper explored the parental theme throughout her career. In the 1850s, she published the often-anthologised 'The Slave Mother' on the evils of family separation, and in her postbellum poems, such as 'The Mother's Blessing', extolled familial joys.[31]

During the Reconstruction and post-Reconstruction period, she delivered many speeches to African American associations, offering sermonic entreaties on topics such as temperance, education, thrift, industry and self-improvement. 'Enlightened Motherhood' was one of such uplift speeches, delivered in 1892 at a meeting of the Brooklyn Literary Society. Expressing its concern with aspirational respectability and the ideal known as 'republican motherhood', the lecture encouraged mothers to teach their sons temperance and sexual purity, drawing attention to double standards relating to issues of moral behaviour and sexual purity across the genders.[32]

Source

Frances E. W. Harper, *Brighter Coming Day: A Frances Ellen Watkins Harper Reader* (New York: Feminist Press of City University of New York, 1989).

It is nearly thirty years since an emancipated people stood on the threshold of a new era, facing an uncertain future[33] – a legally unmarried race, to be taught the sacredness of the marriage relations; an ignorant people, to be taught to read

---

31. Frances E. W. Harper, *Brighter Coming Day: A Frances Ellen Watkins Harper Reader* (New York: The Feminist Press, 1989), p. 137.
32. See Michael Stancliff, *Frances Ellen Watkins Harper: African American Reform Rhetoric and the Rise of a Modern Nation State* (Routledge: New York, 2011).
33. The Thirteenth Amendment to the US Constitution, the measure abolishing slavery, was passed by Senate in April 1864 and by the House in January 1865.

of the Christian law and to learn to comprehend more fully the claims of the gospel of the Christ of Calvary. A homeless race, to be gathered into homes of peaceful security and to be instructed how to plant around their firesides the strongest batteries against sins that degrade and the race vices that demoralize. A race unversed in the science of government and unskilled in the just administration of law, to be translated from the old oligarchy of slavery into the new common-wealth of freedom, and to whose men came the right to exchange the fetters on their wrists for the ballots in their right hands – a ballot which, if not vitiated by fraud or restrained by intimidation, counts just as much as that of the most talented and influential man in the land.

While politicians may stumble on the barren mountain of fretful controversy, and men, lacking faith in God and the invisible forces which make for righteousness, may shrink from the unsolved problems of the hour, into the hands of Christian women comes the opportunity of serving the ever blessed Christ, by ministering to His little ones and striving to make their homes the brightest spots on earth and the fairest types of heaven. The school may instruct and the church may teach, but the home is an institution older than the church and antedates schools, and that is the place where children should be trained for useful citizenship on earth and a hope of holy companionship in heaven.

Every mother should endeavor to be a true artist. I do not mean by this that every woman should be a painter, sculptor, musician, poet, or writer, but the artist who will write on the table of childish innocence thoughts she will not blush to see read in the light of eternity and printed amid the archives of heaven, that the young may learn to wear them as amulets around their hearts and throw them as bulwarks around their lives, and that in the hour of temptation and trial the voices from home may linger around their paths as angles of guidance, around their steps, and be incentives to deeds of high and holy worth.

. . .

Are there not women, respectable women, who feel that it would wring their hearts with untold anguish, and bring their gray hairs in sorrow to the grave, if their daughters should trail the robes of their womanhood in the dust, yet who would say of their sons, if they were trampling their manhood down and fettering their souls with cords of vice, 'O, well, boys will be boys, and young men will sow their wild oats.'

I hold that no woman loves social purity as it deserves to be loved and valued, if she cares for the purity of her daughters and not her sons; who would gather her dainty robes from contact with the fallen woman and yet greet with smiling lips and clasp with warm and welcoming hands the author of her wrong and ruin. How many mothers to-day shrink from a double standard for society which can ostracise the woman and condone the offense of the man? How many mothers say within their hearts, 'I intend to teach my boy to be as pure in his life, as chaste in his conversation, as the young girl who sits at my side encircled in the warm clasp of loving arms?' How many mothers strive to have their boys shun the gilded saloon as they would the den of a deadly serpent? Not the mother who thoughtlessly sends her child to the saloon for a beverage to make merry with her friends. How many mothers teach their boys to shrink in horror from the fascinations of women, not as God made them, but as sin has degraded them?

To-night, if you and I could walk through the wards of various hospitals at home and abroad, perhaps we would find hundreds, it may be thousands, of young men awaiting death as physical wrecks, having burned the candle of their lives at both ends. Were we to bend over their dying couches with pitying glances, and question them of their lives, perhaps numbers of them could tell you sad stories of careless words from thoughtless lips, that tainted their imaginations and sent their virus through their lives; of young eyes, above which God has made the heavens so eloquent with His praise, and the earth around so poetic with His ideas, turning from the splendor of the magnificent sunsets or glorious early dawns, and finding allurement in the dreadful fascinations of sin, or learning to gloat over impure pictures and vile literature. Then, later on, perhaps many of them could say, 'The first time I went to a house where there were revelry and song, and the dead were there and I knew it not, I went with men who were older than myself; men, who should have showed me how to avoid the pitfalls which lie in the path of the young, the tempted, and inexperienced, taught me to gather the flowers of sin that blossom around the borders of hell.'

. . .

The work of the mothers of our race is grandly constructive. It is for us to build above the wreck and ruin of the past more stately temples of thought and action. Some races have been overthrown, dashed in pieces, and destroyed; but to-day the world is needing, fainting, for something better than the results of arrogance, aggressiveness, and indomitable power. We need mothers who are capable of being character builders, patient, loving, strong, and true, whose homes will be uplifting power in the race. This is one of the greatest needs of the hour. No race can afford to neglect the enlightenment of its mothers.

9. Oscar Wilde, 'Testimony at Indecency Trial' (London, 1895)

The extract below records the climactic moment of one of the most prominent British trials of the late nineteenth century. In April 1895, the Anglo-Irish novelist, playwright, poet and celebrity representative of the Aesthetic Movement, Oscar Wilde (1854–1900), stood accused of violating laws forbidding 'acts of gross indecency between men' in his affair with the author Lord Alfred Douglas (1870–1945). Known for his biting wit, flamboyant dress and arch conversation, Wilde was one of the most recognisable transatlantic personalities of his day, rendering his trial an international spectacle.

The extract below from the court transcript contains the most famous exchange from the fourth day of the trial, on 3 April. The moment turned on Wilde's reading of a key phrase in Douglas's poem, 'The Two Loves': 'the love that dare not speak its name'. Called upon to defend its alleged indecency, Wilde offered a brief defence of his affections and attachments. Denying that it referred to intercourse, he instead situated same-sex love within a grand intellectual tradition, using artistic, literary and philosophical precedent to challenge normative late Victorian definitions of the 'natural', and dismissing the reductive comprehension of his accusers.

Famously, his rhetorical gifts were unable to save him. He was convicted of sodomy and served two years in prison, the last eighteen months being spent at Reading Gaol, leaving him chastened and bankrupt. At the time, the Wilde trial had the effect of sharpening the pressure on homosexuality in transatlantic literary society. But the legacy of Wilde's words in favour of 'the noblest forms of affection' in the London courtroom have transcended their immediate context, to inspire generations of activists fighting for LGBTQ equality.

Source

Tim Coates (ed.), *The Trials of Oscar Wilde 1895: Transcript Excerpts from the Trials at the Old Bailey, London, During April and May 1895* (London: Stationery Office, 2001).

Mr. C. F. Gill (cross-examining) – Listen, Mr. Wilde, I shall keep you only a very short time in the witness box. [Counsel read the following poem from *The Chameleon*.][34]

'Last night unto my bed methought there came
Our lady of strange dreams, and from an urn
She poured live fire, so that mine eyes did burn
At sight of it. Anon the floating flame
Took many shapes, and one cried: I am Shame
That walks with Love, I am most wise to turn
Cold lips and limbs to fire; therefore discern
And see my loveliness, and praise my name.
And afterwards, in radiant garments dressed
With sound of flutes and laughing of glad lips,
A pomp of all the passions passed along
All the night through; till the white phantom ships
Of dawn sailed in. Whereat I said this song,
"Of all sweet passions Shame is loveliest."'

---

34. 'In Praise of Shame' (1894), in Caspar Wintermans, *Alfred Douglas: A Poet's Life and His Finest Work* (London: Peter Owen, 2006), p. 221.

G – Is that one of the beautiful poems?

Sir Edward Clarke (Wilde's defence lawyer) –That is not one of Mr. Wilde's.

Mr. Gill –I am not aware that I said it was.

Sir Edward Clarke – I thought you would be glad to say it was not.

Mr. Justice Charles – I understand that was a poem by Lord Alfred Douglas.

Mr. Gill – Yes, my lord, and one which the witness described as a beautiful poem. The other beautiful poem is the one that follows immediately and precedes 'The Priest and the Acolyte.'[35]

G – Your view, Mr. Wilde, is that the 'shame' mentioned here is that shame which is a sense of modesty?

W – That was the explanation given to me by the person who wrote it. The sonnet seemed to me obscure.

G – During 1893 and 1894 you were a good deal in the company of Lord Alfred Douglas?

W – Oh, yes.

G – Did he read that poem to you?

W – Yes.

G – You can, perhaps, understand that such verses as these would not be acceptable to the reader with an ordinarily balanced mind?

W – I am not prepared to say. It appears to me to be a question of taste, temperament and individuality. I should say that one man's poetry is another man's poison! (Laughter.)

G – I daresay! The next poem is one described as 'Two Loves.' It contains these lines:

> '"Sweet youth,
> Tell me why, sad and sighing, dost thou rove
> These pleasant realms? I pray thee tell me sooth,
> What is thy name?" He said, "My name is Love,"
> Then straight the first did turn himself to me,
> And cried, "He lieth, for his name is Shame.
> But I am Love, and I was wont to be
> Alone in this fair garden, till he came
> Unasked by night; I am true Love, I fill
> The hearts of boy and girl with mutual flame."
> Then sighing said the other, "Have thy will,
> I am the Love that dare not speak its name".'

G – Was that poem explained to you?

W – I think that is clear.

G – There is no question as to what it means?

W – Most certainly not.

---

35. 'Two Loves' (1894), in Wintermans, *Alfred Douglas*, p. 220.

G – Is it not clear that the love described relates to natural love and unnatural love?

W – No.

G – What is the 'Love that dare not speak its name'?

W – 'The Love that dare not speak its name' in this century is such a great affection of an elder for a younger man as there was between David and Jonathan,[36] such as Plato made the very basis of his philosophy,[37] and such as you find in the sonnets of Michelangelo and Shakespeare.[38] It is that deep, spiritual affection that is as pure as it is perfect. It dictates and pervades great works of art like those of Shakespeare and Michelangelo, and those two letters of mine, such as they are. It is in this century misunderstood, so much misunderstood that it may be described as the 'Love that dare not speak its name,' and on account of it I am placed where I am now. It is beautiful, it is fine, it is the noblest form of affection. There is nothing unnatural about it. It is intellectual, and it repeatedly exists between an elder and a younger man, when the elder man has intellect, and the younger man has all the joy, hope and glamour of life before him. That it should be so the world does not understand. The world mocks at it and sometimes puts one in the pillory for it.

(Loud applause, mingled with some hisses.)

Mr. Justice Charles – If there is the slightest manifestation of feeling I shall have the Court cleared. There must be complete silence preserved.

G – Then there is no reason why it should be called 'Shame'?

W – Ah, that, you will see, is the mockery of the other love, love which is jealous of friendship and says to it, 'You should not interfere.'

10. Anna Rüling, 'The Women's Movement and the Homosexual Problem' (Berlin, 1904)

In October 1904, before a meeting of the Scientific Humanitarian Committee at the Prinz Albrecht Hotel in Berlin, the Hamburg-born writer and activist Theodora Anna Sprüngli (1880–1953), better known under her pseudonym Anna Rüling, delivered a speech now seen as a foundational document of the LGBTQ movement.[39]

---

36. The First Book of Samuel records the intense homosocial relationship between the eldest son of Saul in the Kingdom of Israel, Jonathan, and David, Saul's successor.

37. Same-sex relationships between men were common in ancient Greece, and a key theme of the *Symposium* (c.385–370 BCE) of Plato (c.428–348 BCE).

38. Though most celebrated as a painter and sculptor, the Florentine artist Michelangelo (1475–1564) also composed over 300 sonnets and madrigals, many of which can be read as addressing same-sex romantic friendship. They bear comparison to those sonnets (numbers 1–126) of William Shakespeare (1564–1616) addressed to the 'fair youth'.

39. Christiane Leidinger, '"Anna Rüling": A Problematic Foremother of Lesbian Herstory', *Journal of the History of Sexuality*, 13:4 (October 2004), pp. 477–99.

Rüling saw that, whilst the international women's movement was gaining momentum, it was doing so by ignoring lesbian involvement within its ranks. She insisted that a unity between their common struggle towards self-determination was a 'cultural historical necessity' and a 'duty' of all female reformers. Using 'urning', a term for homosexuals coined by pioneering same-sex rights activist Karl Heinrich Ulrichs (1825–95), Rüling explicitly turned against the sexual–pathological image of a distinct homosexual 'species', and argued for equal opportunities in education and employment.[40] One of the few examples in this anthology from beyond the Anglo-American tradition, its progressive rhetoric prefigures many of the arguments and approaches made in gender theory over a century later.

Source

Robert B. Ridinger, *Speaking for Our Lives: Historic Speeches and Rhetoric for Gay and Lesbian Rights 1892–2000* (Hoboken: Taylor and Francis, 2014).

Ladies and Gentlemen,

The Women's Movement is a historical and cultural necessity. Homosexuality is a historical and cultural necessity, and homosexuality is an obvious and natural bridge between man and woman.[41]

Today this is an undisputed scientific fact which the ignorant and impatient cannot dispute. Many people have asked how I came to this conclusion and could utter the truth about historical and cultural and natural and historical concepts in one breath, two things which on the surface seem to be opposites.

The interest to research the reason for this extended viewpoint is that people in general, when the matter concerns homosexuals, think only of male Urnings and overlook how many female homosexuals there are. They are, of course, less discussed because they – I was just about to say 'unfortunately' – have had no unjust cause to fight against, such as penal code paragraphs which arise out of having false moral views.

No cruel justice menaces women nor does the penitentiary if they follow their natural instincts. But the mental pressure which Urnings suffer is just as great, indeed even greater than the yoke which their male fellow-sufferers must bear.

---

40. Karl H. Ulrichs, *Forschungen über das Räthsel der Mannmännlichen Liebe* (Leipzig: Schleiz, 1864).
41. By saying this, she was building on the publication, earlier that year, of seminal writings by German feminist Johanna Elberskirchen (1864–1943), who had initiated a conversation about the rights of homosexual women.

To the world which judges by outward appearances they are even more obvious than the female Urning. Only too often they are overwhelmed by people's moralized misunderstandings. In our total social life, however, Uranian women are at least just as important as their male counterparts because they influence our lives in many ways, even if they are not discussed.

If people would just observe, they would soon come to the conclusion that homosexuality and the Women's Movement do not stand opposed to each other, but rather they aid each other reciprocally to gain rights and recognition, and to eliminate the injustice which condemns them on this earth.

. . .

The so-called 'moderate' tendency will not help homosexuals one bit for the simple reason that deeds of this kind have no tendency at all. Victory will come as a sign of radicalism, and we expect that the radicals will change the direction and for once make it honestly and openly recognized: indeed, there is a great number of Urnings among us, and we owe them a word of thanks for their efforts and their work and for many a fine success.

I do not mean to say that all questions of the Women's Movement will be handled from the homosexual viewpoint, just as I do not ascribe all this success to the Urnings or even a greater portion of it – that would be just as insane as it is wrong to take no notice at all of the homosexual problem.

. . .

The Women's Movement is fighting for the rights of free individuals and of self-determination. Therefore, it must recognize the despised spell which society casts on Uranians even today, which oppresses their rights. It is its duty to take a stand and fight the battle on the side of the Uranians as they do for unwed mothers, women workers and many others who need it, and to fight for their rights and for their freedom in their battle against old-fashioned false opinions of morality. For it is really immoral to render a morality which is the worst immorality when women have inalienable rights torn from them and when they now must struggle in bloody battle to recover them; when Uranians have inalienable human rights to their kind of love torn from them, a love which is just as pure and noble as heterosexual love, when they are good people who so love.

There are as many good people among homosexuals as among so-called 'normal' people. Most of all, I would like to avoid the appearance of estimating homosexuals too highly. I can assure you, ladies and gentlemen, I will not do that – I am well aware of the problems of homosexuality, but I also recognize its good side.

Therefore, I would like to say that Uranians are no better or no worse than heterosexuals – they should not be treated differently, but only in a different way.

To conclude my statements, I would like to emphasize again that homosexual women have done their part in the greater Women's Movement, that they are mostly responsible for activating the movement.

They have suffered because of their masculine inclinations and natural characteristics, and because of the many, many injustices and hardships caused by laws, society, and the old morality which concerns women.

Without the power and cooperation of the Urnings, the Women's Movement would not be so successful today, which it certainly is – which could be easily proven.

The Women's Movement and the movement for homosexual rights have thus far traveled on a dark road which has posted many obstacles in their way. Now it will become brighter and brighter around us and in the hearts of the people. This is not to say that the work of securing the rights of women and of Uranians has come to an end; we are still in the middle of two opposing sides, and many a bloody battle will have to be fought.

There will be many victims of the injustice of laws which will deal the death-blow before both movements have reached their goal – to gain the freedom of each person.

Our ultimate goal will be reached when both movements recognize that they have many common interests for which to fight when it becomes necessary.

And when, at times, as they will, hard times come to either side – that will not be the time for hesitation to stand up in defense against injustice and to march on to victory which will surely be ours. Revelation and truth are like the rising sun in the East – no power can force it out of its orbit. Slowly but surely it rises to its glittering zenith!

Perhaps not today or tomorrow, but in the not too distant future the Women's Movement and Uranians will raise their banners in victory!

Per aspera ad astra![42]

11. Theodore Roosevelt, 'On American Motherhood' (Washington, DC, 1905)

Sexuality and procreation were also issues of growing prominence in the language of national politics. A key example can be found in the rhetoric of US President Theodore Roosevelt (1858–1919)'s speeches on motherhood. An outspoken champion of the doctrine of family in his annual message to Congress in 1906, Roosevelt would chastise middle-class white American women for their 'willful sterility . . . the one sin for which the penalty is national death, race death'.[43]

In a speech before the National Congress of Mothers in Washington, DC, on 13 March 1905, he made the same argument directly to an explicitly female audience. On the eve of women's suffrage, Roosevelt's comments were double-edged. On the one hand, he acknowledged the significant debt that society owed to the moral influence of women and

---

42. 'Through hardship to the stars' (Latin).
43. William Griffith (ed.), *Roosevelt, His Life, Meaning and Messages: Speeches, Letters and Magazine Articles Dealing with the War and Other Vital Topics* (New York: Current Literature, 1919), p. 1064.

the dignity of domestic labour. On the other, he reaffirmed society's expectation that a woman's 'first and greatest duty' was to add to the American family.

Source

Theodore Roosevelt, *Address by President Roosevelt Before the National Congress of Mothers, Washington, March 14, 1905* (Washington: G.P.O., 1905).

In our modern industrial civilization there are many and grave dangers to counterbalance the splendors and the triumphs. It is not a good thing to see cities grow at disproportionate speed relatively to the country; for the small land owners, the men who own their little homes, and therefore to a very large extent the men who till farms, the men of the soil, have hitherto made the foundation of lasting national life in every State; and, if the foundation becomes either too weak or too narrow, the superstructure, no matter how attractive, is in imminent danger of falling.

But far more important than the question of the occupation of our citizens is the question of how their family life is conducted. No matter what that occupation may be, as long as there is a real home and as long as those who make up that home do their duty to one another, to their neighbors and to the State, it is of minor consequence whether the man's trade is plied in the country or in the city, whether it calls for the work of the hands or for the work of the head.

No piled-up wealth, no splendor of material growth, no brilliance of artistic development, will permanently avail any people unless its home life is healthy, unless the average man possesses honesty, courage, common sense, and decency, unless he works hard and is willing at need to fight hard; and unless the average woman is a good wife, a good mother, able and willing to perform the first and greatest duty of womanhood, able and willing to bear, and to bring up as they should be brought up, healthy children, sound in body, mind, and character, and numerous enough so that the race shall increase and not decrease.

There are certain old truths which will be true as long as this world endures, and which no amount of progress can alter. One of these is the truth that the primary duty of the husband is to be the home-maker, the breadwinner for his wife and children, and that the primary duty of the woman is to be the help-mate, the housewife, and mother. The woman should have ample educational advantages; but save in exceptional cases the man must be, and she need not be, and generally ought not to be, trained for a lifelong career as the family breadwinner; and, therefore, after a certain point, the training of the two must normally be different because the duties of the two are normally different. This does not mean inequality of function, but it does mean that normally there must be dissimilarity of function. On the whole, I think the duty of the woman the more important, the more difficult, and the more honorable of the two; on the whole I respect the woman who does her duty even more than I respect the man who does his.

No ordinary work done by a man is either as hard or as responsible as the work of a woman who is bringing up a family of small children; for upon her time and strength demands are made not only every hour of the day but often every hour of the night. She may have to get up night after night to take care of a sick child, and yet must by day continue to do all her household duties as well; and if the family means are scant she must usually enjoy even her rare holidays taking her whole brood of children with her. The birth pangs make all men the debtors of all women. Above all our sympathy and regard are due to the struggling wives among those whom Abraham Lincoln called the plain people,[44] and whom he so loved and trusted; for the lives of these women are often led on the lonely heights of quiet, self-sacrificing heroism.

. . .

There are many good people who are denied the supreme blessing of children, and for these we have the respect and sympathy always due to those who, from no fault of their own, are denied any of the other great blessings of life. But the man or woman who deliberately forego these blessings, whether from viciousness, coldness, shallow-heartedness, self-indulgence, or mere failure to appreciate aright the difference between the all-important and the unimportant, – why, such a creature merits contempt as hearty as any visited upon the soldier who runs away in battle, or upon the man who refuses to work for the support of those dependent upon him, and who tho able-bodied is yet content to eat in idleness the bread which others provide.

The existence of women of this type forms one of the most unpleasant and unwholesome features of modern life.

. . .

To sum up, then, the whole matter is simple enough. If either a race or an individual prefers the pleasure of more effortless ease, of self-indulgence, to the infinitely deeper, the infinitely higher pleasures that come to those who know the toil and the weariness, but also the joy, of hard duty well done, why, that race or that individual must inevitably in the end pay the penalty of leading a life both vapid and ignoble. No man and no woman really worthy of the name can care for the life spent solely or chiefly in the avoidance of risk and trouble and labor. Save in exceptional cases the prizes worth having in life must be paid for,

---

44. A favourite phrase of the former President for the mass public. See, for example, his invocation of the 'patriotic instinct of the plain people' in his 4 July Message to Congress, 1861. For his frequent use of the term see Ward H. Lamon and Dorothy L. Teillard (eds), *Recollections of Abraham Lincoln, 1847–1865* (Lincoln: University of Nebraska Press, 1994), p. 111.

and the life worth living must be a life of work for a worthy end, and ordinarily of work more for others than for one's self.

The woman's task is not easy – no task worth doing is easy – but in doing it, and when she has done it, there shall come to her the highest and holiest joy known to mankind; and having done it, she shall have the reward prophesied in Scripture; for her husband and her children, yes, and all people who realize that her work lies at the foundation of all national happiness and greatness, shall rise up and call her blessed.

3 Slavery and Race

Introduction

The period covered by this book has been termed 'the long emancipation'.[1] In the 1770s, slavery dominated the economies of both Europe and the New World. Yet in little over a hundred years it was effectively absent from both. Though economic self-interest hastened this process, it was also due to a remarkable ideological and moral transformation in which some of the most powerful writers, propagandists and orators played prominent roles. Once the rhetoric of universal rights had become central to nationhood, an examination of its inconsistencies with slavery was inevitable. Once a free black republic in Haiti had been declared in 1804, perceptions of slaves' capacities could never remain the same. Yet this was a debate that had consequences extending far beyond emancipation itself. As Saadiya Hartman puts it, the language of 'slavery undergirded the rhetoric of the republic and equality' to such an extent that, even after its official end, its effects lingered to 'sanction subordination and segregation'.[2] This chapter brings this complex interplay of race and slavery to the fore by putting the language of transatlantic abolitionism back in contact with that surrounding the even more arduous task of promoting racial equality.

The transatlantic struggle over slavery can be split into three key periods, all of which are represented in this chapter's opening part ('Debating Slavery'). The first, in the late eighteenth century, was one of gradualist opposition, culminating in the slave trade's abolition in the British colonies in 1807 and the ban on the importation of slaves to the US the following year. Arguments in this period typically mixed an Enlightenment language of natural rights and moral sensibility with Quaker-influenced objections that slavery contravened what a prominent 1776 pamphlet called 'the laws of God'.[3] To these strains was added a comparative rhetoric of patriotism,

---

1. Ira Berlin, *The Long Emancipation: The Demise of Slavery in the United States* (Cambridge, MA: Harvard University Press, 2015).
2. Saadiya Hartman, *Scenes of Subjection* (New York: Oxford University Press, 1997), p. 121.
3. Granville Sharp, *The Just Limitation of Slavery in the Laws of God: Compared with the Unbounded Claims of the African Traders and British American Slaveholders* (London: B. White, 1776), p. 5.

as when British politician Baron Grenville urged Parliament in 1807 to erase 'the stain impressed by the guilt of such traffic' on the 'character of the country'.[4]

The opening speech, however, is a defence of the trade against these attacks. It offers an extract from the testimony of Liverpool slaver James Penny on slave ship conditions before the 1788 Parliamentary inquiry into the trade. This is followed by the speech (1789) with which William Wilberforce presented his first abolition bill to Parliament, playing a key role in bringing the 'magnitude of the subject' (p. 106) to political prominence. Yet the formerly enslaved were eager to shape the meanings of these events for themselves, and in the 'Thanksgiving Sermon' (1808) that follows Wilberforce, we see pioneer ex-slave preacher Absalom Jones use the Book of Exodus as a hopeful analogy for the 'captivity and bondage' of his own people in America.

The next selections take us to the second decisive phase of abolition of the 1830s. In this decade, the evangelicalism of the Second Great Awakening, the increasing growth of free-market capitalism and a surge in British support re-energised the opposition to slavery in America. 'The slavery agitation had increased apace', recalled an early chronicler; 'it had broken out in Congress on the presentation of anti-slavery petitions. The fire thus kindled spread through the country.'[5] This generation of activists sought a moral reformation through new propaganda media, setting up dedicated abolition newspapers, and hiring paid professional speakers, most importantly fugitive and former slaves, to bring powerful first-hand testimony to audiences across the North and across the Atlantic to audiences throughout Britain and Ireland (Figures 6 and 10). These reformers also developed a newly sharp tone of moral confrontation. Whereas earlier activists had focused on the slave trade, campaigners now placed a firmer emphasis on the brutality of slavery itself, addressed public complicity more directly, and exploited domestic values to shock audiences through depictions of separated slave families. When accused of impropriety, leading reformer William Lloyd Garrison defended this new rhetoric, maintaining that 'strong denunciatory language is consistent with gentleness of spirit, long-suffering and perfect charity'.[6]

These new methods and tone inevitably hardened slavery's apologists. Editorials lambasted the 'mobs of runaway negroes, and run-mad fanatics'

---

4. Baron Grenville, *The Parliamentary Register: Or an Impartial Report of the Debates that Have Occurred in the Two Houses of Parliament* (London: Woodfall, 1807).

5. Archibald Grimké, *William Lloyd Garrison, the Abolitionist* (New York: Funk and Wagnalls, 1891), p. 209.

6. William Lloyd Garrison, 'Harsh Language – Retarding the Cause', *Selections from the Writings and Speeches of William Lloyd Garrison* (Boston: W. F. Walcutt, 1852), p. 101.

offering speeches; meetings were organised in South and North to the offer 'torrents of pro-slavery eloquence'.[7] The most prominent defence came from South Carolina politician John Calhoun, whose famous defence of slavery (1837) as 'a positive good' (p. 113) is extracted below. The 'incendiary spirit' (p. 116) of abolition, he warned, would 'infect' the nation. No text better reveals the merit in these warnings than the transcription that follows of former South Carolina slave heiress Angelina Grimké's 1838 speech in Philadelphia's Pennsylvania Hall, recording the clamour and 'mobocratic spirit' (p. 122) that would burn the venue to the ground the following day (Figure 5).

The pre-Civil War decade of the 1850s was the culminating phase of the struggle against slavery. It is represented below by perhaps the most famous abolition speech of all. Frederick Douglass's lecture before the Rochester Ladies Anti-Slavery Society (1852) brandished 'withering sarcasm, and stern rebuke' (p. 130) against the complacency of his Northern audience for their complicity in the political structures that underpinned the ongoing existence of slavery. In doing so, it was similar to the sermon extracted here from the Brooklyn-based celebrity preacher Henry Ward Beecher (1861), an apocalyptic jeremiad that used the parable of Jesus calming the storms of Lake Galilee to urge his congregation to 'confess and forsake' (p. 133) their national sins, not just against the enslaved but against vanquished Spanish and indigenous Americans. In an era in which even many abolitionists were less than progressive on race, both Douglass and Beecher saw that slavery's effects would linger if persistent racial injustices were left unaddressed.

This speech provides an ideal bridge into the next part of the chapter ('Race and Civil Rights'), which focuses on the fight for racial equality in Britain and America. In Chapter 1, the leading black intellectual W. E. B. Du Bois warned his London audience that the 'color line' (p. 59) would be the defining issue of the twentieth century. But attempts to define this line also dominated nineteenth-century rhetoric. The selection below from the controversial Scottish natural scientist Robert Knox reveals a key means by which prejudices were legitimised via polygenist racial theory, in his lecture series on 'The Races of Man' (late 1840s) that reassured British audiences and a global readership that non-Europeans constituted inferior branches of humankind (Figure 13).

As the rest of the speeches in this chapter show, non-white communities fought back against these damaging falsehoods in multiple ways. Some sought community building, as was the case with David Walker, whose speech here (1828) aimed to 'unite the colored population' through uplift and resistance to racism. Others sought to promote black intellectual achievement. Coming at the end of a remarkable transatlantic career,

---

7. 'Abolition and Sectarian Mobs', *United States Review* (August 1854), p. 103.

Alexander Crummell's speech, 'The American Mind and Black Intellect' (1898), rebuked racial misconceptions to commemorate African American achievements. By the end of the century, with racial terrorism against the free black population at crisis point, activists focused on educating the public about such horrors. The speaking tour of activist Ida B. Wells was a crucial moment, with speeches such as that extracted here (1893) bringing the horrific realities of extra-judicial violence to live audiences.

Part A: Debating Slavery

1. James Penny, 'Testimony in Defence of a Humane Slave Trade' (London, 1788)

Following public pressure from abolitionists, in 1788 the British Government launched an enquiry into the conditions of the slave trade. As part of the enquiry, leading traders were called to testify before Parliament on the conduct of their enterprises. One of these individuals was James Penny (1741–99), a prominent Liverpool merchant active in the African trade since the 1760s.[8] The text below is a key section from Penny's testimony, transcribed in the third person, in which he claimed to be 'impelled, both by humanity and interest, to pay every possible attention both to the preservation of the crew and the slaves'. In his testimony, he detailed the state of the ships under his control, which typically transported between 500 and 600 slaves. Penny was widely thanked by fellow practitioners for this defence of the trade, and even when other merchants gradually abandoned it, he remained a staunch advocate until his death.

Source

Reports of the Lords of the Committee of Council Appointed for the Consideration of All Matters Relating to Trade and Foreign Plantations (Board of Trade, London, 1789).

He has shown to the principal people of the Country in Africa the Accommodations on Board his Ship, and they have held up their Hands, and said, The Slaves in here will sleep better than the Gentlemen do on Shore . . .

That the slaves do not show any great concern when first coming on Board – they frequently express Fears, from an Apprehension of being eaten, which it is the Business of the Traders to remove. – That with respect to the general Manner of treating them on Board, they are comfortably lodged in Rooms fitted up for them, which are washed and fumigated with Vinegar or Lime Juice every Day, and after wards dried with Fires, in which are thrown occasionally Frankincense and Tobacco. They lie on the bare Boards, but the greatest Princes in their own Country lie on their Mats, with a Log of Wood

---

8. Some maintain that his legacy lies behind the name of the famous Penny Lane, the suburban Merseyside street immortalised in the Beatles song, though this claim is disputed. For a thorough investigation of this claim see <https://theprioryandthecastironshore .wordpress.com/2018/10/24/was-penny-lane-really-named-after-the-slave-merchant-james-penny/> (last accessed 29 March 2019).

for their Pillow – The Men slaves are fettered when they first come on Board, from prudential Motives – but during the Passage, if they appear reconciled to their Condition, their Fetters are gradually taken off – The Women, Youths and Children are always at Liberty, and are kept in separate Apartments – The Whole of the Slaves are brought upon Deck every Day, when the Weather permits, about Eight of the Clock – if the Weather is sultry, and there appears the least Perspiration upon their Skins, when they come upon Deck, there are Two Men attending with Cloths to rub them perfectly dry, and another to give them a little Cordial – The Surgeon, or his Mate, also generally attends to wash their Mouths with Vinegar or Lime Juice, in order to prevent Scurvy. After they are on deck, water is handed to them to wash their Hands and Faces – They are then formed into Messes, consisting of Ten to each Mess, and a warm Mess is provided for them, alternately of their own Country Food and of the Pulse carried from Europe for that Purpose, to which Stock Fish, Palm Oil, Pepper etc are added; after that, Water is handed them to drink, and the upper Decks are swept clean, when they have been fed – They are then supplied with Pipes and Tobacco; both Sexes sometimes will smoak.

They are amused with instruments of music peculiar to their own Country, with which he provided them; and when tired of music and Dancing, they then go to Games of Chance – the women are supplied Beads, which they make into Ornaments; and the utmost Attention is paid to the keeping up their Spirit and to indulge them in all their little Humours – Particular attention is paid to them, when sick, and the most airy Part of the Ship is appropriated for the Hospital – That the Surgeon is provided with Medicines and with Wine, and Spices also, for Cordials, when the Sick require it and he is encouraged to take Care of the Sick, by an Allowance of One Shilling Per Head, in Addition to his Wages, and Privilege for every Slave that is brought to the Market, which Privilege conflicts in the Average Value of Two Slaves, in Proportion to the Value of the Whole Cargo – The Reputation of the Captain, the Officers, and Surgeons, and their future Employment, in consequence, depend on the Care they take of the Slaves . . .

He has such confidence in them that he has frequently seen them perfectly reconciled to their Condition, and in Appearance as happy as any of his Crew – [he] is of Opinion, that the Treatment of the Negroes on Board Ships in general employed in this Trade, is equally proper.

2. William Wilberforce, 'Resolutions Respecting the Slave Trade' (London, 1789)

On 12 May 1789, the English social reformer and politician William Wilberforce (1759–1833) made his first major speech on the subject of abolition in the House of Commons. Coming in the same year as the publication of former slave Olaudah Equiano's autobiography,

Wilberforce's address has come to stand as a landmark in mainstream transatlantic abolition.

Born into a wealthy family of Yorkshire wool merchants and entering Parliament at twenty-one, Wilberforce became associated with abolition after his conversion to evangelical Christianity in the mid-1780s. Leading reformers such as Thomas Clarkson conscripted the young MP into becoming an emissary for the movement's political aims. Building on the success of public awareness campaigns by the Committee for the Abolition of the Slave Trade, Wilberforce attempted to pass a Parliamentary bill in 1789. Though the bill was defeated, it succeeded in making slavery an entrenched issue in Parliament. Wilberforce returned to introduce similar bills over the next two decades, culminating in the successful Slave Trade Act in 1807 and, three days before his death in July 1833, the Slavery Abolition Act that finally outlawed the practice in the British Empire.

Framed as appealing not to 'passions' but to only 'cool and impartial reason', Wilberforce's carefully calibrated 1789 speech presented slavery as a morally reprehensible issue of natural justice. It distilled the humanitarian and practical case for immediate abolition through evocative accounts of abjection, stark statistics and the narrative of his own empirical conversion to anti-slavery. When denounced as a radical by the trade's defenders, he remarked that, 'if to be feelingly alive to the sufferings of my fellow-creatures is to be a fanatic, I am one of the most incurable fanatics ever permitted to be at large'.[9]

Source

'Debate on Mr. Wilberforce's Resolutions respecting the Slave Trade', in William Cobbett, *The Parliamentary History of England: From the Norman Conquest in 1066 to the Year 1803*, 36 vols (London: T. Curson Hansard, 1806–20), vol. 28 (1789–91), cols 42–68.

When I consider the magnitude of the subject which I am to bring before the House – a subject, in which the interests, not of this country, nor of Europe alone, but of the whole world, and of posterity, are involved: and when I think, at the same time, on the weakness of the advocate who has undertaken this great cause – when these reflections press upon my mind, it is impossible for me not to feel both terrified and concerned at my own inadequacy to such a task. But when I reflect, however, on the encouragement which I have had,

---

9. Robert I. Wilberforce and Samuel Wilberforce, *The Life of William Wilberforce: Volume 1* (1838) (Cambridge: Cambridge University Press, 2011), p. 290.

through the whole course of a long and laborious examination of this question, and how much candour I have experienced, and how conviction has increased within my own mind, in proportion as I have advanced in my labours; – when I reflect, especially, that however averse any gentleman may now be, yet we shall all be of one opinion in the end; – when I turn myself to these thoughts, I take courage – I determine to forget all my other fears, and I march forward with a firmer step in the full assurance that my cause will bear me out, and that I shall be able to justify upon the clearest principles, every resolution in my hand, the avowed end of which is, the total abolition of the slave trade.

I wish exceedingly, in the outset, to guard both myself and the House from entering into the subject with any sort of passion. It is not their passions I shall appeal to – I ask only for their cool and impartial reason; and I wish not to take them by surprise, but to deliberate, point by point, upon every part of this question. I mean not to accuse any one, but to take the shame upon myself, in common, indeed, with the whole parliament of Great Britain, for having suffered this horrid trade to be carried on under their authority. We are all guilty – we ought all to plead guilty, and not to exculpate ourselves by throwing the blame on others; and I therefore deprecate every kind of reflection against the various descriptions of people who are more immediately involved in this wretched business.

Having now disposed of the first part of this subject, I must speak of the transit of the slaves in the West Indies. This I confess, in my own opinion, is the most wretched part of the whole subject. So much misery condensed in so little room, is more than the human imagination had ever before conceived. I will not accuse the Liverpool merchants:[10] I will allow them, nay, I will believe them to be men of humanity; and I will therefore believe, if it were not for the enormous magnitude and extent of the evil which distracts their attention from individual cases, and makes them think generally, and therefore less feelingly on the subject, they would never have persisted in the trade.

I verily believe therefore, if the wretchedness of any one of the many hundred Negroes stowed in each ship could be brought before their view, and remain within the sight of the African Merchant, that there is no one among them whose heart would bear it. Let any one imagine to himself 6 or 700 of these wretches chained two and two, surrounded with every object that is nauseous and disgusting, diseased, and struggling under every kind of wretchedness!

How can we bear to think of such a scene as this? One would think it had been determined to heap upon them all the varieties of bodily pain, for the purpose of blunting the feelings of the mind; and yet, in this very point (to show the power of human prejudice) the situation of the slaves has been described by

---

10. During the eighteenth century, the port city of Liverpool in Northern England became the major hub for the transatlantic slave trade.

Mr. Norris,[11] one of the Liverpool delegates, in a manner which, I am sure will convince the House how interest can draw a film across the eyes, so thick, that total blindness could do no more; and how it is our duty therefore to trust not to the reasonings of interested men, or to their way of colouring a transaction. 'Their apartments,' says Mr. Norris, 'are fitted up as much for their advantage as circumstances will admit. The right ancle of one, indeed is connected with the left ancle of another by a small iron fetter, and if they are turbulent, by another on their wrists. They have several meals a day; some of their own country provisions, with the best sauces of African cookery; and by way of variety, another meal of pulse, &c. according to European taste. After breakfast they have water to wash themselves, while their apartments are perfumed with frankincense and lime-juice. Before dinner, they are amused after the manner of their country. The song and dance are promoted,' and, as if the whole was really a scene of pleasure and dissipation it is added, that games of chance are furnished. 'The men play and sing, while the women and girls make fanciful ornaments with beads, which they are plentifully supplied with.'[12] Such is the sort of strain in which the Liverpool delegates, and particularly Mr. Norris, gave evidence before the privy council.

What will the House think when, by the concurring testimony of other witnesses, the true history is laid open? The slaves who are sometimes described as rejoicing at their captivity, are so wrung with misery at leaving their country, that it is the constant practice to set sail at night, lest they should be sensible of their departure. The pulse which Mr. Norris talks of are horse beans; and the scantiness, both of water and provision, was suggested by the very legislature of Jamaica in the report of their committee, to be a subject that called for the interference of parliament. Mr. Norris talks of frankincense and lime juice; when surgeons tell you the slaves are stowed so close, that there is not room to tread among them: and when you have it in evidence from sir George Yonge,[13] that even in a ship which wanted 200 of her complement, the stench was intolerable. The song and the dance, says Mr. Norris, are promoted. It had been more fair, perhaps, if he had explained that word promoted. The truth is, that for the sake of exercise, these miserable wretches, loaded with chains, oppressed with disease and wretchedness, are forced to dance by the terror of the lash, and sometimes by the actual use of it. 'I,' says one of the other

---

11. Robert Norris (d.1791) was one of several Liverpool slave traders called to give evidence before Parliament in 1788. Others included James Penny, for whose testimony see above (pp. 104–5).

12. Norris's testimony was published in *Reports of the Lords of the Committee of Council Appointed for the Consideration of All Matters Relating to Trade and Foreign Plantations . . .; Dated the 11th of February, 1788, Concerning the Present State of the Trade to Africa, and Particularly the Trade in Slaves, Etc.* (London: Board of Trade, 1789).

13. George Yonge (1731–1812), British Secretary at War.

evidences, 'was employed to dance the men, while another person danced the women.'

Such, then is the meaning of the word promoted; and it may be observed too, with respect to food, that an instrument is sometimes carried out, in order to force them to eat which is the same sort of proof how much they enjoy themselves in that instance also. As to their singing, what shall we say when we are told that their songs are songs of lamentation upon their departure which, while they sing, are always in tears, insomuch that one captain (more humane as I should conceive him, therefore, than the rest) threatened one of the women with a flogging, because the mournfulness of her song was too painful for his feelings. In order, however, not to trust too much to any sort of description, I will call the attention of the House to one species of evidence which is abso-lutely infallible. Death, at least, is a sure ground of evidence, and the proportion of deaths will not only confirm, but if possible will even aggravate our suspicion of their misery in the transit. It will be found, upon an average of all the ships of which evidence has been given at the privy council, that exclusive of those who perish before they sail, not less than 12½ per cent. perish in the passage. Besides these, the Jamaica report[14] tells you, that not less than 4½ per cent. die on shore before the day of sale, which is only a week or two from the time of landing. One third more die in the seasoning, and this in a country exactly like their own, where they are healthy and happy as some of the evidences would pretend. The diseases, however, which they contract on shipboard, the astrin-gent washes which are to hide their wounds, and the mischievous tricks used to make them up for sale, are, as the Jamaica report says, (a most precious and valuable report, which I shall often have to advert to) one principle cause of this mortality. Upon the whole, however, here is a mortality of about 50 per cent. and this among negroes who are not bought unless (as the phrase is with cattle) they are sound in wind and limb.

How then can the House refuse its belief to the multiplied testimonies before the privy council, of the savage treatment of the negroes in the mid-dle passage? Nay, indeed, what need is there of any evidence? The number of deaths speaks for itself, and makes all such enquiry superfluous. As soon as ever I had arrived thus far in my investigation of the slave trade, I confess to you sir, so enormous so dreadful, so irremediable did its wickedness appear that my own mind was completely made up for the abolition. A trade founded in iniquity, and carried on as this was, must be abolished, let the policy be what it might, – let the consequences be what they would, I from this time determined that I would never rest till I had effected its abolition.

―――――

14. Assembly of Jamaica, *Two Reports from the Committee of the Honourable House of Assembly of Jamaica* (London: B. White and Son, 1789). See also Stephen Fuller, *Notes on the Two Reports from the Committee of the Honourable House of Assembly of Jamaica* (London: Printed and sold by James Phillips, 1789).

3. Absalom Jones, 'A Thanksgiving Sermon' (Philadelphia, 1808)

On 1 January 1808, the US law abolishing the transatlantic slave trade took effect. That date soon became enshrined in the commemorative radical calendar, largely thanks to the work of Absalom Jones (1746–1818), one of the early republic's most important black preachers. With the sermon below, he helped establish the tradition whereby the 'first of January, the day of the abolition of the slave trade in our country, be set apart in every year, as a day of public thanksgiving' and an occasion for reflecting on the history of blacks in America.[15]

The first ordained priest of African descent in the US, Jones rose from slavery to found Philadelphia's Free African Society. Born a slave in Delaware but raised in more liberal Philadelphia, Jones received educational opportunities rare for African Americans of the time. Pennsylvania began the outlawing of slavery in 1780, and through employment as a clerk, Jones managed to purchase his own and his wife's freedom. He became a lay minister of the Methodist Episcopal Church, but persistent racial tension led him to found the Free African Society with fellow black minister Richard Allen as a space in which to hear independent religious services. So popular did he become that rumours circulated that Jones had supernatural abilities to influence the mind of assembled congregations.[16]

On New Year's Day, 1808, hundreds of black Philadelphians had travelled to Saint Thomas's Church. Commemorating the official end of the international slave trade, Jones's sermon helped forged an African American commemorative tradition that would persist for more than a century. In the excerpt below, Jones used the analogy of Jewish captivity in the Book of Exodus as a way of outlining a hopeful teleology for black Americans.

Source

Absalom Jones, *A Thanksgiving Sermon, preached January 1, 1808, in St. Thomas's, or the African Episcopal, Church, Philadelphia: On Account of the Abolition of the African Slave Trade, on that Day, by the Congress of the United States* (Philadelphia: Fry and Kammerer, 1808).

And the Lord said, I have surely seen the affliction of my people which are in Egypt, and have heard their cry by reason of their task-masters; for I know their sorrows; and I am come down to deliver them out of the hand of the Egyptians. – EXODUS, iii. 7–8.

———

15. See David Waldstreicher, *In the Midst of Perpetual Fetes: The Making of American Nationalism, 1776–1820* (Chapel Hill: University of North Carolina Press, 1997), p. 329.
16. See Sidney Kaplan and Emma N. Kaplan, *The Black Presence in the Era of the American Revolution* (Amherst: University of Massachusetts Press, 1989), p. 109.

THESE words, my brethren, contain a short account of some of the circumstances which preceded the deliverance of the children of Israel from their
captivity and bondage in Egypt.[17]

They mention, in the first place, their *affliction*. This consisted in their priva-
tion of liberty: they were slaves to the kings of Egypt, in common with their
other subjects; and they were slaves to their fellow slaves. They were compelled
to work in the open air, in one of the hottest climates in the world; and, probably, without a covering from the burning rays of the sun. Their work was of a
laborious kind: it consisted of making bricks, and travelling, perhaps to a great
distance, for the straw, or stubble, that was a component part of them. Their
work was dealt out to them in tasks, and performed under the eye of vigilant
and rigorous masters, who constantly upbraided them with idleness. The least
deficiency, in the product of their labour, was punished by beating.

Nor was this all. Their food was of the cheapest kind, and contained but
little nourishment: it consisted only of leeks and onions, which grew almost
spontaneously in the land of Egypt. Painful and distressing as these sufferings were, they constituted the smallest part of their misery. While the fields
resounded with their cries in the day, their huts and hamlets were vocal at
night with their lamentations over their sons; who were dragged from the
arms of their mothers, and put to death by drowning, in order to prevent
such an increase in their population, as to endanger the safety of the state by
an insurrection. In this condition, thus degraded and oppressed, they passed
nearly four hundred years.

Ah! who can conceive of the measure of their sufferings, during that time?
What tongue, or pen, can compute the number of their sorrows? To them no
morning or evening sun ever disclosed a single charm: to them, the beauties of
spring, and the plenty of autumn had no attractions: even domestic endearments
were scarcely known to them: all was misery; all was grief; all was despair.

Our text mentions, in the second place that, in this situation, they were
not forgotten by the God of their fathers, and the Father of the human race.
Though, for wise reasons, he delayed to appear in their behalf for several hundred years; yet he was not indifferent to their sufferings. Our text tells us, that
he saw their affliction, and heard their cry: his eye and his ear were constantly
open to their complaint: every tear they shed, was preserved, and every groan
they uttered, was recorded; in order to testify, at a future day, against the
authors of their oppressions. But our text goes further: it describes the Judge
of the world to be so much moved, with what he saw and what he heard, that
he rises from his throne – not to issue a command to the armies of angels that
surrounded him to fly to the relief of his suffering children – but to come down
from heaven, in his own person, in order to deliver them out of the hands of the

---

17. In one of the founding myths of Judaism, known as the Exodus, the children of
Israel were enslaved in Egypt, before being delivered from bondage through the leadership of Moses. Christian abolitionists of the nineteenth century frequently drew upon
this analogy, using the passages from Exodus that Jones elucidates here.

Egyptians. Glory to God for this precious record of his power and goodness: let all the nations of the earth praise him.

Clouds and darkness are round about him, but *righteousness and judgment are the habitation of his throne. O sing unto the Lord a new song, for he hath done marvelous things: his right hand and his holy arm hath gotten him the victory. He hath remembered his mercy and truth toward the house of Israel, and all the ends of the earth shall see the salvation of God.*[18]

The history of the world shows us, that the deliverance of the children of Israel from their bondage, is not the only instance, in which it has pleased God to appear in behalf of oppressed and distressed nations, as the deliverer of the innocent, and of those who call upon his name. He is as unchangeable in his nature and character, as he is in his wisdom and power. The great and blessed event, which we have this day met to celebrate, is a striking proof, that the God of heaven and earth *is the same, yesterday, and to-day, and for ever.*

Yes, my brethren, the nations from which most of us have descended, and the country in which some of us were born, have been visited by the tender mercy of the Common Father of the human race. He has seen the affliction of our countrymen, with an eye of pity. He has seen the wicked arts, by which wars have been fomented among the different tribes of the Africans, in order to procure captives, for the purpose of selling them for slaves.

He has seen ships fitted out from different ports in Europe and America, and freighted with trinkets to be exchanged for the bodies and souls of men. He has seen the anguish which has taken place, when parents have been torn from their children, and children from their parents, and conveyed, with their hands and feet bound in fetters, on board of ships prepared to receive them. He has seen them thrust in crowds into the holds of those ships, where many of them have perished from the want of air. He has seen such of them as have escaped from that noxious place of confinement, leap into the ocean; with a faint hope of swimming back to their native shore, or a determination to seek early retreat from their impending misery, in a watery grave. He has seen them exposed for sale, like horses and cattle, upon the wharves; or, like bales of goods, in warehouses of West India and American sea ports.

He has seen the pangs of separation between members of the same family. He has seen them driven into the sugar, the rice, and the tobacco fields, and compelled to work – in spite of the habits of ease which they derived from the natural fertility of their own country in the open air, beneath a burning sun, with scarcely as much clothing upon them as modesty required. He has seen them faint beneath the pressure of their labours. He has seen them return to their smoky huts in the evening, with nothing to satisfy their hunger but a scanty allowance of roots; and these, cultivated for themselves, on that day only, which God ordained as a day of rest for man and beast. He has seen the

---

18. Psalm 98.

neglect with which their masters have treated their immortal souls; not only in withholding religious instruction from them, but, in some instances, depriving them of access to the means of obtaining it. He has seen all the different modes of torture, by means of the whip, the screw, the pincers, and the red hot iron, which have been exercised upon their bodies, by inhuman overseers: overseers, did I say? Yes: but not by these only.

Our God has seen masters and mistresses, educated in fashionable life, sometimes take the instruments of torture into their own hands, and, deaf to the cries and shrieks of their agonizing slaves, exceed even their overseers in cruelty. Inhuman wretches! though You have been deaf to their cries and shrieks, they have been heard in Heaven.

The ears of Jehovah have been constantly open to them: He has heard the prayers that have ascended from the hearts of his people; and he has, as in the case of his ancient and chosen people the Jews, *come down to deliver* our suffering country-men from the hands of their oppressors. He *came down* into the United States, when they declared, in the constitution which they framed in 1788, that the trade in our African fellow-men, should cease in the year 1808: He *came down* into the British Parliament, when they passed a law to put an end to the same iniquitous trade in May, 1807: *He came down* into the Congress of the United States, the last winter, when they passed a similar law, the operation of which commences on this happy day.

Dear land of our ancestors! thou shalt no more be stained with the blood of thy children, shed by British and American hands: the ocean shall no more afford a refuge to their bodies, from impending slavery: nor shall the shores of the British West India islands, and of the United States, any more witness the anguish of families, parted for ever by a publick sale. For this signal interposition of the God of mercies, in behalf of our brethren, it becomes us this day to offer up our united thanks. Let the song of angels, which was first heard in the air at the birth of our Saviour, be heard this day in our assembly: *Glory to God in the highest,* for these first fruits of *peace upon earth, and good will to man:* O! let us *give thanks unto the Lord:* let us *call upon his name,* and *make known his deeds among the people.* Let us *sing psalms unto him and talk of all his wondrous works.*[19]

4. John Calhoun, 'Slavery, A Positive Good' (Washington, DC, 1837)

In the wake of growing numbers of anti-slavery petitions in the 1830s and 1840s, Jacksonian Democrats in the Senate adopted procedural rules to silence abolitionist agitation. But some pro-slavery politicians saw that the best method to oppose abolition was to confront it directly and, in the words of the famous speech excerpted below, 'reason it down'.

---

19. Psalm 105.

John C. Calhoun (1782–1850) of South Carolina was the most important of such pro-slavery politicians in the decades leading up to the Civil War. Alarmed at the abolitionist's moral fanaticism, he went further than previous defenders of the practice by arguing that slavery was not simply a 'necessary evil' but a 'positive good'. White Southerners, he argued, needed to stop yielding the moral high ground to anti-slavery voices. Instead, in an argument that fused anti-industrial paternalism with new pseudo-scientific ideas about racial inferiority, he made the case that slavery was a superior economic system to the free labour of the North, and 'indispensable to the peace and happiness of both' whites and blacks.

Speeches such as the following, delivered on 6 February 1837, defended the 'gag rule' that prevented discussion of abolition in Congress. But more lastingly, Calhoun's words provided an influential intellectual justification for slavery. His concept of 'positive good' was to become a rhetorical rallying cry for pro-slavery advocates in the decades that followed, particularly after his death in 1850.

Source

John C. Calhoun, *Speeches of John C. Calhoun: Delivered in the Congress of the United States from 1811 to the Present Time* (New York: Harper & Brothers, 1843).

The peculiar institution[20] of the South – that, on the maintenance of which the very existence of the slave-holding States depends, is pronounced to be sinful and odious, in the sight of God and man; and this with a systematic design of rendering us hateful in the eyes of the world – with a view to a general crusade against us and our institutions. This, too, in the legislative halls of the Union; created by these confederated States, for the better protection of their peace, their safety, and their respective institution; – and yet, we, the representatives of twelve of these sovereign States against whom this deadly war is waged, are expected to sit here in silence, hearing ourselves and our constituents day after day denounced, without uttering a word; for if we but open our lips, the charge of agitation is resounded on all sides, and we are held up as seeking to

---

20. This euphemistic phrase for slavery was widely used by Southerners to indicate the distinction between the supposedly benign arrangements of US slavery compared to more brutal systems in other cultures. Calhoun used the phrases 'peculiar labour' in 1828 and 'peculiar domestick institution' in 1830. The leading white abolition William Lloyd Garrison adopted the phrase as part of his rhetorical attacks on slavery in the same year, and it soon acquired an ironic double meaning.

aggravate the evil which we resist. Every reflecting mind must see in all this a state of things deeply and dangerously diseased.

I do not belong to the school which holds that aggression is to be met by concession. Mine is the opposite creed, which teaches that encroachments must be met at the beginning, and that those who act on the opposite principle are prepared to become slaves. In this case, in particular, I hold concession or compromise to be fatal. If we concede an inch, concession would follow concession – compromise would follow compromise, until our ranks would be so broken that effectual resistance would be impossible.

We must meet the enemy on the frontier, with a fixed determination of maintaining our position at every hazard. Consent to receive these insulting petitions, and the next demand will be that they be referred to a committee in order that they may be deliberated and acted upon. At the last session we were modestly asked to receive them, simply to lay them on the table, without any view to ulterior action. I then told the Senator from Pennsylvania (Mr. Buchanan),[21] who so strongly urged that course in the Senate, that it was a position that could not be maintained; as the argument in favor of acting on the petitions if we were bound to receive, could not be resisted. I then said, that the next step would be to refer the petition to a committee, and I already see indications that such is now the intention. If we yield, that will be followed by another, and we will thus proceed, step by step, to the final consummation of the object of these petitions.

We are now told that the most effectual mode of arresting the progress of abolition is, to reason it down; and with this view it is urged that the petitions ought to be referred to a committee. That is the very ground which was taken at the last session in the other House, but instead of arresting its progress it has since advanced more rapidly than ever. The most unquestionable right may be rendered doubtful, if one admitted to be a subject of controversy, and that would be the case in the present instance. The subject is beyond the jurisdiction of Congress – they have no right to touch it in any shape or form, or to make it the subject of deliberation or discussion.

In opposition to this view it is urged that Congress is bound by the con-stitution[22] to receive petitions in every case and on every subject, whether within its constitutional competency or not. I hold the doctrine to be absurd, and do solemnly believe, that it would be as easy to prove that it has the right to abolish slavery, as that it is bound to receive petitions for that purpose. The very existence of the rule that requires a question to be put on the reception of petitions, is conclusive to show that there is no such obligation. It has been a

---

21. James Buchanan, Jr (1791–1868), US Senator for Pennsylvania and ill-fated future Democrat President (1857–61).
22. Specifically, the First Amendment of the US Constitution, which enshrines freedom of speech.

standing rule from the commencement of the Government, and clearly shows the sense of those who formed the constitution on this point. The question on the reception would be absurd, if, as is contended, we are bound to receive; but I do not intend to argue the question; I discussed it fully at the last session, and the arguments then advanced neither have been nor can be answered.

As widely as this incendiary spirit has spread, it has not yet infected this body, or the great mass of the intelligent and business portion of the North; but unless it be speedily stopped, it will spread and work upwards till it brings the two great sections of the Union into deadly conflict. This is not a new impression with me. Several years since, in a discussion with one of the Senators from Massachusetts (Mr. Webster),[23] before this fell spirit had showed itself, I then predicted that the doctrine of the proclamation and the Force Bill, that this Government had a right, in the last resort, to determine the extent of its own powers, and enforce its decision at the point of the bayonet, which was so warmly maintained by that Senator, would at no distant day arouse the dormant spirit of abolitionism. I told him that the doctrine was tantamount to the assumption of unlimited power on the part of the Government, and that such would be the impression on the public mind in a large portion of the Union.

The consequence would be inevitable. A large portion of the Northern States believe slavery to be a sin, and would consider it as an obligation of conscience to abolish it if they should feel themselves in any degree responsible for its continuance, – and that this doctrine would necessarily lead to the belief of such responsibility. I then predicted that would commence as it has with this fanatical portion of society, that they would begin their operations on the ignorant, the weak, the young, and the thoughtless, – and gradually extend upwards till they would become strong enough to obtain political control, when he and others holding the highest stations in society, would, however reluctant, be compelled to yield to their doctrines, or be driven into obscurity. But four years have since elapsed, and all this is already in a course of regular fulfillment.

Standing at the point of time at which we have now arrived, it will not be more difficult to trace the course of future events now than it was then. They who imagine that the spirit now abroad in the North, will die away of itself without a shock or convulsion, have formed a very inadequate conception of its real character; it will continue to rise and spread, unless prompt and efficient measures to stay its progress be adopted. Already it has taken possession of the pulpit, of the schools, and, to a considerable extent, of the press; those great instruments by which the mind of the rising generation will be formed.

However sound the great body of the non-slave-holding States are at present, in the course of a few years they will be succeeded by those who will have

---

23. Daniel Webster (1782–1852), US Senator for Massachusetts for the Whig Party. Here, Calhoun invokes his 1833 debate with Webster over states' rights and the merits of the 'Force Bill' that would allow the President to overrule states that obstructed federal law.

been taught to hate the people and institutions of nearly one-half of this Union, with a hatred more deadly than one hostile nation ever entertained towards another. It is easy to see the end. By the necessary course of events, if left to themselves, we must become, finally, two people. It is impossible under the deadly hatred which must spring up between the two great sections, if the present causes are permitted to operate unchecked, that we should continue under the same political system. The conflicting elements would burst the Union asunder, powerful as are the links which hold it together. Abolition and the Union cannot co-exist. As the friend of the Union I openly proclaim it, – and the sooner it is known the better. The former may now be controlled, but in a short time it will be beyond the power of a man to arrest the course of events. We of the South will not, cannot surrender our institutions. To maintain the existing relations between the two races, inhabiting that section of the Union, is indispensable to the peace and happiness of both. It cannot be subverted without drenching the country in blood, and extirpating one or the other of the races. Be it good or bad, it has grown up with our society and institutions, and is so interwoven with them, that to destroy it would be to destroy us as a people.

But let me not be understood as admitting, even by implication, that the existing relations between the two races in the slaveholding States is an evil: – far otherwise; I hold it to be a good, as it has thus far proved itself to be to both, and will continue to prove so if not disturbed by the fell spirit of abolition. I appeal to facts. Never before has the black race of Central Africa, from the dawn of history to the present day, attained a condition so civilized and so improved, not only physically, but morally and intellectually. It came among us in a low, degraded, and savage condition, and in the course of a few generations it has grown up under the fostering care of our institutions, reviled as they have been, to its present comparatively civilized condition. This, with the rapid increase of numbers, is conclusive proof of the general happiness of the race, in spite of all the exaggerated tales to the contrary.

In the mean time, the white or European race has not degenerated. It has kept pace with its brethren in other sections of the Union where slavery does not exist. It is odious to make comparison; but I appeal to all sides whether the South is not equal in virtue, intelligence, patriotism, courage, disinterestedness, and all the high qualities which adorn our nature. I ask whether we have not contributed our full share of talents and political wisdom in forming and sustaining this political fabric; and whether we have not constantly inclined most strongly to the side of liberty, and been the first to see and first to resist the encroachments of power. In one thing only are we inferior – the arts of gain; we acknowledge that we are less wealthy than the Northern section of this Union, but I trace this mainly to the fiscal action of this Government, which has extracted much from, and spent little among us. Had it been the reverse, – if the exaction had been from the other section, and the expenditure with us, this point of superiority would not be against us now, as it was not at the formation of this Government.

But I take higher ground. I hold that in the present state of civilization, where two races of different origin, and distinguished by color, and other physical differences, as well as intellectual, are brought together, the relation now existing in the slaveholding States between the two, is, instead of an evil, a good – a positive good. I feel myself called upon to speak freely upon the subject where the honor and interests of those I represent are involved. I hold then, that there never has yet existed a wealthy and civilized society in which one portion of the community did not, in point of fact, live on the labor of the other. Broad and general as is this assertion, it is fully borne out by history.

This is not the proper occasion, but if it were, it would not be difficult to trace the various devices by which the wealth of all civilized communities has been so unequally divided, and to show by what means so small a share has been allotted to those by whose labor it was produced, and so large a share given to the nonproducing classes. The devices are almost innumerable, from the brute force and gross superstition of ancient times, to the subtle and artful fiscal contrivances of modern.

I might well challenge a comparison between them and the more direct, simple, and patriarchal mode by which the labor of the African race is, among us, commanded by the European. I may say with truth, that in few countries so much is left to the share of the laborer, and so little exacted from him; or where there is more kind attention paid to him in sickness or infirmities of age. Compare his condition with the tenants of the poor houses in the more civilized portions of Europe – look at the sick, and the old and infirm slave, on one hand, in the midst of his family and friends, under the kind superintending care of his master and mistress, and compare it with the forlorn and wretched condition of the pauper in the poor house.

But I will not dwell on this aspect of the question; I turn to the political; and here I fearlessly assert that the existing relation between the two races in the South, against which these blind fanatics are waging war, forms the most solid and durable foundation on which to rear free and stable political institutions. It is useless to disguise the fact. There is and always has been in an advanced stage of wealth and civilization, a conflict between labor and capital.

The condition of society in the South exempts us from the disorders and dangers resulting from this conflict; and which explains why it is that the political condition of the slaveholding States has been so much more stable and quiet than that of the North. The advantages of the former, in this respect, will become more and more manifest if left undisturbed by interference from without, as the country advances in wealth and numbers. We have, in fact, but just entered that condition of society where the strength and durability of our political institutions are to be tested; and I venture nothing in predicting that the experience of the next generation will fully test how vastly more favorable our condition of society is to that of other sections for free and stable institutions, provided we are not disturbed by the interference of others, or shall have sufficient intelligence and spirit to resist promptly and successfully such interference. It rests with ourselves to meet and repel them.

I look not for aid to this Government, or to the other States; not but there are kind feelings towards us on the part of the great body of the non-slaveholding States; but as kind as their feelings may be, we may rest assured that no political party in those States will risk their ascendency for our safety. If we do not defend ourselves none will defend us; if we yield we will be more and more pressed as we recede; and if we submit we will be trampled under foot. Be assured that emancipation itself would not satisfy these fanatics: – that gained, the next step would be to raise the negroes to a social and political equality with the whites; and that being effected, we would soon find the present condition of the two races reversed. They and their northern allies would be the masters, and we the slaves; the condition of the white race in the British West India Islands, bad as it is, would be happiness to ours. There the mother country is interested in sustaining the supremacy of the European race. It is true that the authority of the former master is destroyed, but the African will there still be a slave, not to individuals but to the community, – forced to labor, not by the authority of the overseer, but by the bayonet of the soldiery and the rod of the civil magistrate.

Surrounded as the slaveholding States are with such imminent perils, I rejoice to think that our means of defense are ample, if we shall prove to have the intelligence and spirit to see and apply them before it is too late. All we want is concert, to lay aside all party differences, and unite with zeal and energy in repelling approaching dangers. Let there be concert of action, and we shall find ample means of security without resorting to secession, or disunion. I speak with full knowledge and a thorough examination of the subject, and for one, see my way clearly.

One thing alarms me – the eager pursuit of gain which overspreads the land, and which absorbs every faculty of the mind and every feeling of the heart. Of all passions avarice is the most blind and compromising – the last to see and the first to yield to danger. I dare not hope that any thing I can say will arouse the South to a due sense of danger; I fear it is beyond the power of mortal voice to awaken it in time from the fatal security into which it has fallen.

5. Angelina Grimké, 'Speech at Pennsylvania Hall' (Philadelphia, 1838)

At a time when women rarely received a hearing on the public stage, a number of pioneering female activists were drawn into the struggle against American slavery. The potential dangers of such interventions were made clear by the events surrounding the 1838 anti-slavery speech by the reformer Angelina Grimké (1806–79) in Philadelphia, an act that provoked mob violence and the symbolic burning to the ground of the venue in which she had made her case.

Born into a large and prominent South Carolina slave-holding family, Angelina and her sister Sarah grew appalled by the inhumanity of slavery, and a powerful conversion to Quakerism led them to renounce their family's views and embrace a life of abolitionist activism in Pennsylvania. Equipped with direct experience of the evils of slave-owning, they brought a unique voice to the struggle, becoming associated with William Lloyd Garrison's wing of the abolition movement. In 1836, Angelina published a frank and personal anti-slavery tract, *An Appeal to the Christian Women of the Southern States* (1836), that helped establish her notoriety and influence. The sisters began to hold abolition meetings for women in New York City and Angelina became the first woman to address the Massachusetts State Legislature. Their speaking career placed them at the frenzied intersection of the equally fraught abolition and women's rights debates, provoking a rebuke from ministers against their 'unwomanly behaviour' and from other anti-slavery campaigners who thought the Grimkés' political action undermined the anti-slavery cause. Unrepentant, they replied by asking 'what then can woman do for the slave when she is herself under the feet of man and shamed into silence?'[24]

Angelina's final and most famous anti-slavery speech took place as part of a four-day abolitionist convention in Pennsylvania Hall, Philadelphia, a venue specifically set up to host abolitionist events. On Wednesday, 16 May 1838, a large anti-abolitionist mob had gathered outside as she began to speak, infuriated at the message, the gender of the speaker and the presence of a mixed-race audience. Angelina managed to finish her lecture, but after the mob returned the following day to burn Pennsylvania Hall to the ground, she never spoke against slavery in public again (Figure 5). The transcript below contains her words, interspersed with accounts of what the newspaper reporter calls the noises of 'mobocratic spirit'.

Source

Sarah M. Grimké, Angelina E. Grimké and Mark Perry, *On Slavery and Abolitionism* (New York: Penguin, 2014).

Men, brethren and fathers – mothers, daughters and sisters, what came ye out for to see? A reed shaken with the wind? Is it curiosity merely, or a deep sympathy with the perishing slave, that has brought this large audience together? *[A yell from the mob without the building.]* Those voices without ought to awaken and call out our warmest sympathies. Deluded beings! 'they know not what

---

24. Gerda Lerner, *The Feminist Thought of Sarah Grimké* (New York: Oxford University Press, 1998), pp. 151–2.

they do.'[25] They know not that they are undermining their own rights and their own happiness, temporal and eternal. Do you ask, 'what has the North to do with slavery?' Hear it – hear it. Those voices without tell us that the spirit of slavery is here, and has been roused to wrath by our abolition speeches and conventions: for surely liberty would not foam and tear herself with rage, because her friends are multiplied daily, and meetings are held in quick succession to set forth her virtues and extend her peaceful kingdom. This opposition shows that slavery has done its deadliest work in the hearts of our citizens. Do you ask, then, 'what has the North to do?' I answer, cast out first the spirit of slavery from your own hearts, and then lend your aid to convert the South. Each one present has a work to do, be his or her situation what it may, however limited their means, or insignificant their supposed influence. The great men of this country will not do this work; the church will never do it. A desire to please the world, to keep the favor of all parties and of all conditions, makes them dumb on this and every other unpopular subject. They have become worldly-wise, and therefore God, in his wisdom, employs them not to carry on his plans of reformation and salvation. He hath chosen the foolish things of the world to confound the wise, and the weak to overcome the mighty.

As a Southerner I feel that it is my duty to stand up here to-night and bear testimony against slavery. I have seen it – I have seen it. I know it has horrors that can never be described. I was brought up under its wing: I witnessed for many years its demoralizing influences, and its destructiveness to human happiness. It is admitted by some that the slave is not happy under the worst forms of slavery. But I have never seen a happy slave. I have seen him dance in his chains, it is true; but he was not happy. There is a wide difference between happiness and mirth. Man cannot enjoy the former while his manhood is destroyed, and that part of the being which is necessary to the making, and to the enjoyment of happiness, is completely blotted out. The slaves, however, may be, and sometimes are, mirthful. When hope is extinguished, they say, 'let us eat and drink, for tomorrow we die.'

[Just then stones were thrown at the windows, – a great noise without, and commotion within.]

What is a mob? What would the breaking of every window be? What would the levelling of this Hall be? Any evidence that we are wrong, or that slavery is a good and wholesome institution ? What if the mob should now burst in upon us, break up our meeting and commit violence upon our persons – would this be any thing compared with what the slaves endure? No, no: and we do not remember them 'as bound with them,' if we shrink in the time of peril, or feel unwilling to sacrifice ourselves, if need be, for their sake. *[Great noise.]* I thank the Lord that there is yet life left enough to feel the truth, even though it rages at it – that conscience is not so completely seared as to be unmoved by the truth of the living God.

———

25. Luke 23: 34.

Many persons go to the South for a season, and are hospitably entertained in the parlor and at the table of the slave-holder. They never enter the huts of the slaves; they know nothing of the dark side of the picture, and they return home with praises on their lips of the generous character of those with whom they had tarried. Or if they have witnessed the cruelties of slavery, by remaining silent spectators they have naturally become callous – an insensibility has ensued which prepares them to apologize even for barbarity. Nothing but the corrupting influence of slavery on the hearts of the Northern people can induce them to apologize for it; and much will have been done for the destruction of Southern slavery when we have so reformed the North that no one here will be willing to risk his reputation by advocating or even excusing the holding of men as property. The South know it, and acknowledge that as fast as our principles prevail, the hold of the master must be relaxed.

[*Another outbreak of mobocratic spirit, and some confusion in the house.*]

How wonderfully constituted is the human mind! How it resists, as long as it can, all efforts made to reclaim from error! I feel that all this disturbance is but an evidence that our efforts are the best that could have been adopted, or else the friends of slavery would not care for what we say and do. The South know what we do. I am thankful that they are reached by our efforts. Many times have I wept in the land of my birth, over the system of slavery. I knew of none who sympathized in my feelings – I was unaware that any efforts were made to deliver the oppressed – no voice in the wilderness was heard calling on the people to repent and do works meet for repentance – and my heart sickened within me.

Oh, how should I have rejoiced to know that such efforts as these were being made. I only wonder that I had such feelings. I wonder when I reflect under what influence I was brought up that my heart is not harder than the nether millstone. But in the midst of temptation I was preserved, and my sympathy grew warmer, and my hatred of slavery more inveterate, until at last I have exiled myself from my native land because I could no longer endure to hear the wailing of the slave. I fled to the land of Penn;[26] for here, thought I, sympathy for the slave will surely be found. But I found it not. The people were kind and hospitable, but the slave had no place in their thoughts. Whenever questions were put to me as to his condition, I felt that they were dictated by an idle curiosity, rather than by that deep feeling which would lead to effort for his rescue.

I therefore shut up my grief in my own heart. I remembered that I was a Carolinian, from a state which framed this iniquity by law.[27] I knew that throughout her territory was continual suffering, on the one part, and continual brutality

---

26. Pennsylvania, founded by William Penn (1644–1718) on a royal charter in 1681 emphasising religious freedoms.
27. As the population of the enslaved rose to become a majority during the early nineteenth century, South Carolina introduced ever more punitive measures to its original 1712 and 1739 slave codes.

and sin on the other. Every Southern breeze wafted to me the discordant tones of weeping and wailing, shrieks and groans, mingled with prayers and blasphemous curses. I thought there was no hope; that the wicked would go on in his wickedness, until he had destroyed both himself and his country. My heart sunk within me at the abominations in the midst of which I had been born and educated. What will it avail, cried I in bitterness of spirit, to expose to the gaze of strangers the horrors and pollutions of slavery, when there is no ear to hear nor heart to feel and pray for the slave. The language of my soul was, 'Oh tell it not in Gath, publish it not in the streets of Askelon.'[28] But how different do I feel now! Animated with hope, nay, with an assurance of the triumph of liberty and good will to man, I will lift up my voice like a trumpet, and show this people their transgression, their sins of omission towards the slave, and what they can do towards affecting Southern mind, and overthrowing Southern oppression.

We may talk of occupying neutral ground, but on this subject, in its present attitude, there is no such thing as neutral ground. He that is not for us is against us, and he that gathereth not with us, scattereth abroad. If you are on what you suppose to be neutral ground, the South look upon you as on the side of the oppressor. And is there one who loves his country willing to give his influence, even indirectly, in favor of slavery – that curse of nations ? God swept Egypt with the besom of destruction, and punished Judea also with a sore punishment, because of slavery.[29] And have we any reason to believe that he is less just now? – or that he will be more favorable to us than to his own 'peculiar people'?

[Shoutings, stones thrown against the windows, &c.]

There is nothing to be feared from those who would stop our mouths, but they themselves should fear and tremble. The current is even now setting fast against them. If the arm of the North had not caused the Bastille of slavery to totter to its foundation, you would not hear those cries. A few years ago, and the South felt secure, and with a contemptuous sneer asked, 'Who are the abolitionists? The abolitionists are nothing?' – Ay, in one sense they were nothing, and they are nothing still. But in this we rejoice, that 'God has chosen things that are not to bring to nought things that are.'

[Mob again disturbed the meeting.]

We often hear the question asked, 'What shall we do?' Here is an opportunity for doing something now. Every man and every woman present may do something by showing that we fear not a mob, and, in the midst of threatenings and revilings, by opening our mouths for the dumb and pleading the cause of those who are ready to perish.

---

28. A invocation of the Second Book of Samuel, 1: 20: 'Tell *it* not in Gath, publish *it* not in the streets of Askelon; lest the daughters of the Philistines rejoice, lest the daughters of the uncircumcised triumph.' Gath and Askelon were two cities in modern-day Palestine, currently occupied by Israel.

29. The Plagues of Egypt, as detailed in the Book of Exodus, were a series of calamities inflicted upon the Egyptians by the God of Israel to allow the Israelites to depart from slavery.

To work as we should in this cause, we must know what Slavery is. Let me urge you then to buy the books which have been written on this subject and read them, and then lend them to your neighbors. Give your money no longer for things which pander to pride and lust, but aid in scattering 'the living coals of truth'[30] upon the naked heart of this nation, – in circulating appeals to the sympathies of Christians in behalf of the outraged and suffering slave. But, it is said by some, our 'books and papers do not speak the truth.' Why, then, do they not contradict what we say? They cannot. Moreover the South has entreated, nay commanded us to be silent; and what greater evidence of the truth of our publications could be desired?

Women of Philadelphia! allow me as a Southern woman, with much attachment to the land of my birth, to entreat you to come up to this work. Especially let me urge you to petition. Men may settle this and other questions at the ballot-box, but you have no such right; it is only through petitions that you can reach the Legislature. It is therefore peculiarly your duty to petition. Do you say, 'It does no good'? The South already turns pale at the number sent. They have read the reports of the proceedings of Congress, and there have seen that among other petitions were very many from the women of the North on the subject of slavery. This fact has called the attention of the South to the subject. How could we expect to have done more as yet? Men who hold the rod over slaves, rule in the councils of the nation: and they deny our right to petition and to remonstrate against abuses of our sex and of our kind. We have these rights, however, from our God. Only let us exercise them: and though often turned away unanswered, let us remember the influence of importunity upon the unjust judge, and act accordingly. The fact that the South look with jealousy upon our measures shows that they are effectual. There is, therefore, no cause for doubting or despair, but rather for rejoicing.

It was remarked in England that women did much to abolish Slavery in her colonies.[31] Nor are they now idle. Numerous petitions from them have recently been presented to the Queen, to abolish the apprenticeship with its cruelties nearly equal to those of the system whose place it supplies. One petition two miles and a quarter long has been presented. And do you think these labors will be in vain? Let the history of the past answer. When the women of these States send up to Congress such a petition, our legislators will arise as did those of England, and say, 'When all the maids and matrons of the land are knocking at our doors

---

30. An invocation of 'Our Countrymen in Chains!' (1834), an abolitionist poem by New England poet John Greenleaf Whittier, in *Anti-Slavery Poems and Songs of Labor and Reform* (London: Macmillan, 1889): 'Up, then, in Freedom's manly part / From graybeard eld to fiery youth / And on the nation's naked heart / Scatter the living coals of Truth!'
31. British women activists, such as the Leicester-born reformer Elizabeth Heyrick (1789–1831), kept the abolition movement alive during the 1820s, urging immediate rather than gradual emancipation in the British colonies through pamphlets, speeches and boycotts.

we must legislate.' Let the zeal and love, the faith and works of our English sisters quicken ours – that while the slaves continue to suffer, and when they shout deliverance, we may feel the satisfaction of having done what we could.

6. Frederick Douglass, 'What to the Slave is July 4th?' (Rochester, New York, 1852)

The most consequential genre of abolition oratory came not from white activists but from those formerly enslaved. The most famous of all was delivered in the summer of 1852, when the social reformer and ex-slave Frederick Douglass (1818–95) was invited by the Ladies' Anti-Slavery Society in Rochester, New York, to deliver its annual Fourth of July address. Before an expectant audience of 600 in the ornate Corinthian Hall, the celebrated orator delivered a speech that David Blight has called 'the rhetorical masterpiece of American abolitionism', taking aim squarely at the complicity of his sympathetic Northern audience.[32]

Douglass was born a slave with the name Frederick Bailey in Maryland, knowing little of his family history or even his exact date of birth. He escaped to the North in 1838, and after settling in Massachusetts, became active in Boston abolitionist circles as a gifted anti-slavery speaker and writer, before travelling to Britain and securing both his freedom and international acclaim. His *Narrative of the Life of Frederick Douglass: An American Slave (1845)* and its two successor memoirs became among the most important of all slave narratives. However, it was his remarkable eloquence as an orator that was his most important asset, on both a practical and a symbolic level. Striking a powerful, handsome figure, with a deep voice that could hold audiences transfixed, and possessed of astonishing rhetorical versatility and virtuosity, he stood as a living rebuke to ideas of racial inferiority.

In 1852, he had been based in Rochester for several years, publishing his own newspaper, *The North Star,* managing abolition events, and assisting in the escape of fugitive slaves to Canada. He typically spent about six months of the year travelling extensively across the North, giving up to seventy lectures during winter seasons across thousands of miles. His invitation to speak in the Corinthian Hall came at a crucial point in the development of slavery in America, as the Fugitive Slave Law of 1850 had turned the pursuit of escaped slaves into a national crisis.

---

32. David Blight, *Frederick Douglass: Prophet of Freedom* (New York: Simon & Schuster, 2018), p. 230.

As Blight puts it, 'Douglass channeled all of this tension into a kind of music . . . a symphony in three movements.'[33] First, he offered conventional but pointedly lavish praise of the genius of the founding fathers. Then, in an abrupt turn signalled by the brandishing of pronouns ('to you', 'your deliverance', 'your national independence'), he offered a stunning rebuke to his listeners, moving briskly to a tone of 'scorching irony', before a third final section argued for an anti-slavery reading of the US Constitution. The speech would reach a national and global audience through reprinting in his own paper and as a pamphlet that he sold at his own lectures. The excerpt below offers a full sense of the first two sections of the speech.

Source

Philip S. Foner (ed.), *Frederick Douglass: Selected Speeches and Writings* (Chicago: Lawrence Hill, 1999), pp. 188–206.

Mr. President, Friends and Fellow Citizens:

He who could address this audience without a quailing sensation, has stronger nerves than I have. I do not remember ever to have appeared as a speaker before any assembly more shrinkingly, nor with greater distrust of my ability, than I do this day. A feeling has crept over me, quite unfavorable to the exercise of my limited powers of speech. The task before me is one which requires much previous thought and study for its proper performance. I know that apologies of this sort are generally considered flat and unmeaning. I trust, however, that mine will not be so considered. Should I seem at ease, my appearance would much misrepresent me. The little experience I have had in addressing public meetings, in country schoolhouses, avails me nothing on the present occasion.

The papers and placards say, that I am to deliver a 4th of July oration. This certainly sounds large, and out of the common way, for it is true that I have often had the privilege to speak in this beautiful Hall, and to address many who now honor me with their presence. But neither their familiar faces, nor the perfect gage I think I have of Corinthian Hall, seems to free me from embarrassment.

The fact is, ladies and gentlemen, the distance between this platform and the slave plantation, from which I escaped, is considerable – and the difficulties to be overcome in getting from the latter to the former, are by no means slight. That I am here to-day is, to me, a matter of astonishment as well as of gratitude. You will not, therefore, be surprised, if in what I have to say I evince no elaborate preparation, nor grace my speech with any high sounding exordium. With

---

33. Blight, *Frederick Douglass*, p. 231.

little experience and with less learning, I have been able to throw my thoughts hastily and imperfectly together; and trusting to your patient and generous indulgence, I will proceed to lay them before you.

This, for the purpose of this celebration, is the 4th of July. It is the birthday of your National Independence, and of your political freedom. This, to you, is what the Passover was to the emancipated people of God. It carries your minds back to the day, and to the act of your great deliverance; and to the signs, and to the wonders, associated with that act, and that day. This celebration also marks the beginning of another year of your national life; and reminds you that the Republic of America is now 76 years old.

I am glad, fellow-citizens, that your nation is so young. Seventy-six years, though a good old age for a man, is but a mere speck in the life of a nation. Three score years and ten is the allotted time for individual men; but nations number their years by thousands. According to this fact, you are, even now, only in the beginning of your national career, still lingering in the period of child-hood. I repeat, I am glad this is so. There is hope in the thought, and hope is much needed, under the dark clouds which lower above the horizon. The eye of the reformer is met with angry flashes, portending disastrous times; but his heart may well beat lighter at the thought that America is young, and that she is still in the impressible stage of her existence. May he not hope that high lessons of wisdom, of justice and of truth, will yet give direction to her destiny? Were the nation older, the patriot's heart might be sadder, and the reformer's brow heavier. Its future might be shrouded in gloom, and the hope of its prophets go out in sorrow.

There is consolation in the thought that America is young. Great streams are not easily turned from channels, worn deep in the course of ages. They may sometimes rise in quiet and stately majesty, and inundate the land, refreshing and fertilizing the earth with their mysterious properties. They may also rise in wrath and fury, and bear away, on their angry waves, the accumulated wealth of years of toil and hardship. They, however, gradually flow back to the same old channel, and flow on as serenely as ever. But, while the river may not be turned aside, it may dry up, and leave nothing behind but the withered branch, and the unsightly rock, to howl in the abyss-sweeping wind, the sad tale of departed glory. As with rivers so with nations.[34]

. . .

Fellow-citizens, pardon me, allow me to ask, why am I called upon to speak here to-day? What have I, or those I represent, to do with your national independence? Are the great principles of political freedom and of natural justice, embodied in that Declaration of Independence, extended to us? and am I,

---

34. Douglass then followed with a seemingly conventional ten-minute section narrating the events of the Revolution and praise for the founder's ideals. The next paragraphs indicate the *volta* or turn in the speech.

therefore, called upon to bring our humble offering to the national altar, and to confess the benefits and express devout gratitude for the blessings resulting from your independence to us?

Would to God, both for your sakes and ours, that an affirmative answer could be truthfully returned to these questions! Then would my task be light, and my burden easy and delightful. For who is there so cold, that a nation's sympathy could not warm him? Who so obdurate and dead to the claims of gratitude, that would not thankfully acknowledge such priceless benefits? Who so stolid and selfish, that would not give his voice to swell the hallelujahs of a nation's jubilee, when the chains of servitude had been torn from his limbs? I am not that man. In a case like that, the dumb might eloquently speak, and the 'lame man leap as an hart.'

But, such is not the state of the case. I say it with a sad sense of the disparity between us. I am not included within the pale of this glorious anniversary! Your high independence only reveals the immeasurable distance between us. The blessings in which you, this day, rejoice, are not enjoyed in common. – The rich inheritance of justice, liberty, prosperity and independence, bequeathed by your fathers, is shared by you, not by me. The sunlight that brought life and healing to you, has brought stripes and death to me. This Fourth of July is yours, not mine. You may rejoice, I must mourn. To drag a man in fetters into the grand illuminated temple of liberty, and call upon him to join you in joyous anthems, were inhuman mockery and sacrilegious irony. Do you mean, citizens, to mock me, by asking me to speak to-day? If so, there is a parallel to your conduct. And let me warn you that it is dangerous to copy the example of a nation whose crimes, lowering up to heaven, were thrown down by the breath of the Almighty, burying that nation in irrecoverable ruin! I can to-day take up the plaintive lament of a peeled and woe-smitten people!

'By the rivers of Babylon, there we sat down. Yea! we wept when we remembered Zion. We hanged our harps upon the willows in the midst thereof. For there, they that carried us away captive, required of us a song; and they who wasted us required of us mirth, saying, Sing us one of the songs of Zion. How can we sing the Lord's song in a strange land? If I forget thee, O Jerusalem, let my right hand forget her cunning. If I do not remember thee, let my tongue cleave to the roof of my mouth.'[35]

Fellow-citizens; above your national, tumultuous joy, I hear the mournful wail of millions! whose chains, heavy and grievous yesterday, are, to-day, rendered more intolerable by the jubilee shouts that reach them. If I do forget, if I do not faithfully remember those bleeding children of sorrow this day, 'may my right hand forget her cunning, and may my tongue cleave to the roof of my mouth!' To forget them, to pass lightly over their wrongs, and to chime in with the popular theme, would be treason most scandalous and shocking, and would make me a reproach before God and the world.

---

35. Psalm 137.

My subject, then fellow-citizens, is AMERICAN SLAVERY. I shall see, this day, and its popular characteristics, from the slave's point of view. Standing, there, identified with the American bondman, making his wrongs mine, I do not hesitate to declare, with all my soul, that the character and conduct of this nation never looked blacker to me than on this 4th of July! Whether we turn to the declarations of the past, or to the professions of the present, the conduct of the nation seems equally hideous and revolting. America is false to the past, false to the present, and solemnly binds herself to be false to the future. Standing with God and the crushed and bleeding slave on this occasion, I will, in the name of humanity which is outraged, in the name of liberty which is fettered, in the name of the constitution and the Bible, which are disregarded and trampled upon, dare to call in question and to denounce, with all the emphasis I can command, everything that serves to perpetuate slavery – the great sin and shame of America! 'I will not equivocate; I will not excuse;' I will use the severest language I can command; and yet not one word shall escape me that any man, whose judgment is not blinded by prejudice, or who is not at heart a slaveholder, shall not confess to be right and just.

But I fancy I hear some one of my audience say, it is just in this circumstance that you and your brother abolitionists fail to make a favorable impression on the public mind. Would you argue more, and denounce less, would you persuade more, and rebuke less, your cause would be much more likely to succeed. But, I submit, where all is plain there is nothing to be argued. What point in the anti-slavery creed would you have me argue? On what branch of the subject do the people of this country need light? Must I undertake to prove that the slave is a man? That point is conceded already. Nobody doubts it. The slaveholders themselves acknowledge it in the enactment of laws for their government. They acknowledge it when they punish disobedience on the part of the slave. There are seventy-two crimes in the State of Virginia, which, if committed by a black man, (no matter how ignorant he be), subject him to the punishment of death; while only two of the same crimes will subject a white man to the like punishment. What is this but the acknowledgement that the slave is a moral, intellectual and responsible being? The manhood of the slave is conceded. It is admitted in the fact that Southern statute books are covered with enactments forbidding, under severe fines and penalties, the teaching of the slave to read or to write. When you can point to any such laws, in reference to the beasts of the field, then I may consent to argue the manhood of the slave. When the dogs in your streets, when the fowls of the air, when the cattle on your hills, when the fish of the sea, and the reptiles that crawl, shall be unable to distinguish the slave from a brute, then will I argue with you that the slave is a man!

For the present, it is enough to affirm the equal manhood of the Negro race. Is it not astonishing that, while we are ploughing, planting and reaping, using all kinds of mechanical tools, erecting houses, constructing bridges, building ships, working in metals of brass, iron, copper, silver and gold; that, while we are reading, writing and cyphering, acting as clerks, merchants and secretaries, having among us lawyers, doctors, ministers, poets, authors, editors, orators and teachers; that, while we are engaged in all manner of enterprises common to other men, digging gold in California, capturing the whale in the Pacific, feeding sheep and cattle on the hill-side, living, moving, acting, thinking, planning, living in families as husbands, wives and children, and, above all, confessing and worshipping the Christian's God, and looking hopefully for life and immortality beyond the grave, we are called upon to prove that we are men!

Would you have me argue that man is entitled to liberty? that he is the rightful owner of his own body? You have already declared it. Must I argue the wrongfulness of slavery? Is that a question for Republicans? Is it to be settled by the rules of logic and argumentation, as a matter beset with great difficulty, involving a doubtful application of the principle of justice, hard to be understood? How should I look to-day, in the presence of Americans, dividing, and subdividing a discourse, to show that men have a natural right to freedom? speaking of it relatively, and positively, negatively, and affirmatively. To do so, would be to make myself ridiculous, and to offer an insult to your understanding. – There is not a man beneath the canopy of heaven, that does not know that slavery is wrong for him.

What, am I to argue that it is wrong to make men brutes, to rob them of their liberty, to work them without wages, to keep them ignorant of their relations to their fellow men, to beat them with sticks, to flay their flesh with the lash, to load their limbs with irons, to hunt them with dogs, to sell them at auction, to sunder their families, to knock out their teeth, to burn their flesh, to starve them into obedience and submission to their masters? Must I argue that a system thus marked with blood, and stained with pollution, is wrong? No! I will not. I have better employments for my time and strength than such arguments would imply.

What, then, remains to be argued? Is it that slavery is not divine; that God did not establish it; that our doctors of divinity are mistaken? There is blasphemy in the thought. That which is inhuman, cannot be divine! Who can reason on such a proposition? They that can, may; I cannot. The time for such argument is passed.

At a time like this, scorching irony, not convincing argument, is needed. O! had I the ability, and could I reach the nation's ear, I would, to-day, pour out a fiery stream of biting ridicule, blasting reproach, withering sarcasm, and stern rebuke. For it is not light that is needed, but fire; it is not the gentle shower, but thunder. We need the storm, the whirlwind, and the earthquake. The feeling of the nation must be quickened; the conscience of the nation must be roused; the propriety of the nation must be startled; the hypocrisy of the nation must be exposed; and its crimes against God and man must be proclaimed and denounced.

What, to the American slave, is your 4th of July? I answer: a day that reveals to him, more than all other days in the year, the gross injustice and cruelty to which he is the constant victim. To him, your celebration is a sham; your boasted liberty, an unholy license; your national greatness, swelling vanity; your sounds of rejoicing are empty and heartless; your denunciations of tyrants, brass fronted impudence; your shouts of liberty and equality, hollow mockery; your prayers and hymns, your sermons and thanksgivings, with all your religious parade, and solemnity, are, to him, mere bombast, fraud, deception, impiety, and hypocrisy – a thin veil to cover up crimes which would disgrace a nation of savages. There is not a nation on the earth guilty of practices, more shocking and bloody, than are the people of these United States, at this very hour.

Go where you may, search where you will, roam through all the monarchies and despotisms of the old world, travel through South America, search out every abuse, and when you have found the last, lay your facts by the side of the everyday practices of this nation, and you will say with me, that, for revolting barbarity and shameless hypocrisy, America reigns without a rival.

7. Henry Ward Beecher, 'Peace, Be Still' Sermon (Brooklyn, 1861)

Henry Ward Beecher (1813–87) was one of the most popular American liberal clergymen of the mid-nineteenth century, and frequently used his enormous influence to preach against slavery. Son of the temperance reformer, Rev. Lyman Beecher, and brother of *Uncle Tom's Cabin* author, Harriet Beecher Stowe, he possessed an oratorical skill, and published sermons and lectures, that made him a prominent and controversial moral critic of his age, described in one recent biography as 'the most famous man in America'.[36]

Born in Connecticut and trained in Ohio, Beecher settled in Brooklyn as pastor of the Congregational Plymouth Church, where he cultivated a flamboyant pulpit style and a theology centred on a revolutionary belief in God's love. By the mid-1850s, he routinely drew weekly crowds of 2,500 and was also a regular speaker on the secular lecture circuit. Over that decade, he had gradually become more emphatic in opposing slavery, raising funds for abolitionist militants, holding mock slave auctions to raise awareness, and delivering passionate abolitionist sermons.

The following shows how Beecher used the pulpit as a platform to situate slavery within the broader context of American national sins. Delivered amidst the growing secession crisis of early 1861 and the looming inevitability of conflict, Beecher addressed a nation 'rolling helplessly in a great tempest', and, like Douglass in 1852, admonished his audience for their complacency and complicity. It was this kind of

---

36. Debby Applegate, *The Most Famous Man in America* (New York: Doublegate, 2006).

performance that led Abraham Lincoln to send Beecher to Britain in 1863 to win over audiences hostile to the Northern cause. In order to give a full sense of Beecher's words, his long text has been excerpted into a series of climactic moments.

Source

Fast Day Sermons: Or, the Pulpit on the State of the Country (New York: Rudd & Carleton, 1861).

A SERMON PREACHED AT PLYMOUTH CHURCH, BROOKLYN, ON THE DAY OF THE NATIONAL FAST, JAN. 4, 1861.

> *And there arose a great storm of wind, and the 'waves beat into the ship, so that it was now full. And he was in the hinder part of the ship, asleep on a pillow: and they awake him, and said unto him, Master, carest thou not that we perish? And he arose and rebuked the wind, and said unto the sea, Peace, be still. And the wind ceased, and there was a great calm.'*
>
> — Mark iv. 37–39.

At the close of a laborious day, our Saviour entered a ship, upon the lake of Gennesaret,[37] to cross to the other side. Wearied by his great tasks of mercy, which had filled the day, he fell asleep. Meantime, a sudden and violent wind, to which that lake is even yet subject, swept down from the hills, and well-nigh overwhelmed them. They were not ignorant of navigation, nor unacquainted with that squally sea. Like good men and true, doubtless, they laid about them. They took to sail, and put out oars, and, heading to the wind, valiantly bore up against the gale, and thought nothing of asking help till they had exerted every legitimate power of their own. But the waves overleaped their slender bulwarks, and filled the little vessel past all bailing. Then, when they had done all that men could do, but not till then, they aroused the sleeping Christ and implored his succor. Not for coming to him, did he rebuke them; but for coming with such terror of despair, saying, Why are ye so fearful? How is it that ye have no faith? He outbreathed upon the winds, and their strength quite forsook them. He looked upon the surly waves, and they hasted back to their caverns. There is no tumult in the heavens, on the earth, nor upon the sea, that Christ's word cannot control. When it pleases God to speak, tempestuous clouds are peaceful as flocks of doves, and angry seas change all their roar to rippling music.

　　This nation is rolling helplessly in a great tempest. The Chief Magistrate in despair calls us to go to the sleeping Saviour, and to beseech his Divine

---

37. Alternative name for the Sea of Galilee.

interference.[38] It may be true that the crew have brought the ship into danger by cowardice or treachery; it may be true that a firm hand on the wheel would even yet hold her head to the wind, and ride out the squall. But what of that? Humiliation and prayer are never out of order. This nation has great sins unrepented of; and whatever may be our own judgment of the wisdom of public men in regard to secular affairs, we cannot deny that in this respect they have hit rarely well. Instead of finding fault with the almost only wise act of many days, let us rather admire with gratitude this unexpected piety of men in high places.

. . .

If at such a solemn crisis as this, men refuse to look at things as they are; to call their sins to remembrance; to confess and forsake them; if they shall cover over the great sins of this people, and confess only in a sentimental way, (as one would solace an evening sadness by playing some sweet and minor melody,) then we may fear that God has indeed forsaken his people. But if we shall honestly confess our real sins; if we propose to cleanse ourselves from them; if we do not make prayer a substitute for action, but an incitement to it; if we rise from our knees this day more zealous for temperance, for honesty, for real brotherhood, for pure and undefiled religion, and for that which is the sum and child of them all, regulating liberty to all men, then will the clouds begin to break, and we shall see the blue shining through, and the sun, ere long, driving away the tumultuous clouds, shall come back in triumph, and like one for a moment cast down but now lifted up for victory.

. . .

But upon a day of national fasting and confession, we are called to consider not alone our individual and social evils, but also those which are national. And justice requires that we should make mention of the sins of this nation on every side, past and present. I should violate my own convictions, if, in the presence of more nearly present and more exciting influences, I should neglect to mention the sins of this nation against the Indian, who, as much as the slave, is dumb, but who, unlike the slave, has almost none to think of him, and to speak of his wrongs. We must remember that we are the only historians of the wrongs of the Indian – we that commit them.

And our history of the Indian nations of this country, is like the inquisitor's history of his own trials of innocent victims. He leaves out the rack, and the groans, and the anguish, and the unutterable wrongs, and puts but his own glozing view in his journal. We have heaped up the account of treachery and cruelty on their part, but we have not narrated the provocations, the grinding

---

38. Having failed to prevent the secession crisis, in his final State of the Union address in December 1860, Democrat President James Buchanan (1857–61) offered up his 'prayer to God . . . that He would preserve the Constitution and the Union throughout all generations' (James Buchanan, *Mr. Buchanan's Administration on the Eve of the Rebellion* (New York: D. Appleton, 1866), p. 115).

intrusions, and the misunderstood interpretations of their policy, on our part. Every crime in the calendar of wrong which a strong people can commit against a weak one, has been committed by us against them. We have wasted their substance; we have provoked their hostility, and then chastised them for their wars; we have compelled them to peace ignominiously; we have formed treaties with them only to be broken; we have defiled their possessions. In our presence they have wilted and wasted. A heathen people have experienced at the side of a Christian nation, almost every evil which one people can commit against another.

Admit the laws of race; admit the laws of advancing civilization as fatal to all barbarism; admit the indocility of the savage; admit the rude edges of violent men who form the pioneer advance of a great people, and the intrinsic difficulties of managing a people whose notions and customs and laws are utterly different from our own, and then you have only explained how the evil has been done, but you have not changed its guilt, nor fact. The mischief has been done, and this is simply the excuse. It is a sorry commentary upon a Christian nation, and indeed, upon religion itself, that the freest and most boastfully religious people on the globe are absolutely fatal to any weaker people that they touch. What would be thought of a man who, when he became converted to Christianity, was dangerous to the next man's pocket? What would be thought of a man who, when he became perfect, was a swindler and a robber? And what must be the nature of that Christianization which makes this Republic a most dangerous neighbor to nations weaker than ourselves? We are respectful to strength, and thieves and robbers to weakness. It is not safe for any to trust our magnanimity and generosity. We have no chivalry. We have avarice; we have haughty arrogance; we have assumptive ways; and we have a desperate determination to live, to think only of our own living, and to sweep with the besom of destruction whatever happens to be where we would put our foot.

Nor is this confined to the Indian. The Mexicans have felt the same rude foot. This nation has employed its gigantic strength with almost no moral restriction. Our civilization has not begotten humanity and respect for others' rights, nor a spirit of protection to the weak.

It is quite in vain to say that the land from which we sprung did the same as we are doing. A wicked daughter is not excused because she had a wicked mother. We boast of the Anglo-Saxon race; and if bone and muscle, an indomitable sense of personal liberty, and a disposition to do what we please, are themes for Christian rejoicing, then the Anglo-Saxon may well rejoice. There are sins that belong to races; there are sins that belong to peoples; there are sins that belong to generations of the same people; and the sins that I have enumerated, are sins that belong to our stock, to our kind. But God never forgets what we most easily forget. Either the moral government over nations is apocryphal, or judgments are yet to be visited upon us for the wrongs done to the Indian.

. . .

We who dwell in the North are not without responsibility for this sin. Its wonderful growth, and the arrogance of its claims, have been in part through our delinquency. And our business to-day is not to find fault with the South, I am not discussing this matter with reference to them at all, but only with reference to our own individual profit. Because the South loved money, they augmented this evil; and because the North loved money, and that quiet which befits industry and commerce, she has refused to insist upon her moral convictions, in days past, and yielded to every demand carrying slavery forward in this nation. You and I are guilty of the spread of slavery unless we have exerted, normally and legitimately, every influence in our power against it. If we have said, 'To agitate the question imperils manufacturing, imperils shipping, imperils real estate, imperils quiet and peace,'[39] and if, then, we have sacrificed purity and honesty, – if we have bought the right to make money here by letting slavery spread and grow there, – we have been doing just the same thing that they have. It has been one gigantic bargain, only working out in different ways, North and South.

It is for us just as much as for them that the slave works; and we acquiesce. We clothe ourselves with the cotton which the slave tills. Is he scorched? is he lashed? does he water the crop with his sweat and tears? It is you and I that wear the shirt and consume the luxury. Our looms and our factories are largely built on the slave's bones. We live on his labor. I confess I see no way to escape a part of the responsibility for slavery. I feel guilty in part for this system. If the relinquishment of the articles which come from slave labor would tend even remotely to abridge or end the evil, I would without hesitation forego every one; but I do not see that it would help the matter. I am an unwilling partner in the slave system. I take to myself a part of the sin; I confess it before God; and pray for some way to be opened by which I may be freed from that which I hate bitterly.

---

39. That is, the arguments against radicalising the slavery issue that prevailed in the North during the 1850s and into the war.

Part B: Race and Civil Rights

8. David Walker, 'The Necessity of a General Union Among Us' (Boston, 1828)

During the early decades of the US republic, various groups of free blacks formed institutions devoted to the idea that slavery and racial oppression were best met through racial solidarity. David Walker (1796–1830) was one of the chief proponents of this ideal of black unity. Born a freeman in North Carolina, he moved to Boston and became a leader of anti-slavery and anti-racist organisations. His most prominent arguments for racial solidarity were made in his *Appeal to the Coloured Citizens of the World* (1829), a vivid pamphlet that urged his fellow American blacks to unite to agitate and unify to fight oppression, warning of bloody insurrection if American slave-holders did not liberate their enslaved. Soon after the pamphlet's publication, Nat Turner's bloody 1831 slave rebellion in Virginia seemed to bear out these prophecies and underline the potential for the unity Walker promoted.

Walker's many public speeches had a similar purpose, urging black audiences to appreciate the crucial links between unity, education and collective advancement. In the December 1828 address below, delivered before the Massachusetts General Colored Association that he had helped found, he told his audience that white aid was insufficient, and that it was time to 'form ourselves into a general body, to protect, aid, and assist each other'. It was an argument that would help shape later expressions of black nationalism and provide the basis for generations of African American moral leadership.

Source

Philip S. Foner and Robert J. Branham, *Lift Every Voice: African American Oratory, 1787–1900* (Tuscaloosa: University of Alabama Press, 1998).

Mr. President, – I cannot but congratulate you, together with my brethren on this highly interesting occasion, the first semi-annual meeting of this Society.[40] When I reflect upon the many impediments though which we have had to conduct its affairs, and see, with emotion of delight, the present degree of eminency to which it has arisen, I cannot, sir, but be of the opinion, that an invisible

---

40. The Massachusetts General Colored Association was established in Boston in 1826 'to promote the welfare of the race by working for the destruction of slavery'.

arm must have been stretched out in our behalf. From the very second conference, which was by us convened, to agitate the proposition respecting the society, to the final consolidation, we were by some, opposed, with an avidity and zeal, which, had it been on the opposite side, would have done great honor to themselves. And, sir, but for the undeviating, and truly patriotic exertions of those who were favorable to the formation of this institution, it might have been this day, in yet unorganized condition.

Did I say in an unorganized condition? Yea, had our opponents their way, the very notion of such an institution might have been obliterated in our minds. How strange it is, to see men of sound sense, and of tolerably good judgment, act so diametrically in opposition to their interest; but I forbear making any further comments on this subject, and return to that for which we are convened.

First then, Mr. President, it is necessary to remark here, at once, that the primary object of this institution, is, to unite the colored population, so far, through the United States of America, as may be practicable and expedient; forming societies, opening, extending, and keeping up correspondences, and not withholding anything which may have the least tendency to ameliorate our miserable condition – with the restrictions, however, of not infringing on the articles of its constitution, or that of the United States of America. Now, that we are disunited, is a fact, that no one of common sense will deny; and, that the cause of which, is a powerful auxiliary in keeping us from rising to the scale of reasonable and thinking beings, none but those who delight in our degradation will attempt to contradict.

Did I say those who delight in our degradation? Yea, sir, glory in keeping us ignorant and miserable, that we might be the better and the longer slaves. I was credibly informed by a gentleman of unquestionable veracity, that a slaveholder upon finding one of his young slaves with a small spelling book in his hand (not opened) fell upon and beat him almost to death, exclaiming, at the same time, to the child, you will acquire better learning than I or any of my family.

I appeal to every candid and unprejudiced mind, do not all such men glory in our miseries and degradations; and are there not millions whose chief glory centres in this horrid wickedness? Now, Mr. President, those are the very humane, philanthropic, and charitable men who proclaim to the world, that the blacks are such a poor, ignorant and degraded species of beings, that, were they set at liberty, they would die for the want of something to subsist upon, and in consequence of which, they are compelled to keep them in bondage, to do them good.

O Heaven! What will not avarice and the love of despotic sway cause men to do with their fellow creatures, when actually in their power? But, to return whence I digressed; it has been asked, in what way will the General Colored Association (or the Institution) unite the colored populations, so far, in the United States, as may be practicable and expedient?

To which enquiry I answer, by asking the following: do not two hundred and eight years'[41] very intolerable sufferings teach us the actual necessity of a general union among us? Do we not know indeed, the horrid dilemma into which we are, and from which, we must exert ourselves, to be extricated? Shall we keep slumbering on, with our arms completely folded up, exclaiming every now and then, against our miseries, yet never do the least thing to ameliorate our condition or that of posterity? Shall we not, by such inactivity, leave, or rather entail a hereditary degradation on our children, but a little, if at all, inferior to that which our fathers, under all their comparative disadvantages and privations, left on us?

In fine, shall we, while almost every other people under Heaven, are making such mighty efforts to better their condition, go around from house to house, enquiring what good associations and societies are going to do us? Ought we not to form ourselves into a general body, to protect, aid, and assist each other to the utmost of our power, with the before mentioned restrictions?

Yes, Mr. President, it is indispensably our duty to try every scheme that we think will have a tendency to facilitate our salvation, and leave the final result to that God, who holds the destinies of people in the hollow of his hand, and who ever has, and will, repay every nation according to its works.

Will any be so hardy as to say, or even to imagine, that we are incapable of effecting any object which may have a tendency to hasten our emancipation, in consequence of the prevalence of ignorance and poverty among us? That the major part of us are ignorant and poor, I am at this time unprepared to deny. But shall this defer us from all lawful attempts to bring about the desired object? Nay, sir, it should rouse us to greater exertions; there ought to be a spirit of emulation and inquiry among us, a hungering and thirsting after religion; there are requisitions, which, if we ever be so happy as to acquire, will fit us for all the departments of life; and, in my humble opinion, ultimately result in rescuing us from an oppression, unparalleled, I had almost said, in the annals of the world.

But some may even think that our white brethren and friends are making such mighty efforts, for the amelioration of our condition, that we may stand as neutral spectators of the work. That we have many good friends yea, very good, among that body, perhaps none but a few of these who have ever read at all will deny; and that many of them have gone, and will go, all lengths for our good, is evident, from the very works of the great, the good, and the godlike Granville Sharpe, Wilberforce, Lundy, and the truly patriotic and lamented Mr. Ashmun, late Colonial Agent of Liberia, who, with a zeal which was only equalled by the goodness of his heart, has lost his life in our cause, and a host of others too numerous to mention: a number of private gentlemen too, who, though they say but little, are nevertheless, busily engaged for good.

---

41. The first enslaved Africans in British America were brought to Jamestown, Virginia, by English colonists in 1619.

Now, all of those great, and indeed, good friends whom God has given us, I do humbly, and very gratefully acknowledge. But, that we should co-operate with them, as far as we are able by uniting and cultivating a spirit of friendship and of love among us, is obvious, from the very exhibition of our miseries, under which we groan.

Two millions and a half of colored people in these United States, more than five hundred thousand of whom are about two-thirds of the way free. Now, I ask, if no more than these last were united (which they must be, or always live as enemies) and resolved to aid and assist each other to the utmost of their power, what mighty deeds would be done by them of the good of our cause?

But, Mr. President, instead of a general compliance with these requisitions, which have a natural tendency to raise us in the estimation of the world, we see, to our sorrow, in the very midst of us, a gang of villains, who, for the paltry sum of fifty or a hundred dollars, will kidnap and sell into perpetual slavery, their fellow creatures! And, too, if one of their fellow sufferers, whose miseries are a little more enhanced by the scourges of a tyrant, should abscond from his pretended owner, to take a little recreation, and unfortunately fall in their way, he is gone! for they will sell him for a glass of whiskey!

Brethren and fellow sufferers, I ask you, in the name of God, and of Jesus Christ, shall we suffer such notorious villains to rest peaceably among us? Will they not take our wives and little ones, more particularly our little ones, when a convenient opportunity will admit, and sell them for money, to slave holders, who will doom them to chains, handcuffs, and even unto death? May God open our eyes on those children of the devil and enemies of all good!

But, sir, this wickedness is scarcely more infernal than that which was attempted a few months since, against the government of our brethren, the Haytiens, by a consummate rogue, who out to have, long since, been haltered, but who, I was recently informed, is nevertheless, received into company among some of our most respectable men, with a kind of brotherly affection which ought to be shown only to a gentleman of honor.

Now, Mr. President, all such mean, and more than disgraceful actions as these, are powerful auxiliaries, which work for our destruction, and which are abhorred in the sight of God and of good men. But, sir, I cannot but bless God for the glorious anticipation of a not very distant period, when these things which now help to degrade us will no more be practiced among the sons of Africa, – for, though this, and perhaps another, generation may not experience the promised blessings of Heaven, yet, the dejected, degraded, and now enslaved children of Africa will have, in spite of all their enemies, to take their stand among the nations of the earth.

And, sir, I verily believe that God has something in reserve for us, which, when he shall have parceled it out upon us will repay us for all our suffering and miseries.

9. Robert Knox, 'Lecture on the Races of Men' (Manchester, 1848)

The public lectures of Scottish zoologist Robert Knox (1791–1862) on 'ethnology' made him one of the most influential popularisers of the mid-Victorian racial pseudo-science. After a career as a professor of anatomy in Edinburgh and Glasgow was cut short due to his involvement in the Burke and Hare body-snatching affair, Knox left university teaching in the late 1840s for a life of public lecturing throughout England before paying audiences. 'At that time,' he recalls, 'I had the great question of race, the all-absorbing question of the day, wholly to myself . . . [and] ample reports were made of my lectures and published in the newspaper press.'[42]

These talks made the essentialist argument that all 'human character, individual, social [and] national', could be traced back to 'the all-pervading, unalterable, physical character of race'.[43] Primarily a polygenist, Knox argued that different races of people were distinct species with different aptitudes and qualities. Though he held progressive abolitionist and anti-colonialist views, his crude characterisations of racial distinctions none the less lent broad intellectual support to anti-Semitism and multiple forms of mainstream nineteenth-century racisms. Upon their publication in 1850, his lectures exerted an enduring transatlantic influence.

Source

Robert Knox, *The Races of Men* (Philadelphia: Lea and Blanchard, 1850).

'There is but one animal' said Geoffroy,[44] 'not many;' and to this vast and philosophic view, the mind of Cuvier[45] himself, towards the close of life, gradually approached. It is, no doubt, the correct one. Applied to man, the doctrine amounts to this, – Mankind is of one family, one origin. In every embryo is the type of all the races of men; the circumstances determining these various races of men, as they now, and have existed, are as yet unknown; but they exist, no doubt, and must be physical; regulated by secondary laws, changing, slowly or suddenly, the existing order of things. The idea of new creations, or of any creation saving that of living matter is wholly inadmissible. The world is composed of matter, not of mind. The circumstances giving rise, then, to the specializations of animal

---

42. Robert Knox, *The Races of Men* (Philadelphia: Lea and Blanchard, 1850), p. xi.
43. Knox, *The Races of Men*, p. xii.
44. Etienne Geoffroy Saint-Hilaire (1772–1844), French naturalist, who established the 'unity of composition' theory, whereby all animals were formed of the same elements.
45. Georges Cuvier (1769–1832), French naturalist and polygenist, who believed in three distinct races: Caucasian, Mongol and Ethiopian.

and vegetable forms, giving them a permanency of some thousand years, are as yet unknown to us, and may for ever remain so; but that is no reason why they should not be inquired into. Some speculations into this, the most important of all human inquiries, will be found in the notes appended to this lecture.

In conclusion: the permanent varieties of men, permanent at least seemingly during the historic period, originate in laws elucidated in part by embryology, by the laws of unity of the organization, in a word, by the great laws of transcendental anatomy. Variety is deformity; deviation from one grand type towards which Nature, by her laws of specialization, constantly aims: those laws which, once established, terminated the reign of chaos. To every living thing they give a specific character, enduring at least for a time; man also has his specific character to endure for a time. Certain forms, certain deviations, in obedience to the great and universal law of unity, are not viable in the existing order of things; but they may become so. If the deformity, that is, a return more or less to unity, be too great, too antagonistic of her specific laws, the individual, whether man or mere animal or plant, ceases to be, and thus the extension of variety of forms, which we call 'deformations,' ceases.

The perfect type of man was discovered by the ancient sculptors of Greece: it cannot be surpassed; all attempts to improve on it have failed. Towards this, nature constantly tends. Certain races seem to be approaching the condition of non-viable races; it would seem as if their course was run: they hold the same position to mankind as the individual or family in whom the laws of unity, superseding in part the laws of specialization have given rise to deformations, monstrosities, incompatible with reproduction, or with individual life. These races may then probably disappear, and this may be the fate of man himself under every form, his intellectual nature notwithstanding.

For millions and millions of years the world rolled through space without him; his absence was not felt; he hopes his presence to be now eternal: Creature of yesterday! Such would have been the language of the ancient saurian,[46] could they have spoken – 'Look at our might, our strength; look at the glorious world around; the vast and beauteous forms which everywhere decorate the earth. This can never come to a close.' But it did, and that frequently too: from the past, judge of the future.

10. Ida B. Wells, 'Lynch Law in All Its Phases' (Boston, 1893)

The murder of black Americans by public mobs, often on the spurious grounds of alleged crimes, was a chief means of domestic terrorism in the post-Reconstruction US. The activist, journalist and researcher Ida B. Wells (1862–1931) emerged in the 1890s as the most important national critic raising awareness of lynching and championing its legal redress.

---

46. Antiquated term for general grouping of reptiles and lizards.

Born into slavery in Mississippi in 1862, Wells raised her brothers and sisters following their parents' death from yellow fever in 1878. Educated briefly at the historically black Rust College before moving to Memphis, she became a teacher before being fired for her agitation against public transport segregation. Turning to a career as journalist, she began by reporting on the People's Grocery Lynchings, in which several associates were murdered. When her writings led to a public backlash, she fled Tennessee for Chicago, where she became a noted public speaker as part of her quest to forge an anti-lynching alliance across national civic institutions and churches, even embarking on two speaking tours of England between 1893 and 1894.

In speeches like that excerpted below, delivered at Boston's Tremont Temple on 13 February 1893, Wells narrated her journey towards activism, and placed lynching within a historical lineage of racial oppression and white resentment. In doing so, she also confronted the complacency of white women in the women's rights movement who ignored lynching. The text below extracts some key moments from her long speech, including the closing invocation of 'My Country! 'Tis of Thee', which anticipated Martin Luther King's identical gesture of redemptive patriotism in his most famous speech seven decades later.

Source

Philip S. Foner and Robert J. Branham, *Lift Every Voice: African American Oratory, 1787–1900* (Tuscaloosa: University of Alabama Press, 1998).

I am before the American people to day through no inclination of my own, but because of a deep seated conviction that the country at large does not know the extent to which lynch law prevails in parts of the Republic nor the conditions which force into exile those who speak the truth. I cannot believe that the apathy and indifference which so largely obtains regarding mob rule is other than the result of ignorance of the true situation. And yet, the observing and thoughtful must know that in one section, at least, of our common country, a government of the people, by the people, and for the people, means a government by the mob; where the land of the free and home of the brave means a land of lawlessness, murder and outrage; and where liberty of speech means the license of might to destroy the business and drive from home those who exercise this privilege contrary to the will of the mob. Repeated attacks on the life, liberty and happiness of any citizen or class of citizens are attacks on distinctive American institutions; such attacks imperiling as they do the foundation of government, law and order, merit the thoughtful consideration of far sighted Americans; not from a standpoint of sentiment, not even so much from a standpoint of justice to a weak race, as from a desire to preserve our institutions.

The race problem or negro question, as it has been called, has been omni-present and all pervading since long before the Afro-American was raised from the degradation of the slave to the dignity of the citizen. It has never been settled because the right methods have not been employed in the solution. It is the Banquo's ghost of politics, religion, and sociology which will not down at the bidding of those who are tormented with its ubiquitous appearance on every occasion. Times without number, since invested with citizenship, the race has been indicted for ignorance, immorality and general worthlessness, declared guilty and executed by its self-constituted judges. The operations of law do not dispose of negroes fast enough, and lynching bees have become the favorite pastime of the South. As excuse for the same, a new cry, as false as it is foul, is raised in an effort to blast race character, a cry which has proclaimed to the world that virtue and innocence are violated by Afro-Americans who must be killed like wild beasts to protect womanhood and childhood.

. . .

On the morning of March 9, the bodies of three of our best young men were found in an old field horribly shot to pieces.[47] These young men had owned and operated the 'People's Grocery,' situated at what was known as the Curve, a suburb made up almost entirely of colored people about a mile from city limits. . . . the mob, in obedience to a plan known to every eminent white man in the city, went to the jail between two and three in the morning, dragged out these young men, hatless and shoeless, put them on the yard engine of the railroad which was in waiting just behind the jail, carried them a mile north of the city limits and horribly shot them to death while the locomotive at a given signal let off steam and blew the whistle to deaden the sound of the firing. 'It was done by unknown men,' said the jury, yet the Appeal Avalanche which goes to press at 3 a.m., had a two column account of the lynching.

. . .

The lawlessness here described is not confined to one locality. In the past ten years over a thousand colored men, women and children have been butchered, murdered and burnt in all parts of the South. The details of these terrible outrages seldom reach beyond the narrow world where they occur. Those who commit the murders write the reports, and hence these blots upon the honor of a nation cause but a faint ripple on the outside world. They arouse no great indignation and call forth no adequate demand for justice. The victims were black, and the reports are so written as to make it appear that the helpless creatures deserved the fate which overtook them. Not so with the Italian lynching of 1891.[48] They were not black men, and

---

47. The People's Grocery Lynchings involved the murder on 9 March 1892 of several black grocers by a mob outside a jail in downtown Memphis.
48. The murder by a mob of eleven Italian Americans in New Orleans on 14 March 1891 for alleged involvement in the murder of a policeman. It is the single largest mass lynching in US history.

three of them were not citizens of the Republic, but subjects of the King of Italy. The chief of police of New Orleans was shot and eleven Italians arrested and charged with the murder; they were tried and the jury disagreed; the good, law abiding citizens of New Orleans thereupon took them from the jail and lynched them at high noon. A feeling of horror ran through the nation at this outrage. All Europe was amazed. The Italian government demanded thorough investigation and redress, and the Federal Government promised to give the matter the consideration which was its due. The diplomatic relations between the two countries became very much strained and for a while war talk was freely indulged. Here was a case where the power of the Federal Government to protect its own citizens and redeem its pledges to a friendly power was put to the test.

. . .

The general government is willingly powerless to send troops to protect the lives of its black citizens, but the state governments are free to use state troops to shoot them down like cattle, when in desperation the black men attempt to defend themselves, and then tell the world that it was necessary to put down a 'race war.'

Persons unfamiliar with the condition of affairs in the Southern States do not credit the truth when it is told them. They cannot conceive how such a condition of affairs prevails so near them with steam power, telegraph wires, and printing presses in daily and hourly touch with the localities where such disorder reigns. In a former generation the ancestors of these same people refused to believe that slavery was the 'league with death and the covenant with hell.' Wm. Lloyd Garrison declared it to be, until he was thrown into a dungeon in Baltimore,[49] until the signal lights of Nat Turner's lit the dull skies of Northampton County, and until sturdy old John Brown made his attack on Harper's Ferry.[50] When freedom of speech was martyred in the person of Elijah Lovejoy at Alton,[51] when the liberty of free discussion in Senate in the Nation's Congress was struck down in the person of the fearless Charles Sumner,[52] the Nation was at last convinced that slavery was not only a monster but a tyrant. That same tyrant is at work under a new name and guise.

. . .

---

49. The abolitionist William Lloyd Garrison was imprisoned for libel in Baltimore in 1830.

50. John Brown (1800–59) was a radical white abolitionist who led an armed insurrection against the Federal armoury at Harper's Ferry, Virginia, in October 1859, aiming to lead an armed slave revolt. He was executed following the failed uprising. The event is seen as a key stepping stone towards the outbreak of civil war in 1861.

51. Newspaper editor and abolitionist Elijah Parish Lovejoy was murdered in Alton, Illinois, in November 1837.

52. Charles Sumner (1811–74), abolitionist US Senator from Massachusetts and, later, an opponent of President Ulysses Grant's compromises on Reconstruction.

The voice of the people is the voice of God, I long with all the intensity of my soul for the Garrison, Douglass, Sumner, Whittier, and Phillips who shall rouse this nation to a demand that from Greenland's icy mountains to the coral reefs of the Southern seas, mob rule shall be put down and equal and exact justice be accorded to every citizen of whatever race, who finds a home within the borders of the land of the free and the home of the brave. Then no longer will our national hymn be sounding brass and a tinkling cymbal, but every member of this great composite nation will be a living, harmonious illustration of the words, and all can honestly and gladly join in singing:

> My country! 'tis of thee,
> Sweet land of liberty
> Of thee I sing.
> Land where our fathers died,
> Land of the Pilgrim's pride,
> From every mountain side
> Freedom does ring.

11. Alexander Crummell, 'The American Mind and Black Intellect' (Washington, DC, 1898)

Though such pseudo-scientific views on race were popular, they were also subject to challenge by black intellectuals throughout the nineteenth century. One of the most powerful of such critiques is contained in the speeches and writings of the American minister and African nationalist Alexander Crummell (1819–98), whose career was devoted to 'Negro elevation' and the repudiation of prevailing pseudo-scientific ideas about black inferiority.

Born a freeman in New York, he had a long career that saw him travel to England in the late 1840s, where he attended Cambridge University, before spending twenty years in Liberia exploring the solution of recolonising American blacks to Africa. Returning to the US in the 1870s, he founded a number of institutions for African American uplift, taught at Howard University and gained renown as a public speaker.

Through his writings and activism, Crummell became a pioneering exponent of pan-African ideas. W. E. B. Du Bois describes how, on hearing the elder man speak, that 'instinctively, I bowed before this man as one bows before the prophets of the world . . . in another age he might have say among the elders of the land in a purple-bordered toga'.[53]

---

53. Quoted in Philip S. Foner and Robert J. Branham, *Lift Every Voice: African American Oratory, 1787–1900* (Tuscaloosa: University of Alabama Press, 1998).

The text below excerpts key passages of the inaugural address he delivered, aged seventy-eight, to the American Negro Academy, in which he both critiques the limitations placed on African American flourishing and celebrates the manifold achievements of black intellect.

Source

Philip S. Foner and Robert J. Branham, *Lift Every Voice: African American Oratory, 1787–1900* (Tuscaloosa: University of Alabama Press, 1998).

For the first time in the history of this nation the colored people of America have undertaken the difficult task, of stimulating and fostering the genius of their race as a distinct and definite purpose. Other and many gatherings have been made, during our own two and a half centuries' residence on this continent, for educational purposes; but ours is the first which endeavors to rise up to the plane of culture. For my own part I have no misgivings either with respect to the legitimacy, the timeliness, or the prospective success of our venture.

The race in the brief period of a generation, has been so fruitful in intellectual product, that the time has come for a coalescence of powers, and for reciprocity alike in effort and appreciation. I congratulate you, therefore, on this your first anniversary. To me it is, I confess, a matter of rejoicing that we have, as a people, reached a point where we have a class of men who will come together for purposes, so pure, so elevating, so beneficent, as the cultivation of mind, with the view of meeting the uses and the needs of our benighted people. I feel that if this meeting were the end of this Academy; if I could see that it would die this very day, I would nevertheless, cry out 'All hail!' even if I had to join in with the salutation 'farewell forever!'

. . .

The American mind has refused to foster and to cultivate the Negro intellect. Join to this a kindred fact, of which there is the fullest evidence. Impelled, at times, by pity, a modicum of schooling and training has been given the Negro; but even this, almost universally, with reluctance, with cold criticism, with microscopic scrutiny, with icy reservation, and at times, with ludicrous limitations.

Cheapness characterizes almost all the dominations of the American people to the Negro: Cheapness, in all the past, has been the regimen provided for the Negro in every line of his intellectual, as well as his lower life. And so, cheapness is to be the rule in the future, as well for his higher, as for his lower life: cheap wages and cheap food, cheap and rotten huts; cheap and dilapidated schools; cheap and stinted weeks of schooling; cheap meeting houses for worship; cheap and ignorant ministers; cheap theological training; and now, cheap learning, culture and civilization! Noble exceptions are found in the grand literary circles in which Mr. Howells moves manifest in his generous editing of our own Paul Dunbar's poems.[54]

But this generosity is not general, even in the world of American letters. You can easily see this in the attempt, now a days, to side track the Negro intellect, and to place it under limitations never laid upon any other class. The elevation of the Negro has been a moot question for a generation past. But even to day what do we find the general reliance of the American mind in determining this question? Almost universally the resort is to material agencies! The ordinary, and sometimes the extraordinary American is unable to see that the struggle of a degraded people for elevation is, in its very nature, a warfare, and that its main weapon is the cultivated and scientific mind.

Ask the great men of the land how this Negro problem is to be solved, and then listen to the answers that come from divers classes of our white fellow citizens. The merchants and traders of our great cities tell us 'The Negro must be taught to work;' and they will pour out their moneys by thousands to train him to toil. The clergy in large numbers, cry out 'Industrialism is the only hope of the Negro;' for this is the bed rock, in their opinion, of Negro evangelization! 'Send him to Manual Labor Schools,' cries out another set of philanthropists. 'Hic haec, hoc,' is going to prove the ruin of the Negro' says the Rev. Steele, an erudite Southern Savant. 'You must begin at the bottom with the Negro,' says another eminent author reached the bottom. Says the Honorable George T. Barnes,[55] of Georgia 'The kind of education the Negro should receive should not be very refined nor classical, but adapted to his present condition:' As though there is to be no future for the Negro.

And so you see that even now, late in the 19th century, in this land of learning and science, the creed is 'Thus far and no farther', i.e. for the American black man. One would suppose from the universal demand for the mere industrialism for this race of ours, that the Negro had been going daily to dinner parties, eating terrapin and indulging in champagne; and returning home at night, sleeping on beds of eiderdown; breakfasting in the morning in his bed, and then having his valet to clothe him daily in purple and fine linen all these 250 years of his sojourn in this land. And then, just now, the American people, tired of all this Negro luxury, was calling him, for the first time, to blister his hands with the hoe, and to learn to supply his needs by sweatful toil in the cotton fields.

----

54. Paul Dunbar (1872–1906) was a black American poet most famous for his verse written in 'negro dialect'.

55. George Thomas Barnes (1833–1901), Georgia state legislator and US Congressman.

Listen a moment, to the wisdom of a great theologian, and withal as great philanthropist, the Rev. Dr. Wayland, of Philadelphia.[56] Speaking, not long since, of the 'Higher Education' of the colored people of the South, he said

'that this subject concerned about 8,000,000 of our fellow citizens, among whom are probably 1,500,000 voters. The education suited to these people is that which should be suited to white people under the same circumstances. These people are bearing the impress which was left on them by two centuries of slavery and several centuries of barbarism. This education must begin at the bottom. It must first of all produce the power of self support to assist them to better their condition. It should teach them good citizenship and should build them up morally. It should be, first, a good English education. They should be imbued with the knowledge of the Bible. They should have an industrial education. An industrial education leads to self support and to the elevation of their condition. Industry is itself largely an education, intellectually and morally, and, above all, an education of character. Thus we should make these people self dependent. This education will do away with pupils being taught Latin and Greek, while they do not know the rudiments of English.'[57]

Just notice the cautious, restrictive, limiting nature of this advice! Observe the lack of largeness, freedom and generosity in it. Dr. Wayland, I am sure, has never specialized just such a regimen for the poor Italians, Hungarians or Irish, who swarm, in lowly degradation, in immigrant ships to our shores. No! for them he wants, all Americans want, the widest, largest culture of the land; the instant opening, not simply of the common schools; and then an easy passage to the bar, the legislature, and even the judgeships of the nation. And they oft times get there. But how different the policy with the Negro. He must have 'an education which begins at the bottom.' 'He should have an industrial education,' &c. His education must, first of all, produce the power of self support, &c. Now, all this thought of Dr. Wayland is all true.

But, my friends, it is all false, too; and for the simple reason that it is only half truth. Dr. Wayland seems unable to rise above the plane of burden bearing for the Negro. He seems unable to gauge the idea of the Negro becoming a thinker. He seems to forget that a race of thoughtless toilers are destined to be forever a race of senseless boys; for only beings who think are men. How pitiable it is

---

56. Heman Lincoln Wayland, son of Francis Wayland (1796–1865), Baptist educator, after whom the Wayland Seminary was named in Washington, DC, founded in 1867 to educate former slaves.

57. Heman Lincoln Wayland, 'Instruction of the Colored Citizens', *Journal of Social Science*, 34 (November 1896): 78–83.

to see a great good man be fuddled by a half truth. For to allege 'Industrialism' to be the grand agency in the elevation of a race of already degraded laborers, is as much a mere platitude as to say, 'they must eat and drink and sleep;' for man cannot live without these habits. But they never civilize man; and civilization is the objective point in the movement for Negro elevation. Labor, just like eating and drinking, is one of the inevitabilities of life; one of its positive necessities. And the Negro has had it for centuries; but it has never given him manhood. It does not now, in wide areas of population, lift him up to moral and social elevation. Hence the need of a new factor in his life. The Negro needs light: light thrown in upon all the circumstances of his life. The light of civilization.

. . .

These cheering occurrences, these demonstrations of capacity, give us the greatest encouragement in the large work which is before this Academy. Let us enter upon that work, this year, with high hopes, with large purposes, and with calm and earnest persistence. I trust that we shall bear in remembrance that the work we have undertaken is our special function; that it is a work which calls for cool thought, for laborious and tireless painstaking, and for clear discrimination; that it promises nowhere wide popularity, or, exuberant eclat; that very much of its ardent work is to be carried on in the shade; that none of its desired results will spring from spontaneity; that its most prominent features are the demands of duty to a needy people; and that its noblest rewards will be the satisfaction which will spring from having answered a great responsibility, and having met the higher needs of a benighted and struggling Race.

4 Faith, Culture and Society

Introduction

Nineteenth-century religious culture was vibrant, energised by evangelical revivals and the flourishing of multiple new sects. Yet, in retrospect, it appears as an age in which faith lost its monopoly as a source of moral guidance. New study of scriptures and advances in science made it more difficult for many educated people to believe in religion's literal truth and to defer to the moral and rhetorical authority of preachers. The rippling effect of new ideas from Charles Fourier, Robert Owen, Charles Darwin and Karl Marx posed unprecedented challenges to faith and hierarchy. Some contemporaries famously perceived these shifts as loss. Matthew Arnold's poem 'Dover Beach' (1867) lamented the 'melancholy, long, withdrawing roar' of 'retreating' faith; Friedrich Nietzsche in 1873 thought 'the waters of religion are ebbing away and leaving behind swamps of stagnant ponds'.[1] The speeches in this chapter allow readers to explore the tensions between faith and two new forces that were filling this vacuum: the veneration of 'culture', and radical anti-hierarchical politics.

Religious ceremonies remained by far the most important means by which individuals experienced live extended speech. The first part of the chapter below ('The Role of Faith') explores the debates over how faith should be harnessed in increasingly plural societies. As the prominence of sermons in the abolition debate of Chapter 3 or the peace movement of Chapter 5 shows, one dominant response was that belief should be placed in the service of combating social ills. Two sermons below offer different visions. Jarena Lee, America's earliest recorded black female preacher, active in 1810s Philadelphia, testifies to the role of faith in sustaining institutions for the oppressed. In the next, the celebrity Baptist preacher prodigy Charles Spurgeon and his widely read sermons, in 1850s London, reveal the role that flamboyant calls to conversion could play, as what one observer called 'circus and theatre'[2] (Figure 11).

---

1. Friedrich W. Nietzsche and R. J. Hollingdale, *Untimely Meditations* (Cambridge: Cambridge University Press, 1997), p. 148.
2. Robert H. Ellison, *The Victorian Pulpit: Spoken and Written Sermons in Nineteenth Century Britain* (London: Associated Universities Press, 1998), p. 141.

This chapter also presents a paean to global ecumenical harmony by Swami Vivekananda, cultural ambassador for Hinduism, at the 1893 Chicago Columbian Exposition. The later nineteenth century was also the first time that a substantial number of public figures openly declared their lack of religious beliefs.[3] In Britain, secularist campaigner and MP Charles Bradlaugh's debates on atheism were public spectacles, matched in the US by his American counterpart Robert Ingersoll, 'The Great Agnostic', whose widely performed lecture on 'The Gods' is contained below.

The next part of the chapter ('Culture and Morality') presents speeches that exemplify the emerging role of art and culture as compensation for the diminished guidance of faith. It is an agenda most commonly associated with Arnold's *Culture and Anarchy* (1868), which argued that, by presenting a vision of perfection, culture could transform raw emotion and give life meaning.[4] The growing middle class found an ideal communal outlet for this quest in the newly emerging lecture circuit, which Ralph Waldo Emerson called 'the true Church of the coming time', in which authors served as lay preachers[5] (Figure 7). Selected below are extracts from his performance of his piece 'Ethics' before a Boston audience in 1837, debuting the secular reimagining of uplift that would become 'Self-Reliance', a seminal text in the history of American individualism. It is followed by a speech from the archetypal Victorian sage, art critic and social reformer John Ruskin, whose lecture 'Traffic' (1864) saw him rebuke a Yorkshire audience that had invited him to offer thoughts on their planned civic building, offering instead a secular sermon on the politics of taste.[6] This is followed by a selection from the young Oscar Wilde's American lecture tour of 1882, on which he introduced audiences to the new philosophy of aestheticism. The final selection comes from the socialist designer and poet William Morris, who used the form to explore the connections between 'Art and Socialism' (1884) in the English Midlands.

One of the aspirations of this reimagining of culture was, argued Arnold, to 'do away with classes; to make the best that has been thought and known in the world current everywhere'.[7] Others had far more radical visions of

---

3. Charles Bradlaugh, *Is the Bible Divine? A Six Nights' Discussion between Mr. Charles Bradlaugh and Mr. Robert Roberts* (London: F. Pitman, 1876).

4. Matthew Arnold, *Culture and Anarchy* (Oxford: Oxford University Press, 2006).

5. Ralph Orth and Alfred R. Ferguson (eds), *Journals and Miscellaneous Notebooks of Ralph Waldo Emerson*, 15 vols (Cambridge, MA: Harvard University Press, 1971), vol. IX, p. 71; see Tom F. Wright, 'Carlyle, Emerson and the Voiced Essay', in Thomas Karshan and Kathryn Murphy (eds), *The Literary Essay* (Oxford: Oxford University Press, 2019).

6. For studies of this genre see John Holloway, *The Victorian Sage: Studies in Argument* (London: Macmillan, 1953) and George Landow, *Elegant Jeremiahs: The Sage from Carlyle to Mailer* (Ithaca: Cornell University Press, 1986).

7. Arnold, *Culture and Anarchy*, p. 52.

how social hierarchies might be challenged. The final part of this chapter, on 'Society and Class', surveys some of the ways that orators throughout the period debated alternatives to monarchy, capital and oligarchy. This was the era of mass movement politics, in which reformers from Corn Law repealers to Chartists and socialists exerted political pressure through rallies and displays of support, addressed by speakers who increasingly framed the issues of the day in terms of economic class.[8]

The first example below comes from the flamboyant radical Henry 'Orator' Hunt, whose 1816 speech before thousands in Clerkenwell, London, presaged the police clampdown at his appearance in St Peter's Field, Manchester, three years later. To others, the egalitarian message and collectivist implications of Hunt's rhetoric, and that of the Chartist generation that followed, embodied the urgent threat of French revolutionary excess. The ruling class duly framed new arguments in its own defence, typified here by Benjamin Disraeli's impassioned support for the stability of feudalism and romantic social Toryism before an audience in his constituency of Shrewsbury in 1843.

The final three selections are all examples of how reformers in Gilded Age America argued back against what they saw as the exploitation of the workers by the forces of capitalism. The first comes from 'America's First Black Socialist', Peter Clark, defending collective action in the face of the Great Railroad Strikes of 1877. Also representing the ferment of left-wing thought in Chicago is anarchist Lucy Parsons, whose national notoriety following her husband's execution for his role in the 1886 Haymarket Riot, and whose speeches like the one below, denouncing capital and government, made her an icon of the *fin-de-siècle* left. The chapter is rounded off with one of the most celebrated speeches in US political history, the keynote address delivered by progressive Democrat leader and Presidential candidate for the election of 1896 William Jennings Bryan, taking aim at the economic injustice of the silver system.

---

8. Mary Fairclough, *The Romantic Crowd: Sympathy, Controversy and Print Culture* (Cambridge: Cambridge University Press, 2013).

Part A: The Role of Faith

1. Jarena Lee, 'My Call to Preach the Gospel' (Maryland, c.1810s)

Jarena Lee (1783–1864) was one of the first African American female preachers in America whose words survive. Born free in New Jersey and working in domestic service since childhood, she experienced a powerful evangelical conversion in her youth and joined former slave Richard Allen's African Methodist Episcopal Church. Experiencing overpowering 'voices' commanding her to preach, she eventually overcame the misgivings of her male associates and began delivering sermons on an itinerary circuit and holding prayer meetings.

For a woman of any race to be granted such authority was highly unusual in this period and her trailblazing placed her in danger. Accompanied by a female companion, Lee later wrote that she 'travelled two thousand three hundred and twenty-five miles, and preached one hundred and seventy-eight sermons'[9] to mixed gatherings of blacks and whites. Her diary records camp meetings at which slaves walked twenty miles to hear her speak. No records of Lee's preaching survive, but the account below of her decision to become a preacher from her 1844 autobiography provides a vivid sense of the sermonising style of the era in American Christianity known as the Second Great Awakening.

Source

Jarena Lee, *Religious Experience and Journal of Mrs. Jarena Lee: Giving an Account of Her Call to Preach the Gospel* (Philadelphia: Printed and published for the author, 1849).

Between four and five years after my sanctification,[10] on a certain time, an impressive silence fell upon me, and I stood as if some one was about to speak to me, yet I had no such thought in my heart. – But to my utter surprise there seemed to sound a voice which I thought I distinctly heard, and most certainly understand, which said to me, 'Go preach the Gospel!' I immediately replied aloud, 'No one will believe me.' Again I listened, and again the same voice seemed to say – 'Preach the Gospel; I will put words in your mouth, and you will turn your enemies to become your friends.'

---

9. Priscilla Pope-Levison, *Turn the Pulpit Loose: Two Centuries of American Women Evangelists* (New York: Palgrave Macmillan, 2016).
10. It is estimated that the events narrated took place in 1817.

At first I supposed that Satan had spoken to me, for I had read that he could transform himself into an angel of light for the purpose of deception. Immediately I went into a secret place, and called upon the Lord to know if he had called me to preach, and whether I was deceived or not; when there appeared to my view the form and figure of a pulpit, with a Bible lying thereon, the back of which was presented to me as plainly as if it had been a literal fact.

In consequence of this, my mind became so exercised, that during the night following, I took a text and preached in my sleep. I thought there stood before me a great multitude, while I expounded to them the things of religion. So violent were my exertions and so loud were my exclamations, that I awoke from the sound of my own voice, which also awoke the family of the house where I resided. Two days after I went to see the preacher in charge of the African Society, who was the Rev. Richard Allen,[11] the same before named in these pages, to tell him that I felt it my duty to preach the gospel. But as I drew near the street in which his house was, which was in the city of Philadelphia, my courage began to fail me; so terrible did the cross appear, it seemed that I should not be able to bear it. Previous to my acting out to go to see him, so agitated was my mind, that my appetite for my daily food failed me entirely. Several times on my way there, I turned back again; but as often I felt my strength again renewed, and I soon found that the nearer I approached to the house of the minister, the less was my fear. Accordingly, as soon as I came to the door, my fears subsided, the cross was removed, all things appeared pleasant – I was tranquil.

I now told him, that the Lord had revealed it to me, that I must preach the gospel. He replied, by asking, in what sphere I wished to move in? I said, among the Methodists. He then replied, that a Mrs. Cook, a Methodist lady, had also some time before requested the same privilege; who, it was believed, had done much good in the way of exhortation, and holding prayer meetings; and who had been permitted to do so by the verbal license of the preacher in charge at the time. But as to women preaching, he said that our Discipline knew nothing at all about it – that it did not call for women preachers. This I was glad to hear, because it removed the fear of the cross – but no sooner did this feeling cross my mind, than I found that a love of souls had in a measure departed from me; that holy energy which burned within me, as a fire, began to be smothered. This I soon perceived.

O how careful ought we to be, lest through our by-laws of church government and discipline, we bring into disrepute even the word of life. For as unseemly as it may appear now-a-days for a woman to preach, it should be remembered that nothing is impossible with God. And why should it be thought impossible, heterodox, or improper for a woman to preach? seeing the Saviour died for the woman as well as for the man.

---

11. Richard Allen (1760–1831) founded the African Methodist Episcopal Church, the first black denomination in the United States, in 1794 in Philadelphia.

If the man may preach, because the Saviour died for him, why not the woman? seeing he died for her also. Is he not a whole Saviour, instead of a half one? as those who hold it wrong for a woman to preach, would seem to make it appear.

Did not Mary first preach the risen Saviour, and is not the doctrine of the resurrection the very climax of Christianity – hangs not all our hope on this, as argued by St Paul?[12] Then did not Mary, a woman, preach the gospel? for she preached the resurrection of the crucified son of God.

But some will say that Mary did not expound the Scripture, therefore, she did not preach, in the proper sense of the term. To this I reply, it may be that the term preach in those primitive times, did not mean exactly what it is now made to mean; perhaps it was a great deal more simple then, than it is now – if it were not, the unlearned fishermen could not have preached the gospel at all, as they had no learning.

To this it may be replied, by those who are determined not to believe that it is right for a woman to preach, that the disciples, though they were fishermen and ignorant of letters too, were inspired so to do. To which I would reply, that though they were inspired, yet that inspiration did not save them from showing their ignorance of letters and of man's wisdom; this the multitude soon found out, by listening to the remarks of the envious Jewish priests. If then, to preach the gospel, by the gift of heaven, comes by inspiration solely, is God straitened: must he take the man exclusively? May he not, did he not, and can he not inspire a female to preach the simple story of the birth, life, death, and resurrection of our Lord, and accompany it too with power to the sinner's heart? As for me, I am fully persuaded that the Lord called me to labor according to what I have received, in his vineyard. If he has not, how could he consistently hear testimony in favor of my poor labors, in awakening and converting sinners?

2. Charles Spurgeon, 'Compel Them to Come In' (London, 1858)

Charles Haddon Spurgeon (1834–92) was one of Victorian England's best-known ministers. Born in rural Essex and largely self-educated, he converted to the Baptist Church as a teenager and began a remarkable career as a preacher prodigy, becoming chief minister at London's largest Baptist place of worship, New Park Street Church, while still in his early twenties. His flamboyant and combative sermons became enormously popular and the congregation soon outgrew its original venue, moving to ever larger premises throughout the capital (Figure 11). One observer at Spurgeon's meetings records 'a congregation consisting of

---

12. In Romans 16, Paul emphasised the key role of women in the Christian movement.

10,000 souls, streaming into the hall, mounting the galleries, humming, buzzing, and swarming – a mighty hive of bees – eager to secure at first the best places' before Spurgeon began speaking and 'a low, concentrated thrill and murmur of devotion, which seemed to run at once, like an electric current, through the breast of everyone present, and by this magnetic chain the preacher held us fast bound for about two hours'.[13]

However, Spurgeon was a divisive figure. Though some thought him the greatest British orator of his age, others criticised his theatrical 'animosity' towards his audience as sacrilegious and he was subject to critical media attacks throughout his career. His sermons were regularly reprinted and widely circulated. The example excerpted below from 1858 on a line from Luke 14: 23 (*'And the lord said unto the servant, Go out into the highways and hedges, and compel them to come in, that my house may be filled'*) gives an insight into how Spurgeon's plain-speaking pulpit style fused self-effacing candour with confrontational rebuke, as he called on all sinners to repent and enter the life of Jesus.

Source

C. H. Spurgeon, *Twelve Popular Sermons* (London: Passmore & Alabaster, 1860).

And now to the work – directly to the work. Unconverted, unreconciled, unregenerate men and women, I am to COMPEL YOU TO COME IN. Permit me first of all to accost you in the highways of sin and tell you over again my errand. The King of heaven this morning sends a gracious invitation to you. He says, 'As I live, saith the Lord, I have no pleasure in the death of him that dieth, but had rather that he should turn unto me and live:' 'Come now, and let us reason together, saith the Lord, though your sins be as scarlet they shall be as wool; though they be red like crimson they shall be whiter than snow.'

Dear brother, it makes my heart rejoice to think that I should have such good news to tell you, and yet I confess my soul is heavy because I see you do not think it good news, but turn away from it, and do not give it due regard. Permit me to tell you what the King has done for you. He knew your guilt, he foresaw that you would ruin yourself. He knew that his justice would demand your blood, and in order that this difficulty might be escaped, that his justice might have its full due, and that you might yet be saved, Jesus Christ hath died. Will you just for a moment glance at this picture. You see that man there on his knees in the garden of Gethsemane, sweating drops of blood. You see this next: you see

---

13. Walter Thorburry, *Old and New London: A Narrative of Its History, Its People, and Its Places* (London: Cassell, Petter, Galpin, 1881), p. 290.

that miserable sufferer tied to a pillar and lashed with terrible scourges, till the shoulder bones are seen like white islands in the midst of a sea of blood. Again you see this third picture; it is the same man hanging on the cross with hands extended, and with feet nailed fast, dying, groaning, bleeding; methought the picture spoke and said, 'It is finished.' Now all this hath Jesus Christ of Nazareth done, in order that God might consistently with his justice pardon sin; and the message to you this morning is this – 'Believe in the Lord Jesus Christ and thou shalt be saved.' That is trust him, renounce thy works, and thy ways, and set thine heart alone on this man, who gave himself for sinners.

Well brother, I have told you the message, what sayest thou unto it? Do you turn away? You tell me it is nothing to you; you cannot listen to it; that you will hear me by-and-by; but you will go your way this day and attend to your farm and merchandize. Stop brother, I was not told merely to tell you and then go about my business. No; I am told to compel you to come in; and permit me to observe to you before I further go, that there is one thing I can say – and to which God is my witness this morning, that I am in earnest with you in my desire that you should comply with this command of God. You may despise your own salvation, but I do not despise it; you may go away and forget what you shall hear, but you will please to remember that the things I now say cost me many a groan ere I came here to utter them. My inmost soul is speaking out to you, my poor brother, when I beseech you by him that liveth and was dead, and is alive for evermore, consider my master's message which he bids me now address to you.

But do you spurn it? Do you still refuse it? Then I must change my tone a minute. I will not merely tell you the message, and invite you as I do with all earnestness, and sincere affection – I will go further. Sinner, in God's name I command you to repent and believe. Do you ask me whence my authority? I am an ambassador of heaven. My credentials, some of them secret, and in my own heart; and others of them open before you this day in the seals of my ministry, sitting and standing in this hall, where God has given me many souls for my hire. As God the everlasting one hath given me a commission to preach his gospel, I command you to believe in the Lord Jesus Christ; not on my own authority, but on the authority of him who said, 'Go ye into all the world and preach the gospel to every creature;'[14] and then annexed this solemn sanction, 'He that believeth and is baptized shall be saved, but he that believeth not shall be damned.' Reject my message, and remember 'He that despised Moses's law, died without mercy under two or three witnesses: of how much sorer punishment, suppose ye, shall he be thought worthy, who hath trodden under foot the Son of God.' An ambassador is not to stand below the man with whom he deals, for we stand higher. If the minister chooses to take his proper rank, girded with the omnipotence of God, and anointed with his holy unction, he

---

14. Mark 16: 15.

is to command men, and speak with all authority compelling them to come in: 'command, exhort, rebuke with all long-suffering.'

But do you turn away and say you will not be commanded? Then again will I change my note. If that avails not, all other means shall be tried. My brother, I come to you simple of speech, and I exhort you to flee to Christ. O my brother, dost thou know what a loving Christ he is? Let me tell thee from my own soul what I know of him. I, too, once despised him. He knocked at the door of my heart and I refused to open it. He came to me, times without number, morning by morning, and night by night; he checked me in my conscience and spoke to me by his Spirit, and when, at last, the thunders of the law prevailed in my conscience, I thought that Christ was cruel and unkind. O I can never forgive myself that I should have thought so ill of him. But what a loving reception did I have when I went to him. I thought he would smite me, but his hand was not clenched in anger but opened wide in mercy. I thought full sure that his eyes would dart lightning-flashes of wrath upon me; but, instead thereof, they were full of tears. He fell upon my neck and kissed me; he took off my rags and did clothe me with his righteousness, and caused my soul to sing aloud for joy; while in the house of my heart and in the house of his church there was music and dancing, because his son that he had lost was found, and he that was dead was made alive.

I exhort you, then, to look to Jesus Christ and to be lightened. Sinner, you will never regret, – I will be bondsman for my Master that you will never regret it, – you will have no sigh to go back to your state of condemnation; you shall go out of Egypt and shall go into the promised land and shall find it flowing with milk and honey. The trials of Christian life you shall find heavy, but you will find grace will make them light. And as for the joys and delights of being a child of God, if I lie this day you shall charge me with it in days to come. If you will taste and see that the Lord is good, I am not afraid but that you shall find that he is not only good, but better than human lips ever can describe.

3. Robert Ingersoll, 'The Gods' (Fairbury, Illinois, 1873)

Amid the political and scientific upheavals of the late nineteenth century, the seeds of a renewed rhetoric of secular humanism was emerging. When Robert Ingersoll (1833–99) debuted a new lecture on 'The Gods' in Fairbury, Illinois, in 1873, the local Peoria *Democrat* newspaper accused him of seeking 'to overthrow the very foundations upon which rest our entire system of morals . . . he is an enemy of man as well as God'.

Known with both affection and scorn as 'The Great Agnostic', Ingersoll was one of the most popular orators of his age and a key figure in American atheism, whom thousands would come to hear make the case against organised belief.[15] The son of a Methodist minister, Ingersoll rose to become Republican Attorney General of Illinois before turning his talents for public speaking to the lecture circuit. Lecturing made him a major celebrity, crisscrossing the nation speaking before packed houses on topics ranging from Shakespeare to civil rights.

However, his most consequential theme was the rational case for agnosticism. An early populariser of Charles Darwin and a tireless advocate of science and reason, Ingersoll gave many speeches that ridiculed religion, while counselling respect for the dignity of believers. His unorthodox religious views cost him the political career he craved, but speeches such as the one extracted below continue to provide a model for the humanist and atheistic movements today.

Source

Robert G. Ingersoll, *The Works of Robert G. Ingersoll* (New York: Dresden, 1901).

EACH nation has created a god, and the god has always resembled his creators. He hated and loved what they hated and loved, and he was invariably found on the side of those in power. Each god was intensely patriotic, and detested all nations but his own. All these gods demanded praise, flattery, and worship. Most of them were pleased with sacrifice, and the smell of innocent blood has ever been considered a divine perfume. All these gods have insisted upon having a vast number of priests, and the priests have always insisted upon being supported by the people, and the principal business of these priests has been to boast about their god, and to insist that he could easily vanquish all the other gods put together.

These gods have been manufactured after numberless models, and according to the most grotesque fashions. Some have a thousand arms, some a hundred heads, some are adorned with necklaces of living snakes, some are armed with clubs, some with sword and shield, some with bucklers, and some have wings as a cherub; some were invisible, some would show themselves entire, and some would only show their backs; some were jealous, some were foolish, some turned themselves into men, some into swans, some into bulls, some into doves, and some into Holy Ghosts, and made love to the beautiful daughters of men. Some were married – all ought to have been – and some were considered as old bachelors from all eternity. Some had children, and the children were

---

15. Orvin P. Larson, *American Infidel: The Life of Robert Ingersoll* (New York: Pickle Partners, 2016).

turned into gods and worshiped as their fathers had been. Most of these gods were revengeful, savage, lustful, and ignorant. As they generally depended upon their priests for information, their ignorance can hardly excite our astonishment.

These gods did not even know the shape of the worlds they had created, but supposed them perfectly flat. Some thought the day could be lengthened by stopping the sun, that the blowing of horns could throw down the walls of a city, and all knew so little of the real nature of the people they had created, that they commanded the people to love them. Some were so ignorant as to suppose that man could believe just as he might desire, or as they might command, and that to be governed by observation, reason, and experience was a most foul and damning sin. None of these gods could give a true account of the creation of this little earth. All were woefully deficient in geology and astronomy. As a rule, they were most miserable legislators, and as executives, they were far inferior to the average of American presidents.

These deities have demanded the most abject and degrading obedience. In order to please them, man must lay his very face in the dust. Of course, they have always been partial to the people who created them, and have generally shown their partiality by assisting those people to rob and destroy others, and to ravish their wives and daughters.

Nothing is so pleasing to these gods as the butchery of unbelievers. Nothing so enrages them, even now, as to have some one deny their existence.

. . .

Reason, Observation and Experience – the Holy Trinity of Science – have taught us that happiness is the only good; that the time to be happy is now, and the way to be happy is to make others so. This is enough for us. In this belief we are content to live and die. If by any possibility the existence of a power superior to, and independent of, nature shall be demonstrated, there will then be time enough to kneel. Until then, let us stand erect.

Notwithstanding the fact that infidels in all ages have battled for the rights of man, and have at all times been the fearless advocates of liberty and justice, we are constantly charged by the church with tearing down without building again. The church should by this time know that it is utterly impossible to rob men of their opinions. The history of religious persecution fully establishes the fact that the mind necessarily resists and defies every attempt to control it by violence. The mind necessarily clings to old ideas until prepared for the new. The moment we comprehend the truth, all erroneous ideas are of necessity cast aside.

A surgeon once called upon a poor cripple and kindly offered to render him any assistance in his power. The surgeon began to discourse very learnedly upon the nature and origin of disease; of the curative properties of certain medicines; of the advantages of exercise, air and light, and of the various ways in which health and strength could be restored. These remarks were so full of good sense, and discovered so much profound thought and accurate knowledge, that the cripple, becoming thoroughly alarmed, cried out, 'Do not, I pray you, take away my crutches. They are my only support, and without them I should be miserable indeed!' 'I am not going,' said the surgeon, 'to take away your crutches. I am going to cure you, and then you will throw the crutches away yourself.'

For the vagaries of the clouds the infidels propose to substitute the realities of earth; for superstition, the splendid demonstrations and achievements of science; and for theological tyranny, the chainless liberty of thought.

We do not say that we have discovered all; that our doctrines are the all in all of truth. We know of no end to the development of man. We cannot unravel the infinite complications of matter and force. The history of one monad is as unknown as that of the universe; one drop of water is as wonderful as all the seas; one leaf, as all the forests; and one grain of sand, as all the stars.

We are not endeavoring to chain the future, but to free the present. We are not forging fetters for our children, but we are breaking those our fathers made for us. We are the advocates of inquiry, of investigation and thought. This of itself, is an admission that we are not perfectly satisfied with all our conclusions. Philosophy has not the egotism of faith. While superstition builds walls and creates obstructions, science opens all the highways of thought. We do not pretend to have circumnavigated everything, and to have solved all difficulties, but we do believe that it is better to love men than to fear gods; that it is grander and nobler to think and investigate for yourself than to repeat a creed. We are satisfied that there can be but little liberty on earth while men worship a tyrant in heaven. We do not expect to accomplish everything in our day; but we want to do what good we can, and to render all the service possible in the holy cause of human progress. We know that doing away with gods and supernatural persons and powers is not an end. It is a means to an end: the real end being the happiness of man.

Felling forests is not the end of agriculture. Driving pirates from the sea is not all there is of commerce.

We are laying the foundations of the grand temple of the future – not the temple of all the gods, but of all the people – wherein, with appropriate rites, will be celebrated the religion of Humanity. We are doing what little we can to hasten the coming of the day when society shall cease producing millionaires and mendicants – gorged indolence and famished industry – truth in rags, and superstition robed and crowned. We are looking for the time when the useful shall be the honorable; and when Reason, throned upon the world's brain, shall be the King of Kings, and God of Gods.

4. Swami Vivekananda, 'Address at the World's Parliament of Religions' (Chicago, 1893)

When Chicago held its famous World's Columbian Exposition in 1893, it also hosted the World Parliament of Religions, an unprecedented inter-faith dialogue event. One of the most notable speakers was Swami Vivekananda (1863–1902), the Indian spiritual leader and prominent disseminator of Hindu ideas in the West. Born to an upper-caste family in Bengal and educated in Western philosophy and Christianity, Vivekananda became a leading social reformer devoted to spreading education among the lower castes, and a public intellectual dedicated to raising Western understanding of Hinduism.

Below are two of the short addresses he made to the Chicago convention, including his celebrated opening speech, and a parable on mutual tolerance delivered a few days later to the same audience.

Source
Vivekananda, *Chicago Addresses* (Calcutta: Advaita Ashram, 1904).

'Opening Address'

Sisters and Brothers of America.

[At this moment came the three minute standing ovation from the audience of 7,000][16]

It fills my heart with joy unspeakable to rise in response to the warm and cordial welcome which you have given us. I thank you in the name of the most ancient order of monks in the world; I thank you in the name of the mother of religions; and I thank you in the name of millions and millions of Hindu people of all classes and sects.

My thanks also to some of the speakers on this platform who, referring to the delegates from the Orient, have told you that these men from far-off nations may well claim the honor of bearing to different lands the idea of toleration.

I am proud to belong to a religion which has taught the world both tolerance and universal acceptance. We believe not only in universal toleration but we accept all religions as true. I am proud to belong to a nation which has sheltered the persecuted and the refugees of all religions and all nations of the earth. I am proud to tell you that we have gathered in our bosom the purest remnant of the Israelites who came to Southern India[17] and took refuge with us in the very year in which their holy temple was shattered to pieces by Roman tyranny. I am proud to belong to the religion which has sheltered and is still fostering the remnant of the grand Zoroastrian nation.[18]

---

16. The Parliament of Religions took place in the World's Congress Auxiliary Building, which is now the Art Institute of Chicago.
17. Malabar Jews are the oldest Jewish community in India, present in modern-day Kerala as early as the twelfth century.
18. Zoroastrianism is the ancient Persian religion that shares many similarities with early forms of Hinduism.

I will quote to you brethren a few lines from a hymn which I remember to have repeated from my earliest childhood, which is every day repeated by millions of human beings: 'As the different streams having their sources in different places all mingle their water in the sea, so, O Lord, the different paths which men take through different tendencies, various though they appear, crooked or straight, all lead to Thee.'

The present convention, which is one of the most august assemblies ever held, is in itself a vindication, a declaration to the world of the wonderful doctrine preached in the Gita: 'Whosoever comes to me, though whatsoever form, I reach him; all men are struggling through paths which in the end lead to me.'

Sectarianism, bigotry, and its horrible descendant, fanaticism, have long possessed this beautiful Earth. They have filled the earth with violence, drenched it often and often with human blood, destroyed civilization, and sent whole nations to despair. Had it not been for these horrible demons, human society would be far more advanced than it is now.

But their time is come; and I fervently hope that the bell that tolled this morning in honor of this convention may be the death-knell of all fanaticism, of all persecutions with the sword or with the pen, and of all uncharitable feelings between persons wending their way to the same goal.

. . .

'Why we Disagree'

I will tell you a little story. You have heard the eloquent speaker who has just finished say, 'Let us cease from abusing each other,' and he was very sorry that there should be always so much variance.

But I think I should tell you a story which would illustrate the cause of this variance. A frog lived in a well. It had lived there for a long time. It was born there and brought up there, and yet was a little, small frog. Of course the evolutionists were not there then to tell us whether the frog lost its eyes or not, but, for our story's sake, we must take it for granted that it had its eyes, and that it every day cleansed the water of all the worms and bacilli that lived in it with an energy that would do credit to our modern bacteriologists. In this way it went on and became a little sleek and fat. Well, one day another frog that lived in the sea came and fell into the well.

'Where are you from?'

'I am from the sea.'

'The sea! How big is that? Is it as big as my well?' and he took a leap from one side of the well to the other.

'My friend,' said the frog of the sea, 'how do you compare the sea with your little well?'

Then the frog took another leap and asked, 'Is your sea so big?'

'What nonsense you speak, to compare the sea with your well!'

'Well, then,' said the frog of the well, 'nothing can be bigger than my well; there can be nothing bigger than this; this fellow is a liar, so turn him out.'

That has been the difficulty all the while.

I am a Hindu. I am sitting in my own little well and thinking that the whole world is my little well. The Christian sits in his little well and thinks the whole world is his well. The Mohammedan sits in his little well and thinks that is the whole world. I have to thank you of America for the great attempt you are making to break down the barriers of this little world of ours, and hope that, in the future, the Lord will help you to accomplish your purpose.

Part B: **Culture and Morality**

5. Ralph Waldo Emerson, 'Ethics' (Boston, 1837)

Ralph Waldo Emerson (1809–82) was one of the most influential figures in American literary history. He was the guiding spirit of the Transcendentalist philosophical movement, and his rhetoric helped shape the cultural nationalism of the Jacksonian era. After abandoning a promising Boston preaching career, he developed a reputation as an essayist, poet and prolific public lecturer on the speaking network known as the American 'Lyceum Movement', a type of institution named after the Athenian teaching ground of the Greek philosopher Aristotle. By the 1840s, he had become one of the transatlantic circuit's most celebrated speakers, performing in lecture rooms and town halls across the US, and on a triumphant tour of Britain during 1847–8.[19]

In February 1837, the year of the publication of his most famous work, *Nature,* Emerson delivered a series of lectures on 'The Philosophy of History' at the Masonic Temple in Boston. His talk on 'Ethics' was one of several speeches in which he developed material that would eventually see publication under the title 'Self-Reliance' in his *Essays: First Series (1841).* These inspirational reflections on the potential of the democratic self would live on beyond the lecture hall to become one of the major social texts of American individualism, informing later strains of thought ranging from anti-slavery to libertarianism, and from business culture to the modern rhetoric of self-help. By returning to the original lecture source here, the following excerpts from the 16 February script give a sense of the idiosyncratic diction, sonically patterned prose and digressive looseness experienced by his original lyceum audiences.

Source

Ralph W. Emerson, *The Early Lectures of Ralph Waldo Emerson,* ed. Stephen E. Whicher (Cambridge, MA: Belknap Press, 1964).

Thus in all ways the human soul goes forth to make its law and refuses to accept any influence than spiritual. Foolish men encumber life with artificial forms and weave evermore the web of pretension and hypocrisy. The soul substitutes always being for seeming, as in petrifaction a particle of stone replaces a particle

---

19. See Tom F. Wright, *Lecturing the Atlantic: Speech, Print and an Anglo-American Commons* (Oxford: Oxford University Press, 2017).

of wood. But all the art of the plausible is vain. Manner never did the work of matter. 'What hath he done?' is the divine question which searches men and transpierces the paper shield of every false reputation. A fop may sit in any chair of the world nor be distinguished for his hour from Homer and Washington; but there can never be any doubt concerning the respective abilities of human beings when we seek the truth. Pretension may sit still, but cannot act. Pretension never feigned an act of real greatness. Pretension never wrote an *Iliad*; nor drove back Xerxes; nor Christianized the world; nor abolished slavery.[20]

The obvious inference from these laws is the one maxim which makes the whole Ethics of the Mind, Self-Trust, that is, not a faith in man's own whim or conceit as if he were quite severed from all other beings and acted on his own private account, but a perception that the mind common to the Universe is disclosed to the individual through his own nature. Ascend a mile where you will and the barometer indicates the same levity of air. Rise to a certain height of thought and you behold and predict that which is true for all men in all times. Nothing is sacred but the integrity of one's mind. Absolve yourself and you shall have the suffrage of the world. Stick by yourself and mankind shall leap and run to be of your opinion. Speak your privatest thought and it shall be universal sentiment, for always the inmost becomes the outmost, and our first thought the Last Judgement. That statement only is fit to be made public which you have got at attempting to satisfy your own curiosity. The place where you are is your workyard. The work you can do is your office. The friend you love is your ordained yokefellow. Insist on yourself, never imitate. For your own gift you can present every moment with all the force of a lifetime's cultivation, but can sustain it on the basis of the world but of the adopted talent of another, you have only an extemporaneous half possession.

Be true to yourself. I have seen boys in their play put a shovel under the feet of one of their mates and trip him up. The boy standing on the shovel resembles the man's state who does not rely upon himself. The sincere man who does without second thought that which he is prompted to do, stands upon the basis of the world; he is not an individual so much as he is the hands and the tongue of nature itself. Could he be wholly of this mind he would be strictly omnipotent because his will conspiring with the divine will, his will being the mere effluence of the Reason, he would behold what he willed done.

To believe your own thought – to believe that what is true for you, in your private heart, is true for all men, – that is genius. Familiar as the voice of the mind is to each, the highest merit we ascribe to Moses, Plato, and Milton,[21] is that they set at nought books and traditions, and spoke not what other men,

---

20. In addition to the reference to Homer, Emerson here invokes the fate of Xerxes the Great (ruled 486–465 BCE), King of the Persian Achaemenid Empire, defeated by the Greeks in 480 BCE.

21. The Abrahamic prophet Moses; the ancient Greek philosopher Plato (c.427–347 BCE); and the English Puritan poet John Milton (1608–74).

but what they thought − . Yet this principle, in practical life as arduous as in the intellectual, may serve for the whole distinction betwixt men. It is the harder because you will always find those who think they know what is your duty better than you know it yourself. It is easy in the world to live after the world's opinion. It is easy in solitude to live after our own. But the great man is he who in the midst of the crowd keeps with perfect sweetness the independence of solitude.

Whilst thus the sufficient role of Ethics is comprised in the Stoical precept, Reverence Thyself, explained by Christianity that in the heart of man, is the sanctions and reward that goes along with it, is the perfect system of Compensation which pervades nature, and which though too subtle and simple to be reduced to a science and formally taught, yet finds utterance in a thousand proverbs, in old oracles, in fables and in history.

An eye for an eye; a tooth for a tooth; blood for blood; measure for measure; love for love; Give and it shall be given you. He that watereth shall be watered himself. 'What will you have?' Quoth God; 'pay for it and take it.' Who doth not work, shall not eat. Nothing venture, nothing have. It is written on the tomb of a Shah of Persia. 'Thou shalt be paid exactly for what thou hast done; no more; no less' − Curses are chickens that come home to roost. − Thefts never enrich. Alms never impoverish, and Murder will speak out of stone walls. Self-abasement is self-exaltation. Giving is receiving. The lover is loved.

. . .

And so it always is, the good institution, statute or action which you project now must meet the brunt of passion and ignorance, but slowly it shall find friends, and when you are not in the earth it shall survive and be owned by good and bad alike, and according to what sincere benefit is in it, shall flourish and multiply and nations repose in its shade. Sufficient unto the brave good man is his own purpose and his own superiority to the hostility of the world.

6. John Ruskin, 'Traffic' (Bradford, 1864)

In Britain, a comparative culture of public lectures by prominent figures grew up as part of the Mechanics Institute movement, of particular importance in the industrial cities of Scotland and Northern England. These venues offered some of the foremost public intellectuals of the day a medium through which to engage directly with the public. The text below captures a famous moment when the eminent Victorian cultural critic John Ruskin (1819–1900) did just this, confronting an audience of merchants in Bradford, Yorkshire, with a strident critique of popular taste.

Passionate about reforming the moral and social condition of his 'blind and wandering fellow-men', through an education in art and aesthetics, Ruskin became one of the Victorian era's most influential and controversial critics. In this capacity, in 1864 he was invited by the civic leaders of Bradford to speak before the town to give his opinion on potential designs for their new wool exchange. Instead of addressing this brief, Ruskin launched instead into an invective on the very premise of their invitation, sternly challenging what he saw as his industrial audience's hypocrisy and exploring the relationship between capitalism, taste and morality.

Source

John Ruskin, *The Crown of Wild Olive: Three Lectures on Work, Traffic and War* (London: Smith, Elder, 1866).

My good Yorkshire friends, you asked me down here among your hills that I might talk to you about this Exchange you are going to build:[22] but earnestly and seriously asking you to pardon me, I am going to do nothing of the kind. I cannot talk, or at least can say very little, about this same Exchange. I must talk of quite other things, though not willingly; – I could not deserve your pardon, if when you invited me to speak on one subject, I wilfully spoke on another. But I cannot speak, to purpose, of anything about which I do not care; and most simply and sorrowfully I have to tell you, in the outset, that I do not care about this Exchange of yours.

If, however, when you sent me your invitation, I had answered, 'I won't come, I don't care about the Exchange of Bradford,' you would have been justly offended with me, not knowing the reasons of so blunt a carelessness. So I have come down, hoping that you will patiently let me tell you why, on this, and many other such occasions, I now remain silent, when formerly I should have caught at the opportunity of speaking to a gracious audience.

In a word, then, I do not care about this Exchange, – because you don't; and because you know perfectly well I cannot make you. Look at the essential circumstances of the case, which you, as business men, know perfectly well, though perhaps you think I forget them. You are going to spend 30,000£, which to you, collectively, is nothing; the buying of a new coat is, as to the cost of it, a much more important matter of consideration to me than building a new Exchange is to you. But you think you may as well have the right thing for your money. You know there are a great many odd styles of architecture about; you don't want to do anything ridiculous; you hear of me, among others, as a respectable architectural man-milliner: and you send for me, that I may tell you

---

22. The Bradford Wool Exchange was eventually built in Venetian Gothic style between 1864 and 1867, much to Ruskin's dismay.

the leading fashion; and what is, in our shops, for the moment, the newest and sweetest thing in pinnacles.

Now, pardon me for telling you frankly, you cannot have good architecture merely by asking people's advice on occasion. All good architecture is the expression of national life and character; and it is produced by a prevalent and eager national taste, or desire for beauty. And I want you to think a little of the deep significance of this word 'taste;' for no statement of mine has been more earnestly or oftener controverted than that good taste is essentially a moral quality. 'No,' say many of my antagonists, 'taste is one thing, morality is another. Tell us what is pretty; we shall be glad to know that; but preach no sermons to us.'

Permit me, therefore, to fortify this old dogma of mine somewhat. Taste is not only a part and an index of morality – it is the ONLY morality. The first, and last, and closest trial question to any living creature is, 'What do you like?' Tell me what you like, and I'll tell you what you are. Go out into the street, and ask the first man or woman you meet, what their 'taste' is, and if they answer candidly, you know them, body and soul. 'You, my friend in the rags, with the unsteady gait, what do you like?' 'A pipe and a quartern of gin.' I know you. 'You, good woman, with the quick step and tidy bonnet, what do you like?' 'A swept hearth and a clean tea-table, and my husband opposite me, and a baby at my breast.' Good, I know you also. 'You, little girl with the golden hair and the soft eyes, what do you like?' 'My canary, and a run among the wood hyacinths.' 'You, little boy with the dirty hands and the low forehead, what do you like?' 'A shy at the sparrows, and a game at pitch-farthing.' Good; we know them all now. What more need we ask?

'Nay,' perhaps you answer: 'we need rather to ask what these people and children do, than what they like. If they do right, it is no matter that they like what is wrong; and if they do wrong, it is no matter that they like what is right. Doing is the great thing; and it does not matter that the man likes drinking, so that he does not drink; nor that the little girl likes to be kind to her canary, if she will not learn her lessons; nor that the little boy likes throwing stones at the sparrows, if he goes to the Sunday school.' Indeed, for a short time, and in a provisional sense, this is true. For if, resolutely, people do what is right, in time they come to like doing it. But they only are in a right moral state when they have come to like doing it; and as long as they don't like it, they are still in a vicious state. The man is not in health of body who is always thirsting for the bottle in the cupboard, though he bravely bears his thirst; but the man who heartily enjoys water in the morning and wine in the evening, each in its proper quantity and time. And the entire object of true education is to make people not merely do the right things, but enjoy the right things – not merely industrious, but to love industry – not merely learned, but to love knowledge – not merely pure, but to love purity – not merely just, but to hunger and thirst after justice.

But you may answer or think, 'Is the liking for outside ornaments, – for pictures, or statues, or furniture, or architecture, – a moral quality?' Yes, most surely, if a rightly set liking. Taste for any pictures or statues is not a moral quality, but taste for good ones is. Only here again we have to define the word 'good.' I don't mean by 'good,' clever – or learned – or difficult in the doing. Take a picture by Teniers, of sots quarrelling over their dice: it is an entirely clever picture; so clever that nothing in its kind has ever been done equal to it; but it is also an entirely base and evil picture. It is an expression of delight in the prolonged contemplation of a vile thing, and delight in that is an 'unmannered,' or 'immoral' quality. It is 'bad taste' in the profoundest sense – it is the taste of the devils. On the other hand, a picture of Titian's, or a Greek statue, or a Greek coin, or a Turner landscape, expresses delight in the perpetual contemplation of a good and perfect thing. That is an entirely moral quality – it is the taste of the angels. And all delight in art, and all love of it, resolve themselves into simple love of that which deserves love. That deserving is the quality which we call 'loveliness' – (we ought to have an opposite word, hateliness, to be said of the things which deserve to be hated); and it is not an indifferent nor optional thing whether we love this or that; but it is just the vital function of all our being.

What we like determines what we are, and is the sign of what we are; and to teach taste is inevitably to form character. As I was thinking over this, in walking up Fleet Street the other day, my eye caught the title of a book standing open in a bookseller's window. It was – 'On the necessity of the diffusion of taste among all classes.' 'Ah,' I thought to myself, 'my classifying friend, when you have diffused your taste, where will your classes be? The man who likes what you like, belongs to the same class with you, I think. Inevitably so. You may put him to other work if you choose; but, by the condition you have brought him into, he will dislike the other work as much as you would yourself. You get hold of a scavenger, or a costermonger, who enjoyed the Newgate Calendar[23] for literature, and 'Pop goes the Weasel' for music. You think you can make him like Dante and Beethoven? I wish you joy of your lessons; but if you do, you have made a gentleman of him: – he won't like to go back to his costermongering.'

And so completely and unexceptionally is this so, that, if I had time to-night, I could show you that a nation cannot be affected by any vice, or weakness, without expressing it, legibly, and for ever, either in bad art, or by want of art; and that there is no national virtue, small or great, which is not manifestly expressed in all the art which circumstances enable the people possessing that virtue to produce.

7. Oscar Wilde, 'Art of the English Renaissance' (New York City, 1882)

Following in the wake of Charles Dickens a generation earlier, Oscar Wilde (1854–1900) was the most famous British author to tour the American lecture circuit. Aged just twenty-seven, he arrived in the US in 1881, intending to offer a series of lectures on the modern Aesthetic

---

23. A lowbrow popular publication reporting on crimes in London.

Movement, and hoping to encourage an appreciation for beauty in a country seen as overly devoted to commercial pursuits.

For his American audiences, Wilde inhabited the part of the aesthete, complete with flamboyant lecturing costume that guaranteed that he was widely covered and parodied in the popular press. In a carefully stage-managed trip, he entertained fashionable East Coast audiences familiar from the pages of Edith Wharton, yet also found time to have well-publicised encounters across the breadth of society, including famously drinking whisky with miners in Colorado.

The first speech of his tour was delivered before a standing room-only crowd at Chickering Hall, Manhattan, who heard the speech excerpted below. The standard version of events is that Wilde easily won an initially hostile audience over. Yet, as Michele Mendelssohn has revealed, this was largely a myth. His initial New York audiences found him 'painful' and compared his faltering delivery to that of a 'schoolboy'.[24] Gradually, his performances improved and, thanks to an unexpected demand for his speeches, Wilde extended his tour to over a year, carrying his secular sermons on aesthetics to audiences across America.

Source

Oscar Wilde, *Essays and Lectures* (London: Methuen, 1908).

IN the lecture which it is my privilege to deliver before you to-night I do not desire to give you any abstract definition of beauty at all.[25] For we who are working in art cannot accept any theory of beauty in exchange for beauty itself, and, so far from desiring to isolate it in a formula appealing to the intellect, we, on the contrary, seek to materialise it in a form that gives joy to the soul through the senses. We want to create it, not to define it. The definition should follow the work: the work should not adapt itself to the definition.

Nothing, indeed, is more dangerous to the young artist than any conception of ideal beauty: he is constantly led by it either into weak prettiness or lifeless abstraction: whereas to touch the ideal at all you must not strip it of vitality. You must find it in life and re-create it in art.

While, then, on the one hand I do not desire to give you any philosophy of beauty – for, what I want to-night is to investigate how we can create art, not how we can talk of it – on the other hand, I do not wish to deal with anything like a history of English art.

---

24. Michele Mendelssohn, *Making Oscar Wilde* (Oxford: Oxford University Press, 2018), p. 68.

25. Wilde's more critical listeners complained that this was an example of apophasis: the rhetorical device whereby a speaker brings up a subject by denying it.

To begin with, such an expression as English art is a meaningless expression. One might just as well talk of English mathematics. Art is the science of beauty, and Mathematics the science of truth: there is no national school of either. Indeed, a national school is a provincial school, merely. Nor is there any such thing as a school of art even. There are merely artists, that is all.

And as regards histories of art, they are quite valueless to you unless you are seeking the ostentatious oblivion of an art professorship. It is of no use to you to know the date of Perugino or the birthplace of Salvator Rosa:[26] all that you should learn about art is to know a good picture when you see it, and a bad picture when you see it. As regards the date of the artist, all good work looks perfectly modern: a piece of Greek sculpture, a portrait of Velasquez[27] – they are always modern, always of our time. And as regards the nationality of the artist, art is not national but universal. As regards archaeology, then, avoid it altogether: archaeology is merely the science of making excuses for bad art; it is the rock on which many a young artist founders and shipwrecks; it is the abyss from which no artist, old or young, ever returns. Or, if he does return, he is so covered with the dust of ages and the mildew of time, that he is quite unrecognisable as an artist, and has to conceal himself for the rest of his days under the cap of a professor, or as a mere illustrator of ancient history. How worthless archaeology is in art you can estimate by the fact of its being so popular. Popularity is the crown of laurel which the world puts on bad art. Whatever is popular is wrong.

As I am not going to talk to you, then, about the philosophy of the beautiful, or the history of art, you will ask me what I am going to talk about. The subject of my lecture to-night is what makes an artist and what does the artist make; what are the relations of the artist to his surroundings, what is the education the artist should get, and what is the quality of a good work of art.

Now, as regards the relations of the artist to his surroundings, by which I mean the age and country in which he is born. All good art, as I said before, has nothing to do with any particular century; but this universality is the quality of the work of art; the conditions that produce that quality are different. And what, I think, you should do is to realise completely your age in order completely to abstract yourself from it; remembering that if you are an artist at all, you will be not the mouthpiece of a century, but the master of eternity, that all art rests on a principle, and that mere temporal considerations are no principle at all; and that those who advise you to make your art representative of the nineteenth century are advising you to produce an art which your children, when you have them, will think old-fashioned. But you will tell me this is

---

26. Pietro Perugino (c.1446–1523) was an Umbrian School painter of the Italian Renaissance. Salvator Rosa (1615–73) was an Italian Baroque painter, whose dark scenes proved highly influential on painters of the Romantic Movement.
27. Diego Velázquez (c.1599–1660), Spanish painter of the Baroque period.

an inartistic age, and we are an inartistic people, and the artist suffers much in this nineteenth century of ours.

Of course he does. I, of all men, am not going to deny that. But remember that there never has been an artistic age, or an artistic people, since the beginning of the world. The artist has always been, and will always be, an exquisite exception. There is no golden age of art; only artists who have produced what is more golden than gold.

WHAT, you will say to me, the Greeks? were not they an artistic people? Well, the Greeks certainly not, but, perhaps, you mean the Athenians, the citizens of one out of a thousand cities. Do you think that they were an artistic people? Take them even at the time of their highest artistic development, the latter part of the fifth century before Christ, when they had the greatest poets and the greatest artists of the antique world, when the Parthenon rose in loveliness at the bidding of a Phidias,[28] and the philosopher spake of wisdom in the shadow of the painted portico, and tragedy swept in the perfection of pageant and pathos across the marble of the stage. Were they an artistic people then? Not a bit of it. What is an artistic people but a people who love their artists and understand their art? The Athenians could do neither.

How did they treat Phidias? To Phidias we owe the great era, not merely in Greek, but in all art – I mean of the introduction of the use of the living model. And what would you say if all the English bishops, backed by the English people, came down from Exeter Hall[29] to the Royal Academy[30] one day and took off Sir Frederic Leighton[31] in a prison van to Newgate on the charge of having allowed you to make use of the living model in your designs for sacred pictures?

Would you not cry out against the barbarism and the Puritanism of such an idea? Would you not explain to them that the worst way to honour God is to dishonour man who is made in His image, and is the work of His hands; and, that if one wants to paint Christ one must take the most Christlike person one can find, and if one wants to paint the Madonna, the purest girl one knows? Would you not rush off and burn down Newgate, if necessary, and say that such a thing was without parallel in history?

Without parallel? Well, that is exactly what the Athenians did. In the room of the Parthenon marbles, in the British Museum, you will see a marble shield on the wall. On it there are two figures; one of a man whose face is half hidden, the other of a man with the godlike lineaments of Pericles. For having done this,

---

28. Phidias (c.480–430 BCE), Greek sculptor who decorated the Acropolis but was later imprisoned and executed by his political enemies.
29. The major central London meeting hall of the mid-nineteenth century.
30. The Royal Academy in London was the pre-eminent visual arts institution of Wilde's era.
31. Frederic Leighton (1830–96), English sculptor, painter and President of the Royal Academy.

for having introduced into a bas relief, taken from Greek sacred history, the image of the great statesman who was ruling Athens at the time, Phidias was flung into prison and there, in the common gaol of Athens, died, the supreme artist of the old world.

And do you think that this was an exceptional case? The sign of a Philistine age is the cry of immorality against art, and this cry was raised by the Athenian people against every great poet and thinker of their day – Aeschylus, Euripides, Socrates.[32] It was the same with Florence in the thirteenth century. Good handicrafts are due to guilds, not to the people. The moment the guilds lost their power and the people rushed in, beauty and honesty of work died. And so, never talk of an artistic people; there never has been such a thing.

8. William Morris, 'Art and Socialism' (Leicester, 1884)

Though now most famous as a designer, writer and translator, William Morris (1834–96) was also one of the most prominent late Victorian political lecturers. After establishing his reputation as a poet from the 1850s onwards, Morris turned to socialism decisively in the 1880s, and began to devote much of his energy to travelling around Britain delivering speeches to a wide variety of types of groups, from working-men's meetings in parks and on street corners to more conventional middle-class literary societies.

The talk below is an example of an address to the latter of these audiences, the Leicester Secular Society, a group devoted to the promotion of rationalism and free speech. Where many of his contemporaries saw 'art and socialism', as Norman Kelvin puts it 'for Morris it was no paradox, for there was for him no possible separation between art and politics'.[33] The extract below, from the lecture delivered on 23 February 1884, encapsulates how he framed his thinking on this matter, and his well-known view of work as the source of human meaning rather than a mere means of obtaining a livelihood. Only socialism, Morris told his audiences, could restore work to its proper, central position.

Source

William Morris, *The Works of William Morris*, ed. May Morris, vol. XXIII (London: Longman, Green, 1915), pp. 192–214.

---

32. Three tragedians and philosophers from fifth-century BCE classical Athens, whose public turned upon them.

33. Norman Kelvin (ed.), *William Morris on Art and Socialism* (Mineola, NY: Dover, 1999), p. 4.

My friends, I want you to look into the relations of Art to Commerce, using the latter word to express what is generally meant by it; namely, that system of competition in the market which is indeed the only form which most people now-a-days suppose that Commerce can take.

Now whereas there have been times in the world's history when Art held the supremacy over Commerce; when Art was a good deal, and Commerce, as we understand the word, was a very little; so now on the contrary it will be admitted by all, I fancy, that Commerce has become of very great importance and Art of very little.

. . .

> In a properly ordered state of Society every man willing to work should be ensured –
> First – Honourable and fitting work;
> Second – A healthy and beautiful house;
> Third – Full leisure for rest of mind and body.

Now I don't suppose that anybody here will deny that it would be desirable that this claim should be satisfied: but what I want you all to think is that it is *necessary* that it be satisfied; that unless we try our utmost to satisfy it, we are but part and parcel of a society founded on robbery and injustice, condemned by the laws of the universe to destroy itself by its own efforts to exist for ever. Furthermore, I want you to think that as on the one hand it is possible to satisfy this claim, so on the other hand it is impossible to satisfy it under the present plutocratic system, which will forbid us even any serious attempt to satisfy it: the beginnings of Social Revolution must be the foundations of the re-building of the Art of the People, that is to say of the Pleasure of Life.

To say ugly words again. Do we not *know* that the greater part of men in civilized societies are dirty, ignorant, brutal – or at best, anxious about the next week's subsistence – that they are in short *poor?* And we know, when we think of it, that this is unfair.

It is an old story of men who have become rich by dishonest and tyrannical means, spending in terror of the future their ill-gotten gains liberally and in charity as 'tis called: nor are such people praised; in the old tales 'tis thought that the devil gets them after all. An old story – but I say '*De te fabula*' – of *thee* is the story told: *thou* art the man!

I say that we of the rich and well-to-do classes are daily doing it likewise: unconsciously, or half consciously it may be, we gather wealth by trading on the hard necessity of our fellows, and then we give driblets of it away to those of them who in one way or other cry out loudest to us. Our poor laws, our hospitals, our charities, organized and unorganized, are but tubs thrown to the whale; blackmail paid to lame-foot justice, that she may not hobble after us too fast.

When will the time come when honest and clear-seeing men will grow sick of all this chaos of waste, this robbing of Peter to pay Paul, which is the essence of Commercial war? When shall we band together to replace the system whose motto is 'The devil take the hindmost' with a system whose motto shall be really and without qualification 'One for all and all for one?'

Who knows but the time may be at hand, but that we now living may see the beginning of that end which shall extinguish luxury and poverty? when the upper, middle, and lower classes shall have melted into one class, living contentedly a simple and happy life.

That is a long sentence to describe the state of things which I am asking you to help to bring about: the abolition of slavery is a shorter one and means the same thing. You may be tempted to think the end not worth striving for on one hand; or on the other to suppose, each one of you, that it is so far ahead, that nothing serious can be done towards it in our own time, and that you may as well therefore sit quiet and do nothing: let me remind you how only the other day in the lifetime of the youngest of us many thousand men of our own kindred gave their lives on the battle-field to bring to a happy ending a mere episode in the struggle for the abolition of slavery: they are blessed and happy, for the opportunity came to them, and they seized it and did their best, and the world is the wealthier for it; and if such an opportunity is offered to us shall we thrust it from us that we may sit still in ease of body, in doubt, in disease of soul? These are the days of combat: who can doubt that as he hears all round him the sounds that betoken discontent and hope and fear in high and low, the sounds of awakening courage and awakening conscience? These, I say, are the days of combat, when there is no external peace possible to an honest man; but when for that very reason the internal peace of a good conscience founded on settled convictions is the easier to win, since action for the cause is offered us.

Or, will you say that here in this quiet, constitutionally governed country of England there is no opportunity for action offered to us: if we were in gagged Germany, in gagged Austria, in Russia where a word or two might land us in Siberia or the prison or fortress of Peter and Paul – why then, indeed –

Ah! my friends, it is but a poor tribute to offer on the tombs of the martyrs of liberty, this refusal to take the torch from their dying hands! Is it not of Goethe it is told, that on hearing one say he was going to America to begin life again, he replied, 'Here is America, or nowhere!' So for my part I say, 'Here is Russia, or nowhere.'

To say the governing classes in England are not afraid of freedom of speech, *therefore* let us abstain from speaking freely, is a strange paradox to me. Let us on the contrary press in through the breach which valiant men have made for us: if we hang back we make their labours, their sufferings, their deaths of no account.

Believe me we shall be shown that it is all or nothing: or will anyone here tell me that a Russian moujik[34] is in a worse case than a sweating tailor's wage-slave? Do not let us deceive ourselves, the class of victims exists here as in Russia.

---

34. Russian peasant or serf.

There are fewer of them? May be – then are they of themselves more helpless, and so have more need of our help.

And how can we of the middle classes, we the capitalists and our hangers-on, help them? By renouncing our class, and on all occasions when antagonism rises up between the classes casting in our lot with the victims: with those who are condemned at the best to lack of education, refinement, leisure, pleasure and renown; and at the worst to a life lower than that of the most brutal of savages – in order that the system of competitive Commerce may endure.

There is *no* other way: and this way I tell you plainly, will in the long run give us plentiful occasion for self-sacrifice without going to Russia. I feel sure that in this assembly there are some who are steeped in discontent with the miserable anarchy of the century of Commerce: to them I offer a means of renouncing their class by supporting a Socialist propaganda in joining the Democratic Federation, which I have the honour of representing before you, and which I believe is the only body in this country which puts forward constructive Socialism as its program.

This to my mind is opportunity enough for those of us who are discontented with the present state of things and long for an opportunity of renunciation; and it is very certain that in accepting the opportunity you will have at once to undergo some of the inconveniences of martyrdom, though without gaining its dignity at present. You will at least be mocked and laughed at by those whose mockery is a token of honour to an honest man; but you will, I don't doubt it, be looked on coldly by many excellent people, not *all* of whom will be quite stupid. You will run the risk of losing position, reputation, money, friends even: losses which are certainly pin pricks to the serious martyrdom I have spoken of; but which none the less do try the stuff a man is made of – all the more as he can escape them with little other reproach of cowardice than that which his own conscience cries out at him.

Nor can I assure you that you will for ever escape scot-free from the attacks of open tyranny. It is true that at present Capitalist Society only looks on Socialism in England with dry grins. But remember that the body of people who have for instance ruined India, starved and gagged Ireland, and tortured Egypt, have capacities in them – some ominous signs of which they have lately shown – for openly playing the tyrants' game nearer home.

So on all sides I can offer you a position which involves sacrifice; a position which will give you your 'America' at home, and make you inwardly sure that you are at least of some use to the cause: and I earnestly beg you, those of you who are convinced of the justice of our cause, not to hang back from active participation in a struggle which – who ever helps or who ever abstains from helping – must beyond all doubt end at last in Victory!

Part C: Society and Class

9. Henry 'Orator' Hunt, 'Speech at Spa Fields' (London, 1816)

On a November Friday in 1816, over 10,000 unemployed workers and demobilised army veterans gathered in a park in Clerkenwell, London, as a man in a white top hat spoke for two hours from the window of a public house, denouncing the evils of high prices, over-taxation and the greed of the elite. The speaker was Henry Hunt (1773–1835), flamboyant icon of early nineteenth-century radicalism. A Wiltshire-born gentleman farmer, he had become radicalised during the Napoleonic Wars towards the cause of universal suffrage and annual parliaments. To achieve these aims, he became a pioneer of the tactic of 'mass pressure' or the peaceful mobilisation of public opinion for radical reform, and began to address many mass rallies and outdoor meetings across the country. Hunt's mannered persona, including the white top hat (intended to indicate purity of purpose), earned him the disparaging name 'Orator Hunt' from the Conservative wit Robert Southey, a moniker meant to discredit him as a vainglorious demagogue.[35]

Hunt's address at Spa Fields was the largest of several given that year, including those at major reform meetings in Birmingham, Blackburn, Nottingham, Stockport and Macclesfield. Aware of the nervousness of authorities who lurked at the meetings' fringes, he urged non-violent resistance. Aside from some minor skirmishes, the November Spa Fields meeting was relatively peaceful. However, the movement was increasingly subject to disruption by police. Three years later, in August 1819, when Hunt spoke before 80,000 people at St Peter's Fields in Manchester, local magistrates ordered yeoman cavalry to break up the meeting by charging the crowd, killing eleven people and injuring hundreds. The event soon became known as Peterloo through analogy to the previous year's culminating battle against Napoleon. Hunt was imprisoned for his involvement, cementing his place as a martyr of reform and inspiration to the next generation of Chartist leaders.[36]

Source

William Hone, *The Meeting in Spa Fields: Hone's Authentic and Correct Account . . . of All the Proceedings* (London: W. Hone, 1816).

---

35. Quoted in Robert K. Lapp, *Contest for Cultural Authority: Hazlitt, Coleridge, and the Distresses of the Regency* (Detroit: Wayne State University Press, 1999), p. 119.
36. Jacqueline Riding, *Peterloo: The Story of the Manchester Massacre* (London: Head of Zeus, 2018).

I have no doubt but that this assembly has also heard of many great public meetings having been held in the City of London: one was convened at the Mansion House, another was a Common Council and a third a Common Hall. Gentlemen, I have the honour of being a Liveryman myself;[37] and where I have the power to exercise the indisputable right of an Englishman upon public occasions, there I attend, not for the purpose of differing with one man or the other, but fairly and manfully to come forward before my countrymen, and deliver to them the sentiments of my heart. There have been several attempts made by various persons to prevent me from giving utterance to my feelings; but they know very little of my character, if they think that I am to be put down by calumny, reproaches, or ill names. There may be a great number of persons who may think proper to attack me at this meeting, and you have been attacked for having met there.

Every man has his little private feelings: but standing before such a Meeting as this is, if I were to insult it by giving way to any personal considerations, by making one word of reply to these little petty dabblers in politics, I should be unworthy of your notice. Let them alone, and we shall see they will soon shew what they are. I have therefore done with them: but whenever any of them shall do more for the public good than I have done, I will bow with submission, and worship them; but *until* that day arrives, I shall continue in the same path, and do my duty as an Englishman, and then I need fear no man.

The Meeting at the Mansion House has, I believe the same object as ourselves, although they adopted different course of proceedings. Charity is among the best of virtues, and the first of duties; but where is the Englishman, or the Christian, who is not at all times ready to assist a fellow countryman in distress? Which, however, would you prefer, a penny-worth of soup, or a pennyworth of your own earnings ? [*Applause*]

But, while we give charity its due, I shall tell you an incident which occurred lately in a soup-shop in Wigan, in Lancashire, where a meeting was called to relieve public distress. Into that meeting came a poor weaver, with his work dress on, his shirt sleeves rolled up, his black arms exposed; but he had an honest heart: 'Here I am', said he; 'for three months, myself, a wife and four children, have not tasted an atom of flesh, and we'll die every one of us before we take your soup' – 'Well, honest fellow, what do you want?' – 'Want, want!' said he, 'why, I am an Englishman: give me my rights, and I want no more.' [*Applause*]

This was true English spirit. Reform is what is wanted, to relieve the country from the taxation under which it now groans, by giving the people an adequate representation of their own House. I hope you are all of the weaver's mind, and prepared to die, before you will accept the soup in the shape of charity. It is however, a mortifying (I should rather say, an insulting) sight to see a nest of opulent bankers of government contractors, of these who have fattened on

———

37. A member of the City of London's ancient trade associations and guilds. Henry Hunt was a member of the Worshipful Company of Loriners, or leather manufacturers.

the plunder of the people of England, who have heaped together immense fortunes during a long period of national calamity and distress, meeting together
and endeavouring to impress your minds with a sense of their public charity! I
call such a meeting a base attempt to impose a cheat on you. Suppose one of
your customers (if any of you be shopkeepers or traders) was to owe you five
pounds, and after having offered your bill to him for payment, you were to be
told he could not pay it that day, would you think that a sufficient reason to
deter you from calling on him again and again for it? I am sure you could not.
Will any man, then, or can any man say that you, as Englishmen, be so base to
yourselves and your country, so forgetful of your obligations to your posterity
and yourselves, as to sink down in apathy to your interests merely because your
first application was slighted?

Gentlemen, I put it to your understandings, and to your hearts, whether
such a slight thrown on you should not rather stimulate you to unwearied
exertions, till by the exertion you put your enemies to shame. I am told we had
Police Magistrates here to attend our Meeting last time. I hope they are here
to-day: for I am sure nobody will say of them that they will create disorder;
and therefore I only wish to see your peaceable conduct. [*Here some confusion
again, for a moment or two, took place*] Gentlemen this another of the bugaboos
to frighten you; but never mind it. We had, I am told, foot soldiers, cavalry, and
artillery, here.

I hope the artillery is here to-day; for if so, we will oppose to them the artillery
of truth, reason, and justice, the artillery of irresistible arguments. If all the artillery in Europe were this moment before me, and if I was to be told by them that
unless I gave over speaking they would instantly put the flambeau to the touch-
hole and blow me to atoms, I should not desist, provided my conscience told me
my conduct was consistent with the love I ought to bear to the constitution of my
country. They can torment a man many ways, but it is a high satisfaction to know
that they can only kill him once. As the press described last time to be only 4 or
5000, good God! what will they make these numbers tomorrow? I am sure there
are 30 000 here who cannot hear me, besides those who do hear. I propose, that
when Parliament meets, which I am told will be on the 28th of January, we shall
then present a Petition[38] to the Honourable House of Commons, corrupt as it
is, in a way which must show them that the sentiments of the Petitioners are the
sentiments of the People at large. As that House are in the habit of saying 'O, this
or that Petition is only signed by 4 or 5000, I propose the whole of us shall sign it
[*Yes, we shall*]. As a Member must take it to the House, I believe he may take one
end of it there, while we are signing the other here. The only difficulty is, how shall
we find parchment to write these names on; for if we write all on parchment, I
believe we shall make lawyers idle for a twelve month.

---

38. The purpose of the Spa Field meeting was to raise support for a petition to be delivered
to the Prince Regent, urging electoral reform.

I regard not any trouble, or care, or expenses in coming here; and I shall subscribe with pleasure my mite to buy parchment; and I hope a Committee will be formed to raise subscriptions. For the same end, I came this day eight or ten miles in my carriage to meet you; and while those milk-and-water sops in Cheapside[39] are talking to their neighbours about their politics, I could come, in the time they are doing so, from the city of Bristol.[40] I am a private country gentleman, with a small fortune, but I take care to live within my means and spend whatever I do for my poor countrymen, that they may share in it.

I have ordered my servant to come by-and-bye, with my horse, as I mean to ride home, for two reasons: first, to show you I am not a child in leading strings, but am as able to ride as walk; my second reason is I wish to show you and the people of London, that I never find it necessary, when abroad, to afleet any concealment, or to inclose my cares in a bullet proof carriage.

I must, however, declare, that the worst way of supporting any cause is by acts of violence; these afford to our enemies the surest means of casting disgrace upon it, and enable every man to say 'How bad must be a cause which is supported by men of this description!' Who is there among you base and wicked enough to invade the rights and property of his neighbours? Who is there among you base enough to surrender his own? –

I shall not detain you longer than by reading the Resolutions, which I hope you will adopt unanimously. They are the production of myself, as I have given my whole time to the subject, excepting a morning or two when I go out a sporting. They hit the very point you want; and by hearing them I am sure you will approve of them.

10. Benjamin Disraeli, 'In Defence of the Feudal System' (Shrewsbury, 1843)

Motivated by alarm at the rise of class politics and shocked by the economic and moral condition of the poor, the short-lived but prominent 'Young England' movement of Conservative politicians, writers and thinkers centring around future Prime Minister Benjamin Disraeli blamed the decline of the Tory Party under Robert Peel's leadership. Taking their inspiration from comparable movements such as 'Young Ireland', 'Young Germany' and 'Young Italy', their solutions centred on an idealised vision of a revitalised aristocracy motivated by social duty to protect the poor from what they saw as the exploitative rising middle class.

---

39. That is, the ineffectual discussions taking place among the liverymen in Mansion House on London's Cheapside street.
40. Hunt owned a brewery business in Bristol and had developed a strong following at public meetings there.

The speech selected below, made by Disraeli to his electors in Shrewsbury in 1843, offered one such argument, taking aim at the paralysis of traditional Tory attitudes and making the case for romantic social Toryism. Its ostensible target is the views of Richard Cobden and the Anti-Corn Law League, who sought to destroy the ascendancy of the aristocracy, whom they regarded as idle and parasitical. But it also provided a broad overview of reformist Conservative principles, arguing for a monarchy above party squabbles, a spirit of *noblesse oblige* among the aristocracy, and a paternalistic vision of British class relations.

Source

Joseph Hendershot Park, *British Prime Ministers of the Nineteenth Century: Policies and Speeches* (New York: New York University Press, 1916), pp. 204–9.

Gentlemen, we hear a great deal in the present day upon the subject of the feudal system. I have heard from the lips of Mr. Cobden – no, I have not heard him say it, as I was not present to hear the celebrated speech he made in Drury Lane Theatre[41] – but we have all heard how Mr. Cobden, who is a very eminent person, has said, in a very memorable speech, that England was the victim of the feudal system, and we have all heard how he has spoken of the barbarism of the feudal system, and of the barbarous relics of the feudal system. Now, if we have any relics of the feudal system, I regret that not more of it is remaining. Think one moment – and it is well you should be reminded of what this is, because there is no phrase more glibly used in the present day than 'the barbarism of the feudal system.' Now, what is the fundamental principle of the feudal system, gentlemen? It is that the tenure of all property shall be the performance of its duties. Why, when [William] the Conqueror carved out parts of the land, and introduced the feudal system, he said to the recipient, 'You shall have that estate, but you shall do something for it: you shall feed the poor; you shall endow the Church; you shall defend the land in case of war; and you shall execute justice and maintain truth to the poor for nothing.'

It is all very well to talk of the barbarities of the feudal system, and to tell us that in those days when it flourished a great variety of gross and grotesque circumstances and great miseries occurred but these were not the result of the feudal system; they were the result of the barbarism of the age. They existed not from the feudal system, but in spite of the feudal system. The principle of

41. The Anti-Corn Law League, under Liberal leader Richard Cobden (1804–65), launched with a series of meetings at this London theatre.

the feudal system, the principle which was practically operated upon, was the noblest principle, the grandest, the most magnificent and benevolent that was ever conceived by sage, or ever practised by patriot.

Why, when I hear a political economist, or an Anti-Corn-Law Leaguer, or some conceited Liberal reviewer come forward and tell us, as a grand discovery of modern science, twitting and taunting, perhaps, some unhappy squire who cannot respond to the alleged discovery – when I hear them say, as the great discovery of modern science, that 'Property has its duties as well as its rights,' my answer is that that is but a feeble plagiarism of the very principle of that feudal system which you are always reviling. Let me next tell those gentlemen who are so fond of telling us that property has its duties as well as its rights, that labour also has rights as well as its duties; and when I see masses of property raised in this country which do not recognize that principle; when I find men making fortunes by a method which permits them (very often in a very few years) to purchase the lands of the old territorial aristocracy of the country, I cannot help remembering that those millions are accumulated by a mode which does not recognize it as a duty 'to endow the Church, to feed the poor, to guard the land, and to execute justice for nothing.'

And I cannot help asking myself, when I hear of all this misery, and of all this suffering; when I know that evidence exists in our Parliament of a state of demoralisation in the once happy population of this land, which is not equalled in the most barbarous countries, which we suppose the more rude and uncivilised in Asia are – I cannot help suspecting that this has arisen because property has been permitted to be created and held without the performance of its duties.

Now, I want to ask the gentlemen who are members of the Anti-Corn-Law League, the gentlemen who are pressing on the Government of the country, on the present occasion, the total repeal and abolition of the Corn Laws – I want to know whether they have soberly considered how far they are personally responsible for this degraded state of our population. And I want them to consider this most important point, which has never yet been properly brought before any deliberative assembly – how far the present law of succession and inheritance in land will survive – if that falls – if we recur to the Continental system of parcelling out landed estates – I want to know how long you can maintain the political system of the country.

. . .

Before I sit down I do not wish to close without an observation on those who are always finding fault with the humbler classes of the community – who at the same time charitably say they are not responsible for their deterioration. I confess that, as far as I can form an opinion, the deterioration of society is not to be found only among the labourers of the country. It is not in the squalid dwellings; it is not in the miserable details of sickening poverty, that this deterioration may be found; but, in my opinion, that heroic nobility which formed this country, and that spirited gentry which has so often come forward to vindicate our rights or to defend our liberties, and which have also been the main source of our commercial greatness – for it is the nobility and gentry of the land who have founded our greatest colonies – in my opinion the present race is deficient in those qualities.

There are, however, great exceptions to be made, even in the higher classes of the country; but there is a miserable philosophy of the day which ascribes everything to 'the spirit of the age' – that thinks nothing is to be done by the influence of individual character, which is, after all, the only inducement to great actions, the only spur to great achievements. That opinion is much too prevalent; and there is no question that it is not merely among the lower classes that we find a lack of those great qualities which hitherto have always been associated with the noble, national character of England.

11. Peter H. Clark, 'Socialism: The Remedy for the Evils of Society' (Cincinnati, 1877)

By the 1860s, collectivist economic ideas had taken on the identity of 'socialism'. As the next extract testifies, such beliefs came to transcend cultural and racial distinctions. Known as 'America's First Black Socialist', Peter Humphries Clark (1829–1925) was a schoolteacher and author who became a key figure in the new US labour movement.[42] Born free in Cincinnati and receiving a wide-ranging education, he had been a conductor on the Underground Railroad for escaped slaves before the Civil War, had written for Frederick Douglass's *North Star* and founded a teachers' union for black teachers in Cincinnati. After the war, Clark joined the Workers Party of the United States (WPUS) upon its founding in 1876, and later ran for Congress in 1878 under the banner of the Social Labor Party of America.

The occasion for the speech below was the Great Railroad Strike of 1877, the largest labour confrontation in US history to that date. Dozens of strikers and non-striking workers were killed, millions of dollars' worth of property was burned, and hundreds of factories were closed by strikers, leading President Rutherford B. Hayes to deploy federal troops. Clark delivered the words below on 22 July to a crowd of striking rail workers, outlining his belief that the industrial action was part of a broader class struggle that would lead to the fundamental transformation of the American economic system.

Source

'The Socialistic Meeting', *The Cincinnati Daily Enquirer*, 23 July 1877.

42. Nikki M. Taylor, *America's First Black Socialist: The Radical Life of Peter H. Clark* (Lexington: University of Kentucky Press, 2013).

If I had the choosing of a motto for this meeting, I should select the words of the patriotic and humane Abraham Lincoln, 'With malice toward none, with charity for all, with firmness in the right as God gives us to see the right.'[43] These words, so full of that charity which we should exercise toward each other, are especially suited to this day and time, when wrongs long condemned have at last been resisted and men are bleeding and dying in the busy center of our population, and all over the land other men, with heated passions, are assembling to denounce the needless slaughter of innocent men who, driven by want, have appealed to force for that justice which was otherwise refused to them ...

. . .

Observe how all civilized communities pass from a condition of what is called prosperity to one of depression and distress. Observe how continually these fluctuations occur; how the intervals between them grow shorter; how each one is more violent than the last, the distress produced more widespread. Observe, too, that after each the number of capitalists decrease, while those who remain grow more wealthy and more powerful, while those who have failed join the great army of workers who hang forever on the ragged edge of pauperism.

The so called periods of prosperity are more properly periods of unrestrained speculation. Money accumulates in the hands of the capitalists, [through] some governmental device as a tariff or the issue of greenbacks. This abundance tempts men to embark on business enterprises which seem to promise rich returns. For a time all goes well, shops are crowded with busy men, and all [are] ready to say, 'Behold how prosperous we are!' But there comes a check to all this. The manufacturers begin to talk about a glutted market. There has been overproduction. There comes the period of sharp competition. Prices are reduced, goods are sold at below cost, then comes the crash, bosses fail, shops are closed, men are idle, and the miserable workmen stand forth, underbidding each other in the labor market. If the competition be too sharp, they resort to strikes as in the present instance. Then comes violence, lawlessness, bloodshed and death.

People who talk of the anarchy of socialism surely cannot have considered these facts. If they had, they would have discovered not a little of anarchy on their side of the question.

It is folly to say that a condition of poverty is a favorable one, and to point to men who have risen to affluence from that condition. For one man who is strong through the hindrances of poverty, there are ten thousand who fail. If you take ten thousand men and weigh them with lead and cast them into the midst of Lake Erie, a few may swim out but the majority will be drowned.

This condition of poverty is not a favorable one either for the individual or for the nation. Especially is it an unfavorable condition for a nation whose government lies in the hands of all its citizens. A monarchy or an aristocracy can

---

43. A key line from Lincoln's second inaugural address, 4 March 1865, in Washington, DC.

afford to have the mass of its citizens steeped in poverty and ignorance. Not so in a republic. Here every man should be the owner of wealth enough to render him independent of the threats or bribes of the demagogue. He should be the owner of wealth enough to give leisure for that study which will qualify him to study and understand the deep questions of public policy which are continually demanding solution. The more men there are who have this independence, this leisure, the safer we are as a nation, reduce the number, and the fewer there are, the more dangerous the situation. So alarming has been the spread of ignorance and poverty in the past generation, that whole cities in our land whose states, indeed are at the mercy of an ignorant rabble who have no political principle except to vote for the men who pay the most on election days and who promise to make the biggest dividend of public stealing. This is sadly true, nor is the Negro, scarcely ten years from slavery, the chief sinner in this respect.

That this evil of poverty is partially curable, at least, I am justified in thinking, because I find each of the great political parties offering remedies for the hard times and the consequent poverty. Many wise men, learned in political economy, assure us that their doctrines, faithfully followed, will result in a greater production of wealth and a more equal division of the same. But as I have said before, there is but one efficacious remedy proposed, and that is found in Socialism.

The present industrial organization of society has been faithfully tried and has proven a failure. We get rid of the king, we get rid of the aristocracy, but the capitalist comes in their place, and in the industrial organization and guidance of society his little finger is heavier than their loins. Whatever Socialism may bring about, it can present nothing more anarchical than is found in Grafton, Baltimore and Pittsburgh today.[44]

. . .

The government must control capital with a strong hand. It is merely the accumulated results of industry, and there would be no justice should a few score bees in the hive take possession of the store of honey and dole it out to the workers in return for services which added to their superabundant store. Yet such is the custom of society.

Future accumulations of capital should be held sacredly for the benefit of the whole community. Past accumulations may be permitted to remain in private hands until, from their very uselessness, they will become a burden which their owners will gladly surrender.

Machinery too, which ought to be a blessing but is proving to be a curse to the people should be taken in hand by the government and its advantages distributed to all. Captain Cutter[45] wrote in his song of steam:

Soon I intend ye may go and play, While I manage this world myself.

---

44. Stations along the rail line between Pennsylvania, West Virginia and Maryland.
45. George Washington Cutter (1809–65) was a Kentuckian poet, hero of the Mexican War, and author of *Song of Steam and Other Poems* (1857).

Had he written, ye may go and starve, it would have been nearer the truth. Machinery controlled in the interests of labor would afford that leisure for thought, for self culture, for giving and receiving refining influences, which are so essential to the full development of character. 'The ministry of wealth' would not be confined to a few, but would be a benefit to all.

Every railroad in the land should be owned or controlled by the government. The title of private owners should be extinguished, and the ownership vested in the people. All a road will need to meet will be a running expense and enough to replace waste. The people can then enjoy the benefit of travel, and where one man travels now, a thousand will travel then. There will be no strikes, for the men who operate the road will be the recipient of its profits.

Finally, we want governmental organization of labor so that ruinous competition and ruinous overproduction shall equally be avoided, and these commercial panics which sweep over and engulf the world will be forever prevented.

It will be objected that this is making our government a machine for doing for the citizen everything which can be more conveniently done by combined than by individual effort. Society has already made strides in the direction of Socialism. Every drop of water we draw from hydrants, the gas that illumines our streets at night, the paved streets upon which we walk, our parks, our schools, our libraries, are all outgrowths of the Socialistic principle. In that direction lies safety.

Choose ye this day which course ye shall pursue.

Let us, finally, not forget that we are American citizens, that the right of free speech and of a free press is enjoyed by us. We are exercising today the right to assemble and complain of our grievances. The courts of the land are open to us, and we hold in our hands the all compelling ballot.

There is no need for violent counsels or violent deeds. If we are patient and wise, the future is ours.

12. Lucy Parsons, 'I am an Anarchist' (Kansas City, 1886)

Chicago-based Lucy González Parsons (1853–1942) was one of the first ethnic minority women to rise to prominence in American radical movements primarily composed of white males. Probably born into slavery on a Texas plantation, of mixed African American and Mexican heritage, she married Albert Parsons, an ex-Confederate soldier turned radical left-wing Republican, in the early 1870s and moved north to the boom city of Chicago. Both became active in labour causes, and Lucy's career as an activist would continue into the late 1930s.

However, she will always be most associated with the events of November 1886, known as the Haymarket Affair. Following a disturbance at an anarchist rally, in which an explosive was thrown into police lines, killing seven officers and four civilians, Lucy and her husband were both arrested, along with many other anarchists; Albert was one of four found guilty and executed in November the following year.

Even before the trial, Parson's speeches throughout the Chicago area had earned her the name 'the windiest woman in windy city history'. Within hours of Albert's incarceration in October 1886, Lucy set off on a speaking tour of the nation, championing anarchism, the defendants' innocence and freedom of speech. By February 1887, she had delivered forty-three speeches in seventeen states, becoming a First Amendment *cause célèbre* and gaining notoriety for her unapologetic radicalism. Repeatedly barred from speaking in booked auditoria, she often spoke in the open air, and generated feverish newspaper coverage for speeches such as that excerpted below, from a meeting on 21 December 1886.

Source

Lucy Parsons, *Freedom, Equality and Solidarity: Writing and Speeches 1878–1937* (Chicago: Charles Kerr, 2004).

I am an anarchist. I suppose you came here, the most of you, to see what a real, live anarchist looked like. I suppose some of you expected to see me with a bomb in one hand and a flaming torch in the other, but are disappointed in seeing neither.

If such has been your ideas regarding an anarchist, you deserved to be disappointed. Anarchists are peaceable, law abiding people. What do anarchists mean when they speak of anarchy? Webster[46] gives the term two definitions: chaos and the state of being without political rule. We cling to the latter definition. Our enemies hold that we believe only in the former.

Do you wonder why there are anarchists in this country, in this great land of liberty, as you love to call it? Go to New York. Go through the byways and alleys of that great city. Count the myriads starving; count the multiplied thousands who are homeless; number those who work harder than slaves and live on less and have fewer comforts than the meanest slaves. You will be dumbfounded by your discoveries, you who have paid no attention to these poor, save as objects of charity and commiseration. They are not objects of charity, they are the victims of the rank injustice that permeates the system of government, and of political economy that holds sway from the Atlantic to the Pacific.

Its oppression, the misery it causes, the wretchedness it gives birth to, are found to a greater extent in New York than elsewhere. In New York, where not

---

46. Webster's dictionaries are the series of authoritative guides to US English usage, named after the lexicographer Noah Webster (1758–1843).

many days ago two governments united in unveiling a statue of liberty, where a hundred bands played that hymn of liberty, 'The Marseillaise.'[47] But almost its equal is found among the miners of the West, who dwell in squalor and wear rags, that the capitalists, who control the earth that should be free to all, may add still further to their millions! Oh, there are plenty of reasons for the existence of anarchists.

But in Chicago they do not think anarchists have any right to exist at all. They want to hang them there, lawfully or unlawfully. You have heard of a certain Haymarket meeting. You have heard of a bomb. You have heard of arrests and of succeeding arrests effected by detectives. Those detectives! There is a set of men nay, beasts for you! Pinkerton detectives! They would do anything. I feel sure capitalists wanted a man to throw that bomb at the Haymarket meeting and have the anarchists blamed for it. Pinkerton could have accomplished it for him.

. . .

The bomb at Chicago sounded the downfall of the wage system of the nineteenth century. Why? Because I know no intelligent people will submit to despotism. The first means the diffusion of power. I tell no man to use it. But it was the achievement of science, not of anarchy, and would do for the masses. I suppose the press will say I belched forth treason. If I have violated any law, arrest me, give me a trial, and the proper punishment, but let the next anarchist that comes along ventilate his views without hindrance. Well, the bomb exploded, the arrests were made and then came that great judicial farce, beginning on June 21. The jury was impaneled. Is there a Knight of Labor[48] here? Then know that a Knight of Labor was not considered competent enough to serve on that jury. 'Are you a Knight of Labor?' 'Have you any sympathy with labor organizations?' were the questions asked each talisman. If an affirmative answer was given, the talisman was bounced. It was not are you a Mason, a Knight Templar? O, no! [Great applause.]

I see you read the signs of the times by that expression. Hangman Gary, miscalled judge, ruled that if a man was prejudiced against the defendants, it did not incapacitate him for serving on the jury. For such a man, said Hangman Gary, would pay closer attention to the law and evidence and would be more apt to render a verdict for the defense. Is there a lawyer here? If there is he knows such a ruling is without precedent and contrary to all law, reason or common sense. In the heat of patriotism the American citizen sometimes drops a tear for the nihilist of Russia. They say the nihilist can't get justice, that he is condemned without trial. How much more should he weep for his next door neighbor, the anarchist, who is given the form of trial under such a ruling. There were 'squealers' introduced as witnesses for the prosecution.

---

47. The national anthem of France, adopted by the French National Convention in 1795, and named after its adoption by army volunteers marching to Paris from Marseille.
48. A moderate, non-anarchist, non-socialist labour federation active in the US since the 1860s.

There were three of them. Each and every one was compelled to admit they had been purchased and intimidated by the prosecution. Yet Hangman Gary held their evidence as competent. It came out in the trial that the Haymarket meeting was the result of no plot, but was caused in this wise. The day before the wage slaves in McCormick's factory had struck for eight hours' labor,[49] McCormick, from his luxurious office, with one stroke of the pen by his idle, beringed fingers, turned 4,000 men out of employment. Some gathered and stoned the factory. Therefore they were anarchists, said the press.

But anarchists are not fools; only fools stone buildings. The police were sent out and they killed six wage slaves. You didn't know that. The capitalistic press kept it quiet, but it made a great fuss over the killing of some policemen. Then these crazy anarchists, as they are called, thought a meeting ought to be held to consider the killing of six brethren and to discuss the eight hour movement. The meeting was held. It was peaceable. When Bonfield[50] ordered the police to charge those peaceable anarchists, he hauled down the American flag and should have been shot on the spot. While the judicial farce was going on the red and black flags were brought into court, to prove that the anarchists threw the bomb. They were placed on the walls and hung there, awful specters before the jury.

What does the black flag mean? When a cable gram says it was carried through the streets of a European city it means that the people are suffering – that the men are out of work, the women starving, the children barefooted. But, you say, that is in Europe. How about America? The *Chicago Tribune* said there were 30,000 men in that city with nothing to do. Another authority said there were 10,000 barefooted children in mid winter. The police said hundreds had no place to sleep or warm. Then President Cleveland[51] issued his Thanksgiving proclamation and the anarchists formed in procession and carried the black flag to show that these thousands had nothing for which to return thanks. When the Board of Trade, that gambling den, was dedicated by means of a banquet, $30 a plate, again the black flag was carried, to signify that there were thousands who couldn't enjoy a 2 cent meal.

But the red flag, the horrible red flag, what does that mean? Not that the streets should run with gore, but that the same red blood courses through the veins of the whole human race. It meant the brotherhood of man. When the red flag floats over the world the idle shall be called to work. There will be an end of prostitution for women, of slavery for man, of hunger for children. Liberty has been named anarchy.

If this verdict is carried out it will be the death knell of America's liberty. You and your children will be slaves.

---

49. In the Spring of 1886, workers at the McCormick Harvesting Machine Company in Chicago demanded an eight-hour working day and went on strike. The company locked out the workers and hired strike-breakers.
50. John Bonfield, notoriously brutal Chicago police inspector.
51. Grover Cleveland's first term as President for the Democrats was 1885–9.

You will have liberty if you can pay for it. If this verdict is carried out, place the flag of our country at half mast and write on every fold 'shame.' Let our flag be trailed in the dust. Let the children of workingmen place laurels to the brow of these modern heroes, for they committed no crime.

Break the two fold yoke. Bread is freedom and freedom is bread.

13. William Jennings Bryan, 'The Cross of Gold Speech' (Chicago, 1896)

On 9 July 1896, at the Democratic National Convention in Chicago, Nebraska politician William Jennings Bryan (1860–96) delivered what is widely seen as one of the greatest speeches in American political history. Pitting Eastern financial interests against the agrarian South and mid-West, it was a powerful expression of what was known as the 'free silver' argument. Rapturously received by delegates, it saw Bryan selected as Democratic Presidential candidate, the youngest major party nominee in US history.

Since the depression of the 1870s, in which farmers had been particularly badly affected, there had been growing calls in US politics for reform in how currency was managed, with many advocating for the free coinage of silver to help raise prices for crops. First the Greenback Party and then the Populist Party galvanised an anti-monopoly message of nationalisation of transport and the break-up of major banks, and the unlimited coinage of silver to use as money in addition to the gold-backed currency already in circulation.

By the 1896 election, elements of this 'free silver' programme had become part of the Democrat's message, and at the nominating convention Bryan used an impassioned speech to became the cause's most powerful champion.[52] In the subsequent election, Bryan revolutionised the role of oratory in national politics, pioneering the national stumping tour when he spoke to an audience of 5 million people in 600 speeches across twenty-seven states. In November, however, the Democrats were beaten by William McKinley's Republicans, beginning the series of defeats that Bryan would suffer as nominee in 1900, and again in 1908.

Source

Official Proceedings of the Democratic National Convention Held in Chicago, Illinois, July 7, 8, 9, 10, and 11, 1896 (Logansport, IN, 1896), pp. 226–34. Reprinted in *The Annals of America*, vol. 12, *1895–1904: Populism, Imperialism, and Reform* (Chicago: Encyclopedia Britannica, 1968), pp. 100–5.

---

52. Gerard N. Magliocca, *The Tragedy of William Jennings Bryan: Constitutional Law and the Politics of Backlash* (New Haven, CT: Yale University Press, 2011).

We say in our platform that we believe that the right to coin money and issue money is a function of government. We believe it. We believe it is a part of sovereignty and can no more with safety be delegated to private individuals than can the power to make penal statutes or levy laws for taxation.

Mr. Jefferson, who was once regarded as good Democratic authority, seems to have a different opinion from the gentleman who has addressed us on the part of the minority. Those who are opposed to this proposition tell us that the issue of paper money is a function of the bank and that the government ought to go out of the banking business. I stand with Jefferson rather than with them, and tell them, as he did, that the issue of money is a function of the government and that the banks should go out of the governing business.

They complain about the plank which declares against the life tenure in office. They have tried to strain it to mean that which it does not mean. What we oppose in that plank is the life tenure that is being built up in Washington which establishes an office-holding class and excludes from participation in the benefits the humbler members of our society . . .

Let me call attention to two or three great things. The gentleman from New York says that he will propose an amendment providing that this change in our law shall not affect contracts which, according to the present laws, are made payable in gold. But if he means to say that we cannot change our monetary system without protecting those who have loaned money before the change was made, I want to ask him where, in law or in morals, he can find authority for not protecting the debtors when the act of 1873[53] was passed when he now insists that we must protect the creditor. He says he also wants to amend this platform so as to provide that if we fail to maintain the parity within a year that we will then suspend the coinage of silver. We reply that when we advocate a thing which we believe will be successful we are not compelled to raise a doubt as to our own sincerity by trying to show what we will do if we are wrong.

I ask him, if he will apply his logic to us, why he does not apply it to himself. He says that he wants this country to try to secure an international agreement. Why doesn't he tell us what he is going to do if they fail to secure an international agreement? There is more reason for him to do that than for us to expect to fail to maintain the parity. They have tried for thirty years – thirty years – to secure an international agreement, and those are waiting for it most patiently who don't want it at all.

Now, my friends, let me come to the great paramount issue. If they ask us here why it is we say more on the money question than we say upon the tariff question, I reply that if protection has slain its thousands the gold standard has slain its tens of thousands. If they ask us why we did not embody all these things in our platform which we believe, we reply to them that when we have restored

---

53. The Coinage Act of 1873 that set monetary standards in the US.

the money of the Constitution, all other necessary reforms will be possible, and that until that is done there is no reform that can be accomplished.

Why is it that within three months such a change has come over the sentiments of the country? Three months ago, when it was confidently asserted that those who believed in the gold standard would frame our platforms and nominate our candidates, even the advocates of the gold standard did not think that we could elect a President; but they had good reasons for the suspicion, because there is scarcely a state here today asking for the gold standard that is not within the absolute control of the Republican Party.

But note the change. Mr. McKinley[54] was nominated at St. Louis upon a platform that declared for the maintenance of the gold standard until it should be changed into bimetallism by an international agreement. Mr. McKinley was the most popular man among the Republicans; and everybody three months ago in the Republican Party prophesied his election. How is it today? Why, that man who used to boast that he looked like Napoleon, that man shudders today when he thinks that he was nominated on the anniversary of the Battle of Waterloo. Not only that, but as he listens he can hear with ever increasing distinctness the sound of the waves as they beat upon the lonely shores of St. Helena.

Why this change? Ah, my friends. is not the change evident to anyone who will look at the matter? It is because no private character, however pure, no personal popularity, however great, can protect from the avenging wrath of an indignant people the man who will either declare that he is in favor of fastening the gold standard upon this people, or who is willing to surrender the right of self-government and place legislative control in the hands of foreign potentates and powers ...

We go forth confident that we shall win. Why? Because upon the paramount issue in this campaign there is not a spot of ground upon which the enemy will dare to challenge battle. Why, if they tell us that the gold standard is a good thing, we point to their platform and tell them that their platform pledges the party to get rid of a gold standard and substitute bimetallism. If the gold standard is a good thing, why try to get rid of it? If the gold standard, and I might call your attention to the fact that some of the very people who are in this convention today and who tell you that we ought to declare in favor of international bimetallism and thereby declare that the gold standard is wrong and that the principles of bimetallism are better – these very people four months ago were open and avowed advocates of the gold standard and telling us that we could not legislate two metals together even with all the world.

I want to suggest this truth, that if the gold standard is a good thing we ought to declare in favor of its retention and not in favor of abandoning it; and

---

54. William McKinley (1843–1901) was President for the Republican Party from 1897 until his assassination in 1901.

if the gold standard is a bad thing, why should we wait until some other nations are willing to help us to let it go?

Here is the line of battle. We care not upon which issue they force the fight. We are prepared to meet them on either issue or on both. If they tell us that the gold standard is the standard of civilization, we reply to them that this, the most enlightened of all nations of the earth, has never declared for a gold standard, and both the parties this year are declaring against it. If the gold standard is the standard of civilization, why, my friends, should we not have it? So if they come to meet us on that, we can present the history of our nation. More than that, we can tell them this, that they will search the pages of history in vain to find a single instance in which the common people of any land ever declared themselves in favor of a gold standard. They can find where the holders of fixed investments have.

Mr. Carlisle[55] said in 1878 that this was a struggle between the idle holders of idle capital and the struggling masses who produce the wealth and pay the taxes of the country; and my friends, it is simply a question that we shall decide upon which side shall the Democratic Party fight. Upon the side of the idle holders of idle capital, or upon the side of the struggling masses? That is the question that the party must answer first; and then it must be answered by each individual hereafter. The sympathies of the Democratic Party, as described by the platform, are on the side of the struggling masses, who have ever been the foundation of the Democratic Party.

There are two ideas of government. There are those who believe that if you just legislate to make the well-to-do prosperous, that their prosperity will leak through on those below. The Democratic idea has been that if you legislate to make the masses prosperous their prosperity will find its way up and through every class that rests upon it.

You come to us and tell us that the great cities are in favor of the gold standard. I tell you that the great cities rest upon these broad and fertile prairies. Burn down your cities and leave our farms, and your cities will spring up again as if by magic. But destroy our farms and the grass will grow in the streets of every city in the country.

My friends, we shall declare that this nation is able to legislate for its own people on every question without waiting for the aid or consent of any other nation on earth, and upon that issue we expect to carry every single state in the Union.

I shall not slander the fair state of Massachusetts nor the state of New York by saying that when citizens are confronted with the proposition, 'Is this nation able to attend to its own business?' – I will not slander either one by saying that the people of those states will declare our helpless impotency as a nation to attend to our own business. It is the issue of 1776 over again. Our ancestors,

---

55. John G. Carlisle (1834–1910), prominent Democrat politician.

when but 3 million, had the courage to declare their political independence of every other nation upon earth. Shall we, their descendants, when we have grown to 70 million, declare that we are less independent than our forefathers? No, my friends, it will never be the judgment of this people. Therefore, we care not upon what lines the battle is fought. If they say bimetallism is good but we cannot have it till some nation helps us, we reply that, instead of having a gold standard because England has, we shall restore bimetallism, and then let England have bimetallism because the United States have.

If they dare to come out in the open field and defend the gold standard as a good thing, we shall fight them to the uttermost, having behind us the producing masses of the nation and the world. Having behind us the commercial interests and the laboring interests and all the toiling masses, we shall answer their demands for a gold standard by saying to them, you shall not press down upon the brow of labor this crown of thorns. You shall not crucify mankind upon a cross of gold.

5 Empire and Manifest Destiny

Introduction

Modern colonialism and imperialism were the most distinctive political features of the nineteenth century. Between American independence and World War One, Britain's vast global constellation of possessions gradually became a formal 'empire'. For the US, though born through anti-imperial rebellion, its first century was also one of relentless expansionism, an era of continental conquest that gave way in the 1890s to overseas adventurism.[1] Both polities needed to explain these changes to an enlarged voting public, and both needed to determine how best to deal with the populations that came under their control. This chapter surveys the debate over the conduct of empire in the US and Britain, with parts dedicated to the particular trans-atlantic resonance of the questions arising from British rule in Ireland, and to the moral issue of indigenous rights. Reading across two different national–imperial styles suits the inherently comparative strain to how empires explained and debated themselves, with acute sensitivity to exceptions and analogies. And it allows us to see how harmful worldviews were enshrined through layers of argument and language at once subtle and insidious.

Unabashed jingoistic rhetoric seems familiar to us as a signature tone of the age. Yet, whereas in 'The White Man's Burden' (1899), British poet Rudyard Kipling encouraged the proud embrace of imperial projects with 'open speech and simple', in reality, the language of imperialism was perhaps the most grandly euphemistic of all contained in this book.[2] Evasions and abstractions allowed those making the case for expansion, invasion and domination to obscure the arbitrariness and brutality of empire.[3] Half-understood concepts ('internationalism' or 'cosmopolitanism', p. 214); a faux-rational lexicon

---

1. The notion of formal and informal empires is broken down usefully in Paul A. Kramer, 'Power and Connection: Imperial Histories of the United States in the World', *The American Historical Review*, 116:5 (December 2011).

2. Rudyard Kipling, 'The White Man's Burden', *McClure's Magazine*, 12 (February 1899).

3. For a recent study of imperial rhetoric see Martin Thomas and Richard Toye, *Arguing About Empire: Imperial Rhetoric in Britain and France, 1882–1956* (Oxford: Oxford University Press, 2017).

('annexation' and 'improvements', p. 204); natural metaphors ('waves of civilization', p. 230): all enabled publics to detach from the horrors being committed in their name and to focus instead on economics and geopolitics. A masculinist and racialised register of paternalism, duty and glory helped frame Eurocentric exceptionalisms. Whether loosely or explicitly, religious justifications threaded through these arguments, underpinning the discourse of missionary duty and, most famously of all, the phrase 'Manifest Destiny', the seminal slogan for the providential right of Anglo-American possession of the North American continent.[4]

Though far less prominent, a number of important rhetorical traditions during the period covered by this book pushed back against this imperial ideology. As Bernard Porter puts it, 'the imperial theme had always had its counterpoint of protest'.[5] Both from within groups at the receiving end of invasion, settlement and exploitation, and from home-front publics in the metropole, a wide variety of observers used an array of settings to outline their case against expansion and empire. Though 'anti-imperialism' coalesced as a *fin-de-siècle* movement, for much of the century it was more often an offshoot of broader reform agendas, including abolition (see Chapter 3), forms of nationalism (see Chapter 1), and the peace movement (see Chapter 6). Their arguments provide an under-appreciated and sometimes surprising counter-current to the prevailing discourse of the day.[6] Objections ranged from simple humanitarianism to economic, political and practical, including misgivings about unintended domestic consequences, fears of over-reach, and ethnic or racial pollution. Though opposition to empire might mobilise the same language of outrage as the anti-slavery or gender equality cause, it also drew strategically upon a language of respectability and national honour, one of many ways in which colonised and indigenous peoples reimagined the very tropes of pro-imperial propaganda.

This chapter's first part ('Opposing Empire') reveals the diversity of these voices. The first piece comes from a delegation of Cherokee women (1817) counselling their male counterparts to resist further Anglo-American encroachment rather than yield to the temptation of compromise. This is followed by an oral proclamation (1846) issued thirty years later by Mexican General Francisco Mejía as he faced the imminent US 'usurpation', focusing on the hypocrisy of how Manifest Destiny 'shamelessly derides the very principles invoked' (p. 203) in the Declaration of Independence. In the next

---

4. The origins of this use of the phrase lie in John O'Sullivan, 'Annexation', *United States Magazine and Domestic Review*, July–August 1845.

5. Bernard Porter, *Critics of Empire: British Radicals and the Imperial Challenge*, revised edn (London: I. B. Tauris, 2008).

6. Michael P. Cullinane, *Liberty and American Anti-Imperialism, 1898–1909* (New York: Palgrave Macmillan, 2012).

speech (1848), South Carolina Senator John Calhoun, who appeared in Chapter 3 as an outspoken apologist for slavery, returns to argue against Mexican expansion, on the anti-pollution basis that it involved 'placing colored races on an equality with the white race' (p. 205). Moving on to Britain's involvement in India, we turn to the famous House of Commons speech (1858) delivered by John Bright, presenting a case for imperial retreat that is equal parts Quaker moral crusade, paternalism and free trade liberalism. The final speech (1900) in this part of the chapter offers an extract from Democrat Presidential candidate William Jennings Bryan's patriotic moral case for the 'paralysing impact' of America's embryonic colonial policy on domestic life.

In Britain in the 1870s, the country faced with growing domestic criticism and new rivalries from Germany and Japan, 'empire' needed to be defended as a conscious policy. This led to the period of renewed assertion known as the New Imperialism, explored in the next part of the chapter ('Defending Empire'). Benjamin Disraeli's speech (1872) at London's Crystal Palace is selected here as a paramount expression of this resurgent rhetoric, pitting global 'cosmopolitan' greatness against meagre, merely 'national', parochialism. Twenty years later, with the US joining the imperial fray, Theodore Roosevelt offered an even more strident, gendered defence of empire's potential in 'uplifting mankind', rejecting those who made 'a pretence of humanitarianism, to hide and cover their timidity.' (p. 215). It was a case whose racial underpinnings were made even clearer in the next speech, in which Albert Beveridge promised global 'regeneration', should the white race act as 'master-organiser of the world' (p. 217).

The third part of the chapter ('The Irish Question') focuses on one territorial dispute whose implications played out on both sides of the Atlantic. The first speech (1843) comes from one of legendary statesman Daniel O'Connell's 'monster meetings' in rural Ireland, to which hundreds of thousands travelled to hear him make the case for Irish freedoms. As Wendell Phillips told a meeting in Boston in 1840, 'the voice of O'Connell, which now shakes the three kingdoms, has poured across the waters as a thunder-peal for the cause of liberty in our land'.[7] Yet the following selection reveals the push-back that such influence could produce, in the form of nativist Philadelphia politician Lewis Levin's open-air speech (1844) attacking the growing Papist threat of the urban Irish diaspora, words that incited violent ethnic riots. Finally, we turn to Prime Minister Gladstone's stirring and ultimately unsuccessful attempt to persuade the House of Commons to pass his Irish Home Rule Bill of 1886.

As many of the speeches in this chapter show, arguments about empire were essentially human rights debates. The culminating part ('Indigenous

---

7. 'Address from the People of Ireland', *The Anti-Slavery Reporter*, 20 April 1842.

Rights') brings this key issue to the fore, by exploring the diverse ways in which justice for colonised peoples was debated and framed. First is a speech from President Andrew Jackson (1830), the politician most associated with Native American oppression, presenting his 'Indian Removal' policy before Congress using the Lockean justification of appropriating land from the unproductive 'wandering savage' (p. 231). A few years later in Boston, we see Pequot intellectual William Apess deliver his landmark 'Eulogy for King Philip' (1836), introducing white audiences to a new vision of indigenous history and sovereignty. Taking an entirely different tone, we turn to Mark Twain's widely performed lecture on 'Our Fellow Savages of the Sandwich Islands' (1868), which uses deadpan satire as a stern rebuke to missionary prejudices towards the peoples of the Pacific. The chapter ends with a seminal moment in British political history, as the first ever MP from the Indian subcontinent, Dadabhai Naoroji, brought the perspective of the colonised to the House of Commons in his maiden speech (1893).

Part A: Opposing Empire

1. Nanye'hi et al., 'Cherokee Women Address Their Nation' (Georgia, 1817)

In the first two decades of the nineteenth century, successive US administrations pressured the Cherokee to sell lands that had once covered seven Southern states. In this petition from May 1817, read before the Cherokee Council in what is now Georgia, a female delegation urged their husbands, sons and fathers to resist the further surrender of tribal lands. As clan mothers, women held prominent positions in Cherokee culture, their close association with nature and the soil serving as a basis for respect and authority, the women even participating in treaty negotiations.

Their plea ends with the reading of a message from Nanye'hi (c.1783–1822), also known Nancy Ward, one of the leading figures of the southeastern Cherokee, who was too elderly to attend Council. Nanye'hi had spent a lifetime urging conciliation between settlers and the Cherokee, and earned the respect of settler delegations for her persuasive oratory.[8] Below we see this veteran ambassador symbolically add her voice to those arguing that male leaders should not cede any more territory but rather should embrace agriculture in order to prevent removal. In less than two decades, the Cherokee would be forcibly moved west in what became known as the Trail of Tears of 1836–8.

Source

Cherokee Women to Cherokee Council, 2 May 1817, series 1, Andrew Jackson Presidential Papers, Microfilm reel 22. Library of Congress, Manuscripts Division.

The Cherokee ladies now being present at the meeting of the chiefs and warriors in council have thought it their duties as mothers to address their Chiefs and warriors now assembled.

Our beloved children and head men of the Cherokee nation[9] we address you warriors in council. We have raised all of you on the land which we now

---

8. Laura E. Donaldson, '"But we are your mothers, you are our sons": Gender, Sovereignty and the Nation in Early Cherokee Women's Writing', in Cheryl Suzack (ed.), *Indigenous Women and Feminism* (Vancouver: University of British Columbia Press, 2010).

9. The *Constitution and Laws of the Cherokee Nation* (1875) notes that 'our fathers have existed as a separate and distinct Nation . . . from a period extending into antiquity' (William P. Boudinot, D. H. Ross and Joseph A. Scales, *Constitution and Laws of the Cherokee Nation* (St Louis: R. & T.A. Ennis, printers, 1875)).

have, which God gave us to inhabit and to raise provisions. We know that our country has once been extensive, but by repeated sales has become circumscribed to a small tract, and [we] never have thought it our duty to interfere in the disposition of it till now. If a father and mother was to sell all their lands which they had to depend on, which their children had to raise their living on, which would be indeed bad & to be removed to another country. We do not wish to go to an unknown country to which we have understood some of our children wish to go to over the Mississippi, but this act of our children would be like destroying their mothers.

Your mothers, your sisters, ask and beg of you not to part with any more of our land.[10] We say ours. You are our descendants; take pity on our request. But keep it for our growing children, for it was the good will of our creator to place us here, and you know our father, the great president[11] will not allow his white children to take our country away. Only keep your hand off of paper talks for it's our own country. For if it was not, they would not ask you to put your hands to paper, for it would be impossible to remove us all. For as soon as one child is raised, we have others in our arms, for such is our situation & will consider our circumstance.

Therefore, children, don't part with any more of our lands but continue on it and enlarge your farms. Cultivate and raise corn & cotton and your mothers and sisters will make clothing for you which our father the president has recommended to us all. We don't charge anybody for selling any lands, but we have heard such intentions of our children. But your talks become true at last; it was our desire to forewarn you all not part with our lands.

Nanye'hi to her children: Warriors take pity and listen to the talks of your sisters. Although I am very old yet cannot but pity the situation in which you will have hear of their minds. I have great many grand children which I wish them to do well on our land.

2. Francisco Mejía, 'Proclamation Against American Usurpation' (Matamoros, 1846)

General Francisco Mejía (c.1795–c.1852) was a veteran of the Mexican independence movement and the subsequent anti-colonial struggles of the 1820s against Spain. By the mid-1840s, he was faced with a new territorial threat from the Americans to the north, who were contesting increasing amounts of land.

---

10. This reference to the land as 'ours' may reflect an earlier gender division of labour in which women were the agriculturalists; see Nancy F. Cott, Jeanne Boydston, Ann Braude, Lori Ginzberg and Molly Ladd-Taylor, *Root of Bitterness: Document of the Social History of American Women* (Boston: Northeastern University Press, 1966), p. 177.

11. James Monroe was sworn in as US President in March 1817.

When Zachary Taylor's US army marched to the Rio Grande in early 1846, Mejía was stationed at Matamoros on the southern side of the river, and had this famous proclamation read to his troops on 18 March, reviewing the history of Mexican–American relations concerning Texas and charging the US with illegal conduct. Though he was superseded by other commanders, his speech remains a key document of Mexican resistance to the war that would break out in April 1846, concluding two years later with the loss of vast tracts of land to the US.

Source

Steven R. Butler (ed.), *A Documentary History of the Mexican War* (Richardson, TX: Descendants of Mexican War Veterans, 1995), p. 25.

The general-in-chief of the forces assembled against the enemy, to the inhabitants of this department and the troops under his command.

FELLOW-CITIZENS: – The annexation of the department of Texas to the United States,[12] projected and consummated by the tortuous policy of the cabinet of the Union, does not yet satisfy the ambitious desires of the degenerate sons of Washington. The civilized world[13] has already recognized in that act all the marks of injustice, iniquity, and the most scandalous violation of the rights of nations. Indelible is the stain which will for ever darken the character for virtue falsely attributed to the people of the United States; and posterity will regard with horror their perfidious conduct, and the immorality of the means employed by them to carry into effect that most degrading depredation. The right of conquest has always been a crime against humanity; but nations jealous of their dignity and reputation have endeavoured at least to cover it by the splendour of arms and the prestige of victory. To the United States, it has been reserved to put in practice dissimulation, fraud, and the basest treachery, in order to obtain possession, in the midst of peace, of the territory of a friendly nation, which generously relied upon the faith of promises and the solemnity of treaties.

The cabinet of the United States does not, however, stop in its career of usurpation. Not only does it aspire to the possession of the department of Texas, but it covets also the regions on the left bank of the Rio Bravo. Its army, hitherto for some time stationed at Corpus Christi, is now advancing to take

---

12. The Republic of Texas declared independence from the Republic of Mexico in March 1836, and joined the United States of America in December 1845.
13. A potential invocation of Jefferson's address of a 'candid world' in the US Declaration of Independence.

possession of a large part of Tamaulipas; and its vanguard has arrived at the Arroya Colorado, distant eighteen leagues from this place. What expectations, therefore, can the Mexican government have of treating with an enemy, who, whilst endeavouring to lull us into security, by opening diplomatic negotiations, proceeds to occupy a territory which never could have been the object of the pending discussion? The limits of Texas are certain and recognized; never have they extended beyond the river Nueces; notwithstanding which, the American army has crossed the line separating Tamaulipas from that department. Even though Mexico could forget that the United States urged and aided the rebellion of the former colonists,[14] and that the principle, giving to an independent people the right to annex itself to another nation, is not applicable to the case, in which the latter has been the protector of the independence of the former, with the object of admitting it into its own bosom; even though it could be accepted as an axiom of international law, that the violation of every rule of morality and justice might serve as a legitimate title for acquisition; nevertheless, the territory of Tamaulipas would still remain beyond the law of annexation, sanctioned by the American Congress; because that law comprises independent Texas, the ground occupied by the rebellious colony, and in no wise includes other departments, in which the Mexican government has uninterruptedly exercised its legitimate authority.

Fellow-countrymen: With an enemy which respects not its own laws, which shamelessly derides the very principles invoked by it previously, in order to excuse its ambitious views, we have no other resource than arms. We are fortunately always prepared to take them up with glory, in defence of our country; little do we regard the blood in our veins, when we are called on to shed it in vindication of our honour, to assure our nationality and independence. If to the torrent of devastation which threatens us it be necessary to oppose a dike of steel, our swords will form it; and on their sharp points will the enemy receive the fruits of his anticipated conquest. If the banks of the Panuco have been immortalized by the defeat of an enemy, respectable and worthy of the valour of Mexico, those of the Bravo shall witness the ignominy of the proud sons of the north, and its deep waters shall serve as the sepulchre for those who dare to approach it. The flame of patriotism which burns in our hearts will receive new fuel from the odious presence of the conquerors; and the cry of Dolores[15] and Iguala[16] shall be re-echoed with harmony to our ears, when we take up our march to oppose our naked breasts to the rifles of the hunters of the Mississippi.

---

14. Volunteers from the US undertook much of the fighting in the Texas Revolution of 1835–6.

15. For the brief revolutionary speech known as 'The Cry of Dolores' ('El Grito de Dolores') see Chapter 1 (p. 52).

16. The Plan of Iguala was a revolutionary proclamation promulgated in February 1821.

3. John Calhoun, 'Mexican Annexation and the "White Race"' (Washington, DC, 1848)

When American troops prevailed over Mexican forces in 1848, peace negotiations focused on how much of Mexico would be incorporated into the US. Among the arguments made against incorporation were those that expressed the fear that territorial acquisitions would transform the republic for the worse. The most important of these was delivered by John C. Calhoun (1782–1850), Senator for South Carolina, Vice President under John Quincy Adams and Andrew Jackson, and one of the era's most prominent pro-slavery advocates. During the 1840s, he shifted from being a supporter of Mexican annexation to a fierce sceptic of the Mexican–American War, declaring to Congress in May 1846 that 'when I look on and see that we are rushing upon the most tremendous event . . . I am in a state of wonder and deep alarm'.[17]

His reasons were in part constitutional and in part concerned with sectional interests. He argued that territorial expansion amounted to a dangerous expansion of Federal power, threatening the republic's economic future and undermining the power of the Southern states. However, as this contribution to a Senate debate opposing the incorporation of Mexican lands makes clear, racial anxieties were also central to his anti-imperialist stance: specifically, the concern that bringing non-white peoples into the country would imperil 'the free white race'.

Source
The Congressional Globe, 6 January 1848.

'RESOLVED, That to conquer Mexico and to hold it, either as a province or to incorporate it into the Union, would be inconsistent with the avowed object for which the war has been prosecuted;[18] a departure from the settled policy of the Government; in conflict with its character and genius; and in the end subversive of our free and popular institutions.'

. . . it is without example or precedent, either to hold Mexico as a province, or to incorporate her into our Union. No example of such a line of policy can be found. We have conquered many of the neighboring tribes of Indians, but we have never thought of holding them in subjection – never of incorporating them into our Union. They have either been left as an independent people amongst us, or been driven into the forests.

---

17. *The Congressional Globe*, 12 May 1846.
18. The declaration of war against Mexico in May 1846 was officially on the basis of self-defence against incursions across the Rio Grande.

I know further, sir, that we have never dreamt of incorporating into our Union any but the Caucasian race – the free white race. To incorporate Mexico, would be the very first instance of the kind of incorporating an Indian race; for more than half of the Mexicans are Indians, and the other is composed chiefly of mixed tribes. I protest against such a union as that! Ours, sir, is the Government of a white race.

The greatest misfortunes of Spanish America are to be traced to the fatal error of placing these colored races on an equality with the white race.[19] That error destroyed the social arrangement which formed the basis of society. The Portuguese and ourselves have escaped – the Portuguese at least to some extent – and we are the only people on this continent which have made revolutions without being followed by anarchy. And yet it is professed and talked about to erect these Mexicans into a Territorial Government, and place them on an equality with the people of the United States. I protest utterly against such a project.

Sir, it is a remarkable fact, that in the whole history of man, as far as my knowledge extends, there is no instance whatever of any civilized colored races being found equal to the establishment of free popular government, although by far the largest portion of the human family is composed of these races. And even in the savage state we scarcely find them anywhere with such government, except it be our noble savages – for noble I will call them. They, for the most part, had free institutions, but they are easily sustained among a savage people. Are we to overlook this fact? Are we to associate with ourselves as equals, companions, and fellow-citizens, the Indians and mixed race of Mexico? Sir, I should consider such a thing as fatal to our institutions.

4. John Bright, 'Opposition to India Policy' (London, 1858)

In the 1850s, Great Britain was consolidating its control over its South Asian territories, following the Indian Rebellion of 1857. Prime Minister Lord Palmerston introduced a bill to transfer control of the territories from the East India Company to the British Crown, an arrangement that would become known as the British Raj. At this crucial juncture, various forms of anti-imperialist arguments were being made against such an authoritarian presence in the region. One of the most prominent came from the English Quaker politician John Bright (1811–89), a leading figure in nineteenth-century British liberal radicalism. A famously effective public speaker, described by Henry Adams as 'the first orator in the world', his speeches helped direct

---

19. A racial caste system was officially abolished under Mexican independence in 1821.

Parliamentary feeling on issues ranging from Catholic emancipation, voting reform and anti-slavery to repeal of the Corn Laws.[20]

Bright was also one of the era's most eloquent opponents of British Empire, part of a 'Manchester School' of liberalism that argued against imperial expansion in favour of free-trade separatism. In this speech to the House of Commons on 24 June 1858, he outlined a series of practical and moral objections to imperial policy in Asia and urged for a transformation of British rule. Unlike fellow liberal anti-imperialists such as Cobden, who maintained a pessimistic view of the 'hopeless' case of India, Bright fostered an approach that was practical and reform-orientated, citing the Roman Empire's infrastructural programme as inspiration and arguing for a new posture of free trade over military domination.

Source
Hansard, House of Commons, 24 June 1858.

But how long does England propose to govern India?[21] Nobody answers that question, and nobody can answer it. Be it 50, or 100, or 500 years, does any man with the smallest glimmering of common sense believe that so great a country, with its twenty different nations and its twenty languages, can ever be bound up and consolidated into one compact and enduring empire? I believe such a thing to be utterly impossible. We must fail in the attempt if ever we make it, and we are bound to look into the future with reference to that point.

The Presidency of Madras, for instance, having its own Government, would in fifty years become one compact State, and every part of the Presidency would look to the city of Madras as its capital, and to the Government of Madras as its ruling power. If that were to go on for a century or more, there would be five or six Presidencies of India built up into so many compact States; and if at any future period the sovereignty of England should be withdrawn, we should leave so many Presidencies built up and firmly compacted together, each able to support its own independence and its own Government; and we should be able to say we had not left the country a prey to that anarchy and discord which I believe to be inevitable if we insist on holding those vast territories with the idea of building them up into one great empire. But I am obliged to admit that mere machinery is not sufficient in this case, either with respect to my own scheme or to that of the noble Lord (Lord Stanley).[22] We want something else

20. Bernard Porter, *Critics of Empire: British Radicals and the Imperial Challenge* (London: I. B. Tauris, 2008), p. 13.
21. British dominion over India is usually dated to the Battle of Plassey in 1757.
22. Edward Henry Stanley, Early of Derby (1826–93), proposed a Government of India Act transferring power over India to the British Crown.

than mere clerks, stationery, despatches, and so forth. We want what I shall designate as a new feeling in England, and an entirely new policy in India. We must in future have India governed, not for a handful of Englishmen, not for that Civil Service whose praises are so constantly sounded in this House. You may govern India, if you like, for the good of England, but the good of England must come through the channels of the good of India.

There are but two modes of gaining anything by our connection with India. The one is by plundering the people of India, and the other by trading with them. I prefer to do it by trading with them. But in order that England may become rich by trading with India, India itself must become rich, and India can only become rich through the honest administration of justice and through entire security of life and property.

Now, as to this new policy, I will tell the House what I think the Prime Minister should do. He ought, I think, always to choose for his President of the Board of Control or his Secretary of State for India, a man who cannot be excelled by any other man in his Cabinet, or in his party, for capacity, for honesty, for attention to his duties, and for knowledge adapted to the particular office to which he is appointed. If any Prime Minister appoint an inefficient man to such an office, he will be a traitor to the Throne of England. That officer, appointed for the qualities I have just indicated, should, with equal scrupulousness and consciousness, make the appointments, whether of the Governor-General, or (should that office be abolished) of the Governors of the Presidencies of India. Those appointments should not be rewards for old men simply because such men have done good service when in their prime, nor should they be rewards for mere party service, but they should be appointments given under a feeling that interests of the very highest moment, connected with this country, depend on those great offices in India being properly filled. The same principles should run throughout the whole system of government; for unless there be a very high degree of virtue in all these appointments, and unless our great object be to govern India well and to exalt the name of England in the eyes of the whole Native population, all that we have recourse to in the way of machinery will be of very little use indeed.

I admit that this is a great work; I admit, also, that the further I go into the consideration of this question, the more I feel that it is too large for me to grapple with, and that every step we take in it should be taken as if we were men walking in the dark. We have, however, certain great principles to guide us, and by their light we may make steps in advance, if not fast, at any rate sure. But we start from an unfortunate position. We start from a platform of conquest by force of arms extending over a hundred years. There is nothing in the world worse than the sort of foundation from which we start. The greatest genius who has shed lustre on the literature of this country has said, 'There is no sure foundation set on blood'; and it may be our unhappy fate, in regard to India, to demonstrate the truth of that saying. We are always subjugators, and we must be viewed with hatred and suspicion. I say we must look at the thing as it is, if we are to see our exact position, what our duty is, and what chance there is of our retaining India and of governing it for the advantage of its people. Our difficulties have been enormously increased by the revolt. The people of India have only seen England in its worst form in that country. They have seen it in its military power, its exclusive Civil Service, and in the supremacy of a handful of foreigners. When Natives of India come to this country, they are delighted with England and with Englishmen. They find themselves treated with a kindness, a consideration, a respect, to which they were wholly strangers in their own country; and they cannot understand how it is that men who are so just, so attentive to them here, sometimes, indeed too often, appear to them in a different character in India. I remember that the Hon. Frederic Shore, who wrote some thirty years since, stated, in his able and instructive book, that even in his time the conduct of the English in India towards the Natives was less agreeable, less kindly, less just than it had been in former years; and in 1853, before the Committee presided over by the hon. Member for Huntingdon (Mr. T. Baring), evidence was given that the feeling between the rulers and the ruled in India was becoming every year less like what could be desired.

. . .

Now, perhaps I may be told that I am proposing strange things, quite out of the ordinary routine of government. I admit it. We are in a position that necessitates something out of the ordinary routine. There are positions and times in the history of every country, as in the lives of individuals, when courage and action are absolute salvation; and now the Crown of England, acting by the advice of the responsible Ministers, must, in my opinion, have recourse to a great and unusual measure in order to allay the anxieties which prevail throughout the whole of India. The people of India do not like us, but they scarcely know where to turn if we left them. They are sheep literally without a shepherd. They are people whom you have subdued, and who have the highest and strongest claims upon you – claims which you cannot forget – claims which, if you do not act upon, you may rely upon it that, if there be a judgment for nations – as I believe there is – as for individuals, our children in no distant generation must pay the penalty which we have purchased by neglecting our duty to the populations of India.

5. William Jennings Bryan, 'Imperialism' (Kansas City, 1900)

In 1898, the US Government had annexed Cuba, Puerto Rico, the Philippines, Guam and Hawaii as part of the Spanish–American War, an event that many see as the onset of the mature imperialist phase in American political history. Proponents of American expansion, such as President McKinley, made a case for empire that fused ideas of Manifest Destiny with a rhetoric of modern internationalism.

In the Presidential election of 1900, the Democratic Party candidate, William Jennings Bryan (1860–1925), made opposition to such imperialist ambitions a central campaign issue. Though Bryan had initially supported the war, its conduct and outcome had led him to see imperialism as a moral crisis for the American people. Before an audience of 50,000 people at the Democratic National Convention in Kansas City, Missouri, on 8 August 1900, Bryan outlined this anti-imperialist creed, arguing in Jeffersonian terms that it was impossible for America to become a colonial power without undermining its crucial moral identity and destiny. Bryan lost the 1900 election and the US retained its new territorial possessions, though Cuba became independent once more in 1902.

Source

William Jennings Bryan, 'Imperialism', in *Under Other Flags: Travels, Lectures, Speeches* (Lincoln, NE: Woodruff-Collins Printing Co., 1904).

Mr. Chairman and Members of the Notification Committee:

I shall, at an early day, and in a more formal manner, accept the nomination which you tender, and shall at that time discuss the various questions covered by the Democratic platform. It may not be out of place, however, to submit a few observations at this time upon the general character of the contest before us and upon the question which is declared to be of paramount importance in this campaign.

. . .

Those who would have this Nation enter upon a career of empire must consider, not only the effect of imperialism on the Filipinos, but they must also calculate its effects upon our own nation. We cannot repudiate the principle of self-government in the Philippines without weakening that principle here.

Lincoln said that the safety of this Nation was not in its fleets, its armies, or its forts, but in the spirit which prizes liberty as the heritage of all men, in all lands, everywhere, and he warned his countrymen that they could not destroy this spirit without planting the seeds of despotism at their own doors.

Even now we are beginning to see the paralyzing influence of imperialism. Heretofore this Nation has been prompt to express its sympathy with those who were fighting for civil liberty. While our sphere of activity has been limited to the Western Hemisphere, our sympathies have not been bounded by the seas. We have felt it due to ourselves and to the world, as well as to those who were struggling for the right to govern themselves, to proclaim the interest which our people have, from the date of their own independence, felt in every contest between human rights and arbitrary power.

. . .

Our opponents, conscious of the weakness of their cause, seek to confuse imperialism with expansion, and have even dared to claim Jefferson as a supporter of their policy. Jefferson spoke so freely and used language with such precision that no one can be ignorant of his views. On one occasion he declared: 'If there be one principle more deeply rooted than any other in the mind of every American, it is that we should have nothing to do with conquest.' And again he said: 'Conquest is not in our principles; it is inconsistent with our government.'[23]

The forcible annexation of territory to be governed by arbitrary power differs as much from the acquisition of territory to be built up into States as a monarchy differs from a democracy. The Democratic party does not oppose expansion when expansion enlarges the area of the Republic and incorporates land which can be settled by American citizens, or adds to our population people who are willing to become citizens and are capable of discharging their duties as such.

The acquisition of the Louisiana territory, Florida, Texas and other tracts which have been secured from time to time enlarged the republic and the Constitution followed the flag into the new territory. It is now proposed to seize upon distant territory already more densely populated than our own country and to force upon the people a government for which there is no warrant in our Constitution or our laws.

. . .

I can conceive of a national destiny surpassing the glories of the present and the past – a destiny which meets the responsibility of today and measures up to the possibilities of the future. Behold a republic, resting securely upon the foundation stones quarried by revolutionary patriots from the mountain of eternal truth – a republic applying in practice and proclaiming to the world the self-evident propositions that all men are created equal; that they are endowed with inalienable rights; that governments are instituted among men to secure these rights, and that governments derive their just powers from the consent of the governed.[24]

Behold a republic in which civil and religious liberty stimulate all to earnest endeavor and in which the law restrains every hand uplifted for a neighbour's injury – a republic in which every citizen is a sovereign, but in which no one cares to wear a crown. Behold a republic standing erect while empires all around are bowed beneath the weight of their own armaments – a republic whose flag is loved while other flags are only feared. Behold a republic increasing in population, in wealth, in strength and in influence, solving the problems of civilization and hastening the coming of an universal brotherhood – a republic

---

23. Thomas Jefferson, 'Queries as to the Rights and Duties of the United States Under her Treaties with France', in H. A. Washington (ed.), *The Writings of Thomas Jefferson: Being His Autobiography, Correspondence, Reports, Messages, Addresses, and Other Writings, Official and Private* (Cambridge: Cambridge University Press, 2011), p. 412.
24. Much of these sentences comes directly from the Declaration of Independence.

which shakes thrones and dissolves aristocracies by its silent example and gives light and inspiration to those who sit in darkness. Behold a republic gradually but surely becoming the supreme moral factor in the world's progress and the accepted arbiter of the world's disputes – a republic whose history, like the path of the just, 'is as the shining light that shineth more and more unto the perfect day.'[25]

---

25. Proverbs 4: 18.

Part B: Defending Empire

6. Benjamin Disraeli, 'The Maintenance of Empire' (London, 1872)

Faced with an emergent challenge from German expansionism, the future of empire returned as a key theme in 1870s British politics. One of those eager to shape public opinion on the imperial question was former Conservative Prime Minister and Chancellor of the Exchequer Benjamin Disraeli (1804–81). In 1872, he was out of office, having been defeated in 1868 in the general election by William Ewart Gladstone's Liberal Party. Earlier in his career, Disraeli had called the empire 'a millstone round our necks', but during this period in opposition, his views underwent a transition that saw him adopt a renewed enthusiasm for empire as a popular banner that might return the Tories to power.

His famous speech at the Crystal Palace in South London, before a banquet of the National Union of Conservative and Constitutional Associations on 24 June 1872, was a key milestone in this shift and became one of the most influential expressions of what became known as the 'New Imperialism'.[26] Delivered in a locale chosen for its symbolism, harking back to the high Victorian glories of the Great Exhibition a generation before, the speech pledged renewed faith in the value of the empire, proclaiming that it was the duty of the Conservative Party to maintain it.[27] There was political capital to be gained from such an embrace of imperial jingoism, and Disraeli's Conservatives were returned to government in the election of February 1874.

Source

Thomas E. Kebbel (ed.), *Selected Speeches of the late Right Honourable the Earl of Beaconsfield* (Longman: London, 1882).

Gentlemen, there is another and second great object of the Tory party. If the first is to maintain the institutions of the country, the second is, in my opinion, to uphold the empire of England. If you look to the history of this country since the advent of Liberalism[28] – forty years ago – you will find that there has been no effort so continuous, so subtle, supported by so much energy, and carried

---

26. Bernard Porter, *The Absent-Minded Imperialists: Empire, Society, and Culture in Britain* (Oxford: Oxford University Press, 2006), p. 111.

27. Stanley R. Stembridge, 'Disraeli and the Millstones', *Journal of British Studies*, 5: 1 (November 1965), p. 122.

28. A 'Liberal Party' first emerged in Britain in the late 1830s.

on with so much ability and acumen, as the attempts of Liberalism to effect the disintegration of the empire of England.

And, gentlemen, of all its efforts, this is the one which has been the nearest to success. Statesmen of the highest character, writers of the most distinguished ability, the most organized and efficient means, have been employed in this endeavour. It has been proved to all of us that we have lost money by our colonies. It has been shown with precise, mathematical demonstration that there never was a jewel in the crown of England that was so truly costly as the possession of India. How often has it been suggested that we should at once emancipate ourselves from this incubus. Well, that result was nearly accomplished. When those subtle views were adopted by the country under the plausible plea of granting self-government to the colonies, I confess that I myself thought that the tie was broken.

Not that I for one object to self-government. I cannot conceive how our distant colonies can have their affairs administered except by self-government. But self-government, in my opinion, when it was conceded, ought to have been conceded as a part of a great policy of imperial consolidation. It ought to have been accompanied by an imperial tariff, by securities for the people of England for the enjoyment of unappropriated lands which belonged to the sovereign as their trustee, and by a military code which should have precisely defined the means and the responsibilities by which the colonies should be defended, and by which, if necessary, this country should call for aid from the colonies themselves. It ought, further, to have been accompanied by the institution of some representative council in the metropolis, which would have brought the colonies into constant and continuous relations with the home government.

All this, however, was omitted because those who advised that policy – and I believe their convictions were sincere – looked upon the colonies of England, looked upon our connection with India, as a burden upon this country, viewing everything in a financial aspect, and totally passing by those moral and political considerations which make nations great, and by the influence of which alone men are distinguished from animals.

Well, what has been the result of this attempt during the reign of Liberalism for the disintegration of empire? It has entirely failed. But how has it failed? Through the sympathy of the colonies with the mother country. They have decided that the empire shall not be destroyed, and in my opinion no minister in this country will do his duty who neglects any opportunity of reconstructing as much as possible our colonial empire, and of responding to those distant sympathies which may become the source of incalculable strength and happiness to this land. Therefore, gentlemen, with respect to the second great object of the Tory party also – the maintenance of the Empire – public opinion appears to be in favour of our principles ...

When you return to your homes, when you return to your counties and your cities, you must tell to all those whom you can influence that the time is at hand, that, at least, it cannot be far distant, when England will have to decide between national and cosmopolitan principles. The issue is not a mean one. It is whether you will be content to be a comfortable England, modelled and moulded upon continental principles and meeting in due course an inevitable fate, or whether you will be a great country, – an imperial country – a country where your sons, when they rise, rise to paramount positions, and obtain not merely the esteem of their countrymen, but command the respect of the world.

7. Theodore Roosevelt, 'The Strenuous Life' (Chicago, 1899)

Just as the rhetoric of the 'New Imperialism' transformed British discussions of empire, pro-imperialist language came to characterise mainstream US politics at the century's close. No figure is more associated with this language than Theodore Roosevelt (1858–1919). He had been one of America's most ardent imperialists for the previous decade and was resourceful in mounting a case for empire that rhetorically linked it to a broader cultural mission. When running as McKinley's Vice President on the 1900 Republican ticket, Roosevelt's countless stump speeches routinely mounted a stirring defence of the Spanish–American War and its territorial acquisitions. Arguing against what he saw as the *faux* humanitarianism of Democrat leader William Jennings Bryan, Roosevelt took the American empire as his signature theme.

The address below, made before the Hamilton Club in Chicago on 10 April 1899, embodies this message. In a register of unblinking optimism, Roosevelt updates the tropes of Manifest Destiny for a new global era, fusing American exceptionalist ideas with a secular emphasis on masculine bodily endeavour, drawn in part from his own experience of transcending childhood infirmity. The speech made front pages around the country and confirmed him as one of the key political figures of his generation.[29]

Source

Theodore Roosevelt, *Letters and Speeches*, ed. Louis Auchincloss (New York: Library of America, 2004).

In speaking to you, men of the greatest city of the West, men of the State which gave to the country Lincoln and Grant, men who preeminently and distinctly embody all that is most American in the American character I wish to preach, not the doctrine of ignoble ease, but the doctrine of the strenuous life. The life of toil and effort, of labor and strife; to preach that highest form of success

---

29. Kathleen Dalton, *Theodore Roosevelt: A Strenuous Life* (New York: Random House, 2002), p. 186.

which comes, not to the man who desires mere easy peace, but to the man who does not shrink from danger, from hardship or from bitter toil, and who out of these wins the splendid ultimate triumph.

. . .

In the West Indies and the Philippines alike we are confronted by most difficult problems. It is cowardly to shrink from solving them in the proper way; for solved they must be, if not by us, then by some stronger and more manful race. If we are too weak, too selfish, or too foolish to solve them, some bolder and abler people must undertake the solution. Personally, I am far too firm a believer in the greatness of my country and the power of my countrymen to admit for one moment that we shall ever be driven to the ignoble alternative.

The problems are different for the different islands. Porto Rico is not large enough to stand alone. We must govern it wisely and well, primarily in the interest of its own people. Cuba is, in my judgment, entitled ultimately to settle for itself whether it shall be an independent state or an integral portion of the mightiest of republics. But until order and stable liberty are secured, we must remain in the island to insure them, and infinite tact, judgment, moderation, and courage must be shown by our military and civil representatives in keeping the island pacified, in relentlessly stamping out brigandage, in protecting all alike, and yet in showing proper recognition to the men who have fought for Cuban liberty. The Philippines offer a yet graver problem. Their population includes halfcaste and native Christians, warlike Moslems, and wild pagans. Many of their people are utterly unfit for self-government, and show no signs of becoming fit. Others may in time become fit but at present can only take part in self-government under a wise supervision, at once firm and beneficent. We have driven Spanish tyranny from the islands. If we now let it be replaced by savage anarchy, our work has been for harm and not for good. I have scant patience with those who fear to undertake the task of governing the Philippines, and who openly avow that they do fear to undertake it, or that they shrink from it because of the expense and trouble; but I have even scanter patience with those who make a pretense of humanitarianism to hide and cover their timidity and who cant about 'liberty' and the 'consent of the governed,' in order to excuse themselves for their unwillingness to play the part of men. Their doctrines, if carried out, would make it incumbent upon us to leave the Apaches of Arizona to work out their own salvation, and to decline to interfere in a single Indian reservation. Their doctrines condemn your forefathers and mine for ever having settled in these United States.

England's rule in India and Egypt has been of great benefit to England, for it has trained up generations of men accustomed to look at the larger and loftier side of public life. It has been of even greater benefit to India and Egypt. And finally, and most of all, it has advanced the cause of civilization. So, if we do our duty aright in the Philippines, we will add to that national renown which is the highest and finest part of national life, will greatly benefit the people of the Philippine Islands, and, above all, we will play our part well in the great work of uplifting mankind. But to do this work, keep ever in mind that we must show in a very high degree the qualities of courage, of honesty, and of good judgment. Resistance must be stamped out. The first and all-important work to be done is to establish the supremacy of our flag. We must put down armed resistance before we can accomplish anything else, and there should be no parleying, no faltering, in dealing with our foe. As for those in our own country who encourage the foe, we can afford contemptuously to disregard them; but it must be remembered that their utterances are not saved from being treasonable merely by the fact that they are despicable.

When once we have put down armed resistance, when once our rule is acknowledged, then an even more difficult task will begin, for then we must see to it that the islands are administered with absolute honesty and with good judgment. If we let the public service of the islands be turned into the prey of the spoils politician, we shall have begun to tread the path which Spain trod to her own destruction. We must send out there only good and able men, chosen for their fitness, and not because of their partisan service, and those men must not only administer impartial justice to the natives and serve their own government with honesty and fidelity, but must show the utmost tact and firmness, remembering that, with such people as those with whom we are to deal, weakness is the greatest of crimes, and that next to weakness comes lack of consideration for their principles and prejudices.

I preach to you, then, my countrymen, that our country calls not for the life of ease but for the life of strenuous endeavor. The twentieth century looms before us big with the fate of many nations. If we stand idly by, if we seek merely swollen, slothful ease and ignoble peace, if we shrink from the hard contests where men must win at hazard of their lives and at the risk of all they hold dear, then the bolder and stronger peoples will pass us by, and will win for themselves the domination of the world. Let us therefore boldly face the life of strife, resolute to do our duty well and manfully; resolute to uphold righteousness by deed and by word; resolute to be both honest and brave, to serve high ideals, yet to use practical methods. Above all, let us shrink from no strife, moral or physical, within or without the nation, provided we are certain that the strife is justified, for it is only through strife, through hard and dangerous endeavor, that we shall ultimately win the goal of true national greatness.

8. Albert J. Beveridge, 'The Philippines Are Ours Forever' (Washington, DC, 1900)

Like Roosevelt, fellow Republican politician Albert J. Beveridge (1862–1927) combined progressivism with an often contradictory commitment to imperialism. A lawyer from the Mid-West, his political rise in the late 1890s was a direct result of his strident advocacy of American expansion overseas, a belief underpinned by the twin concerns of nationalism and commercial expansion. In a famous 1898 speech entitled 'March of the Flag', he poured scorn on the idea of self-determination for Spain's former colonies, asking 'shall we save them from these nations to give them the self-rule of tragedy? It would be like giving a razor to a babe and telling it to shave itself.'[30]

Elected to the Senate for Indiana in 1899, he travelled to the Philippines to witness conditions first-hand, and came back to Washington to persuade his colleagues that America must accept its place as a world power. This 9 January 1900 speech before Congress was typical of a messianic strain of pro-imperialist rhetoric, systematically refuting prominent misgivings about what the new age of American empire might bring.

Source

'Our Philippine Policy, Senator Alfred J. Beveridge', *Congressional Record, Senate*, 9 January 1900, pp. 704–11.

Mr. President, this question is deeper than any question of party politics; deeper than any question of the isolated policy of our country even; deeper even than any question of constitutional power. It is elemental. It is racial. God has not been preparing the English-speaking and Teutonic peoples for a thousand years for nothing but vain and idle self-contemplation and self-admiration. No! He has made us the master organizers of the world to establish system where chaos reigns. He has given us the spirit of progress to overwhelm the forces of reaction throughout the earth. He has made us adepts in government that we may administer government among savage and senile peoples. Were it not for such a force as this the world would relapse into barbarism and night. And of all our race He has marked the American people as His chosen nation to finally lead in the regeneration of the world. This is the divine mission of America, and it holds for us all the profit, all the glory, all the happiness possible to man. We are trustees of the world's progress, guardians of its righteous peace. The judgment of the Master is upon us: 'Ye have been faithful over a few things; I will make you ruler over many things.'

What shall history say of us? Shall it say that we renounced that holy trust, left the savage to his base condition, the wilderness to the reign of waste, deserted duty, abandoned glory, forgot our sordid profit even, because we feared our strength and read the charter of our powers with the doubter's eye and the quibbler's mind? Shall it say that, called by events to captain and command the proudest, ablest, purest race of history in history's noblest work, we declined

---

30. Albert J. Beveridge, *The Meaning of the Times and Other Speeches* (Indianapolis: Bobbs Merrill, 1908), p. 25.

that great commission? Our fathers would not have had it so. No! They founded no paralytic government, incapable of the simplest acts of administration. They planted no sluggard people, passive while the world's work calls them. They established no reactionary nation. They unfurled no retreating flag.

That flag has never paused in its onward march. Who dares halt it now – now, when history's largest events are carrying it forward; now, when we are at last one people, strong enough for any task, great enough for any glory destiny can bestow? How comes it that our first century closes with the process of consolidating the American people into a unit just accomplished, and quick upon the stroke of that great hour presses upon us our world opportunity, world duty, and world glory, which none but the people welded into an invisible nation can achieve or perform?

Blind indeed is he who sees not the hand of God in events so vast, so harmonious, so benign. Reactionary indeed is the mind that perceives not that this vital people is the strongest of the saving forces of the world; that our place, therefore, is at the head of the constructing and redeeming nations of the earth; and that to stand aside while events march on is a surrender of our interests, a betrayal of our duty as blind as it is base. Craven indeed is the heart that fears to perform a work so golden and so noble; that dares not win a glory so immortal.

Do you tell me that it will cost us money? When did Americans ever measure duty by financial standards? Do you tell me of the tremendous toil required to overcome the vast difficulties of our task? What mighty work for the world, for humanity, even for ourselves has ever been done with ease? Even our bread must we eat by the sweat of our faces. Why are we charged with power such as no people ever knew if we are not to use it in a work such as no people ever wrought? Who will dispute the divine meaning of the fable of the talents?

Do you remind me of the precious blood that must be shed, the lives that must be given, the broken hearts of loved ones for their slain? And this is indeed a heavier price than all combined. And, yet, as a nation, every historic duty we have done, every achievement we have accomplished has been by the sacrifice of our noblest sons. Every holy memory that glorifies the flag is of those heroes who have died that its onward march might not be stayed. It is the nation's dearest lives yielded for the flag that makes it dear to us; it is the nation's most precious blood poured out for it that makes it precious to us. That flag is woven of heroism and grief, of the bravery of men and women's tears, of righteousness and battle, of sacrifice and anguish, of triumph and of glory. It is these which make our flag a holy thing.

Part C: The Irish Question

9. Daniel O'Connell, 'Ireland Shall be Free' (Mullaghmast, Ireland, 1843)

During the 1830s and early 1840s, a remarkable campaign was waged by the Repeal Association to return Ireland to legislative independence and establish a Parliament in Dublin. The rapid growth the movement enjoyed was due in no small part to having one of the nineteenth century's greatest orators at its helm. Daniel O'Connell (1775–1847) was a former lawyer who founded the Catholic Association in 1823 and entered Westminster following the Catholic Emancipation Act of 1829, before leading the Repeal Association. At the heart of the movement's efforts were a series of enormous open-air events known as 'monster meetings' held across Ireland, at which O'Connell, known affectionately as 'The Liberator', addressed crowds with a combined total of more than 700,000 people. 'You will scarcely meet in Ireland a peasant', reported the British journalist James Grant, 'who has not heard Mr O'Connell speak.'[31]

O'Connell picked locations with historical connections, the last and most memorable being Mullaghmast in County Kildare, the site of an 1857 massacre of Irish gentry by the English army. From early on Saturday, supporters from every corner of Ireland converged on the small town, with boarding houses booked out within a ten-mile radius of the meeting place. On the morning of the event, the Liberator's procession passed through villages and towns, the roadsides lined with cheering crowds. Mounting a large platform especially assembled for the event in the meeting field, the sixty-eight-year-old orator addressed a sea of supporters with the words below. Though only a fraction could hear him speak, these words were widely reprinted and circulated. As a result of these meetings, O'Connell was arrested for conspiracy and imprisoned for three months.

Source

Lewis Copeland, Lawrence W. Lamm and Stephen J. McKenna, *The World's Great Speeches* (Mineola, NY: Dover, 1999).

---

31. James Grant, *Impressions of Ireland and the Irish, 1844*, 2 vols (London: Cunningham, 1844), vol. II, pp. 199–200.

At Mullaghmast (and I have chosen this for this obvious reason), we are on the precise spot where English treachery – aye, and false Irish treachery, too – consummated a massacre[32] that has never been imitated, save in the massacre of the Mamelukes by Mahomet Ali.[33] It was necessary to have Turks atrocious enough to commit a crime equal to that perpetrated by Englishmen. But do not think that the massacre at Mullaghmast was a question between Protestants and Catholics – it was no such thing. The murdered persons were to be sure Catholics, but a great number of the murderers were also Catholics, and Irishmen, because there were then, as well as now, many Catholics who were traitors to Ireland. But we have now this advantage, that we have many honest Protestants joining us[34] – joining us heartily in hand and heart, for old Ireland and liberty. I thought this a fit and becoming spot to celebrate, in the open day, our unanimity in declaring our determination not to be misled by any treachery. Oh, my friends, I will keep you clear of all treachery – there shall be no bargain, no compromise with England – we shall take nothing but repeal, and a parliament in College Green.

You will never, by my advice, confide in any false hopes they hold out to you; never confide in anything coming from them, or cease from your struggle, no matter what promise may be held out to you, until you hear me say I am satisfied; and I will tell you where I will say that – near the statue of King William, in College Green. No, we came here to express our determination to die to a man, if necessary, in the cause of old Ireland. We came to take advice of each other, and above all, I believe you came here to take my advice. I can tell you, I have the game in my hand – I have the triumph secure – I have the repeal certain, if you but obey my advice.

[Great cheers, and cries of 'We will obey you in anything.']

I will go slow – you must allow me to do so – but you will go sure. No man shall find himself imprisoned or persecuted who follows my advice. I have led you thus far in safety; I have swelled the multitude of repealers until they are identified with the entire population, or nearly the entire population of the land, for seven eighths of the Irish people are now enrolling themselves repealers.

[Cheers and cries of more power to you.]

I don't want more power; I have power enough, and all I ask of you is to allow me to use it. I will go on quietly and slowly, but I will go on firmly, and with a certainty of success. I am now arranging a plan for the formation of the Irish House of Commons.

. . .

---

32. In late 1577, the Lord Deputy of Ireland summoned hundreds of members of leading families under false pretences to Mullaghmast in County Kildare, where they were ambushed and massacred.

33. In 1811, Muhammad Ali, the Ottoman Viceroy of Egypt, conducted a similar massacre of unsuspecting Mameluke notables in Cairo.

34. The Repeal Association enjoyed support from a number of eminent Anglo-Irish Protestants, including Sir John Gray and James Haughton.

Yes, my friends, for this purpose I must get some time. I worked the present repeal year tolerably well. I believe no one in January last, would believe
that we could have such a meeting within the year as the Tara demonstration. You may be sure of this – and I say it in the presence of him who will
judge me – that I never will willfully deceive you. I have but one wish under
heaven, and that is for the liberty and prosperity of Ireland. I am for leaving
England to the English, Scotland to the Scotch, but we must have Ireland for
the Irish.

I will not be content until I see not a single man in any office, from the lowest
constable to the Lord Chancellor, but Irishmen. This is our land, and we must
have it. We will be obedient to the Queen, joined to England by the golden link
of the Crown, but we must have our own parliament, our own bench, our own
magistrates, and we will give some of the shoneens[35] which now occupy the
bench leave to retire, such as those lately appointed by Sugden.[36] He is a pretty
boy, sent here from England; but I ask, did you ever hear such a name as he has
got? I remember, in Wexford, a man told me he had a pig at home which he was
so fond of that he would call it Sugden. No: we shall get judicial independence
for Ireland. It is for this purpose we are assembled here to-day, as every countenance I see around me testifies. If there is any one here who is for the Union,
let him say so. Is there anybody here for the repeal?

[Cries of 'all, all,' and loud cheering.]

Yes, my friends, the Union was begot in iniquity – it was perpetrated in
fraud and cruelty. It was no compact, no bargain, but it was an act of the
most decided tyranny and corruption that was ever yet perpetrated. Trial by
jury was suspended – the right of personal protection was at an end – courts
martial sat throughout the land – and the county of Kildare, among others,
flowed with blood.

Oh, my friends, listen now to the man of peace, who will never expose
you to the power of your enemies. In 1798 there were some brave men, some
valiant men, to head the people at large, but there were many traitors, who left
the people in the power of their enemies.[37] The Curragh of Kildare afforded
an instance of the fate which Irishmen were to expect, who confided in their
Saxon enemies. Oh, it was an ill-organized, a premature, a foolish, and an absurd
insurrection ; but you have a leader now who never will allow you to commit
any act so foolish or so destructive.

How delighted do I feel with the thorough conviction which has come
over the minds of the people, that they could not gratify your enemies more
than by committing a crime. No; our ancestors suffered for confiding in the

---

35. A derogatory Gaelic term for Irish people who imitate English ways.
36. Edward Sugden, English-born Lord Chancellor of Ireland between 1841 and 1846.
37. In the Irish Rebellion of 1798, the United Irishmen rose up against British rule, but
failed in part due to the withdrawal of support by the French.

English, but we never will confide in them. They suffered for being divided amongst themselves. There is no division amongst us. They suffered for their own dissensions – for not standing man to man by each other's side. We shall stand peaceably side by side in the face of every enemy.

. . .

Yes, among the nations of the earth, Ireland stands number one in the physical strength of her sons, and in the beauty and purity of her daughters. Ireland, land of my forefathers, how my mind expands, and my spirit walks abroad in something of majesty, when I contemplate the high qualities, inestimable virtues, the true purity and piety, and religious fidelity of the inhabitants of your green fields and productive mountains. Oh, what a scene surrounds us! – It is not only the countless thousands of brave and active and peaceable and religious men that are here assembled, but nature herself has written her character with the finest beauty in the verdant plains that surround us.

Let any man run round the horizon with his eye, and tell me if created man ever produced anything so green and so lovely, so undulating, so teeming with production. The richest harvests that any land can produce are those reaped in Ireland; and then here are the sweetest meadows, the greenest fields, the loftiest mountains, the purest streams, the noblest rivers, the most capacious harbours – and her water power is equal to turn the machinery of the whole world. Oh, my friends, it is a country worth fighting for – it is a country worth dying for; but above all, it is a country worth being tranquil, determined, submissive and docile; for disciplined as you are in obedience to those who are breaking the way, and trampling down the barriers between you and your constitutional liberty, I will see every man of you having a vote, and every man protected by the ballot from the agent or landlord. I will see labour protected, and every title to possession recognized, when you are industrious and honest. I will see prosperity again throughout your land – the busy hum of the shuttle and the tinkling of the smithy shall be heard again. We shall see the nailer employed even until the middle of the night, and the carpenter covering himself with his chips. I will see prosperity in all its gradations spreading through a happy, contented, religious land.

I will hear the hymn of a happy people go forth at sunrise to God in praise of his mercies – and I will see the evening sun set down amongst the uplifted hands of a religious and free population. Every blessing that man can bestow and religion can confer upon the faithful heart, shall spread throughout the land. Stand by me – join with me – I will say be obedient to me, and Ireland shall be free.

10. Lewis C. Levin, 'The Papist Threat' (Philadelphia, 1844)

On the other side of the Atlantic, where an Irish diaspora continued to swell in major East Coast cities, many Americans took inspiration from the rhetoric of O'Connell. However, the increasing prominence of the Irish Question and Catholicism in US urban life also provoked a powerful backlash. The following speech by the nativist Pennsylvania politician Lewis Charles Levin represents this response at its most incendiary. As part of a campaign against immigration from Catholic countries and against what was seen as an extension of Papist political power, he became chief spokesman for a start-up political party calling itself the American Republican Party, which later became the Native American Party.

In May of 1844, Levin sparked a mass riot in downtown Philadelphia by attempting to give an anti-immigrant speech in the heart of an Irish-Catholic neighbourhood in Philadelphia. After being chased out of the area, Levin returned the following night, accompanied by thousands of protesters, who rioted and burnt down Irish homes and Catholic churches. Levin was later arrested for incitement to riot but never charged. The following speech, which was published as a pamphlet in general circulation, was typical of the tenor of anti-Irish Nativist rhetoric of the period.

Source

Lewis Charles Levin, *A Lecture on Irish Repeal and Elucidation of the Fallacy of its Principles and in Proof of its Pernicious Tendency, in its Moral, Religious and Political Aspects* (Philadelphia [no publisher], 1844).

Repeal! Irish Repeal! O'Connell and the Irish Catholics! Emancipation for Ireland. The Queen! The Pope! Irish Independence! O'Connell and Sedition! The Arrest of the Liberator! The Conspiracy crushed. 'If O'Connell suffers, Peel dies!' Another grand rally for old Ireland! Slavery and the President of the United States! His Holiness the Pope, and the degraded American people who give countenance to slavery!

These are a few of the watchwords of the times, that strike upon the ear of an American patriot, in the middle of the nineteenth century! The sounds are strange. They strike us with surprise. Nay, they appal us with apprehension. The Pope! the Queen! Irish Catholics and African slavery! What a cluster of ill-assorted associations, to be wound up with the name of Daniel O'Connell, Sedition, Conspiracy, and Arrest! Do we really live in the middle of the 19th century? Are we truly awake, or is all this a frightful dream? Is this the chosen land of liberty? Was it here, that the rights of man were erected on a foundation of blood? Was it here that Washington said, in the tones of a father – 'Shun the brawls of Europe'? How is this? The fair land of liberty become the battle-ground of kings, tyrants, popes and their political myrmidons? Why all this din and turmoil? Is the Republic in danger? Have the monarchs and popes of Europe hired wretches to insult us? Incendiaries to stir us up to riot? Slanderers to defile our freedom? Monarchists to scold us for slavery – themselves the slaves they pity? Or, have we lost the recollections of liberty, and sent to Europe for a supply of royal tutors to instruct us in the rights of man? How is this?

. . .

Genius and Ireland are but two names to denote the same thing; but Ireland and Popery are two deadening influences always fatal to her genius. Why, oh! why, will men hug to their bosoms the slimy serpent whose cold embrace is – death? Why, oh! Ireland, do you not rise like a disenthralled spirit, from the tomb of superstition, regenerated, vigorous, pure, manly! Casting off the fetters of an Iron Church, which crushes thought, tramples out the sparks of emulation from the glowing mind, and scatters ignorance, as well as indolence, throughout thy Heaven-blest land? Awake! – benighted, deluded, enslaved men! – awake to the glorious liberty of mind! Fulfil your destiny of greatness! Look upon the American People! Slandered by your Arch Deceiver! – abused, villified, insulted! Look upon them, proud and erect in the God-like attitude of the rights of man, scorning and trampling under their feet the tyrannous power of Church and State! Look upon them who hold the Pope to be a rank usurper on the rights of man – a wanton violator of the laws of God! Look upon them, and say: – Could they have acquired Liberty and Independence, had they been the white slaves of his holiness, the Pope? Think you the Declaration of American Independence would ever have seen the light, or its consummation ever have blazed through the world, if Thomas Jefferson had been an emissary of his Holiness, or George Washington had been a Daniel O'Connell?

Start not at this question. It is one suggested by common sense. American independence was the work of a little band of patriots, not one fifth the number of the population of Ireland. They, too, were oppressed by the persecutions of power, bigotry, and the unholy combination of Church and State. But they were not slaves to Papal power. They boasted 'liberty of conscience,' which to obtain and preserve, had driven them to horde with the untamed savage; and to battle to the death, with royal troops armed by the hand of monarchy to scourge rebellion.

Had this little American band, a handful of men compared to Ireland's overflowing population, been Roman Catholics, under the guidance of the Pope, what would have been their fate? Instead of a great Washington, some O'Connell would have sprung up among us, with a beggar's bag in his hand, asking for an Independence Fund! He would have mounted logs, casks, and market stalls, making glorious speeches to the members of an 'Independence Association;' with three cheers for liberty, followed by a rich repast, an elegant dinner, a sumptuous supper, or a splendid entertainment, where another speech would wind up the day's labor, exhorting the people to send on the Rent, and not let the 'Liberator'[38] starve. This would have been the farce of one day. And what the stage-play of another? Why,

---

38. Daniel O'Connell.

the 'Association of Liberty,' would assemble in the Hall of Independence: adopt a petition to her most gracious majesty; indite a missive to his holiness, the Pope; read the correspondence of the friends of America from distant climes, remitting their shillings and pence to support the orators of freedom. Then pass a resolution, unanimously, never to disturb the peace; never to fire a rifle; never to draw a sword; never to handle a pitchfork! But to depend on the gracious clemency of her most gracious majesty, to accord us the boon of Independence, as a consequence of our resolving never to fight for it!

. . .

Trace Repeal back one step, and whence does it flow? From the Papal throne. From that throne, unlike all others, built upon power, Religious and Temporal – Spiritual and Political. The Power which makes man a slave, and transforms Kings into Fiends – Priests into Tormentors – a People into Drones – a Country into a Desert. A Flower which extinguishes the fire on the Altar of Domestic Love – in a form peculiar, fatal, revolting! Snatching its votaries away from the homage of nature, – to the cold Convent – the repulsive Abbey – the gloomy cell of the anchorite – the horrid dungeons of the Inquisition, and the demoralizing edict of Celibacy. Stirring up Sedition, Rebellion and Civil War, as the only means of extending a power which reason revolts from, and persuasion fails to diffuse. Which mankind have resisted, in every age, at the peril and under the penalty of the cannon's mouth, the edge of the sword, the fire of the faggot, the torments of the stake, and the tortures of the rack!

Intelligence! Education! Knowledge! upborne on these pinions, no people can fear the inroads of Despotism, or shrink appalled from the monarchists of power. In vain will superstition plot, if an unshackled press, remains free to speak. In vain will Demagogues attempt to hoodwink the masses, if thought and reason be left free, to discuss truth, inquire into facts, investigate principles, and expose error, denounce fraud, reveal hypocrisy, and point out villainy to execration and contempt. A free Press, untrammelled thought and intrepid speech, are the true and potent champions of Liberty. Light, glorious, immortal, sublime light – is the Guardian Angel of the best gifts of heaven to man.

11. William E. Gladstone, 'Government of Ireland Bill' (London, 1886)

Under the leadership of Charles Stewart Parnell (1846–91) in the 1880s, the Irish Home Rule movement came as close as ever to securing self-government for Ireland. Liberal Prime Minister William Ewart Gladstone (1809–98) was a central figure in this attempt to find a legislative solution to the Irish Question. He had long been fixated on attempts to give Ireland greater sovereignty, had backed Peel's repeal of the Corn Laws, and upon becoming Premier for the first time in 1869, it is reported that his first response was to declare that 'my mission is to pacify Ireland'.[39] His 1869 Irish Church Act helped end the Protestant domination of Ireland, but his major effort came in his third term as Prime Minister with his ill-fated Government of Ireland Bill in 1886, which proposed the creation of a devolved assembly in Dublin.

On 7 June 1886, at the age of seventy-six, Gladstone introduced the bill into the Commons in a speech lasting over three hours. Urging the House to heed the 'voice' of Ireland and couching his proposal in a teleological language of tides and progress, he depicted Home Rule as the next stage of imperial evolution following the encouraging precedent set by the 1867 confederation of Canada. 'At last came the Old Man's speech, as vigorous as ever and in beautiful voice,' recalled his Cabinet Minister, Leonard Courtney, 'but it was a losing speech.'[40] The vote split the Liberal Party, with key members of his own party opting to defend the Union, and Ireland would not see Home Rule until 1922, following much upheaval.

Source

Hansard, House of Commons, 7 June 1886, CCCVI [3d Ser.], 1215–40.

What is the case of Ireland at this moment? Have honourable Gentlemen considered that they are coming into conflict with a nation? Can anything stop a nation's demand, except its being proved to be immoderate and unsafe? But here are multitudes, and, I believe, millions upon millions, out-of-doors, who feel this demand to be neither immoderate nor unsafe. In our opinion, there is but one question before us about this demand. It is as to the time and circumstance of granting it. There is no question in our minds that it will be granted, We wish it to be granted in the mode prescribed by Mr. Burke, Mr. Burke said, in his first speech at Bristol –

> 'I was true to my old-standing invariable principles, that all things which came from Great Britain should issue as a gift of her bounty and beneficence rather than as claims recovered against struggling litigants, or at least, if your beneficence obtained no credit in your concessions, yet that they should appear the salutary provisions of your wisdom and foresight – not as things wrung from you with your blood by the cruel gripe of a rigid necessity.'[41]

39. Quoted in Peter John Jagger, *Gladstone* (London: Bloomsbury, 1998).
40. Leonard Courtney, journal entry for 8 June 1886, quoted in G. P. Gooch, *Life of Lord Courtney* (London: Macmillan, 1920).
41. Edmund Burke to the electors of Bristol, 3 November 1774, in *The Works of the Right Honourable Edmund Burke*, vol. 2 (London: Henry G. Bohn, 1855), p. 135.

The difference between giving with freedom and dignity on the one side, with acknowledgment and gratitude on the other, and giving under compulsion – giving with disgrace, giving with resentment dogging you at every step of your path – this difference is, in our eyes, fundamental, and this is the main reason not only why we have acted, but why we have acted now. This, if I understand it, is one of the golden moments of our history – one of those opportunities which may come and may go, but which rarely return, or, if they return, return at long intervals, and under circumstances which no man can forecast. There have been such golden moments even in the tragic history of Ireland, as her poet says[42] –

> 'One time the harp of Innisfail
> Was tuned to notes of gladness.'

And then he goes on to say –

> 'But yet did oftener tell a tale
> Of more prevailing sadness.'

But there was such a golden moment – it was in 1795 – it was on the mission of Lord Fitzwilliam. At that moment it is historically clear that the Parliament of Grattan was on the point of solving the Irish problem.[43] The two great knots of that problem were – in the first place, Roman Catholic Emancipation; and, in the second place, the Reform of Parliament. The cup was at her lips, and she was ready to drink it, when the hand of England rudely and ruthlessly dashed it to the ground in obedience to the wild and dangerous intimations of an Irish faction.

'*Ex illo fluere ac retro sublapsa referri, Spes Danaum.*'[44]

There has been no great day of hope for Ireland, no day when you might hope completely and definitely to end the controversy till now – more than 90 years. The long periodic time has at last run out, and the star has again mounted into the heavens. What Ireland was doing for herself in 1795 we at length have done. The Roman Catholics have been emancipated – emancipated after a woeful disregard of solemn promises through 29 years, emancipated slowly, sullenly, not from goodwill, but from abject terror, with all the fruits and consequences which will always follow that method of legislation. The second problem has been also solved, and the representation of Ireland has been thoroughly reformed; and I am thankful to say that the franchise was given to Ireland on the re-adjustment of last year with a free heart, with an open hand, and the gift of that franchise was the last act required to make the success of Ireland in her final effort absolutely sure.

---

42. Denys Shyne Lawlor (1808–87), 'The Harp of Innisfail'.
43. William Fitzwilliam, the Whig Lord Lieutenant of Ireland, pledged a Bill for Catholic Emancipation to Irish MP Henry Grattan in 1795, but the offer was withdrawn by King George III.
44. 'From then onwards the tide of fortune left the shores of Troy and ebbed faster than it flowed earlier' (Latin); from Virgil, *Aeneid*, Book II.

We have given Ireland a voice: we must all listen for a moment to what she says. We must all listen – both sides, both Parties, I mean as they are, divided on this question – divided, I am afraid, by an almost immeasurable gap. We do not undervalue or despise the forces opposed to us. I have described them as the forces of class and its dependents; and that as a general description – as a slight and rude outline of a description – is, I believe, perfectly true. I do not deny that many are against us whom we should have expected to be for us. I do not deny that some whom we see against us have caused us by their conscientious action the bitterest disappointment. You have power, you have wealth, you have rank, you have station, you have organization. What have we? We think that we have the people's heart; we believe and we know we have the promise of the harvest of the future.

As to the people's heart, you may dispute it, and dispute it with perfect sincerity. Let that matter make its own proof. As to the harvest of the future, I doubt if you have so much confidence, and I believe that there is in the breast of many a man who means to vote against us to-night a profound misgiving, approaching even to a deep conviction, that the end will be as we foresee, and not as you do – that the ebbing tide is with you and the flowing tide is with us. Ireland stands at your bar expectant, hopeful, almost suppliant. Her words are the words of truth and soberness. She asks a blessed oblivion of the past and in that oblivion our interest is deeper than even hers.

My right honourable Friend the Member for East Edinburgh (Mr. Goschen)[45] asks us to-night to abide by the traditions of which we are the heirs. What traditions? By the Irish traditions? Go into the length and breadth of the world, ransack the literature of all countries, find, if you can, a single voice, a single book, find, I would almost say, as much as a single newspaper article, unless the product of the day, in which the conduct of England towards Ireland is anywhere treated except with profound and bitter condemnation. Are these the traditions by which we are exhorted to stand? No; they are a sad exception to the glory of our country. They are a broad and black blot upon the pages of its history; and what we want to do is to stand by the traditions of which we are the heirs in all matters except our relations with Ireland, and to make our relations with Ireland to conform to the other traditions of our country. So we treat our traditions – so we hail the demand of Ireland for what I call a blessed oblivion of the past. She asks also a boon for the future; and that boon for the future, unless we are much mistaken, will be a boon to us in respect of honour, no less than a boon to her in respect of happiness, prosperity, and peace.

Such, Sir, is her prayer. Think, I beseech you, think well, think wisely, think, not for the moment, but for the years that are to come, before you reject this Bill.

---

45. George Goschen (1831–1907), a leading figure in the Liberal Unionist Party, which broke with the Liberal Party in 1886 in response to Gladstone's Home Rule plans.

Part D: Indigenous Rights

12. Andrew Jackson, 'Speech to Congress on Indian Removal' (Washington, DC, 1830)

The policies of Andrew Jackson (1767–1845) in the early 1830s marked a new era in Indian–Anglo-American relations. Before entering politics, the man who would become the figure most associated with the oppression of indigenous populations had proved himself, through his ability to exact ruthless military victories over native armies. Upon becoming President in 1829, he began to develop his policy, known as 'Indian Removal', by which native peoples were forced to abandon ancestral homelands in the southeastern US for new territories west of the Mississippi.

The Indian Removal Act divided the nation but, despite strong northeastern opposition, was passed in May 1830. In his annual speech to Congress on 6 December of that year, Jackson further outlined the moral and practical basis for his policy. Claiming 'friendly feeling' to the 'aborigines of the country', he presented westward expansion in terms of paternalistic benevolence towards peoples who lacked the capacity for self-determination. Moreover, he presented this relocation as little different to the transatlantic passage of European Americans such as those in his audience and his own Scots–Irish parents. Indian Removal was enforced under Jackson and Martin Van Buren, culminating in the expulsions and devastating forced migrations known to the Cherokee as the 'Trail of Tears'.

Source

Citation: President Jackson's Message to Congress 'On Indian Removal', 6 December 1830; Records of the United States Senate, 1789–1990; Record Group 46; National Archives and Records Administration.

It gives me pleasure to announce to Congress that the benevolent policy of the Government, steadily pursued for nearly thirty years, in relation to the removal of the Indians beyond the white settlements is approaching to a happy consummation. Two important tribes[46] have accepted the provision made for their removal at the last session of Congress, and it is believed that their example will induce the remaining tribes also to seek the same obvious advantages.

---

46. A minority of Cherokee had begun to migrate to Arkansas. The Choctaw signed the Treaty of Dancing Rabbit Creek in September 1830. However, most other major tribes took longer to accept the terms. The Chickasaw signed the Treaty of Pontotoc Creek and the Seminoles the Treaty of Payne's Landing in 1832; the Cherokee agreed to removal in the Treaty of New Echota in 1835.

The consequences of a speedy removal will be important to the United States, to individual States, and to the Indians themselves. The pecuniary advantages which it promises to the Government are the least of its recommendations. It puts an end to all possible danger of collision between the authorities of the General and State Governments on account of the Indians. It will place a dense and civilized population in large tracts of country now occupied by a few savage hunters. By opening the whole territory between Tennessee on the north and Louisiana on the south to the settlement of the whites it will incalculably strengthen the southwestern frontier and render the adjacent States strong enough to repel future invasions without remote aid. It will relieve the whole State of Mississippi and the western part of Alabama of Indian occupancy, and enable those States to advance rapidly in population, wealth, and power. It will separate the Indians from immediate contact with settlements of whites; free them from the power of the States; enable them to pursue happiness in their own way and under their own rude institutions; will retard the progress of decay, which is lessening their numbers, and perhaps cause them gradually, under the protection of the Government and through the influence of good counsels, to cast off their savage habits and become an interesting, civilized, and Christian community.

What good man would prefer a country covered with forests and ranged by a few thousand savages to our extensive Republic, studded with cities, towns, and prosperous farms embellished with all the improvements which art can devise or industry execute, occupied by more than 12,000,000 happy people, and filled with all the blessings of liberty, civilization and religion?

The present policy of the Government is but a continuation of the same progressive change by a milder process. The tribes which occupied the countries now constituting the Eastern States were annihilated or have melted away to make room for the whites. The waves of population and civilization are rolling to the westward, and we now propose to acquire the countries occupied by the red men of the South and West by a fair exchange, and, at the expense of the United States, to send them to land where their existence may be prolonged and perhaps made perpetual.

Doubtless it will be painful to leave the graves of their fathers; but what do they more than our ancestors did or than our children are now doing? To better their condition in an unknown land our forefathers left all that was dear in earthly objects. Our children by thousands yearly leave the land of their birth to seek new homes in distant regions. Does Humanity weep at these painful separations from everything, animate and inanimate, with which the young heart has become entwined?

Far from it. It is rather a source of joy that our country affords scope where our young population may range unconstrained in body or in mind, developing the power and facilities of man in their highest perfection. These remove hundreds and almost thousands of miles at their own expense, purchase the lands they occupy, and support themselves at their new homes from the moment of their arrival. Can it be cruel in this Government when, by events which it cannot control, the Indian is made discontented in his ancient home to purchase his lands, to give him a new and extensive territory, to pay the expense of his removal, and support him a year in his new abode? How many thousands of our own people would gladly embrace the opportunity of removing to the West on such conditions! If the offers made to the Indians were extended to them, they would be hailed with gratitude and joy.

And is it supposed that the wandering savage[47] has a stronger attachment to his home than the settled, civilized Christian? Is it more afflicting to him to leave the graves of his fathers than it is to our brothers and children? Rightly considered, the policy of the General Government toward the red man is not only liberal, but generous. He is unwilling to submit to the laws of the States and mingle with their population. To save him from this alternative, or perhaps utter annihilation, the General Government kindly offers him a new home, and proposes to pay the whole expense of his removal and settlement.

13. William Apess, 'Eulogy for King Philip' (Boston, 1836)

Amidst the turmoil of Jacksonian removal, representatives of the indigenous communities attempted to push back against popular misconceptions of their plight. In 1836, the Pequot writer and activist William Apess (1798–1839) made one such attempt in a noted public lecture in Boston, offering a strident and important reframing of New England history, and emphasising the importance of colonial genocide to America's destiny. Born in Massachusetts of mixed Pequot and Anglo-American origins, Apess was ordained a Methodist minister before publishing one of the earliest Native American biographies, *A Son of the Forest* (1829). During the early 1830s, he led a revolt against the Massachusetts Commonwealth in favour of Native American rights and published the landmark essay 'An Indian's Looking-Glass for the White Man' (1833).

---

47. This pointed phrase, interchangeable with 'the hunter state', encapsulates the fundamental justification used for the conquest of under-utilised land. As President James Monroe (1758–1831) had argued in his first message to Congress in December 1817, 'the hunter state can exist only in the vast uncultivated desert. It yields to the more dense and compact form and great force of civilized population; and of right it ought to yield, for the earth was given to mankind to support the greatest number of which it is capable, and no tribe of people have a right to withhold from the wants of others more than is necessary for their own support and comfort' (Stanislaus M. Hamilton (ed.), *The Writings of James Monroe: Including a Collection of His Public and Private Papers and Correspondence Now for the First Time Printed* (New York: G. P. Putnam's Sons, 1898), p. 40).

His speech before the Boston audience was entitled 'Eulogy on King Philip'. It offered a political account of the wars of the 1670s between the English colonists and the Wampanoag chief Metacomet (c.1639–76), known as 'King Philip'. As Jill Lepore has written, Apess shrewdly exploited the growing fascination with the heroism of indigenous historical figures to press claims for political equality, and his shaping of public memory in speeches like this helped underpin the efforts of New England tribal groups such as the Mashpee to secure recognition and self-government.[48] The following text consists of the opening and the close of a lecture in which Apess used the defence of a controversial historical figure as a means of reflecting on competing visions of history and on the destiny of Native American citizenship.

Source

Barry O'Connell, *On Our Own Ground: The Complete Writings of William Apess, a Pequot* (Amherst: University of Massachusetts Press, 2002).

I do not arise to spread before you the fame of a noted warrior, whose natural abilities shone like those of the great and mighty Philip of Greece, or of Alexander the Great, or like those of Washington – whose virtues and patriotism are engraven on the hearts of my audience. Neither do I approve of war as being the best method of bowing to the haughty tyrant, Man, and civilizing the world. No, far from me be such a thought. But it is to bring before you beings made by the God of Nature, and in whose hearts and heads he has planted sympathies that shall live forever in the memory of the world, whose brilliant talents shone in the display of natural things, so that the most cultivated, whose powers shown with equal luster, were not able to prepare mantles to cover the burning elements of an uncivilized world. What, then? Shall we cease to mention the mighty of the earth, the noble work of God?

Yet those purer virtues remain untold. Those noble traits that marked the wild man's course lie buried in the shades of night; and who shall stand? I appeal to the lovers of liberty. But those few remaining descendants who now remain as the monument of the cruelty of those who came to improve our race and correct our errors – and as the immortal Washington lives endeared and engraven on the hearts of every white in America, never to be forgotten in time – even such is the immortal Philip[49] honored, as held in memory by the

48. Jill Lepore, *The Name of War: King Philip's War and the Origins of American Identity* (New York: Vintage, 1999), p. 225.
49. Wampanoag chief Metacomet (c.1639–76).

degraded but yet grateful descendants who appreciate his character; so will every patriot, especially in this enlightened age, respect the rude yet all accomplished son of the forest, that died a martyr to his cause, though unsuccessful, yet as glorious as the American Revolution. Where, then, shall we place the hero of the wilderness?

Justice and humanity for the remaining few prompt me to vindicate the character of him who yet lives in their hearts and, if possible, melt the prejudice that exists in the hearts of those who are in the possession of his soil, and only by the right of conquest – is the aim of him who proudly tells you, the blood of a denominated savage runs in his veins. It is, however, true that there are many who are said to be honorable warriors, who, in wisdom of their civilized legislation, think it no crime to wreak their vengeance upon whole nations and communities, until the fields are covered with blood and the rivers turned into purple fountains, while groans, like distant thunder, are heard from the wounded and the tens of thousands of the dying, leaving helpless families depending on their cares and sympathies for life; while a loud response is heard floating through the air from the ten thousand Indian children and orphans, who are left to mourn the honorable acts of a few – civilized men.

Now, if we have common sense and ability to allow the difference between the civilized and the uncivilized, we cannot but see that one mode of warfare is as just as the other; for while one is sanctioned by authority of the enlightened and cultivated men, the other is an agreement according to the pure laws of nature, growing out of natural consequences; for nature has her defense for every beast of the field; even the reptiles of the earth and the fishes of the sea have their weapons of war. But thou frail man was made for a nobler purpose – to live, to love, and adore his God, and do good to his brother – for this reason, and this alone, the God of heaven prepared ways and means to blast anger, man's destroyer, and cause the Prince of Peace to rule, that man might swell those blessed notes. My image is of God; I am not a beast.

But as all men are governed by animal passions who are void of the true principles of God, whether cultivated or uncultivated, we shall now lay before you the true character of Philip, in relation to those hostilities between himself and the whites; and in so doing, permit me to be plain and candid.

. . .

What sad tales are these for us to look upon the massacre of our dear fathers, mothers, brothers,[50] and sisters; and if we speak, we are then called savages for complaining. Our affections for each other are the same as yours; we think as much of ourselves as you do of yourselves. When our children are sick, we do all we can for them; they lie buried deep in our affections; if they

---

50. King Philip's War (1675–8) saw over 1,000 colonists killed, twelve settler towns destroyed and one-tenth of all military-aged men lost. Native American losses were far greater, with up to 80 per cent of the population of the region lost.

die, we remember it long and mourn in after years. Children also cleave to their parents; they look to them for aid; they do the best they know how to do for each other; and when strangers come among us, we use them as well as we know how; we feel honest in whatever we do; we have no desire to offend anyone. But when we are so deceived, it spoils all our confidence in our visitors. And although I can say that I have some dear, good friends among white people, yet I eye them with a jealous eye, for fear they will betray me. Having been deceived so much by them, how can I help it? Being brought up to look upon white people as being enemies and not friends, and by the whites treated as such, who can wonder?

Yes, in vain have I looked for the Christian to take me by the hand and bid me welcome to his cabin, as my fathers did them, before we were born; and if they did, it was only to satisfy curiosity and not to look upon me as a man and a Christian. And so all of my people have been treated, whether Christians or not. I say, then, a different course must be pursued, and different laws must be enacted, and all men must operate under one general law. And while you ask yourselves, 'What do they, the Indians, want?' you have only to look at the unjust laws made for them and say, 'They want what I want,' in order to make men of them, good and wholesome citizens. And this plan ought to be pursued by all missionaries or not pursued at all. That is not only to make Christians of us, but men, which plan as yet has never been pursued. And when it is, I will then throw my might upon the side of missions and do what I can to favor it. But this work must begin here first, in New England.

Having now closed, I would say that many thanks is due from me to you, though an unworthy speaker, for your kind attention; and I wish you to understand that we are thankful for every favor; and you and I have to rejoice that we have not to answer for our fathers' crimes; neither shall we do right to charge them one to another. We can only regret it, and flee from it; and from henceforth, let peace and righteousness be written upon our hearts and hands forever, is the wish of a poor Indian.

14. Mark Twain, 'Our Fellow Savages of the Sandwich Islands' (San Francisco, 1868)

His acidic wit and ability to combine deceptively offhand comedy with social commentary made the author known as Mark Twain one of the icons of American culture. Born Samuel Clemens (1835–1910) in Missouri, he worked as a printer's apprentice and as a riverboat pilot up and down the Mississippi. He is famous for the fiction and journalism that brought the life of that river to a global audience with humour and sharp wit. But Twain was also a strident critic of American imperialism and the treatment of the indigenous peoples of the world. He first rose to fame in the late 1860s, thanks to a celebrated lecture attacking American chauvinism and violence overseas, a piece sometimes entitled 'Our Fellow Savages of the Sandwich Islands'.

In 1866, Twain had spent five months in the Sandwich Islands (Hawaii) as correspondent for the *Sacramento Union* newspaper in California. The mordant and acerbic pieces he sent home were widely reprinted in the West and helped establish his reputation as a socially engaged humourist. He capitalised upon this early success by turning to the speaking circuit, where his speeches presented reflections on his travels in ways that mocked the pretensions of fellow 'traveller–philosopher' performers such as Bayard Taylor.[51] Between 1866 and 1873, Twain gave the 'Sandwich Islands' speech almost 100 times throughout the US and Britain. Audiences thrilled at being wrong-footed by his deadpan style, and by the ways in which he packaged what was a typically trenchant denunciation of missionary excesses and xenophobic views.

Source

Paul Fatout (ed.), *Mark Twain Speaking* (Des Moines: University of Iowa Press, 1976).

These islands were discovered some eighty or ninety years ago by Captain Cook, though another man came very near discovering them before, and he was diverted from his course by a manuscript found in a bottle.[52] He wasn't the first man who has been diverted by suggestions got out of a bottle. When these islands were discovered the population was about 400,000, but the white man came and brought various complicated diseases, and education, and civilization, and all sorts of calamities, and consequently the population began to drop off with commendable activity. Forty years ago they were reduced to 200,000, and the educational and civilizing facilities being increased they dwindled down to 55,000, and it is proposed to send a few more missionaries and finish them. It isn't the education or civilization that has settled them; it is the imported diseases, and they have all got the consumption and other reliable distempers, and

---

51. See Paul Fatout, *Mark Twain Speaking* (Des Moines: University of Iowa Press, 1976), pp. 224–5. For more on the genre Twain was satirising see Tom F. Wright, 'The Results of Locomotion: Bayard Taylor and the Travel Lecture in the Nineteenth Century United States', *Studies in Travel Writing*, 14:2 (2010), 111–34.

52. In January 1778, British explorer Captain James Cook (1729–79) was the first European to land on the archipelago he would name 'the Sandwich Islands' after his patron, John Montagu (1744–1814), Earl of Sandwich. Cook was murdered by Hawaiian natives on his third visit to the island group.

to speak figuratively, they are retiring from business pretty fast. When they pick up and leave we will take possession as lawful heirs.

There are about 3,000 white people in the islands; they are mostly Americans. In fact they are the kings of the Sandwich Islands; the monarchy is not much more than a mere name. These people stand as high in the scale of character as any people in the world, and some of them who were born and educated in those islands don't even know what vice is. A Kanaka or a native is nobody unless he has a princely income of $75 annually, or a splendid estate worth $100. The country is full of office-holders and office-seekers; there are plenty of such noble patriots. Of almost any party of three men, two would be office-holders and one an office-seeker. In a little island half the size of one of the wards of St. Louis, there are lots of noblemen, princes and men of high degree, with grand titles, holding big offices, receiving immense salaries – such as ministers of war, secretaries of the navy, secretaries of state and ministers of justice. They make a fine display of uniforms, and are very imposing at a funeral. That's the country for a petty hero to go to, he would soon have the conceit taken out of him. There are so many of them that a nobleman from any other country would be nobody. They only lionize their own people, and therefore they lionize everybody.

. . .

These natives are very hospitable people indeed – very hospitable. If you want to stay a few days and nights in a native's cabin you can stay and welcome. They will do everything they possibly can to make you comfortable. They will feed you on baked dog, or poi, or raw fish, or raw salt pork, fricasseed cats – all the luxuries of the season. Everything the human heart can desire, they will set before you. Perhaps now, this isn't a captivating feast at first glance, but it is offered in all sincerity, and with the best motives in the world, and that makes any feast respectable whether it is palatable or not. But if you want to trade, that's quite another matter – that's business! And the Kanucker is ready for you. He is a born trader, and he will swindle you if he can. He will lie straight through, from the first word to the last. Not such lies as you and I tell, but gigantic lies, lies that awe you with their grandeur, lies that stun you with their imperial impossibility. He will sell you a molehill at the market price of a mountain, and will lie it up to an altitude that will make it cheap at the money. If he is caught, he slips out of it with an easy indifference that has an unmistakable charm about it.

One peculiarity of these Kanakas is that nearly every one of them has a dozen mothers – not natural ones – I haven't got down yet where I can make such a statement as that – but adopted mothers. They have a custom of calling any woman mother they take a liking to – no matter what her color or politics – and it is possible for one native to have a thousand mothers if his affections are liberal and stretchy, and most of them are. This custom breeds some curious incidents. A California man went down there and opened a sugar plantation. One of his hands came and said he wanted to bury his mother. He gave him permission. Shortly after he came again with the same request. 'I thought you buried her last week,' said the gentleman. 'This is another one,' said the native. 'All right,' said the gentleman, 'go and plant her.' Within a month the man wanted to bury some more mothers. 'Look here,' said the planter, 'I don't want to be hard on you in your affliction, but it appears to me that your stock of mothers holds out pretty well. It interferes with business, so clear out, and never come back until you have buried every mother you have in the world.'

They are an odd sort of people, too. They can die whenever they want to. That's a fact. They don't mind dying any more than a jilted Frenchman does. When they take a notion to die they die, and it don't make any difference whether there is anything the matter with them or not, and they can't be persuaded out of it. When one of them makes up his mind to die, he just lays down and is just as certain to die as though he had all the doctors in the world hold of him. A gentleman in Hawaii asked his servant if he wouldn't like to die and have a big funeral. He said yes, and looked happy, and the next morning the overseer came and said, 'That boy of yours laid down and died last night and said you were going to give him a fine funeral.'

. . .

The land that I have tried to tell you about lies out there in the midst of the watery wilderness, in the very heart of the almost soilless solitudes of the Pacific. It is a dreamy, beautiful, charming land. I wish I could make you comprehend how beautiful it is. It is a land that seems ever so vague and fairy-like when one reads about it in books, peopled with a gentle, indolent, careless race.[53]

It is Sunday land. The land of indolence and dreams, where the air is drowsy and things tend to repose and peace, and to emancipation from the labor, and turmoil, and weariness, and anxiety of life.

15. Dadabhai Naoroji, 'Maiden Speech in Parliament' (London, 1893)

Dadabhai Naoroji (1825–1917) was one of the founders of the modern Indian freedom struggle and the first Asian MP to sit in the British Houses of Parliament. Born in Mumbai in 1825, he left a promising university career for England in the 1850s, founding a cotton trading company and teaching at University College London. In 1867, he founded the East India Association to combat prevailing views of Asian inferiority and was instrumental in its merging with the Indian National Association to become the Indian National Congress.

Following Naoroji's unsuccessful 1886 candidacy for the Liberal Party in the London seat of Holborn, Lord Salisbury the Prime Minister remarked that English constituencies were not ready to elect a

---

53. It seems likely that Twain is employing the well-worn colonial trope of the indolent, 'lazy native' ironically, taking aim at its empty moralism and chauvinism.

'black man'. Yet Naoroji's prominence amongst reformers and the general public continued to grow, and with the support of the suffrage movement he was eventually elected as Liberal MP for Clerkenwell in 1892, joining Gladstone's government. As the *Manchester Guardian* noted, India would now 'be able to speak through him to the House of Commons and to the world with their own voice.'[54] Taking the oath of office on the *Khordeh Avesta*, the Zoroastrian sacred text, he made his maiden speech in February 1893, outlining his vision for the relationship of metropole to colony and his belief in the 'golden thread' holding India to Britain.

Source

Dadabhai Naoroji, *Dadabhai Naoroji's Speeches and Writings* (Madras: G. A. Natesan, 1917).

Mr. Naoroji said it might be thought rather rash and unwise on his part to stand up in this House so soon after his admission, but his excuse was that he was under a certain necessity to do so. A very great and unique event had happened in connection with India. For the first time in the history of British rule in India, an Indian was admitted into this House as a member for an English constituency. *(Cheers.)*

The spirit of British rule, the instinct of British justice and generosity, when Britain first took the matter of Indian government seriously in hand about the beginning of this century, deliberately decided that India should be governed on the lines of British freedom and justice. Steps were taken without any hesitation to introduce Western education, civilization, and political institutions into that country. The result was that aided by a noble language, the youth of India began to be educated, a great movement of political thought set in, and a new life was infused into the country which had been decaying for centuries.

They had given to India freedom of speech and enabled Indians to stand before their British rulers and to represent their case in clear and open language whenever they felt aggrieved in any matter, and the ultimate result, so to speak, was that an Indian stood before them in this House, a member of the Parliament of the British Empire able to state his views openly and freely. The glory and credit of this great event, which had thrilled India from one end to the other, the new life, the joy, and ecstasy of India at the present moment – all was theirs. He stood there in the name of India to thank British rulers that

---

54. 'Mr. Dadabhai Naoroji', *The Manchester Guardian*, 26 July 1892. Available at: <https://www.theguardian.com/theguardian/2013/jul/26/election-naoroji-finsbury-1892> (last accessed 10 July 2019).

they had made it possible for an Indian to stand before this House with the conviction – though he had no numbers of votes behind him to influence its action – that whenever he had any grievance to bring forward supported by just and proper reasons he would always find a large number of other members ready to support him and to concede the justice that he asked. *(Cheers.)*

The name of Central Finsbury would never be forgotten by India. The event of his election had strengthened the loyalty and attachment of India ten times more than if 100,000 European soldiers had been sent to protect that country. *(Cheers.)*

The moral force of which the right honourable Member for Mid Lothian[55] spoke was the golden thread by which India was held by the British Power; as long as India was satisfied with the justice and honour of Britain, so long would the Indian Empire endure.[56] He hoped the connection between England and India, which formed in fact five-sixths of the British Empire, might continue long and with benefit to both countries. *(Cheers.)*

---

55. Former Prime Minister and Liberal MP for Mid Lothian, William Ewart Gladstone (1809–98).

56. In 1892, the British Parliament introduced the Indian Councils Act, increasing the involvement of the Indian people in the legislative process.

6 War and Peace

Introduction

War and peace are the oldest subjects of rhetoric; Aristotle's *Rhetoric* considered them 'one of the chief subjects of all deliberation'.[1] With the legitimacy of foreign engagements increasingly seen as reliant upon the consent of the governed, the period covered by this book saw more such deliberation than ever before. Public justifications for, and objections to, foreign engagements were part of a maturing political and diplomatic world order, whilst a nascent peace movement offered fresh challenge to militarism and its relationships to the individual. It was a spirit that Immanuel Kant had helped define in his influential *Perpetual Peace*, arguing that 'the vast grave' of global war could be avoided only through liberal constitutions, trade and peace federations acting to restrain the 'stream of those hostile passions which fear the law'. However, these aspirations inevitably had to compete with the renewed energy that nationalism and imperialism gave to the 'passions' of ancient martial rhetoric. Despite the consoling myths of 'Pax Britannica' or the 'Hundred Years' Peace' of 1815–1914, this was a century of constant conflict for both Britain and America, who fought internal rebellions and enforced coercive imperial regimes, all the while deliberating the very meaning of peace and war.[2]

This book opened with examples of war rhetoric that revealed key strategies and tensions. Those arguing for war against Britain or France assembled bellicose arguments using hyperbole and ideas of inevitability, with conflict framed as an inevitable response to 'tyranny' (p. 50) and injuries and usurpations (p. 44). Such rhetoric relied upon ushering in what Giorgio Agamben calls a 'state of exception', in which the pull of conflict transcends normal considerations – as Cicero put it, 'in times of war, law falls silent'.[3]

---

1. Aristotle, *The Art of Rhetoric*, trans. Robin Waterfield (Oxford: Oxford University Press, 2018), p.16.
2. Karl Polanyi, *Great Transformation: The Political and Economic Origins of Our Time* (London: V. Gollancz, 1946).
3. Giorgio Agamben, *States of Exception* (Chicago: University of Chicago Press, 2008); *silent enim lēgēs inter arma*, in Cicero's 'Pro Milone', quoted in P. MacKendrick, *The Speeches of Cicero* (London: Duckworth, 1995).

A growing problem for such attempts as the century progressed, however, was that the centralising logic of conflict was increasingly at odds with the pluralist ideals of liberal democracies. This relied upon the mobilisation of racial, ethnocentric or territorial prejudices. But it also rested upon subtler forms of justification. We can see a direct line between Jefferson's sleight of hand in the Declaration, suggesting that the colonists must 'acquiesce in the necessity' of war, and Lincoln's legalistic claim in his Second Inaugural (1865) to 'accept war' rather than 'make war'.

As British peace activist Jonathan Dymond complained in an 1823 pamphlet, most people believed in war as they did 'in the rising of the sun, without any idea than that it is part of the ordinary processes'.[4] But from the foundation of peace societies in the 1810s onwards, an articulate minority expressed the view that war and violence were unjustifiable, and that international relations could be pursued in a rational, pacific manner.[5] Inspired variously by Quaker traditions, evangelical revivals, Enlightenment rationalism or free trade, these advocates protested against specific wars and war in general through speeches, boycotts and petitions. Arguments ranged from the claim that war brutalised and promoted moral decline, to the sense that it was a consequence of masculinity.[6] Those opposed to war were often engaged in acts of redefinition, shifting horizons of empathy to consider what counted as 'war' for average citizens or for the colonised, and opposition to war was framed in terms of jeremiadic apocalypticism and messianic optimism, but also in terms that rested upon ideas of barbarism, diving the world into civilised and uncivilised.

The first part of this chapter ('America's Path to Disunion') collects a series of speeches whose language traces the unravelling of the American republic that came together in Chapter 1.[7] In Massachusetts Senator Daniel Webster's 'Reply to Hayne' speech of 1830, the prospect that awaits if the 'bonds that make unite us are "broken asunder"' is figured as an 'abyss'

---

4. Anon. [Jonathan Dymond], *An Enquiry into the Accordance of War with the Principles of Christianity* (London: Longman, Hurst, 1823).

5. For studies of the British context see Martin Ceadel, *The Birth of the Peace Movement, 1730–1854* (New York: Clarendon Press, 1996); Martin Ceadel, *Semi-detached Idealists: The British Peace Movement and International Relations, 1854–1945* (Oxford: Oxford University Press, 2007); and C. Roland Marchand, *The American Peace Movement and Social Reform, 1898–1918* (Princeton: Princeton University Press, 1973).

6. Carolyn Eastman, 'Fight Like a Man: Gender and Rhetoric in the Early Nineteenth Century American Peace Movement', *American Nineteenth-Century History*, 10:3 (2009), 247–71.

7. For a survey of earlier approaches to this material see David Zarefsky, 'Rhetorical Interpretations of the American Civil War', *Quarterly Journal of Speech*, 81:1 (1995), 108–20.

(p. 246). Eight years later, in the next speech given before the Springfield, Illinois, lyceum, the young Abraham Lincoln adopted a series of similarly foreboding metaphors to warn about the escalating temper of national politics. Looking back at the words of John Calhoun, Angelina Grimké and others in Chapters 3 and 5 can help explain to readers the transformation we see by the time of the next speech (1856), Charles Sumner's sexually charged denunciation of Southern pro-slavery politicians that was to lead to his savage beating on the floor of the Senate. On the cusp of war, the final speech here contains the era's most enduring image of all, Lincoln's characterisation of the Union in an address to the Illinois State Capitol as a 'house divided against itself' (p. 255).

Once war was declared, the central rhetorical struggle was that of defining its significance and symbolism. Was it the last stand of aristocratic nobility against a commercial cabal? Was it the triumph of abolitionist fanaticism, the cleansing of moral wrongs or simply the inevitable process of nation-building? In the next part of the chapter ('The Meaning of the American Civil War'), British observers and Americans in North and South offered such readings in speeches that are best read as exercises in storytelling, narrating the journey of the republic to the impasse and deliberating over its future. The first attempt is from Confederate Vice President Alexander Stephens, whose speech (1861) in Savannah, Georgia, held up white supremacy as the 'cornerstone' of the break-away nation. Though accurately reflecting a key strand of Southern thinking, Stephens's words were soon disowned by his superior, Jefferson Davis. The same was true of the similarly unguarded words of British Chancellor of the Exchequer William E. Gladstone, speaking the following year in Newcastle, where he appeared to recognise that the Confederacy had 'made a nation' (p. 263).

It was against these rival efforts at defining the Union cause that Lincoln offered the most celebrated narrative of his own. At the battlefield cemetery in Gettysburg, Pennsylvania, his brief address (1863) framed the conflict as a 'new birth of freedom' (p. 267) (Figure 8).[8] The final speech in this part of the chapter attempts much the same thing. Following the Emancipation Proclamation of 1863, slavery was now central to the war. With an eye to shaping the postwar debate, in a Manhattan speech in 1864, Frederick Douglass praised the moral 'grandeur and vastness' (p. 271) of the conflict, arguing that the 'mission of the war' could not be complete until former slaves had full citizenship rights and were free of all racial discrimination.

The final section ('Pacifisms and Non-Violence') places anti-war speeches back into a broader lineage that served as an undercurrent to the century. In the first, Boston reformer Hannah Mather Crocker uses the sermon form to

---

8. Gary Wills, *Lincoln at Gettysburg: The Words that Remade America* (New York: Simon and Schuster, 2011).

critique both the War of 1812 and 'the great evil of war' more broadly. It is followed by fellow New Englander Henry David Thoreau's lecture (1848) debuting his case for civil disobedience against state coercion, a speech that would become one of the most enduring rhetorical monuments of Transcendentalism and shape traditions of non-violent resistance throughout the world during the next century. The next speech takes us to the House of Commons, and to Quaker MP John Bright's celebrated 'Angel of Death Speech', arguing against British involvement in the Crimean conflict. During the last decades of the century, an even more explicit and programmatic pacifism took root, particularly in working-class socialist movements. The chapter, and the book, closes with one such example, Russian émigré Emma Goldman's attack on what she terms 'Patriotism, A Menace to Liberty', a lecture that she delivered throughout the 1900s, expressing ideas that would see her deported during the Great War.

Part A: America's Path to Disunion

1. Daniel Webster, 'Second Reply to Hayne' (Washington, DC, 1830)

In 1830, during the issue known as the South Carolina Nullification Crisis, Democrat Senator Robert Hayne of South Carolina had accused the industrial North of harming the export economy of the slave-owning South and encroaching on its independence. Rather than being an aggregate body, he argued that the nation was simply an association of sovereign bodies, from which individual states could withdraw at will.

On 26 January, eager spectators crowded the galleries and Senate floor to hear the response of Massachusetts senator Daniel Webster (1782–1852). His epic two-day reply made the debate more than just an argument over tariffs or a contest between two celebrated speakers. Rather, the exchange became an important showcase for competing visions for the nation, with Webster's contribution offering a transcendent statement of what has been called the 'rhetoric of stewardship' underpinning the ideal of the Union.[9] His words came to be seen as one of the great Senate speeches. Through mass reprinting it became a rhetorical touchstone, its cadences studied by generations of school students and its foreboding phrases reverberating through the following decades' slow drift towards sectional conflict.

Source

Daniel Webster, *The Great Orations and Senatorial Speech of Daniel Webster* (New York: W. M. Hayward, 1853).

... This leads us to inquire into the origin of this government and the source of its power. Whose agent is it? Is it the creature of the State legislatures, or the creature of the people? If the government of the United States be the agent of the State governments, then they may control it, provided they can agree in the manner of controlling it; if it be the agent of the people, then the people alone can control it, restrain it, modify, or reform it. It is observable enough, that the doctrine for which the honorable gentleman contends leads him to the necessity of maintaining, not only that this general government is the creature of the States, but that it is the creature of each of the States severally, so that each may assert the power for itself of determining whether it acts within the limits of its authority. It is the servant of four-and-twenty masters, of different will

---

9. Wayne Fields, 'The Reply to Hayne: Daniel Webster and the Rhetoric of Stewardship', *Political Theory*, 11:1 (February 1983).

and different purposes and yet bound to obey all. This absurdity (for it seems no less) arises from a misconception as to the origin of this government and its true character. It is, Sir, the people's Constitution, the people's government, made for the people, made by the people, and answerable to the people.[10]

The people of the United States have declared that the Constitution shall be the supreme law.[11] We must either admit the proposition, or dispute their authority. The States are, unquestionably, sovereign, so far as their sovereignty is not affected by this supreme law. But the State legislatures, as political bodies, however sovereign, are yet not sovereign over the people. So far as the people have given the power to the general government, so far the grant is unquestionably good, and the government holds of the people, and not of the State governments. We are all agents of the same supreme power, the people. The general government and the State governments derive their authority from the same source. Neither can, in relation to the other, be called primary, though one is definite and restricted, and the other general and residuary. The national government possesses those powers which it will be shown the people have conferred upon it, and no more.

... By this the supremacy of the Constitution and laws of the United States is declared. The people so will it. No State law is to be valid which comes in conflict with the Constitution, or any law of the United States passed in pursuance of it. But who shall decide this question of interference? To whom lies the last appeal? This, Sir, the Constitution itself decides also, by declaring, 'That the judicial power shall extend to all cases arising under the Constitution and laws of the United States.' These two provisions cover the whole ground. They are, in truth, the keystone of the arch! With these it is a government; without them it is a confederation. In pursuance of these clear and express provisions, Congress established, at its very first session, in the judicial act, a mode for carrying them into full effect, and for bringing all questions of constitutional power to the final decision of the Supreme Court. It then, Sir, became a government. It then had the means of self-protection; and but for this, it would, in all probability, have been now among things which are past. Having constituted the government, and declared its powers, the people have further said, that, since somebody must decide on the extent of these powers, the government shall itself decide; subject always, like other popular governments, to its responsibility to the people ...

I have not allowed myself, Sir, to look beyond the Union, to see what might lie hidden in the dark recess behind. I have not coolly weighed the

---

10. This sentence was, of course, later paraphrased by Abraham Lincoln in the Gettysburg Address.
11. The 'Supremacy Clause' of the US Constitution (Article VI, Clause 2) established federal law as 'the supreme Law of the Land; and the Judges in every State shall be bound thereby'.

chances of preserving liberty when the bonds that unite us together shall be broken asunder. I have not accustomed myself to hang over the precipice of disunion, to see whether, with my short sight, I can fathom the depth of the abyss below; nor could I regard him as a safe counsellor in the affairs of this government, whose thoughts should be mainly bent on considering, not how the Union may be best preserved, but how tolerable might be the condition of the people when it should be broken up and destroyed. While the Union lasts, we have high, exciting, gratifying prospects spread out before us and our children.

Beyond that I seek not to penetrate the veil. God grant that in my day, at least, that curtain may not rise! God grant that on my vision never may be opened what lies behind! When my eyes shall be turned to behold for the last time the sun in heaven, may I not see him shining on the broken and dishonored fragments of a once glorious Union; on States dissevered, discordant, belligerent; on a land rent with civil feuds, or drenched, it may be, in fraternal blood! Let their last feeble and lingering glance rather behold the gorgeous ensign of the republic, now known and honored throughout the earth, still full high advanced, its arms and trophies streaming in their original lustre, not a stripe erased or polluted, not a single star obscured, bearing for its motto, no such miserable interrogatory as 'What is all this worth?' nor those other words of delusion and folly, 'Liberty first and Union afterwards';[12] but everywhere, spread all over in characters of living light, blazing on all its ample folds, as they float over the sea and over the land, and in every wind under the whole heavens, that other sentiment, dear to every true American heart, – Liberty and Union, now and for ever, one and inseparable!

2. Abraham Lincoln, 'The Lyceum Address' (Springfield, Illinois, 1838)

Abraham Lincoln (1809–65) was the sixteenth President of the US, serving from 1861 until his assassination in April 1865. Born into rural poverty in Kentucky, Lincoln moved as a young man to Illinois and became an outstanding local lawyer in the state capital Springfield, before entering national politics. Through agility in legislative machinations and astute stewardship of the military conduct of the Civil War, he is considered the outstanding figure responsible for the preservation of the Union. His rhetorical gifts also helped to shape its moral mission. Though having little formal education, Lincoln is now celebrated as one of the masters of nineteenth-century political language, and his

---

12. This is a broad encapsulation of Hayne's states' rights position in his previous contribution to the debate.

speeches as Illinois Congressman and Senatorial candidate, and later as President, are celebrated as among the most important examples of public eloquence, marking its shift towards a recognisably modern epigrammatic concision.

On 27 January 1838, the twenty-eight-year-old delivered a speech before the lyceum in Springfield that offers a glimpse into his evolving ideas about the structural flaws of the Union. As his law partner William Herndon recalls, 'we had a society in Springfield, which contained and commanded all the culture and talent of the place . . . its meetings were public, and reflected great credit on the community.' Lincoln's speech 'created for the young orator a reputation which soon extended beyond the limits of the locality in which he lived'.[13] Alarmed by recent lynchings of African Americans and mob violence against abolitionists, Lincoln used his speech to reflect upon the dangers to the future of the republic of extra-legal violence. The following text excerpts the opening and closing sections of his remarks.

Source

Abraham Lincoln, *The Collected Works of Abraham Lincoln*, vol. 2, ed. Roy P. Basler, Lloyd A. Dunlap and Marion D. Pratt (New Brunswick, NJ: Rutgers University Press, 1953).

As a subject for the remarks of the evening, *the perpetuation of our political institutions*, is selected.

In the great journal of things happening under the sun, we, the American People, find our account running, under date of the nineteenth century of the Christian era. – We find ourselves in the peaceful possession, of the fairest portion of the earth, as regards extent of territory, fertility of soil, and salubrity of climate. We find ourselves under the government of a system of political institutions, conducing more essentially to the ends of civil and religious liberty, than any of which the history of former times tells us. We, when mounting the stage of existence, found ourselves the legal inheritors of these fundamental blessings. We toiled not in the acquirement or establishment of them – they are a legacy bequeathed us, by a *once* hardy, brave, and patriotic, but *now* lamented and departed race of ancestors. Theirs was the task (and nobly they performed it) to possess themselves, and through themselves, us, of this goodly land; and to uprear upon its hills and its valleys, a political

---

13. William Herndon, *Herndon's Lincoln: The True Story of a Great Life, Vol. 1* (Chicago: Belford, Clarke, 1889), p. 193.

edifice of liberty and equal rights; 'tis ours only, to transmit these, the former, unprofaned by the foot of an invader; the latter, undecayed by the lapse of time and untorn by usurpation, to the latest generation that fate shall permit the world to know. This task of gratitude to our fathers, justice to ourselves, duty to posterity, and love for our species in general, all imperatively require us faithfully to perform.

How then shall we perform it? – At what point shall we expect the approach of danger? By what means shall we fortify against it? – Shall we expect some transatlantic military giant, to step the Ocean, and crush us at a blow? Never! – All the armies of Europe, Asia and Africa combined, with all the treasure of the earth (our own excepted) in their military chest, with a Buonaparte for a commander, could not by force, take a drink from the Ohio, or make a track on the Blue Ridge, in a trial of a thousand years.

At what point then is the approach of danger to be expected? I answer, if it ever reach us, it must spring up amongst us. It cannot come from abroad. If destruction be our lot, we must ourselves be its author and finisher. As a nation of freemen, we must live through all time, or die by suicide.

I hope I am over wary; but if I am not, there is, even now, something of ill-omen, amongst us. I mean the increasing disregard for law which pervades the country; the growing disposition to substitute the wild and furious passions, in lieu of the sober judgment of Courts; and the worse than savage mobs, for the executive ministers of justice. This disposition is awfully fearful in any community; and that it now exists in ours, though grating to our feelings to admit, it would be a violation of truth, and an insult to our intelligence, to deny. Accounts of outrages committed by mobs, form the every-day news of the times.[14] They have pervaded the country, from New England to Louisiana; – they are neither peculiar to the eternal snows of the former, nor the burning suns of the latter; – they are not the creature of climate – neither are they confined to the slave-holding, or the non-slave-holding States. Alike, they spring up among the pleasure hunting masters of Southern slaves, and the order loving citizens of the land of steady habits. – Whatever, then, their cause may be, it is common to the whole country.

. . .

Another reason which *once was*, but which, to the same extent, is *now no more*, has done much in maintaining our institutions thus far. I mean the powerful influence which the interesting scenes of the revolution had upon the *passions* of the people as distinguished from their judgment. By this influence, the jealousy, envy, and avarice, incident to our nature, and so common to a state of peace, prosperity, and conscious strength, were, for the time, in a great measure smothered and rendered inactive; while the deep-rooted

---

14. The most recent incident Lincoln invokes was the murder of newspaper editor and abolitionist Elijah Parish Lovejoy in Alton, Illinois, in November 1837.

principles of *hate*, and the powerful motive of *revenge*, instead of being turned against each other, were directed exclusively against the British nation. And thus, from the force of circumstances, the basest principles of our nature, were either made to lie dormant, or to become the active agents in the advancement of the noblest cause – that of establishing and maintaining civil and religious liberty.

But this state of feeling *must fade, is fading, has faded*, with the circumstances that produced it.

I do not mean to say, that the scenes of the revolution *are now* or *ever will* be entirely forgotten; but that like every thing else, they must fade upon the memory of the world, and grow more and more dim by the lapse of time. In history, we hope, they will be read of, and recounted, so long as the bible shall be read; – but even granting that they will, their influence *cannot be* what it heretofore has been. Even then, they *cannot be* so universally known, nor so vividly felt, as they were by the generation just gone to rest. At the close of that struggle, nearly every adult male had been a participator in some of its scenes. The consequence was, that of those scenes, in the form of a husband, a father, a son or brother, a *living history* was to be found in every family – a history bearing the indubitable testimonies of its own authenticity, in the limbs mangled, in the scars of wounds received, in the midst of the very scenes related – a history, too, that could be read and understood alike by all, the wise and the ignorant, the learned and the unlearned. – But *those* histories are gone. They *can* be read no more forever. They *were* a fortress of strength; but, what invading foeman could *never do*, the silent artillery of time *has done*; the leveling of its walls. They are gone. – They *were* a forest of giant oaks; but the all-resistless hurricane has swept over them, and left only, here and there, a lonely trunk, despoiled of its verdure, shorn of its foliage; unshading and unshaded, to murmur in a few gentle breezes, and to combat with its mutilated limbs, a few more ruder storms, then to sink, and be no more.

They *were* the pillars of the temple of liberty; and now, that they have crumbled away, that temple must fall, unless we, their descendants, supply their places with other pillars, hewn from the solid quarry of sober reason. Passion has helped us; but can do so no more. It will in future be our enemy. Reason, cold, calculating, unimpassioned reason, must furnish all the materials for our future support and defence. – Let those materials be moulded into *general intelligence, sound morality*, and in particular, *a reverence for the constitution and laws*: and, that we improved to the last; that we remained free to the last; that we revered his name to the last; that, during his long sleep, we permitted no hostile foot to pass over or desecrate his resting place; shall be that which to learn the last trump shall awaken our WASHINGTON.

Upon these let the proud fabric of freedom rest, as the rock of its basis; and as truly as has been said of the only greater institution, '*the gates of hell shall not prevail against it.*'

3. Charles Sumner, 'The Crime Against Kansas' (Washington, DC, 1856)

On 18 May 1856, in a stifling and crowded Senate, the member for Massachusetts, Charles Sumner (1811–74), began a two-day, five-hour, carefully memorised speech, arguing that Kansas should be admitted to the Union as a free state. Sumner was a prominent anti-slavery politician representing, successively, the Whig Party, Free Soil Party and radical wing of the new Republicans. Noted as an academic lawyer and powerful orator, the tall and commanding Sumner cut a flamboyant figure in the Senate of the 1850s. However, history will always remember him most for the physical savagery that this speech provoked.

Delivered slowly and with caustic sarcasm, the speech singled out two Democrat senators – Stephen Douglas of Illinois and Andrew Butler of South Carolina – for scorn, using provocatively sexual imagery to charge the latter with taking 'a mistress . . . who, though ugly to others, is always lovely to him; though polluted in the sight of the world, is chaste in his sight – I mean', added Sumner, 'the harlot, Slavery'. It served as a gauntlet thrown down for the South and, as he intended, Sumner's denunciations infuriated his opponents. As Christopher Hanlon argues, to many Southern observers, anger at the speech was not just about the larger issue of slavery, but about what was perceived as the improper abolitionist use of transatlantic media, since his words were explicitly designed for global transmission through print networks.[15]

Two days later, as the chamber was almost empty after closing for the day, Sumner was sitting at his desk signing envelopes containing copies of the printed speech, ready for the international transmission for which his words were clearly designed. Preston Brooks, a South Carolina House member related to Senator Butler, entered the chamber with a heavy cane and confronted Sumner with the offence taken on his kin's behalf: 'Mr. Sumner, I have read your speech twice over carefully. It is a libel on South Carolina, and Mr. Butler, who is a relative of mine.' As Sumner began to stand up, Brooks beat him severely with a gold-headed, thick gutta-percha cane until he was unconscious. This Senate floor bloodshed galvanised both sides of the sectional crisis. Sumner became a martyr in an outraged North and the issue energised the Republican party; Brooks was venerated for his valour across the South. The former slowly recovered from his injuries but kept away from the Senate for almost three years. In the mean time,

---

15. Christopher Hanlon, 'Embodied Eloquence, the Sumner Assault, and the Transatlantic Cable', *American Literature*, 82:3 (2010), 489.

along with the simultaneous unrest that Summer in Kansas, the caning of Sumner become a stark confirmation of the likelihood of conflict and made plain the violence that rose ever closer to the surface of political rhetoric. The following text contains some key sections of Sumner's lengthy address.

Source

Charles Sumner, *The Works of Charles Sumner*, vol. IV (Boston: Lee and Shepard, 1870–3), pp. 125–249.

MR. PRESIDENT,

– You are now called to redress a great wrong. Seldom in the history of nations is such a question presented. Tariffs, army bills, navy bills, land bills, are important, and justly occupy your care; but these all belong to the course of ordinary legislation. As means and instruments only, they are necessarily subordinate to the conservation of Government itself. Grant them or deny them, in greater or less degree, and you inflict no shock. The machinery of Government continues to move. The State does not cease to exist. Far otherwise is it with the eminent question now before you, involving the peace of the whole country, with our good name in history forevermore.

Take down your map, Sir, and you will find that the Territory of Kansas, more than any other region, occupies the middle spot of North America, equally distant from the Atlantic on the east and the Pacific on the west, from the frozen waters of Hudson's Bay on the north and the tepid Gulf Stream on the south, – constituting the precise geographical centre of the whole vast Continent. To such advantages of situation, on the very highway between two oceans, are added a soil of unsurpassed richness, and a fascinating, undulating beauty of surface, with a health-giving climate, calculated to nurture a powerful and generous people, worthy to be a central pivot of American institutions. A few short months have hardly passed since this spacious Mediterranean country was open only to the savage,[16] who ran wild in its woods and prairies; and now it has drawn to its bosom a population of freemen larger than Athens crowded within her historic gates . . .

Against this Territory, thus fortunate in position and population, a Crime has been committed which is without example in the records of the Past.[17] Not in plundered provinces or in the cruelties of selfish governors will you find its parallel . . .

---

16. Kansas was first settled by European Americans in 1827.
17. Following the 1854 Kansas–Nebraska Act, which had laid open the possibility of Kansas becoming a slave state, pro- and anti-slavery supporters had been engaged in violent confrontations over the territory's future.

The wickedness which I now begin to expose is immeasurably aggravated by the motive which prompted it. Not in any common lust for power did this uncommon tragedy have its origin. It is the rape of a virgin Territory, compelling it to the hateful embrace of Slavery; and it may be clearly traced to a depraved desire for a new Slave State, hideous offspring of such a crime, in the hope of adding to the power of Slavery in the National Government. Yes, Sir, when the whole world, alike Christian and Turk, is rising up to condemn this wrong, making it a hissing to the nations, here in our Republic, force – ay, Sir, FORCE – is openly employed in compelling Kansas to this pollution, and all for the sake of political power. There is the simple fact, which you will vainly attempt to deny, but which in itself presents an essential wickedness that makes other public crimes seem like public virtues.

This enormity, vast beyond comparison, swells to dimensions of crime which the imagination toils in vain to grasp, when it is understood that for this purpose are hazarded the horrors of intestine feud, not only in this distant Territory, but everywhere throughout the country. The muster has begun. The strife is no longer local, but national. Even now, while I speak, portents lower in the horizon, threatening to darken the land, which already palpitates with the mutterings of civil war ...

Such is the Crime which you are to judge. The criminal also must be dragged into the day, that you may see and measure the power by which all this wrong is sustained. From no common source could it proceed. In its perpetration was needed a spirit of vaulting ambition which would hesitate at nothing; a hardihood of purpose insensible to the judgment of mankind; a madness for Slavery, in spite of Constitution, laws, and all the great examples of our history; also consciousness of power such as comes from the habit of power; a combination of energies found only in a hundred arms directed by a hundred eyes; a control of Public Opinion through venal pens and a prostituted press; an ability to subsidize crowds in every vocation of life, – the politician with his local importance, the lawyer with his subtle tongue, and even the authority of the judge on the bench, – with a familiar use of men in places high and low, so that none, from the President to the lowest border postmaster, should decline to be its tool: all these things, and more, were needed, and they were found in the Slave Power of our Republic. There, Sir, stands the criminal, unmasked before you, heartless, grasping, and tyrannical, with an audacity beyond that of Verres, a subtlety beyond that of Machiavel, a meanness beyond that of Bacon, and an ability beyond that of Hastings.[18] Justice to Kansas can be secured only by the prostration of this influence; for this is the Power behind – greater than any President – which succors and sustains the Crime ...

---

18. Gaius Verres (c.120–43 BCE), Roman magistrate known for his corrupt rule of Sicily. Niccolò Machiavelli (1469–1527), Italian diplomat and philosopher, whose cynical counsel to potential leaders in *The Prince* (1513) made him a byword for deceitful rule. Francis Bacon (1561–1626), English philosopher often criticised for a supposed coldness of spirit. Warren Hastings (1732–1818), English statesman and Governor-General of India from 1774 to 1785, beset by accusations of corruption.

Such is the Crime and such the criminal which it is my duty to expose; and, by the blessing of God, this duty shall be done completely to the end. But this will not be enough. The Apologies which, with strange hardihood, are offered for the Crime must be torn away, so that it shall stand forth without a single rag or fig-leaf to cover its vileness. And, finally, the True Remedy must be shown . . .

Before entering upon the argument, I must say something of a general character, particularly in response to what has fallen from Senators who have raised themselves to eminence on this floor in championship of human wrong: I mean the Senator from South Carolina [Mr. Butler][19] and the Senator from Illinois [Mr. Douglas], who, though unlike as Don Quixote and Sancho Panza, yet, like this couple, sally forth together in the same adventure. I regret much to miss the elder Senator from his seat; but the cause against which he has run a tilt, with such ebullition of animosity, demands that the opportunity of exposing him should not be lost; and it is for the cause that I speak. The Senator from South Carolina has read many books of chivalry, and believes himself a chivalrous knight, with sentiments of honor and courage. Of course he has chosen a mistress to whom he has made his vows, and who, though ugly to others, is always lovely to him,[20] – though polluted in the sight of the world, is chaste in his sight: I mean the harlot Slavery . . .

The contest, which, beginning in Kansas, reaches us will be transferred soon from Congress to that broader stage, where every citizen is not only spectator, but actor; and to their judgment I confidently turn. To the People, about to exercise the electoral franchise, in choosing a Chief Magistrate of the Republic,[21] I appeal, to vindicate the electoral franchise in Kansas. Let the ballot-box of the Union, with multitudinous might, protect the ballot-box in that Territory. Let the voters everywhere, while rejoicing in their own rights, help guard the equal rights of distant fellow-citizens, that the shrines of popular institutions, now desecrated, may be sanctified anew, – that the ballot-box, now plundered, may be restored, – and that the cry, 'I am an American citizen,' shall no longer be impotent against outrage. In just regard for free labor, which you would blast by deadly contact with slave labor, – in Christian sympathy with the slave, whom you would task and sell, – in stern condemnation of the Crime consummated on that beautiful soil, – in rescue of fellow-citizens, now subjugated to Tyrannical Usurpation, – in dutiful respect for the early Fathers, whose aspirations are ignobly thwarted, – in the name of the Constitution outraged, of the Laws trampled down, of Justice banished, of Humanity degraded, of Peace destroyed, of Freedom crushed to earth, – and in the name of the Heavenly Father, whose service is perfect freedom, I make this last appeal.

---

19. Senator Andrew Butler (1796–1857), co-author of the Kansas–Nebraska Act (1854) with Senator Stephen Douglas (1813–61), Democrat politician from Illinois and advocate of the 'popular sovereignty' position on slavery.

20. Building on the reference to Miguel de Cervantes's *Don Quixote* above, an implicit comparison is made with the knight's transformation of a sturdy peasant girl into 'Dulcinea', an idealised object of his affections.

21. The 1856 election was held on Tuesday, 4 November 1856.

4. Abraham Lincoln, 'A House Divided' (Springfield, Illinois, 1858)

Lincoln's first speech of national renown was an address made in June 1858 at the Republican state convention in the Illinois statehouse in Springfield. Lincoln had been elected to the state legislature, had served in Washington, DC, as Whig Congressman in 1847, and after several career setbacks, joined the new anti-slavery Republican Party in 1856. Accepting the nomination of the party for Senate, Lincoln offered a foreboding verdict on the national political impasse. In a careful analysis of the aftermath of the Kansas–Nebraska Act, the speech accused Illinois Senator Douglas and President Franklin Pierce of conspiring to extend slavery, and claimed that the Dred Scott decision of 1857 had opened the door for slavery to be legal in the North and any future territories.

Widely transcribed in the national papers, in the words of Lincoln's early biographer, the speech 'excited the greatest interest everywhere throughout the free States. The grave peril he so clearly pointed out came home to the people of the North almost with the force of a revolution; and thereafter their eyes were fixed upon the Illinois senatorial campaign with undivided attention'.[22] It was to help propel the forty-nine-year-old provincial politician to national office.

As Lincoln remarked to his law partner, William Herndon, about the speech, 'I want to use some universally known figure, expressed in simple language as universally known, that it may strike home to the minds of men in order to rouse them to the peril of the times.'[23] He did so by drawing on New Testament phraseology to characterise the harm that the increasing incomprehension of Southern and Northern interests was causing for federal unity. In what would become famous as Lincoln's signature style, legalistic forensics, paratactic rhythms and a gift for narrative and apt metaphor combined in a forceful depiction of the nation's political unwinding.

Source

Abraham Lincoln, *The Collected Works of Abraham Lincoln*, vol. 2, ed. Roy P. Basler, Lloyd A. Dunlap and Marion D. Pratt (New Brunswick, NJ: Rutgers University Press, 1953).

---

22. John G. Nicolay, *A Short Life of Abraham Lincoln* (New York: Century, 1904), p. 120.
23. Quoted in Ward H. Lamon and Chauncey F. Black, *The Life of Abraham Lincoln: From His Birth to His Inauguration as President* (Boston: James R. Osgood, 1872), p. 89.

Mr. President and Gentlemen of the Convention:

If we could first know where we are and whither we are tending, we could better judge what to do and how to do it. We are now far into the fifth year since a policy was initiated[24] with the avowed object and confident promise of putting an end to slavery agitation. Under the operation of that policy, that agitation has not only not ceased but has constantly augmented. In my opinion, it will not cease until a crisis shall have been reached and passed. 'A house divided against itself cannot stand.'[25] I believe this government cannot endure, permanently, half slave and half free. I do not expect the Union to be dissolved; I do not expect the house to fall; but I do expect it will cease to be divided. It will become all one thing, or all the other. Either the opponents of slavery will arrest the further spread of it and place it where the public mind shall rest in the belief that it is in the course of ultimate extinction, or its advocates will push it forward till it shall become alike lawful in all the states, old as well as new, North as well as South.

Have we no tendency to the latter condition?

Let anyone who doubts carefully contemplate that now almost complete legal combination – piece of machinery, so to speak – compounded of the Nebraska doctrine and the Dred Scott decision.[26] Let him consider, not only what work the machinery is adapted to do, and how well adapted, but also let him study the history of its construction and trace, if he can, or rather fail, if he can, to trace the evidences of design and concert of action among its chief architects, from the beginning.

The new year of 1854 found slavery excluded from more than half the states by state constitutions and from most of the national territory by congressional prohibition. Four days later commenced the struggle which ended in repealing that congressional prohibition. This opened all the national territory to slavery and was the first point gained.

But, so far, Congress *only* had acted; and an endorsement by the people, real or apparent, was indispensable to save the point already gained and give chance for more.

This necessity had not been overlooked, but had been provided for, as well as might be, in the notable argument of 'squatter sovereignty,'[27] other-wise

---

24. The Kansas–Nebraska Act of 1854, co-authored by Stephen Douglas and Andrew Butler, sought to end division over slavery through popular sovereignty.

25. Matthew 12: 25: 'And Jesus knew their thoughts, and said unto them, Every kingdom divided against itself is brought to desolation; and every city or house divided against itself shall not stand.'

26. In *Dred Scott* v. *John F. A. Sandford* (March 1857), the Supreme Court ruled that Dred Scott, a slave who had resided in a free state and territory, was not entitled to his freedom, and that African Americans were not and could not be US citizens.

27. The name given by enemies of the popular sovereignty provisions of the Kansas–Nebraska Act.

called 'sacred right of self-government,' which latter phrase, though expressive of the only rightful basis of any government, was so perverted in this attempted use of it as to amount to just this: That if any *one* man choose to enslave *another*, no *third* man shall be allowed to object. That argument was incorporated into the Nebraska Bill itself, in the language which follows:

It being the true intent and meaning of this act not to legislate slavery into a territory or state, nor to exclude it therefrom, but to leave the people there-of perfectly free to form and regulate their domestic institutions in their own way, subject only to the Constitution of the United States.

Then opened the roar of loose declamation in favor of 'squatter sovereignty' and 'sacred right of self-government.' 'But,' said opposition members, 'let us amend the bill so as to expressly declare that the people of the territory may exclude slavery.' 'Not we,' said the friends of the measure; and down they voted the amendment.

While the Nebraska Bill was passing through Congress, a law case, involving the question of a Negro's freedom, by reason of his owner having voluntarily taken him first into a free state and then into a territory covered by the congressional prohibition, and held him as a slave for a long time in each, was passing through the United States Circuit Court for the district of Missouri; and both Nebraska Bill and lawsuit were brought to a decision in the same month of May 1854. The Negro's name was Dred Scott, which name now designates the decision finally made in the case. Before the then next presidential election, the law case came to, and was argued in, the Supreme Court of the United States; but the decision of it was deferred until after the election. Still, before the election, Senator Trumbull, on the floor of the Senate, requested the leading advocate of the Nebraska Bill to state his opinion whether the people of a territory can constitutionally exclude slavery from their limits; and the latter answers: 'That is a question for the Supreme Court.'

The election came. Mr. Buchanan was elected, and the endorsement, such as it was, secured. That was the second point gained. The endorsement, however, fell short of a clear popular majority by nearly 400,000 votes, and so, perhaps, was not overwhelmingly reliable and satisfactory. The outgoing President, in his last annual message, as impressively as possible echoed back upon the people the weight and authority of the endorsement. The Supreme Court met again, did not announce their decision, but ordered a reargument.

The presidential inauguration came, and still no decision of the Court; but the incoming President, in his inaugural address, fervently exhorted the people to abide by the forthcoming decision, whatever it might be. Then, in a few days, came the decision.

The reputed author of the Nebraska Bill finds an early occasion to make a speech at this capital endorsing the Dred Scott decision, and vehemently denouncing all opposition to it. The new President, too, seizes the early

occasion of the Silliman letter[28] to endorse and strongly construe that decision, and to express his astonishment that any different view had ever been
entertained!

At length a squabble springs up between the President and the author of
the Nebraska Bill, on the mere question of *fact*, whether the Lecompton constitution[29] was or was not in any just sense made by the people of Kansas; and
in that quarrel the latter declares that all he wants is a fair vote for the people,
and that he cares not whether slavery be voted *down* or voted *up*. I do not
understand his declaration, that he cares not whether slavery be voted down
or voted up, to be intended by him other than as an apt definition of the policy
he would impress upon the public mind – the principle for which he declares
he has suffered so much and is ready to suffer to the end. And well may he
cling to that principle! If he has any parental feeling, well may he cling to it. That
principle is the only shred left of his original Nebraska doctrine.

Under the Dred Scott decision, 'squatter sovereignty' squatted out of existence, tumbled down like temporary scaffolding; like the mold at the foundry,
served through one blast and fell back into loose sand; helped to carry an
election and then was kicked to the winds. His late joint struggle with the
Republicans against the Lecompton constitution involves nothing of the original
Nebraska doctrine. That struggle was made on a point – the right of a people
to make their own constitution – upon which he and the Republicans have
never differed.

The several points of the Dred Scott decision, in connection with Senator
Douglas' 'care not' policy, constitute the piece of machinery in its present state
of advancement. This was the third point gained. The working points of that
machinery are:

First, that no Negro slave, imported as such from Africa, and no descendant of such slave can ever be a citizen of any state in the sense of that term
as used in the Constitution of the United States. This point is made in order
to deprive the Negro, in every possible event, of the benefit of that provision
of the United States Constitution which declares that 'the citizens of each
state shall be entitled to all the privileges and immunities of citizens in the
several states.'

Second, that, 'subject to the Constitution of the United States,' neither
Congress nor a territorial legislature can exclude slavery from any United
States territory. This point is made in order that individual men may fill up the

---

28. In 1857, a group of distinguished men in Connecticut, led by Benjamin Silliman of
Yale University, wrote an open letter to President James Buchanan condemning the use
of military force against American citizens. The President quickly responded, defending
the use of troops against free-state agitators.
29. The Lecompton Constitution was a proposed pro-slavery constitution for the state
of Kansas, drawn up in 1857.

territories with slaves, without danger of losing them as property, and thus enhance the chances of permanency to the institution through all the future.

Third, that whether the holding a Negro in actual slavery in a free state makes him free, as against the holder, the United States courts will not decide, but will leave to be decided by the courts of any slave state the Negro may be forced into by the master. This point is made, not to be pressed immediately but, if acquiesced in for awhile, and apparently endorsed by the people at an election, then to sustain the logical conclusion that what Dred Scott's master might lawfully do with Dred Scott in the free state of Illinois, every other master may lawfully do with any other one, or 1,000 slaves, in Illinois or in any other free state.

Auxiliary to all this, and working hand in hand with it, the Nebraska doctrine, or what is left of it, is to educate and mold public opinion, at least Northern public opinion, not to care whether slavery is voted down or voted up. This shows exactly where we now are; and partially, also, whither we are tending.

It will throw additional light on the latter to go back and run the mind over the string of historical facts already stated. Several things will now appear less dark and mysterious than they did when they were transpiring. The people were to be left 'perfectly free,' 'subject only to the Constitution.' What the Constitution had to do with it, outsiders could not then see. Plainly enough, now, it was an exactly fitted niche for the Dred Scott decision to afterward come in and declare the perfect freedom of the people to be just no freedom at all.

Why was the amendment expressly declaring the right of the people voted down? Plainly enough, now, the adoption of it would have spoiled the niche for the Dred Scott decision. Why was the Court decision held up? Why even a senator's individual opinion withheld till after the presidential election? Plainly enough, now, the speaking out then would have damaged the 'perfectly free' argument upon which the election was to be carried. Why the outgoing President's felicitation on the endorsement? Why the delay of a reargument? Why the incoming President's advance exhortation in favor of the decision? These things look like the cautious patting and petting of a spirited horse preparatory to mounting him when it is dreaded that he may give the rider a fall. And why the hasty after-endorsement of the decision by the President and others?

We cannot absolutely know that all these exact adaptations are the result of preconcert. But when we see a lot of framed timbers, different portions of which we know have been gotten out at different times and places and by different workmen — Stephen, Franklin, Roger, and James, for instance[30] — and when we see these timbers joined together and see they exactly make the frame of a house or a mill, all the tenons[31] and mortises exactly fitting,

---

30. Senator Stephen Douglas; former President Franklin Pierce; Chief Justice Roger Taney; and President James Buchanan.
31. The end of a piece of timber, fitted to a mortice for insertion.

and all the lengths and proportions of the different pieces exactly adapted to their respective places, and not a piece too many or too few, not omitting even scaffolding, or, if a single piece be lacking, we see the place in the frame exactly fitted and prepared yet to bring such piece in – in such a case, we find it impossible not to believe that Stephen and Franklin and Roger and James all understood one another from the beginning, and all worked upon a common plan or draft drawn up before the first blow was struck.

Part B: The Meaning of the American Civil War

5. Alexander Stephens, 'The Cornerstone Speech' (Savannah, Georgia, 1861)

Following the victory of Lincoln's Republicans on a clear abolitionist platform in the November 1860 Presidential election, seven Southern states seceded and established a Confederate States of America in February 1861, with its initial capital in Montgomery, Alabama. There was much disagreement within the seceding states as to the precise objectives of their new nation. One famous articulation was given by the new Confederate Vice President, Alexander Stephens (1812–83), former Governor of Georgia, who delivered an extemporaneous address known as the 'Cornerstone Speech' in Savannah on 21 March.

   Whereas other Confederate leaders gave more equivocal accounts of their view of their project and often focused on issues of states' rights, Stephens placed an uncompromising emphasis on the 'physical, philosophical and moral truth' of racial superiority.[32] Its frank defence of slavery angered the Confederate President, Jefferson Davis, who foresaw the damage it could do. When transcriptions were widely quoted in the transatlantic press, the stark views contained in it helped dissuade Britain and France from recognising the Confederacy. None the less, as Harry V. Jaffa has declared, the rare candour of the Cornerstone Speech 'conveys, more than any other contemporary document, not only the soul of the Confederacy but also of that Jim Crow[33] South that arose from the ashes'.[34]

Source

Alexander H. Stephens, 'Cornerstone Address, March 21, 1861', in Frank Moore (ed.), *The Rebellion Record: A Diary of American Events with Documents, Narratives, Illustrative Incidents, Poetry, etc.*, vol. 1 (New York: O. P. Putnam, 1862), pp. 44–6.

---

32. For more on these divisions see Drew Gilpin Faust, *The Creation of Confederate Nationalism: Ideology and Identity in the Civil War South* (Baton Rouge: Louisiana State University Press, 1988).

33. Jim Crow was the name of the racial caste system that operated in the Southern and border states from the 1870s to the 1960s.

34. Harry V. Jaffa, *A New Birth of Freedom: Abraham Lincoln and the Coming of the Civil War* (New York: Rowman, Littlefield, 2000), p. 223.

The new constitution[35] has put at rest, forever, all the agitating questions relating to our peculiar institution – African slavery as it exists amongst us – the proper status of the negro in our form of civilization.[36] This was the immediate cause of the late rupture and present revolution. Jefferson in his forecast, had anticipated this, as the 'rock upon which the old Union would split.'[37] He was right. What was conjecture with him, is now a realized fact. But whether he fully comprehended the great truth upon which that rock stood and stands, may be doubted. The prevailing ideas entertained by him and most of the leading statesmen at the time of the formation of the old constitution, were that the enslavement of the African was in violation of the laws of nature; that it was wrong in principle, socially, morally, and politically. It was an evil they knew not well how to deal with, but the general opinion of the men of that day was that, somehow or other in the order of Providence, the institution would be evanescent and pass away. This idea, though not incorporated in the constitution, was the prevailing idea at that time. The constitution, it is true, secured every essential guarantee to the institution while it should last, and hence no argument can be justly urged against the constitutional guarantees thus secured, because of the common sentiment of the day. Those ideas, however, were fundamentally wrong. They rested upon the assumption of the equality of races. This was an error. It was a sandy foundation, and the government built upon it fell when the 'storm came and the wind blew.'

Our new government is founded upon exactly the opposite idea; its foundations are laid, its corner-stone rests, upon the great truth that the negro is not equal to the white man; that slavery subordination to the superior race is his natural and normal condition. This, our new government, is the first, in the history of the world, based upon this great physical, philosophical, and moral truth. This truth has been slow in the process of its development, like all other truths in the various departments of science. It has been so even amongst us. Many who hear me, perhaps, can recollect well, that this truth was not generally admitted, even within their day. The errors of the past generation still clung to many as late as twenty years ago. Those at the North, who still cling to these errors, with a zeal above knowledge, we justly denominate fanatics. All fanaticism springs from an aberration of the mind from a defect in reasoning. It is a species of insanity.

---

35. The Confederate States Constitution was adopted on 11 March 1861.

36. In Article I, Section 9(4), the Confederate Constitution stated that 'No bill of attainder, ex post facto law, or law denying or impairing the right of property in negro slaves shall be passed.'

37. The closest Jefferson came to arguing this was his claim following the Missouri Compromise of 1820's expansion of slavery: 'I considered it at once as the knell of the Union' (Letter to John Holmes, 22 April 1820, in Thomas Jefferson, *The Writings of Thomas Jefferson: Being His Autobiography, Correspondence, Reports, Messages, Addresses, and Other Writings, Official and Private*, ed. H. A. Washington (Cambridge: Cambridge University Press, 2011), p. 159).

One of the most striking characteristics of insanity, in many instances, is forming correct conclusions from fancied or erroneous premises; so with the anti-slavery fanatics. Their conclusions are right if their premises were. They assume that the negro is equal, and hence conclude that he is entitled to equal privileges and rights with the white man. If their premises were correct, their conclusions would be logical and just but their premise being wrong, their whole argument fails. I recollect once of having heard a gentleman from one of the northern States, of great power and ability, announce in the House of Representatives, with imposing effect, that we of the South would be compelled, ultimately, to yield upon this subject of slavery, that it was as impossible to war successfully against a principle in politics, as it was in physics or mechanics. That the principle would ultimately prevail. That we, in maintaining slavery as it exists with us, were warring against a principle, a principle founded in nature, the principle of the equality of men.

The reply I made to him was, that upon his own grounds, we should, ultimately, succeed, and that he and his associates, in this crusade against our institutions, would ultimately fail. The truth announced, that it was as impossible to war successfully against a principle in politics as it was in physics and mechanics, I admitted; but told him that it was he, and those acting with him, who were warring against a principle. They were attempting to make things equal which the Creator had made unequal.

In the conflict thus far, success has been on our side, complete throughout the length and breadth of the Confederate States.[38] It is upon this, as I have stated, our social fabric is firmly planted; and I cannot permit myself to doubt the ultimate success of a full recognition of this principle throughout the civilized and enlightened world.

. . .

But to return to the question of the future. What is to be the result of this revolution?

Will every thing, commenced so well, continue as it has begun? In reply to this anxious inquiry, I can only say it all depends upon ourselves. A young man starting out in life on his majority, with health, talent, and ability, under a favoring Providence, may be said to be the architect of his own fortunes. His destinies are in his own hands. He may make for himself a name, of honor or dishonor, according to his own acts. If he plants himself upon truth, integrity, honor and uprightness, with industry, patience and energy, he cannot fail of success. So it is with us. We are a young republic, just entering upon the arena of nations; we will be the architects of our own fortunes. Our destiny, under Providence, is in our own hands. With wisdom, prudence, and statesmanship on the part of our public men, and intelligence, virtue and patriotism on the part of the people, success, to the full measures of our most sanguine hopes, may be looked for.

---

38. In March 1861, South Carolina, Mississippi, Florida, Alabama, Georgia, Louisiana and Texas had seceded.

But if unwise counsels prevail if we become divided if schisms arise, if dissentions spring up if factions are engendered if party spirit, nourished by unholy personal ambition shall rear its hydra head, I have no good to prophesy for you. Without intelligence, virtue, integrity, and patriotism on the part of the people, no republic or representative government can be durable or stable.

We have intelligence, and virtue, and patriotism. All that is required is to cultivate and perpetuate these. Intelligence will not do without virtue. France was a nation of philosophers. These philosophers become Jacobins. They lacked that virtue, that devotion to moral principle, and that patriotism which is essential to good government. Organized upon principles of perfect justice and right-seeking amity and friendship with all other powers – I see no obstacle in the way of our upward and onward progress. Our growth, by accessions from other States, will depend greatly upon whether we present to the world, as I trust we shall, a better government than that to which neighboring States belong. If we do this, North Carolina, Tennessee, and Arkansas cannot hesitate long; neither can Virginia, Kentucky, and Missouri.[39] They will necessarily gravitate to us by an imperious law. We made ample provision in our constitution for the admission of other States; it is more guarded, and wisely so, I think, than the old constitution on the same subject, but not too guarded to receive them as fast as it may be proper. Looking to the distant future, and, perhaps, not very far distant either, it is not beyond the range of possibility, and even probability, that all the great States of the north-west will gravitate this way, as well as Tennessee, Kentucky, Missouri, Arkansas, etc. Should they do so, our doors are wide enough to receive them, but not until they are ready to assimilate with us in principle.

The process of disintegration in the old Union may be expected to go on with almost absolute certainty if we pursue the right course. We are now the nucleus of a growing power which, if we are true to ourselves, our destiny, and high mission, will become the controlling power on this continent. To what extent accessions will go on in the process of time, or where it will end, the future will determine. So far as it concerns States of the old Union, this process will be upon no such principles of reconstruction as now spoken of, but upon reorganization and new assimilation. Such are some of the glimpses of the future as I catch them.

6. William E. Gladstone, 'The South Has Made a Nation' (Newcastle, 1862)

A key question for Lincoln and the North was whether the European powers would recognise the Confederacy. 'Recognition is better to the South than fleets and armies,' warned *The New York Times* in October

---

39. All of these states would indeed secede. West Virginia was created in May 1861, when Unionist northwestern counties of Virginia rejected secession from the Union.

1862; 'if you permit of recognition, you may well make peace.'[40] The conflict had caused significant problems for Britain. In order to stem the crucial cotton trade with Europe, the Union had blockaded Southern ports, and the effects of this put pressure on the British economy, causing widespread unemployment in industrial Northern England and raising American fears of recognition of the South as a legitimate state.

Though hostile to slavery and sensitive to his own family's historic involvement in it, William Ewart Gladstone, the British Chancellor, was far more sympathetic to the Southern cause than either Prime Minister Lord Palmerston or Foreign Minister Lord Russell. On 7 October 1862, in Newcastle, during a tour of the North, Gladstone delivered a speech on the American conflict that, whilst expressing even-handed affinity with the Union, none the less seemed explicitly to recognise the seceding states as a nation (Figure 12).

His position was at odds with that of his colleagues and never became official policy, prevented in part by subsequent Confederate defeats. None the less, it came so close to having a decisive impact on the conflict that Gladstone considered the speech the 'most singular . . . least excusable' error of his career.[41] As one early biographer recorded, his words 'reverberated around the world and caused a profound sensation'.[42] The troubling insights it provided into British thinking were a key contributing factor in Lincoln's readying of the Emancipation Proclamation for issue in January 1863.

Source

'Mr. Gladstone's Speech in Newcastle', *The Times*, 9 October 1862, pp. 7–8.

It is not usual for a Chancellor of the Exchequer to detain a public assembly on questions of foreign policy, but I cannot help briefly alluding to the deplorable, though I think not doubtful, struggle now proceeding in America [*hear hear*]. When exercising my own poor faculties in the matter I have never felt that England had any reason, connected with her own special interests, for desiring the disruption of the American Union. I can understand those who say that it is

40. 'From Great Britain', *The New York Times*, 26 October 1862.
41. John Morley, *The Life of William Ewart Gladstone* (London: MacMillan, 1903), p. 81.
42. Quoted in Morley, *The Life of William Ewart Gladstone*, p. 81.

for the general interest of nations that no state should swell to the dimensions of a continent.

...

When the two parties are in a state of great mutual exasperation, it is not at all unlikely that neutrality will offend both parties, because, in point of fact, that state of mind in which the conduct of the neutral is liable to be judged by either disputant is not a state in which we should expect perfectly impartial conclusions [*hear, hear*]. But what we may expect is, that an honest course of neutrality will eventually be recognised – that the course we have pursued up to this date will be recognised after this struggle shall have passed away, and come to be calmly considered [*applause*].

But if either party have a right in the meantime to find fault, it appears to me to be the Confederates rather than the Federals [*hear, hear*]. If we have deviated at all from neutrality, our course has been against them. We have permitted the exports of arms and warlike stores to the Confederates, whose ports are blockaded and to the Federals, who have perfect freedoms to import whatever they please [*hear*] I believe that course has been right and just: but at any rate we have not had a bias unfavourable to the Northern States.

But I would for a moment make an appeal on behalf of the people of the Northern States as regards our appreciation of their position. Great allowances have to be made, and great allowances for heat and exaggeration under the present circumstances than perhaps could fairly be claimed for other nations. Only consider what has been their previous history. They have never drunk the bitter cup of mortification and disappointment. They had but to will a thing to be done, and it has been done. Their course has been one of prosperity and advancement, without example and without a single break. It is not in human nature a people that has been subject to experience so flattering – so soothing to human self-love – should at once learn to accommodate and to submit itself with a perfect good grace to the circumstances and necessities of our present human condition [*hear*].

We have suffered before. We have gone through the very agonies of that dismemberment, against which the Northern people of the United States have been struggling, We have gone through it, and now we know it is not a bad thing after all [*hear, hear*]. They have not gone through it. All I say is, bear with all we can. Let us keep a kindly temper. Let us not allow ourselves the slightest irritation when we see our policy adversely criticised on the other side of the Atlantic, and let us beware of adverse criticism on this side. They are our kin, and they were, if they are not now, our customers: and we hope they will be our customers again [*applause*].

... We may have our own opinion of slavery. We may be for North or the south; but we have no doubt of this – that Jefferson Davis and the other Confederate leaders have made an army; they are making, it appears, a navy; and they have made what is more than either – they have made a nation [*sensation, following by prolonged cheering*].

7. Abraham Lincoln, 'The Gettysburg Address' (Gettysburg, Pennsylvania, 1863)

Midway through the Civil War, on Thursday, 19 November 1863, President Abraham Lincoln was invited to deliver remarks at the official dedication of the National Cemetery of Gettysburg, Pennsylvania, a site that marked one of the bloodiest and most decisive battles of the war. He was not the featured orator that day, but part of a delegation featuring various eminent politicians from Northern states, and he was to address the crowd after the main speaker, Senator Edward Everett of Massachusetts. Speaking for two hours from a memorised speech, Everett offered an ornate and elaborate evocation of the battle scene, moving many in the audience to tears.

Lincoln was then introduced and his high, penetrating voice rang out for only three minutes as he delivered his concise and tightly composed 273-word speech. Most in the audience expected another long speech, and were surprised when the President sat down after his famous closing lines So surprisingly brief were his remarks that the ceremonial photographer famously did not have time to focus his equipment. As David Herbert-Donald puts it, 'Immediately afterwards, Lincoln may have felt that his Gettysburg address was not successful. "Lamon, that speech won't scour!" he is supposed to have said, referring to the plows used on the western prairies that failed to turn back the heavy soil.'[43] Yet as soon as the short speech was reprinted in newspapers, it began its journey towards its present acclaim for both stylistic achievement and political clarity. The *Chicago Tribune* thought 'the dedicatory remarks by President Lincoln will live among the annals of man'. *Harper's Weekly* thought the 'few words of the President' were 'as simple and felicitous and earnest a word as was ever spoken'.[44] The President was repeatedly asked for autographed copies of the speech in the years that followed.

Yet the vision for the republic outlined in the speech's brief narrative was anything but blandly consensual. By giving precedence to the Declaration of Independence over the Constitution, it attempted to reaffirm American history strongly in terms of the 'proposition' of equality, implicitly rebuking those who saw the Civil War as a conflict primarily about states' rights. This was not lost on critics of such a politics, some of whom quickly denounced what one Democratic newspaper saw as the speech's 'perversion of history'.[45] By framing democratic ideals in

---

43. David Herbert-Donald, *Lincoln* (New York: Simon and Schuster, 2011), p. 464.
44. Quoted in Herbert-Donald, *Lincoln*, p. 465.
45. Wilbur F. Storey, *Chicago Times*, quoted in Herbert-Donald, *Lincoln*, p. 466.

memorable hymnal cadences, including some of the phrases of Webster, seen in an earlier speech in this chapter, the address remains one of the lasting monuments in nineteenth-century rhetoric. It marks the transition, argues Gary Wills, from 'ornate oratorical embellishment' to 'sound-bite' public speaking; it brought the formal ideals of oratory 'into the modern era, where the pace of life does not allow for the leisurely style of Lincoln's rhetorical forebears'.[46]

Source

Abraham Lincoln, Roy P. Basler, Lloyd A. Dunlap and Marion D. Pratt (eds), *The Collected Works of Abraham Lincoln*, vol. 2 (New Brunswick, NJ: Rutgers University Press, 1953).

Four score and seven years ago[47] our fathers brought forth on this continent, a new nation, conceived in Liberty, and dedicated to the proposition that all men are created equal.

Now we are engaged in a great civil war, testing whether that nation, or any nation so conceived and so dedicated, can long endure. We are met on a great battle-field of that war.[48] We have come to dedicate a portion of that field, as a final resting place for those who here gave their lives that that nation might live. It is altogether fitting and proper that we should do this.

But, in a larger sense, we can not dedicate – we can not consecrate – we can not hallow – this ground. The brave men, living and dead, who struggled here, have consecrated it, far above our poor power to add or detract. The world will little note, nor long remember what we say here, but it can never forget what they did here. It is for us the living, rather, to be dedicated here to the unfinished work which they who fought here have thus far so nobly advanced. It is rather for us to be here dedicated to the great task remaining before us – that from these honored dead we take increased devotion to that cause for which they gave the last full measure of devotion – that we here highly resolve that these dead shall not have died in vain – that this nation, under God, shall have a new birth of freedom – and that government of the people, by the people, for the people, shall not perish from the earth.

---

46. Gary Wills, *Lincoln at Gettysburg: The Words that Remade America* (New York: Simon and Schuster, 2011), p. 160.
47. Since the Declaration of Independence in July 1776.
48. The Battle of Gettysburg was fought from 1 to 3 July 1863, an engagement of General George Meade's Union Army of the Potomac against Robert E. Lee's Army of Northern Virginia as they invaded Pennsylvania. Lee's forces were ultimately repelled in the bloodiest battle of the war, with over 50,000 casualties.

8. Frederick Douglass, 'The Mission of the War' (New York City, 1864)

In the third year of the conflict, on 13 January 1864, the African American political leader Frederick Douglass was invited by the Women's Loyal League to deliver a high-profile lecture at the Cooper Union in Manhattan. Though the Civil War was entering its decisive phase, Douglass worried that its objectives and significance were still unclear and that many questions haunted the Northern public. Was this a conflict about states' rights alone? What was the role of the larger issue of slavery? Douglass was also concerned that there was defeatism in the air, with some arguing that Lincoln should make peace and return to the prewar status quo.

Douglass had become the most prominent spokesperson for the African American perspective on the war and had been working with radical Republicans, such as Thaddeus Stevens and Charles Sumner, to maintain the conflict's abolitionist essence. His 1864 Cooper Union speech framed the war decisively as a crusade against slavery, 'a great national opportunity', a 'salutary' education in democratic history, and a moment of 'hope' as much as 'fear'. Moreover, with an eye to shaping the postwar debate, he argued that abolition could not be complete until the former slaves had full citizenship rights and were free of all racial discrimination.

Source

Frederick Douglass, 'The Mission of the War: A Lecture', *New York Tribune*, 14 January 1864, pp. 1–2.

Ladies and Gentlemen: By the mission of the war I mean nothing occult, arbitrary or difficult to be understood, but simply those great moral changes in the fundamental conditions of the people, demanded by the situation of the country plainly involved in the nature of the war, and which, if the war is conducted in accordance with its true character, it is naturally and logically fitted to accomplish.

Speaking in the name of Providence, some men tell me that slavery is already dead, that it expired with the first shot at Sumter. This may be so, but I do not share the confidence with which it is asserted. In a grand crisis like this, we should all prefer to look facts sternly in the face and to accept their verdict whether it bless or blast us. I look for no miraculous destruction of slavery. The war looms before me simply as a great national opportunity, which may be improved to national salvation, or neglected to national ruin. I hope much from the bravery of our soldiers, but in vain is the might of armies if our rulers fail to profit by experience and refuse to listen to the suggestions of wisdom and justice. The most hopeful fact of the hour is that we are now in a salutary school – the school of affliction. If sharp and signal retribution, long protracted, wide-sweeping and overwhelming, can teach a great nation respect for the long-despised claims of justice, surely we shall be taught now and for all time to come. But if, on the other hand, this potent teacher, whose lessons are written in characters of blood and thundered to us from a hundred battlefields shall fail, we shall go down as we shall deserve to go down, as a warning to all other nations which shall come after us.[49] It is not pleasant to contemplate the hour as one of doubt and danger. We naturally prefer the bright side, but when there is a dark side it is folly to shut our eyes to it or deny its existence.

I know that the acorn involves the oak, but I know also that the commonest accident may destroy its potential character and defeat its natural destiny. One wave brings its treasure from the briny deep, but another often sweeps it back to its primal depths. The saying that revolutions never go backward must be taken with limitations. The Revolution of 1848 was one of the grandest that ever dazzled a gazing world.[50] It overturned the French throne, sent Louis Philippe into exile, shook every throne in Europe, and inaugurated a glorious Republic. Looking from a distance, the friends of democratic liberty saw in the convulsion the death of kingcraft in Europe and throughout the world. Great was their disappointment. Almost in the twinkling of an eye, the latent forces of despotism rallied. The Republic disappeared. Her noblest defenders were sent into exile, and the hopes of democratic liberty were blasted in the moment of their bloom. Politics and perfidy proved too strong for the principles of liberty and justice in that contest. I wish I could say that no such liabilities darken the horizon around us. But the same elements are plainly involved here as there. Though the portents are that we shall flourish, it is too much to say that we cannot fail and fall. Our destiny is to be taken out of our own hands. It is cowardly to shuffle our responsibilities upon the shoulders of Providence. I do not intend to argue but to state facts.

We are now wading into the third year of conflict with a fierce and sanguinary rebellion, one which, at the beginning of it, we were hopefully assured by one of our most sagacious and trusted political prophets would be ended in less than ninety days; a rebellion which, in its worst features, stands alone among rebellions a solitary and ghastly horror, without a parallel in the history of any

---

49. An invocation of John Winthrop's famous Puritan sermon, 'A Model of Christian Charity' (1630), delivered on the *Arbella* en route to Massachusetts Bay: 'For we must consider that we shall be as a city upon a hill. The eyes of all people are upon us. So that if we shall deal falsely with our God in this work we have undertaken, and so cause Him to withdraw His present help from us, we shall be made a story and a by-word through the world.'

50. A series of republican uprisings against monarchies across continental Europe and Ireland took place during 1848, none of which was ultimately successful in achieving its aims; most led to more repressive regimes.

nation, ancient or modern; a rebellion inspired by no love of liberty and by no hatred of oppression, as most other rebellions have been, and therefore utterly indefensible upon any moral or social grounds; a rebellion which openly and shamelessly sets at defiance the world's judgment of right and wrong, appeals from light to darkness, from intelligence to ignorance, from the ever-increasing prospects and blessings of a high and glorious civilization to the cold and withering blasts of a naked barbarism; a rebellion which even at this unfinished stage of it counts the number of its slain not by thousands nor by tens of thousands, but by hundreds of thousands; a rebellion which in the destruction of human life and property has rivaled the earthquake, the whirlwind and the pestilence that waketh in darkness and wasteth at noonday. It has planted agony at a million hearthstones, thronged our streets with the weeds of mourning, filled our land with mere stumps of men, ridged our soil with two hundred thousand rudely formed graves and mantled it all over with the shadow of death. A rebellion which, while it has arrested the wheels of peaceful industry and checked the flow of commerce, has piled up a debt heavier than a mountain of gold to weigh down the necks of our children's children. There is no end to the mischief wrought. It has brought ruin at home, contempt abroad, has cooled our friends, heated our enemies and endangered our existence as nation.

Now, for what is all this desolation, ruin, shame suffering and sorrow? Can anybody want the answer? Can anybody be ignorant of the answer? It has been given a thousand times from this and other platforms. We all know it is slavery. Less than a half a million of Southern slaveholders – holding in bondage four million slaves – finding themselves outvoted in the effort to get possession of the United States government, in order to serve the interests of slavery, have madly resorted to the sword – have undertaken to accomplish by bullets what they failed to accomplish by ballots. That is the answer.

. . .

I know that many are appalled and disappointed by the apparently interminable character of this war. I am neither appalled nor disappointed without pretending to any higher wisdom than other men. I knew well enough and often said it: once let the North and South confront each other on the battlefield, and slavery and freedom be the inspiring motives of the respective sections, the contest will be fierce, long and sanguinary. Governor Seymour[51] charges us with prolonging the war, and I say the longer the better if it must be so – in order to put an end to the hell-black cause out of which the rebellion has risen.

Say not that I am indifferent to the horrors and hardships of the war. I am not indifferent. In common with the American people generally, I feel the prolongation of the war a heavy calamity, private as well as public. There are vacant spaces at my hearthstone which I shall rejoice to see filled again by the boys

---

51. Horatio Seymour (1810–86), Democrat Governor of New York in 1853–4 and 1863–4, and a fierce critic of Lincoln's war policy.

who once occupied them, but which cannot be thus filled while the war lasts, for they have enlisted 'during the war.'

But even from the length of this struggle, we who mourn over it may well enough draw some consolation when we reflect upon the vastness and grandeur of its mission. The world has witnessed many wars – and history records and perpetuates their memory – but the world has not seen a nobler and grander war than that which the loyal people of this country are now waging against the slaveholding rebels. The blow we strike is not merely to free a country or continent, but the whole world, from slavery; for when slavery fails here, it will fall everywhere. We have no business to mourn over our mission. We are writing the statutes of eternal justice and liberty in the blood of the worst of tyrants as a warning to all aftercomers. We should rejoice that there was normal life and health enough in us to stand in our appointed place, and do this great service for mankind.

. . .

The hour is one of hope as well as danger. But whatever may come to pass, one thing is clear: The principles involved in the contest, the necessities of both sections of the country, the obvious requirements of the age, and every suggestion of enlightened policy demand the utter extirpation of slavery from every foot of American soil, and the enfranchisement of the entire colored population of the country. Elsewhere we may find peace, but it will be a hollow and deceitful peace. Elsewhere we may find prosperity, but it will be a transient prosperity. Elsewhere we may find greatness and renown, but if these are based upon anything less substantial than justice they will vanish, for righteousness alone can permanently exalt a nation.

I end where I began – no war but an Abolition war; no peace but an Abolition peace; liberty for all, chains for none; the black man a soldier in war, a laborer in peace; a voter at the South as well as at the North; America his permanent home, and all Americans his fellow countrymen. Such, fellow citizens, is my idea of the mission of the war. If accomplished, our glory as a nation will be complete, our peace will flow like a river, and our foundation will be the everlasting rocks.

Part C: Pacifisms and Non-Violence

9. Hannah Mather Crocker, 'Fast Sermon Against the War' (Boston, 1812)

The peace movement in the early US was powerfully religious in impulse. Anti-war arguments were often made through sermons drawing upon the traditional form of the 'jeremiads', lamenting the moral state of society and prophesying its imminent downfall.[52] Such sermons enjoyed a resurgence during the Revolutionary period and particularly in the era of the 'War of 1812' (1812–15) against Great Britain.

One intriguing example of this period's anti-war rhetoric was a sermon dated as delivered in August 1812 by Hannah Mather Crocker (1752–1829). A descendant of the Mather dynasty of prominent New England Puritan ministers, Crocker became one of early America's most vocal advocates for women's rights. In the sermon below we see her invoking a tradition practised by earlier generations of her family in offering a 'fast day sermon'. Like many others, she saw 'Madison's War' as bringing neither political nor religious benefit to the republic. Crocker moved from concern about a just war to a litany of sins against materialism, extortion and oppression, to illustrate how the people of 'God's Israel' had gone astray. It helped model a peace movement that placed women's influence at the heart of civil society.

However, it is not clear that Mather ever delivered this sermon. Since women were forbidden from preaching, she presented the piece under the *nom de plume* of 'Increase Mather Jr. of the Inner Temple', adopting the persona of the male public speaker.

Source

Hannah M. Crocker and Constance J. Post, *Observations on the Real Rights of Women and Other Writings* (Lincoln: University of Nebraska Press, 2011).

Preached at Mr. Madison's Fast Day, August 20, 1812

My Respected Hearers,

We have this day assembled in the house of the Lord in compliance with and direction of the head government of this Nation. As specified by proclamation thro' the medium of the public newspapers, it may be expected by them that we join in fervent prayer for the divine blessing to attend the present war.

---

52. The classic study of which remains Sacvan Bercovitch, *American Jeremiad* (Madison: University of Wisconsin Press, 1978).

But every judicious person must be sensible it is the duty of a wise Nation to seek direction of heaven before they engage in a war. If they do not, but rush into one without seeking direction from him who is the wise ruler and disposer of all events of Mankind, we can have no reason to expect a blessing will attend the undertaking till we have sought out heaven to direct our path. I feel very confident no war can be justifiable in the eye of the God of peace except a defensive one. And when his people are labouring under the yoke of tyranny and oppression, it is the duty of such a people to call on the Lord and be of good courage and commit their cause to him if a just one.

We may expect a blessing will attend us, if we fervently pray [to] him to appear on our behalf, that he would protect us and break us to pieces the power of every cruel and proud oppressor, for wherefore go we forth except the Lord go with us.

Now if any nation do go forth in a rash manner, not first seeking direction of heaven as to the justness of the cause, it may indeed be called a war of passion, or the rage of men in power. God forbid this nation, as a people, should engage in such a war, for which reason I have chosen for our present meditation these words

> Numbers the 22 chapter 12 verse
> And God said unto Balaam thou shalt not go with them, thou
> shalt not curse the people for they are blessed

I would recommend to you, my hearers, to read the whole of this chapter, when you return to your own houses, that you may take into view the wonderful interposition of divine providence of behalf of this ancient people Israel. Now at that time they, the Children of Israel, were many, and Moab was sore afraid of them, and Balak the son of Zippor was king of the Moabites at the time. And Moab was greatly intimidated and sore afraid, on account of the vast number of the Children of Israel, whom it seems had pitched their tents on the plains of Moab, on this side of Jordan, by Jericho. Now Balak, tho' he was irrupted to a degree of desperation, yet he had not the hardiness or imprudence to wage war against the Israelites till he had secured Balaam in his interest, as he supposed him to be a prophet, or one versed in divination.

In the first place we shall take notice of the unhappy situation of the Moabites and their poor king Balak, that they could not call on the God of Israel as the God of their Fathers, and they dare not for their cause was a bad one. For it doth not appear that the Israelites made any war upon them but were quiet in their own tents. But such was the pride of Moab and Balak.

. . .

If we humble ourselves under his mighty hand, he can and will turn their machinations from the curse of war to peace. War is always a sore judgement to a Nation and never ought to be resorted to, till no other refuge is left to preserve our lives, and Liberty. Then it is our duty to stand fast in the Liberty wherewith God has made us free, and trust in him to deliver us from all our enemies. We, my hearers, of these United States, have ever been peculiar care of a most kind and gracious God. Has he not upheld us, from our first settlement to the present day? When we have had reason to think our vessel had nearly foundered, did not he that raised up a Joshua[53] of old, has he not raised up a Washington in our own remembrance? He can yet save our American Israel.

For if the God of peace bless us, we need not fear the wrath of Man. We have reason to hope much from the wisdom, and prudence, of the head rulers of this State . We have reason to think heaven directed our choices in a ruler for peace. We have reason to bless God we have yet peace so far, that we are preserved from intestine war among ourselves in this part of our land. We have reason to bless God for the faithfulness of our Clergy for they are heard to say, almost to a man, peace be within your walls, prosperity in all your dwellings. From these things we may be encouraged and hope the wrath, indication and horror of war will soon pass over if we will take the advice of Isiah, to God's own people. ...

I must be plain and explicit here, for I wish the meanest capacity to comprehend our present situation. For some years past we have been the happiest people on the Globe; we have been blessed with every favour heaven could bestow on a favoured people, but we have done evil in the sight of the Lord. We have gone astray from the living God. We have forsaken the path of our ancestors, we have gone astray from the living God and have worshipped the Idols of silver and gold. We have made haste to be rich. Our land groans under the Yoke of extortion and oppression[54] and tis for our follies and sinfulness we are now involved in a war, which is indeed a gloomy scene. And as it appears a war of party and the rage of men in power, nothing can save us from intestine animosity but the good sense of the people attended with a divine blessing. For God almighty's sake, don't let party spirit prevail among us and destroy all our happiness. Let us bear in mind [that] if we differ in opinion, we also differ in our looks; and we can no more make men think alike than we can them look alike. Our frames, our whole organisation, are so different, tis impossible we should think just alike. But we can all be so far orthodox as to do good to our fellow creatures. We can love and show mercy and walk humbly before God. If we differ in some points respecting religion or politics, we can all bear in mind that our country was settled on the firm basis of liberty, freedom and independence for the free enjoyment of civil, and religious privileges but not licentiousness.

Let us then, by hearers, continue firm in the real interest of our beloved Country. Let us unite in one body for the joint interest of all its members. For we are indeed a very great and numerous people, and the Lord Jehovah will not as yet give us up if we do not provoke him by our sins and follies, which are indeed very

---

53. In the Hebrew Bible's Book of Joshua, the eponymous figure leads the Israelite tribes after the death of Moses.

54. A reference to slavery, still active in the Southern states, though it had been abolished in Massachusetts in 1783.

great. It behooves us then, my friends, to forsake every evil way. Let me beg of you to begin by paying more regard to family government. If we do not, tis greatly to be feared our Children will not be found walking in the path of our venerable ancestors. We of these New England States have been blessed in a most particular manner in having wise and good Men to rule over us. We now call on all Magistrates to perform their duty, to restrain all profaneness, and debauchery in the land. It is now indeed a crying sin in our land and calls loudly for reformation. Tis reformation alone can save the city. If every one will consider and do his part, we may yet be that happy people whose God is Jehovah. Be yet encouraged, my friends, for I doubt not we can find ten righteous ones amongst us.

Let us all then join heart and hand and do justly, love and show mercy and put our trust in the God of our Fathers, for he is ever Merciful. I have been Young, tho' I am now old. And I can say I have never seen the righteous Man forsaken, or his seed. Tho' reduced to begging bread, the God of Jacob has been their support. Fear not then, my people, tho' an host should encamp against thee, and Balak and Balaam go forth to curse us with an ill judged war, yet the Lord will take a gracious care of his own people and will meet their enemies in the way. He can turn the curse of war into the blessing of peace. It is our duty to be firm, trusting in the Lord, commit all of affairs to him who ruleth among the nations and can turn the hearts of Men from the curse of war to peace. When he sees us fully humbled under his correcting hand, he can, and will, put a stop to Balaam's career and turn his curse into a blessing and cause him to say in such language as this: tho' Balak would give me his house full of silver and gold, I cannot go beyond the commandment of the Lord –

Don't let us rail so much at second causes but look to the great first cause who has permitted the great evil of war in our country. He has been pleased to permit it for our chastisement, for we have indeed been very ungrateful for the mercies we have enjoyed. Turn then, my people, return unto the path of your ancestors. Seek the Lord, whilst he may be found, fervently commit the cause of your country and your wholesales to his guidance and protection in and thro' his beloved son Jesus Christ, who is able to keep what we commit unto him, and to his name be adoration and praise.

Amen

10. Henry David Thoreau, 'Resistance to Civil Government' (Concord, Massachusetts, 1848)

In July of 1846, while living in his famous semi-isolation in woods near Concord, Massachusetts, the twenty-nine-year-old nature writer and philosopher Henry David Thoreau (1817–62) was arrested for non-payment of the poll tax and sent to Concord jail. He had refused to pay a levy that he saw as supporting the recently declared war against

Mexico and thus tacitly underpinning the possible expansion of slavery. Thoreau spent one night behind bars before an anonymous benefactor paid his bill.

The episode has been the subject of much apocryphal myth-making, and its meaning fought over by various political traditions. Yet though a largely symbolic gesture, the incident of Thoreau's imprisonment was to result in one of his greatest rhetorical creations. Eighteen months later, he used this incident as the basis for two lectures that he delivered at the Concord Lyceum, combined under the title 'Resistance to Civil Government' and often republished as 'Civil Disobedience'.

Though often seen merely as a defence of the rights of individuals, the speech can also be read as a landmark in American peace rhetoric. It has long been renowned for its influence on pacifists, most famously the non-violence of Emma Goldman, Gandhi, anti-Nazi resisters and Martin Luther King. Thoreau's key theme was the priority of individual conscience over government in moral matters, and the resultant duty of the individual to withdraw financial support from an over-reaching militaristic government. He ridicules modern warfare, dismissing soldiers as mere machines in the service of 'some unscrupulous man of power', and the government as mere machinery bent to the will of a single man.

Drawing upon Christian and Confucian ethics, its emphatically individualistic language of non-compliance and non-cooperation offered a fresh perspective on ideas of 'Non-Resistance' that had been debated in reform and abolitionist circles during the previous decade. And though its subject was the Mexican conflict, the background fury of the piece is best read as a response to the realisation that similarly stark moral choices faced all American citizens as the issue of slavery infected all areas of politics, both North and South.

Source

Henry David Thoreau, 'Resistance to Civil Government', in *Aesthetic Papers*, ed. Elizabeth P. Peabody (Boston: The Editor, 1849).

... Under a government which imprisons any unjustly, the true place for a just man is also a prison. The proper place today, the only place which Massachusetts has provided for her freer and less desponding spirits, is in her prisons, to be put out and locked out of the State by her own act, as they have already put themselves out by their principles. It is there that the fugitive slave, and the Mexican prisoner on parole, and the Indian come to plead the wrongs of his race should find them; on that separate, but more free and honorable, ground, where the State places those who are not with her, but against her – the only house in a slave State in which a free man can abide with honor. If any think that their influence would be lost there, and their voices no longer afflict the ear of the State, that they would not be as an enemy within its walls, they do not know by how much truth is stronger than error, nor how much more eloquently and effectively he can combat injustice who has experienced a little in his own person. Cast your whole vote, not a strip of paper merely, but your whole influence. A minority is powerless while it conforms to the majority; it is not even a minority then; but it is irresistible when it clogs by its whole weight. If the alternative is to keep all just men in prison, or give up war and slavery, the State will not hesitate which to choose. If a thousand men were not to pay their tax-bills this year, that would not be a violent and bloody measure, as it would be to pay them, and enable the State to commit violence and shed innocent blood. This is, in fact, the definition of a peaceable revolution, if any such is possible. If the tax-gatherer, or any other public officer, asks me, as one has done, 'But what shall I do?' my answer is, 'If you really wish to do anything, resign your office.' When the subject has refused allegiance, and the officer has resigned his office, then the revolution is accomplished. But even suppose blood should flow. Is there not a sort of blood shed when the conscience is wounded? Through this wound a man's real manhood and immortality flow out, and he bleeds to an everlasting death. I see this blood flowing now.

I have contemplated the imprisonment of the offender, rather than the seizure of his goods – though both will serve the same purpose – because they who assert the purest right, and consequently are most dangerous to a corrupt State, commonly have not spent much time in accumulating property. To such the State renders comparatively small service, and a slight tax is wont to appear exorbitant, particularly if they are obliged to earn it by special labor with their hands. If there were one who lived wholly without the use of money, the State itself would hesitate to demand it of him.

But the rich man – not to make any invidious comparison – is always sold to the institution which makes him rich. Absolutely speaking, the more money, the less virtue; for money comes between a man and his objects, and obtains them for him; and it was certainly no great virtue to obtain it. It puts to rest many questions which he would otherwise be taxed to answer; while the only new question which it puts is the hard but superfluous one, how to spend it. Thus his moral ground is taken from under his feet. The opportunities of living are diminished in proportion as what are called the 'means' are increased. The best thing a man can do for his culture when he is rich is to endeavor to carry out those schemes which he entertained when he was poor. Christ answered the Herodians according to their condition. 'Show me the tribute-money,'[55]

---

55. Matthew 22: 19. 'Shew me the tribute money. And they brought unto him a penny.' Herodians were followers of Herod Antipas, Tetrarch of Galilee from 4 BCE to 39 CE.

said he; – and one took a penny out of his pocket; – if you use money which has the image of Caesar on it, and which he has made current and valuable, that is, if you are men of the State, and gladly enjoy the advantages of Caesar's government, then pay him back some of his own when he demands it. 'Render therefore to Caesar that which is Caesar's, and to God those things which are God's' – leaving them no wiser than before as to which was which; for they did not wish to know.

When I converse with the freest of my neighbors, I perceive that, whatever they may say about the magnitude and seriousness of the question, and their regard for the public tranquillity, the long and the short of the matter is, that they cannot spare the protection of the existing government, and they dread the consequences to their property and families of disobedience to it. For my own part, I should not like to think that I ever rely on the protection of the State. But, if I deny the authority of the State when it presents its tax-bill, it will soon take and waste all my property, and so harass me and my children without end.

This is hard. This makes it impossible for a man to live honestly, and at the same time comfortably, in outward respects. It will not be worth the while to accumulate property; that would be sure to go again. You must hire or squat somewhere, and raise but a small crop, and eat that soon. You must live within yourself, and depend upon yourself always tucked up and ready for a start, and not have many affairs. A man may grow rich in Turkey even, if he will be in all respects a good subject of the Turkish government. Confucius said: 'If a state is governed by the principles of reason, poverty and misery are subjects of shame; if a state is not governed by the principles of reason, riches and honors are the subjects of shame.'[56] No: until I want the protection of Massachusetts to be extended to me in some distant Southern port, where my liberty is endangered, or until I am bent solely on building up an estate at home by peaceful enterprise, I can afford to refuse allegiance to Massachusetts, and her right to my property and life. It costs me less in every sense to incur the penalty of disobedience to the State than it would to obey. I should feel as if I were worth less in that case.

Some years ago, the State met me in behalf of the Church, and commanded me to pay a certain sum toward the support of a clergyman whose preaching my father attended, but never I myself. 'Pay,' it said, 'or be locked up in the jail.' I declined to pay. But, unfortunately, another man saw fit to pay it. I did not see why the schoolmaster should be taxed to support the priest, and not the priest the schoolmaster; for I was not the State's schoolmaster, but I supported myself by voluntary subscription. I did not see why the lyceum should not present its tax-bill, and have the State to back its demand, as well as the Church. However, at the request of the selectmen, I condescended to make some such statement as this in writing: – 'Know all men by these presents, that I, Henry Thoreau, do not wish to be regarded as a member of any incorporated society which I

---

56. Confucius, *Annalects*, 8.13.

have not joined.' This I gave to the town clerk; and he has it. The State, having thus learned that I did not wish to be regarded as a member of that church, has never made a like demand on me since; though it said that it must adhere to its original presumption that time. If I had known how to name them, I should then have signed off in detail from all the societies which I never signed on to; but I did not know where to find a complete list.

I have paid no poll-tax for six years. I was put into a jail once on this account, for one night;[57] and, as I stood considering the walls of solid stone, two or three feet thick, the door of wood and iron, a foot thick, and the iron grating which strained the light, I could not help being struck with the foolishness of that institution which treated me as if I were mere flesh and blood and bones, to be locked up. I wondered that it should have concluded at length that this was the best use it could put me to, and had never thought to avail itself of my services in some way. I saw that, if there was a wall of stone between me and my townsmen, there was a still more difficult one to climb or break through before they could get to be as free as I was. I did not for a moment feel confined, and the walls seemed a great waste of stone and mortar. I felt as if I alone of all my townsmen had paid my tax.

They plainly did not know how to treat me, but behaved like persons who are underbred. In every threat and in every compliment there was a blunder; for they thought that my chief desire was to stand the other side of that stone wall. I could not but smile to see how industriously they locked the door on my meditations, which followed them out again without let or hindrance, and they were really all that was dangerous. As they could not reach me, they had resolved to punish my body; just as boys, if they cannot come at some person against whom they have a spite, will abuse his dog. I saw that the State was half-witted, that it was timid as a lone woman with her silver spoons, and that it did not know its friends from its foes, and I lost all my remaining respect for it, and pitied it.

Thus the State never intentionally confronts a man's sense, intellectual or moral, but only his body, his senses. It is not armed with superior wit or honesty, but with superior physical strength. I was not born to be forced. I will breathe after my own fashion. Let us see who is the strongest. What force has a multitude? They only can force me who obey a higher law than I. They force me to become like themselves. I do not hear of men being forced to have this way or that by masses of men. What sort of life were that to live? When I meet a government which says to me, 'Your money or your life,' why should I be in haste to give it my money? It may be in a great strait, and not know what to

---

57. On 23 July 1846, Thoreau was on an errand in Concord, where he encountered Sam Staples, the Concord constable, tax collector and jailer. For several years, Thoreau had refused to pay the poll tax (imposed on all males 20–70 years old) to protest against the institution of slavery. Staples took the opportunity to ask him to pay his back taxes, and when Thoreau refused, he was politely escorted to jail. See Laura Dassow Walls, *Henry David Thoreau: A Life* (Chicago: University of Chicago Press, 2017), pp. 140–1.

do: I cannot help that. It must help itself; do as I do. It is not worth the while to snivel about it. I am not responsible for the successful working of the machinery of society. I am not the son of the engineer. I perceive that, when an acorn and a chestnut fall side by side, the one does not remain inert to make way for the other, but both obey their own laws, and spring and grow and flourish as best they can, till one, perchance, overshadows and destroys the other. If a plant cannot live according to its nature, it dies; and so a man.

11. John Bright, 'Angel of Death Speech' (London, 1855)

As we saw from his strident opposition to imperialism in Chapter 5, the leading British radical John Bright (1811–89) regularly used his oratorical gifts to try to mobilise Parliament against the prevailing views of mid-Victorian administrations. His Quakerism and his belief in the pacifying force of free trade combined to form a prominent strain of anti-war thought. Through not a strict pacifist, he opposed the conflicts of his day from a practical and moral sense of militarism's futility. His most famous speech on such themes occurred on 23 February 1855, in the midst of British involvement against the Russian Empire in the Crimea.

Following the ill-fated Battle of Balaclava and the Charge of the Light Brigade in late 1854, public opinion had moved against the British role in the war. The Liberal–Whig coalition of the Prime Minister, the Earl of Aberdeen, had fallen in January 1855, to be replaced by a government led by Lord Palmerston. Bright addressed a House of Commons divided on whether to continue its involvement in the Crimea. Denouncing the war as anti-Christian, contrary to the principles of free trade and harmful to British interests, he claimed that it was simply 'a gigantic system of outdoor relief for the aristocracy'.

At the speech's close came the rhetorical flourish for which it became famous: the invocation of the 'angel of death', an allusion to the Bible story found in Exodus, where God sent his angel to kill the first-born children of Egypt but spared any Israelite who painted his door posts with blood. Afterwards, Benjamin Disraeli told him, 'I would give all that I ever had to have delivered that speech.'[58] Yet though the public mood on the Crimea had cooled, Bright's hard-line views still ran counter to popular opinion and he was to lose his seat as MP for Manchester in 1857.

Source

John Bright, *Speeches on Questions of Public Policy*, vol. I (London: Macmillan, 1868).

---

58. Quoted in George B. Smith, *The Life and Speeches of John Bright* (London: Hodder and Stoughton, 1881), p. 282.

Now, there are some Gentlemen not far from me – there are men who write in the public press – there are thousands of persons in the United Kingdom at this moment – and I learn with astonishment and dismay that there are persons even in that grave assembly which we are not allowed to specify by a name in this House[59] – who have entertained dreams – impracticable theories – expectations of vast European and Asiatic changes, of revived nationalities, and of a new map of Europe, if not of the world, as a result or an object of this war.[60]

And it is from those Gentlemen that we hear continually, addressed to the noble Lord the Member for Tiverton,[61] terms which I cannot well understand. They call upon him to act, to carry on the war with vigour, and to prosecute enterprises which neither his Government, nor any other Government has ever seriously entertained; but I would appeal to those Gentlemen whether it does not become us – rewarding the true interests and the true honour of the country – if our Government have offered terms of peace to Russia, not to draw back from those terms, not to cause any unnecessary delay, not to adopt any subterfuge to prevent those terms being accepted, not to attempt shuffles of any kind, not to endeavour to insist upon harder terms, and thus make the approach of peace even still more distant than it is at present?

Whatever may be said about the honour of the country in any other relation in regard to this affair, this, at least, I expect every man who hears me to admit – that if terms of peace have been offered they have been offered in good faith, and shall be in honour and good faith adhered to; so that if, unfortunately for Europe and humanity, there should be any failure at Vienna, no man should point to the English Government and to the authorities and rulers of this Christian country, and say that we have prolonged the war and the infinite calamities of which it is the cause. Well, now, I said that I was anxious that the Government of the noble Lord should not be overthrown. Will the House allow me to say why I am so? The noble Lord at the head of the Government has long been a great authority with many persons in this country upon foreign policy. His late colleague, and present envoy to Vienna,[62] has long been a great authority with a large portion of the people of this country upon almost all political questions.

With the exception of that unhappy selection of an ambassador at Constantinople, I hold that there are no men in this country more truly responsible for

---

59. The House of Lords, where previous Prime Minister Lord Aberdeen sat.

60. The Crimean War pitted an alliance of Britain, France, Ottoman Turkey and Sardinia against Russia. Britain joined the conflict to protect its commercial and strategic interests in the Middle East and India.

61. Lord Palmerston, MP for Tiverton, had become Prime Minister for the first time earlier that month following the fall of the Aberdeen administration. He was under pressure to continue to prosecute the conflict in the Crimea, including from members of his own bench such as William Gladstone, who had resigned.

62. Lord John Russell (1792–1878), whom Palmerston had sent as Foreign Minister to Vienna to negotiate with the Russians.

our present position in this war than the noble Lord[63] who now fills the highest office in the State and the noble Lord who is now, I trust, rapidly approaching the scene of his labours in Vienna.

['Hear, hear!' and cries of 'No, no!']

I do not say this now to throw blame upon those noble Lords, because their policy, which I hold to be wrong, they, without doubt, as firmly believe to be right; but I am only stating facts. It has been their policy that they have entered into war for certain objects, and I am sure that neither the noble Lord at the head of the Government nor his late colleague the noble Lord the Member for London[64] will shrink from the responsibility which attaches to them. Well, Sir, now we have those noble Lords in a position which is, in my humble opinion, favourable to the termination of the troubles which exist.

I think that the noble Lord at the head of the Government himself would have more influence in stilling whatever may exist of clamour in this country than any other Member of this House. I think, also, that the noble Lord the Member for London would not have undertaken the mission to Vienna if he had not entertained some strong belief that, by so doing, he might bring the war to an end. Nobody gains reputation by a failure in negotiation, and as that noble Lord is well acquainted with the whole question from beginning to end, I entertain a hope – I will not say a sanguine hope – that the result of that mission to Vienna will be to bring about a peace, to extricate this country from some of those difficulties inseparable from a state of war. There is one subject upon which I should like to put a question to the noble Lord at the head of the Government. I shall not say one word here about the state of the army in the Crimea, or one word about its numbers or its condition. Every Member of this House, every inhabitant of this country, has been sufficiently harrowed with details regarding it.[65]

To my solemn belief, thousands – nay, scores of thousands of persons – have retired to rest, night after night, whose slumbers have been disturbed, or whose dreams have been based upon the sufferings and agonies of our soldiers in the Crimea. I should like to ask the noble Lord at the head of the Government – although I am not sure if he will feel that he can or ought to answer the question – whether the noble Lord the Member for London has power, after discussions have commenced, and as soon as there shall be established good grounds for believing that the negotiations for peace will prove successful, to enter into any armistice? ['No! no!' and 'Hear, hear!']

I know not, Sir, who it is that says 'No, no,' but I should like to see any man get up and say that the destruction of 200,000 human lives lost on all sides during the course of this unhappy conflict is not a sufficient sacrifice. You are

---

63. Lord Palmerston.
64. Lord Russell.
65. The defeats of the British army during the previous year, most notoriously in the Charge of the Light Brigade, had revealed the shortcomings of the military. Coverage of the poor conditions suffered by the army had shocked the public.

not pretending to conquer territory – you are not pretending to hold fortified or unfortified towns; you have offered terms of peace which, as I understand them, I do not say are not moderate; and breathes there a man in this House or in this country whose appetite for blood is so insatiable that, even when terms of peace have been offered and accepted, he pines for that assault in which of Russian, Turk, French, and English, as sure as one man dies, 20,000 corpses will strew the streets of Sebastopol? I say I should like to ask the noble Lord – and I am sure that he will feel, and that this House will feel, that I am speaking in no unfriendly manner towards the Government of which he is at the head – I should like to know, and I venture to hope that it is so, if the noble Lord the Member for London has power, at the earliest stage of these proceedings at Vienna, at which it can properly be done – and I should think that it might properly be done at a very early stage – to adopt a course by which all further waste of human life may be put an end to, and further animosity between three great nations be, as far as possible, prevented?

I appeal to the noble Lord at the head of the Government and to this House; I am not now complaining of the war – I am not now complaining of the terms of peace, nor, indeed, of anything that has been done – but I wish to suggest to this House what, I believe, thousands, and tens of thousands, of the most educated and of the most Christian portion of the people of this country are feeling upon this subject, although, indeed, in the midst of a certain clamour in the country, they do not give public expression to their feelings. Your country is not in an advantageous state at this moment; from one end of the kingdom to the other there is a general collapse of industry. Those Members of this House not intimately acquainted with the trade and commerce of the country do not fully comprehend our position as to the diminution of employment and the lessening of wages. An increase in the cost of living is finding its way to the homes and hearts of a vast number of the labouring population.

At the same time there is growing up – and, notwithstanding what some hon. Members of this House may think of me, no man regrets it more than I do – a bitter and angry feeling against that class which has for a long period conducted the public affairs of this country. I like political changes when such changes are made as the result, not of passion, but of deliberation and reason. Changes so made are safe, but changes made under the influence of violent exaggeration, or of the violent passions of public meetings, are not changes usually approved by this House or advantageous to the country.

I cannot but notice, in speaking to Gentlemen who sit on either side of this House, or in speaking to any one I meet between this House and any of those localities we frequent when this House is up – I cannot, I say, but notice that an uneasy feeling exists as to the news that may arrive by the very next mail from the East. I do not Suppose that your troops are to be beaten in actual conflict with the foe, or that they will be driven into the sea; but I am certain that many homes in England in which there now exists a fond hope that the distant one may return – many such homes may be rendered desolate when the next mail shall arrive.

The angel of death has been abroad throughout the land; you may almost hear the beating of his wings.[66] There is no one, as when the first-born were slain of old, to sprinkle with blood the lintel and the two sideposts of our doors, that he may spare and pass on; he takes his victims from the castle of the noble, the mansion of the wealthy, and the cottage of the poor and the lowly, and it is on behalf of all these classes that I make this solemn appeal. I tell the noble Lord, that if he be ready honestly and frankly to endeavour, by the negotiations to be opened at Vienna, to put an end to this war, no word of mine, no vote of mine, will be given to shake his power for one single moment, or to change his position in this House.

I am sure that the noble Lord is not inaccessible to appeals made to him from honest motives and with no unfriendly feeling. The noble Lord has been for more than forty years a Member of this House. Before I was born, he sat upon the Treasury bench, and he has devoted his life in the service of his country.

He is no longer young, and his life has extended almost to the term allotted to man. I would ask, I would entreat the noble Lord to take a course which, when he looks back upon his whole political career – whatever he may therein find to be pleased with, whatever to regret – cannot but be a source of gratification to him. By adopting that course he would have the satisfaction of reflecting that, having obtained the object of his laudable ambition – having become the foremost subject of the Crown, the director of, it may be, the destinies of his country and the presiding genius in her councils – he had achieved a still higher and nobler ambition; that he had returned the sword to the scabbard – that at his word torrents of blood had ceased to flow – that he had restored tranquillity to Europe, and saved this country from the indescribable calamities of war.

12. Emma Goldman, 'Patriotism, a Menace to Liberty' (San Francisco, 1908)

As seen in Thoreau's speech, some of most powerful nineteenth-century critiques of war rejected militarism as part of a broader rejection of the role of the state. As one of the most famous anarchist activists in *fin-de-siècle* America, Emma Goldman (1869–1940) continued this anti-state pacifist tradition, and was a particularly outspoken critic of the structures of feeling that led citizens from love of nation to martial fervour. Born in Russia, educated in Germany and emigrating to the US in 1886, Goldman became an advocate of free speech, birth control, women's equality and independence, and union organisation (Figure 15).

---

66. A reference to the angel sent out by God to kill enemies of the Israelites, most famously in Exodus 12: 12, to which Bright alludes: 'For I will pass through the land of Egypt this night, and will smite all the firstborn in the land of Egypt, both man and beast; and against all the gods of Egypt I will execute judgment: I *am* the LORD.'

The text below is an excerpt from a speech she would deliver in various forms many times from the 1900s onwards, taking aim at the jingoistic emotions that underpinned the worst tendencies of American overseas expansion. She appeared at Odd Fellows' Hall in San Francisco as an invited speaker of the International Workingmen's Association, one reporter recalling that 'a large crowd was present to hear the fiery utterances as they fell, laden with molten metal, from the speaker's lips'.[67] Expressing such fiercely anti-patriotic views was not without personal risk. Goldman's criticism of the mandatory conscription of young men into the military during World War One was to lead to her two-year imprisonment, followed by her deportation in 1919 to the Soviet Union.

Source

Alix Kates Shulman, *Red Emma Speaks: Selected Writings and Speeches by Emma Goldman* (New York: Random House, 1979).

Men and Women:

What is patriotism? Is it love of one's birthplace, the place of childhood's recollections and hopes, dreams and aspirations? Is it the place where, in childlike naivete, we would watch the passing clouds, and wonder why we, too, could not float so swiftly? The place where we would count the milliard glittering stars, terror-stricken lest each one 'an eye should be,' piercing the very depths of our little souls? Is it the place where we would listen to the music of the birds and long to have wings to fly, even as they, to distant lands? Or is it the place where we would sit on Mother's knee, enraptured by tales of great deeds and conquests? In short, is it love for the spot, every inch representing dear and precious recollections of a happy, joyous and playful childhood?

If that were patriotism, few American men of today would be called upon to be patriotic, since the place of play has been turned into factory, mill, and mine, while deepening sounds of machinery have replaced the music of the birds. No longer can we hear the tales of great deeds, for the stories our mothers tell today are but those of sorrow, tears and grief.

What, then, is patriotism? 'Patriotism, sir, is the last resort of scoundrels,' said Dr. [Samuel] Johnson.[68] Leo Tolstoy, the greatest anti-patriot of our time, defines patriotism as the principle that will justify the training of wholesale

---

67. Candace Falk, *Emma Goldman: A Documentary History of the American Years* (Stanford: Stanford University Press, 2016), p. 327.
68. James Boswell, *Life of Johnson*, ed. R. W. Chapman and P. Rogers (Oxford: Oxford University Press, 1998), p. 615.

murderers;[69] a trade that requires better equipment in the exercise of man-killing than the making of such necessities as shoes, clothing, and houses; a trade that guarantees better returns and greater glory than that of the honest workingman . . .

Indeed, conceit, arrogance and egotism are the essentials of patriotism. Let me illustrate. Patriotism assumes that our globe is divided into little spots, each one surrounded by an iron gate. Those who have had the fortune of being born on some particular spot consider themselves nobler, better, grander, more intelligent than those living beings inhabiting any other spot. It is, therefore, the duty of everyone living on that chosen spot to fight, kill and die in the attempt to impose his superiority upon all the others. The inhabitants of the other spots reason in like manner, of course, with the result that from early infancy the mind of the child is provided with blood-curdling stories about the Germans, the French, the Italians, Russians, etc. When the child has reached manhood he is thoroughly saturated with the belief that he is chosen by the Lord himself to defend his country against the attack or invasion of any foreigner. It is for that purpose that we are clamoring for a greater army and navy, more battleships and ammunition . . .

An army and navy represent the people's toys. To make them more attractive and acceptable, hundreds and thousands of dollars are being spent for the display of toys. That was the purpose of the American government in equipping a fleet and sending it along the Pacific coast, that every American citizen should be made to feel the pride and glory of the United States.[70]

The city of San Francisco spent one hundred thousand dollars for the entertainment of the fleet; Los Angeles, sixty thousand; Seattle and Tacoma, about one hundred thousand . . . Yes, two hundred and sixty thousand dollars were spent on fireworks, theater parties, and revelries, at a time when men, women, and children through the breadth and length of the country were starving in the streets; when thousands of unemployed were ready to sell their labor at any price.

What could not have been accomplished with such an enormous sum? But instead of bread and shelter, the children of those cities were taken to see the fleet, that it may remain, as one newspaper said, 'a lasting memory for the child.'

A wonderful thing to remember, is it not? The implements of civilized slaughter. If the mind of the child is poisoned with such memories, what hope is there for a true realization of human brotherhood?

We Americans claim to be a peace-loving people. We hate bloodshed; we are opposed to violence. Yet we go into spasms of joy over the possibility of projecting dynamite bombs from flying machines upon helpless citizens. We are

---

69. Leo Tolstoy, 'On Patriotism', in *Tolstoy's Writings on Civil Disobedience and Non-Violence* (New York: New American Library, 1968).

70. In 1907, President Theodore Roosevelt ordered the newly enlarged US Navy battle fleet, known as 'The Great White Fleet', to complete a journey around the world as a display of the arrival of America as a major naval power.

ready to hang, electrocute, or lynch anyone, who, from economic necessity, will risk his own life in the attempt upon that of some industrial magnate. Yet our hearts swell with pride at the thought that America is becoming the most powerful nation on earth, and that she will eventually plant her iron foot on the necks of all other nations.

Such is the logic of patriotism.

... Thinking men and women the world over are beginning to realize that patriotism is too narrow and limited a conception to meet the necessities of our time. The centralization of power has brought into being an international feeling of solidarity among the oppressed nations of the world; a solidarity which represents a greater harmony of interests between the workingman of America and his brothers abroad than between the American miner and his exploiting compatriot; a solidarity which fears not foreign invasion, because it is bringing all the workers to the point when they will say to their masters, 'Go and do your own killing. We have done it long enough for you.'

... The proletariat of Europe has realized the great force of that solidarity and has, as a result, inaugurated a war against patriotism and its bloody specter, militarism. Thousands of men fill the prisons of France, Germany, Russia and the Scandinavian countries because they dared to defy the ancient superstition ...

America will have to follow suit. The spirit of militarism has already permeated all walks of life. Indeed, I am convinced that militarism is a greater danger here than anywhere else, because of the many bribes capitalism holds out to those whom it wishes to destroy ...

The beginning has already been made in the schools ... Children are trained in military tactics, the glory of military achievements extolled in the curriculum, and the youthful mind perverted to suit the government. Further, the youth of the country is appealed to in glaring posters to join the Army and the Navy. 'A fine chance to see the world!' cries the governmental huckster. Thus innocent boys are morally shanghaied into patriotism, and the military Moloch[71] strides conquering through the nation ...

When we have undermined the patriotic lie, we shall have cleared the path for the great structure where all shall be united into a universal brotherhood – a truly free society.

---

71. Moloch is a Canaanite deity associated with child sacrifice.

Further Reading

Online Resources

American Rhetoric – a site dedicated to 'Public Rhetoric, political, social, movie and religious speeches and related concepts of and exercises in rhetoric' <https://www.americanrhetoric.com> (last accessed 11 July 2019).

The History Place – Great Speeches Collection <http://www.historyplace.com/speeches/previous.htm> (last accessed 11 July 2019).

'Sounds from the Park', a site dedicated to 'the history and traditions of Britain's last great open air oratory site: Speakers' Corner in Hyde Park, London' <https://soundsfromthepark.on-the-record.org.uk/about-sounds-from-the-park/about-speakers-corner/> (last accessed 11 July 2019).

Voices of Democracy – The U.S. Oratory Project (University of Maryland) <http://voicesofdemocracy.umd.edu> (last accessed 11 July 2019).

General

Barnet Baskerville, *The People's Voice: The Orator in American Society* (Lexington: University Press of Kentucky, 2015).

Carolyn Eastman, *A Nation of Speechifiers: Making an American Public After the Revolution* (Chicago: Chicago University Press, 2009).

Jay Fliegelman, *Declaring Independence: Jefferson, Natural Language & the Culture of Performance* (Stanford: Stanford University Press, 1996).

Sandra M. Gustafson, *Eloquence is Power: Oratory and Performance in Early America* (Chapel Hill: University of North Carolina Press, 2001).

Sandra Gustafson, 'Oral Genres and Print', in Mary Saracino Zboray and Ronald J. Zboray (eds), *Oxford History of Popular Print Culture: Volume Five* (Oxford: Oxford University Press, 2019).

Aled Jones, *Powers of the Press: Newspapers, Power and the Public in Nineteenth-Century England* (London: Routledge, 2016).

Brian MacArthur, *The Penguin Book of Historic Speeches* (London: Penguin, 1995).

Joseph S. Meisel, *Public Speech and the Culture of Public Life in the Age of Gladstone* (New York: Columbia, 2001).

Walter J. Ong, with additional chapters by John Hartley, *Orality and Literacy: The Technologizing of the Word: 30th Anniversary Edition* (London: Routledge, 2012).

Edward G. Parker, *The Golden Age of American Oratory* (Boston: Whittemore, Niles, and Hall, 1857).

Sean Scalmer, *On the Stump: Campaign Oratory and Democracy in the United States, Britain, and Australia* (Toronto: University of Toronto Press, 2017).

Shaun Usher, *Speeches of Note: A Celebration of the Old, New and Unspoken* (London: Hutchison, 2018).

Chapter 1 Nationalisms and Independence

David Armitage, *The Declaration Of Independence: A Global History* (Cambridge, MA: Harvard University Press, 2007).

John E. Ferling, *The Loyalist Mind: Joseph Galloway and the American Revolution* (University Park: Pennsylvania State University Press, 1977).

David Geggus, 'The Haitian Revolution in Atlantic Perspective', in Nicholas Canny and Philip Morgan (eds), *The Oxford Handbook of the Atlantic World: 1450–1850* (Oxford: Oxford University Press, 2011).

Virginia Guedea, 'Miguel Hidalgo y Costilla', in Michael S. Werner (ed.), *Encyclopedia of Mexico* (Chicago: Fitzroy Dearborn, 1997), p. 640.

Catherine Hobbs, *Rhetoric on the Margins of Modernity* (Carbondale: Southern Illinois University Press, 2002).

C. L. R. James, *The Black Jacobins: Toussaint L'Ouverture and the San Domingo Revolution* (London: Secker and Warburg, 1938).

Lloyd Kramer, *Nationalism: Political Cultures in Europe and America 1775–1865* (New York: Twayne, 1998).

E. L. Magoon, *Orators of the American Revolution* (New York: Mason, Baker and Pratt, 1873).

Pauline Maier, *American Scripture: Making the Declaration of Independence* (New York: Vintage/Knopf, 1998).

Frank Moore, *The Patriot Preachers of the American Revolution* (New York: C. T. Evans, 1862).

Christopher Reid, 'Burke as Rhetorician and Orator', in David Dwan (ed.), *The Cambridge Companion to Edmund Buke* (Cambridge: Cambridge University Press).

Chapter 2 Gender, Suffrage and Sexuality

Paula Bartley, *Emmeline Pankhurst* (London: Routledge, 2002).

Susan G. Bell and Karen M. Offen, *Women, Family and Freedom: The Debate in Documents: 1880–1950* (Stanford: Stanford University Press, 1983).

Melba Joyce Boyd, *Discarded Legacy: Politics and Poetics in the Life of Frances E. W. Harper, 1825–1911* (Detroit: Wayne State University Press, 1995).

Sean Brady, *Masculinity and Male Homosexuality in Britain, 1861–1913* (New York: Palgrave, 2009).

Barbara Caine, *Victorian Feminists* (Oxford: Oxford University Press, 1993).

Karlyn Kohrs Campbell, *Women Public Speakers in the United States, 1800–1925: A Bio-Critical Sourcebook* (Westport, CT: Greenwood Press, 1994).

James Daley, *Great Speeches on Gay Rights* (New York: Dover, 2001).

Ellen Carol Dubois and Richard Candida Smith, *Elizabeth Cady Stanton, Feminist as Thinker: A Reader in Documents and Essays* (New York: NYU Press, 2007).

Brian Harrison, *Separate Sphere: Opposition to Women's Suffrage in Britain* (London: Routledge, 1978).

Christiane Leidinger, '"Anna Rüling": A Problematic Foremother of Lesbian Herstory', *Journal of the History of Sexuality*, 13:4 (October 2004): 477–99.

Lucy McDiarmid, 'Oscar Wilde's Speech from the Dock', *Textual Practice*, 15:3 (2010), 447–66.

Sally Gregory McMillen, *Seneca Falls and the Origins of the Women's Rights Movement* (Oxford: Oxford University Press, 2009).

Charles E. Morris, *Queering Public Address: Sexualities in American Historical Discourse* (Columbia: University of South Carolina Press, 2007).

M. J. Naparsteck, *The Trial of Susan B. Anthony: An Illegal Vote, a Courtroom Conviction and a Step Toward Women's Suffrage* (Jefferson, NC: McFarland, 2014).

S. M. Nix, *Women at the Podium: Memorable Speeches in History* (New York: Harper, 2000).

Carla L. Peterson, *Doers of the Word: African-American Women Speakers and Writers in the North (1830–1880)* (New Brunswick, NJ: Rutgers University Press, 1998).

'Sojourner Truth: Compare the Two Speeches', The Sojourner Truth Project. Available at: <https://www.thesojournertruthproject.com> (last accessed 1 April 2019).

Erlene Stetson and Linda David, *Glorying in Tribulation: The Lifework of Sojourner Truth* (East Lansing: Michigan State University Press, 1994).

Elaine Weiss, *The Woman's Hour: The Great Fight to Win the Vote* (New York: Penguin, 2019).

Chapter 3 Slavery and Race

Marc M. Arkin, 'The Federalist Trope: Power and Passion in Abolitionist Rhetoric', *The Journal of American History*, 88:1 (2001), 75–98.

Irving H. Bartlett, *John C. Calhoun: A Biography* (New York: W. W. Norton, 1993).

Mia Bay, *To Tell the Truth Freely: The Life of Ida B. Wells* (New York: Hill & Wang, 2009).

Carol Berkin, *Civil War Wives: The Lives and Times of Angelina Grimké Weld, Varina Howell Davis, and Julia Dent Grant* (New York: Vintage, 2010).

Ira Berlin, *The Long Emancipation: The Demise of Slavery in the United States* (Cambridge, MA: Harvard University Press, 2015).

David Blight, *Frederick Douglass: Prophet of Freedom* (New York: Simon and Schuster, 2018).

Christopher Leslie Brown, *Moral Capital: Foundations of British Abolitionism* (Chapel Hill: University of North Carolina Press, 2006).

Brycchan Carey, *British Abolitionism and the Rhetoric of Sensibility: Writing, Sentiment, and Slavery, 1760–1807* (Basingstoke: Palgrave Macmillan, 2005).

Brion Davis, *Inhuman Bondage: The Rise and Fall of Slavery in the New World* (Oxford: Oxford University Press, 2006).

Lacy K. Ford, *Deliver Us from Evil: The Slavery Question in the Old South, 1787–1840* (New York: Oxford University Press, 2012).

Henry Louis Gates, 'Talkin' Black', in Christopher Ricks and Leonard Michaels (eds), *The State of the Language* (London: Faber and Faber, 1991).

Peter P. Hinks, *To Awaken My Afflicted Brethren: David Walker and the Problem of Antebellum Slave Resistance* (University Park: Pennsylvania State University Press, 1997).

Kristin Hoganson, 'Garrisonian Abolitionists and the Rhetoric of Gender, 1850–1860', *American Quarterly*, 45 (December 1993).

Waldo E. Martin, *The Mind of Frederick Douglass* (Chapel Hill: University of North Carolina Press, 1984).

William Mulligan and Maurice Bric (eds), *A Global History of Anti-Slavery Politics in the Nineteenth Century* (Basingstoke: Palgrave Macmillan, 2013).

Chapter 4 Faith, Culture and Society

Matthew Arnold, *Culture and Anarchy* (Oxford: Oxford University Press, 2006).

Matthew Bevis, *The Art of Eloquence: Byron, Dickens, Tennyson, Joyce* (Oxford: Oxford University Press, 2007).

Charles Bradlaugh, *Is the Bible Divine? A Six Nights' Discussion between Mr. Charles Bradlaugh and Mr. Robert Roberts* (London: F. Pitman, 1876).

Stephen Bullivant and Michael Ruse (eds), *The Oxford Handbook of Atheism* (New York: Oxford University Press, 2013).

Robert H. Ellison, *The Victorian Pulpit: Spoken and Written Sermons in Nineteenth-Century Britain* (London: Associated Universities Press, 1998).

Mary Fairclough, *The Romantic Crowd: Sympathy, Controversy and Print Culture* (Cambridge: Cambridge University Press, 2013).

Nathan O. Hatch, *The Democratization of American Christianity* (New Haven, CT: Yale University Press, 1989).

Martin Hewitt, 'Aspects of Platform Culture in Nineteenth-Century Britain', *Nineteenth-Century Prose*, 29:1 (Spring 2002): 1.

John Holloway, *The Victorian Sage: Studies in Argument* (London: Macmillan, 1953).

Sylvester A. Johnson, *African American Religions, 1500–2000: Colonialism, Democracy, and Freedom* (Cambridge: Cambridge University Press, 2015).

Norman Kelvin (ed.), *William Morris on Art and Socialism* (Mincola, NY: Dover, 1999).

George Landow, *Elegant Jeremiahs: The Sage from Carlyle to Mailer* (Ithaca: Cornell University Press, 1986).

Michele Mendelssohn, *Making Oscar Wilde* (Oxford: Oxford University Press, 2018).

Priscilla Pope-Levison, *Turn the Pulpit Loose: Two Centuries of American Women Evangelists* (New York: Palgrave Macmillan, 2016).

Angela Ray, *The Lyceum and Public Culture in Nineteenth Century America* (East Lansing: Michigan University Press, 2005).

Tom F. Wright, 'Carlyle, Emerson and the Voiced Essay', in Thomas Karshan and Kathryn Murphy (eds), *The Literary Essay* (Oxford: Oxford University Press, 2019).

Tom F. Wright (ed.), *The Cosmopolitan Lyceum: Lecture Culture and the Globe in Nineteenth-Century America* (Amherst: University Massachusetts Press, 2013).

Tom F. Wright, *Lecturing the Atlantic: Speech, Print and an Anglo-American Commons* (Oxford: Oxford University Press, 2017).

Chapter 5 Empire and Manifest Destiny

David Cannadine, *Victorious Century: The United Kingdom 1800–1900* (New York: Allen Lane, 2017).

William Clements, *Oratory in Native North America* (Tucson: University of Arizona Press, 2002).

Robert Foster, *Modern Ireland 1600–1972* (Oxford: Oxford University Press, 2011).

Granville Ganter, *The Collected Speeches of Sagoyewatha, or Red Jacket* (Syracuse: Syracuse University Press, 2006).

Patrick M. Geoghegan, *Liberator: The Life and Death of Daniel O'Connell* (Dublin: Gill & Macmillan, 2012).

Huston Gilmore, '"The shouts of vanished crowds": Literacy, Orality, and Popular Politics in the Campaign to Repeal the Act of Union in Ireland, 1840–1848', *19: Interdisciplinary Studies in the Nineteenth Century*, 18 (2014), 1–27.

Richard H. Immerman, *Empire for Liberty: A History of American Imperialism from Benjamin Franklin to Paul Wolfowitz* (Princeton: Princeton University Press, 2012).

Nathan Jessen, *Populism and Imperialism: Politics, Culture, and Foreign Policy in the American West, 1890–1900* (Lawrence: University of Kansas Press, 2017).

Carolyn Johnston, *Cherokee Women in Crisis; Trail of Tears, Civil War, and Allotment, 1838–1907* (Tuscaloosa: University of Alabama Press, 2003).

Edgar R. Jones, *Selected Speeches on British Foreign Policy, 1738–1914* (Oxford: Oxford University Press, 1914).

Stephen Kinzer, *The True Flag: Theodore Roosevelt, Mark Twain, and the Birth of American Empire* (New York: St Martin's Griffin, 2018).

Lawrence J. McCaffrey, *The Irish Question: Two Centuries of Conflict* (Lexington: University Press of Kentucky, 1995).

Joseph S. Meisel, *Public Speech and the Culture of Public Life in the Age of Gladstone* (New York: Columbia University Press, 2002).

Bernard Porter, *The Absent-Minded Imperialists: Empire, Society, and Culture in Britain* (Oxford: Oxford University Press, 2006).

Bernard Porter, *Critics of Empire: British Radicals and the Imperial Challenge*, revised edn (London: I. B. Tauris, 2008).

Simon J. Potter, 'Empire, Cultures and Identities in Nineteenth- and Twentieth-Century Britain', *History Compass*, 5 (2007), 51–70.

Jacqueline Riding, *Peterloo: The Story of the Manchester Massacre* (London: Head of Zeus, 2018).

Theodore Roosevelt, *Selected Speeches and Writings of Theodore Roosevelt*, ed. Gordon Hutner (New York: Vintage, 2014).

Donald Scott, 'The Popular Lecture and the Creation of a Public in Mid-Nineteenth-Century America', *Journal of American History*, 66:4 (1980), 791–5.

David Spurr, *The Rhetoric of Empire: Colonial Discourse in Journalism, Travel Writing, and Imperial Administration* (Durham, NC: Duke University Press, 1993).

Stanley R. Stembridge, 'Disraeli and the Millstones', *Journal of British Studies*, 5:1 (November 1965), 122–39.

Deborah Gillan Straub, *Voices of Multicultural America: Notable Speeches Delivered by African, Asian, Hispanic and Native Americans, 1790–1995* (New York: Gale Research, 1996).

Martin Thomas and Richard Toye, *Arguing about Empire: Imperial Rhetoric in Britain and France, 1882–1956* (Oxford: Oxford University Press, 2017).

Andrew S. Thompson, Section 9: 'After-Effects', in *The Empire Strikes Back? The Impact of Imperialism on Britain from the Mid-Nineteenth Century* (Harlow: Pearson, 2005), pp. 203–38.

C. A. Weslager, *The Delaware Indians: A History* (New Brunswick, NJ: Rutgers University Press, 2003).

Chapter 6 War and Peace

Robert Blaisdell, *The Civil War: Great Speeches and Documents* (New York: Dover, 2016).

Marin Ceadel, *The Birth of the Peace Movement, 1730–1854* (New York: Clarendon Press, 1996).

Martin Ceadel, *Semi-Detached Idealists: The British Peace Movement and International Relations, 1854–1945* (Oxford: Oxford University Press, 2007).

John W. Chambers, *The Eagle and the Dove: The American Peace Movement and United States Foreign Policy, 1900–1922* (Syracuse: Syracuse University Press, 1991).

'Civil War Monument Speeches', American Battlement Trust. Available at: <https://www.battlefields.org/learn/primary-sources/civil-war-monument-speeches> (last accessed 1 April 2019).

Carolyn Eastman, 'Fight Like a Man: Gender and Rhetoric in the Early Nineteenth-Century American Peace Movement', *American Nineteenth-Century History*, 10:3 (2009), 247–71.

Abraham Lincoln, *Speeches and Writings, 1832–1858*, ed. Don E. Fehrenbacher (New York: Library of America, 1989).

Abraham Lincoln, *Speeches and Writings, 1859–1865* (New York: Library of America, 1989).

James M. McPherson, *Battle Cry of Freedom: The Civil War Era* (Oxford: Oxford University Press, 1988).

C. Roland Marchand, *The American Peace Movement and Social Reform, 1898–1918* (Princeton: Princeton University Press, 1973).

Craig R. Smith, *Daniel Webster and the Oratory of Civil Religion* (Columbia: University of Missouri Press, 2005).

Gary Wills, *Lincoln at Gettysburg: The Words that Remade America* (New York: Simon and Schuster, 2011).

David Zarefsky 'Rhetorical Interpretations of the American Civil War', *Quarterly Journal of Speech*, 81:1 (1995), 108–20.

Index